THE MAPLES

By JAMES H. MAPLESON
COMPLETE

PREFACE.

HAVING been repeatedly urged by numerous friends on both sides of the Atlantic to set forth a few of the difficulties attending the career of an impresario, who, during the last thirty years, has fought many operatic battles, I have undertaken the task, having at the present moment for the first time in my recollection a few weeks of comparative repose before again renewing my lyrical campaigns.

I willingly sat down to the work, trusting that an account of the few partial defeats and the many brilliant victories incident to my life may be found interesting.

This being my first appearance as an author, I am naturally unpractised in the artifices of style familiar to more experienced hands.

Some of my plain statements of facts will not, I fear, be fully appreciated by the personages to whom they refer; and in case they should feel offended by my frankness, I ask their pardon beforehand, convinced that they will readily accord it.

J. H. MAPLESON.
Junior Carlton Club,
21st September, 1888.

CHAPTER I.

QUALIFICATIONS FOR THE CAREER OF IMPRESARIO—MY FIRST APPEARANCE AS VIOLINIST—DÉBUT AS A VOCALIST—DIFFICULTIES AS A CRITIC—ENGAGED AT LODI AND VERONA—RADICAL OPERATION ON MY THROAT—I START AS MUSICAL AGENT—MEETING WITH MR. E. T. SMITH—MANAGEMENT OF DRURY LANE.

BEFORE beginning my thirty years' career as an operatic manager, I had already had a large and varied experience of music in the character of student, critic, violinist, vocalist, composer, concert director, and musical agent. At the age of fourteen I entered the Royal Academy of Music, where the Principal was at that time Cipriani Potter. I took as my first study the violin, my professor being Watson, under whom I made good progress. Harmony I studied under Lucas. My compositions are limited to two pianoforte pieces and a song, which I published soon after leaving the Academy, where I remained about two years.

I made my first public appearance among the first violins at Her Majesty's Theatre, where, during the Jenny Lind seasons of 1848 and a portion of 1849, I played from the same desk as Remenyi, the famous Hungarian violinist. Remenyi, too, shared my rooms, and often kept me up at night by his loud and passionate declamations on the subject of Hungarian independence, and of liberty generally. He had taken part in the revolutionary movement of 1848, and on its collapse had fled for his life to foreign parts. Fortunately, he had his violin to depend upon; and it was in London, I believe, that he first turned his remarkable talent to practical and pecuniary account.

Mr. [afterwards Sir Michael] Costa had left Her Majesty's Theatre two years previously to take part in establishing the Royal Italian Opera at Covent Garden, and the new conductor at Her Majesty's Theatre was our eminent composer M. W. Balfe. It had already occurred to me to quit the comparative obscurity of the orchestra for a brilliant position on the stage; and this idea was encouraged by Balfe, who, during the intervals of operatic business, gave me singing lessons. I also received instruction from Gardoni, the tenor, and Belletti, the baritone. As I had a tenor voice, Gardoni's lessons were particularly useful to me; and I was led to believe by each of my distinguished professors that I had in me the making of a primo tenore.

Long before I had completed my studies as a vocalist, an opportunity, indeed a necessity, for making my first appearance as a singer presented itself. Not to remain idle during the long months separating one opera season from another, I took out in the English Provinces in 1849 a company in which were included Sontag, Calzolari, Belletti, Lablache, and the famous pianist Thalberg. On one occasion, after giving a concert at Salisbury, the whole party paid a visit to Stonehenge, where Sontag sang "Casta diva," and Lablache a portion of Oroveso's solo music among the Druidical remains, so suggestive of the opera of Norma. I have now before me a handsome little clock which Madame Sontag presented to me at the end of the tour. It is inscribed: "To J. H. Mapleson from Madame Sontag (Countess Rossi)." I may mention in connection with this charming vocalist, whose good nature and good temper were on a par with her talent, a peculiarity which will perhaps astonish some of the concert singers of the present day. Instead of avoiding, according to the modern practice, the task of either beginning or ending a concert, she was ready and even anxious to sing both the first piece and the last. "If I do not begin the concert people will not come in time," she would say; "and if I do not end it they will go away before it is over."

In the autumn of 1850 I took on tour a company which included Roger and Madame Viardot, the famous representatives of "John of Leyden" and "Fidès" in Le Prophète. Meyerbeer was in constant correspondence with them. To avoid the expense of postage, he used to send his music written on such fine paper that to be able to read it with any ease it was necessary to place it on a back-ground of ordinary writing paper.

In a subsequent tour my leading tenor was one night for some reason or other not forthcoming. There was no one to replace him, and as I was myself a tenor I plunged boldly into the gap. I sang with success, but it occurred to me even as I was singing that I had need of further instruction. On my return to London I called on Sims Reeves, and sang to him; when he at once recommended me to go to Milan, and place myself under Signor Mazzucato, director and principal professor of singing at the celebrated Conservatorio. Reeves was kind enough to give me a letter to Mazzucato, under whom he had himself studied, with results which need not here be set forth.

Before taking farewell of England in order to go through a three years' course of training in Italy I did a little work as musical critic for a journal called the Atlas, which for years past has ceased to exist, but which, at the time I speak of, enjoyed a good reputation, especially in connection with literary and artistic matters. The proprietor, and ostensible editor, was a well-known journalist, Mr. George Francis, author of "The Orators of the Age," a series of papers which made some stir when, before appearing in book-form, they were published in the pages of Frazer's Magazine. Mr. Francis had, I believe, gained his experience of our British orators in the gallery of the House of Commons, where he was for many years one of the principal reporters of the Times staff. Mr. Francis was also a brilliant foreign correspondent, and it afterwards became a speciality of his to assist and preside at the birth of new journals. His fee as accoucheur on these occasions was, I believe, a considerable one. After a time nothing would satisfy him but to have a paper of his own. He bought the Atlas, and while entrusting most of the editorial work to a Mr. Joyce, who was my immediate chief, appropriated to himself all free admissions that reached the office. Accordingly, when it became my duty to write an account of the first production of Le Prophète at the Royal Italian Opera, I received instructions from my editor about sending in "copy," but was not furnished with a stall. I was to manage, somehow or other, to hear the opera, and I was in any case to send in a notice of it. I endeavoured to buy a ticket, but everything was sold.

In my despair I chanced to meet the American philanthropist, Mr George Peabody, well known by his charitable deeds, and who hastened on this occasion to perform a good work towards me. He assured me that the difficulty which troubled me was not so great as I imagined. It was now late in the afternoon. The performance was to take place that evening, and Mr. Peabody suggested that first of all the best thing I could do was to dine with him at the "Hummums." Thence, after finishing a bottle of excellent port, we walked quietly to the gallery entrance of the opera—at that time under the piazza, next door to the Bedford Hotel—bought our tickets, and found places in the very front row.

Soon, however, I was to start for Milan, where, studying constantly with Professor Mazzucato, I spent nearly three years. Then an engagement was offered to me at Lodi, where I was to make my first appearance on any stage as "Carlo" in Linda di Chamouni.

Manners and customs at the Lodi Opera-house were at that time rather peculiar. Refreshments of all kinds used to be served in the audience department between the acts. Every box was furnished with a little kitchen for cooking macaroni, baking or frying pastry, and so on. The wine of the country was drunk freely, not out of glasses, but in classical fashion from bowls. Attired in the brilliant uniform of my part I was in the middle of the pit draining one of these bowls, when suddenly the signal was given for the rising of the curtain. All seemed lost. But I hurried back to the stage, and fortunately was not very late for my entry.

My success in Lodi was such that I was offered four pounds a month to sing at Verona. Here my first duty was to replace Bettini (not the husband of Madame Trebelli Bettini, but the dramatic tenor of that name) in the important part of "Manrico." Il Trovatore had but lately been brought out, and was then in the first period of its success. I had never heard the work, but the tenor part had been sent to me, and I had to master it in four days, my final study being made in the diligence, with no musical instrument to aid me except a tuning-fork. I studied the part all day and, by the light of a candle, all night, and before I reached Verona knew it perfectly. The prima donna of the cast was Mdlle. Lotti, afterwards known in London and elsewhere as Madame Lotti Della Santa, the second part of her name being derived from her husband, Signor Della Santa, who, during my stay at Verona, played the part of the "Count di Luna" to the "Leonora" of his future wife. Bettini married a sister of Max Maretzek, afterwards well known as conductor and impresario in the United States. I made a sufficiently good impression at Verona to cause Signor Bettini, who on my arrival was seriously ill, to get perfectly well after I had made but two appearances.

Returning to London early in 1854, I gave a grand concert with the following eminent artists:—Mdme. Clara Novello, Miss Dolby, Mr. Sims Reeves, Herr Formes, and Mdme. Arabella Goddard. I also took part in it. My throat, however, had become affected, and after I had been very thoroughly operated upon by Dr. Billing, I found myself deprived alike of tonsils, uvula, and voice.

My path had now been marked out for me. For the future I might be a musical agent, a concert director, or an impresario; but not a vocalist.

In 1855 the two principal members of the touring party I was directing were Miss Hayes and Mdme. Gassier.

In the year 1856 I started a musical agency in the Haymarket, the first established in London. Both Mr. Lumley and Mr. Gye applied to me for singers. As I was well known in Italy, numbers of artists inscribed their names on my books. I did a good business, and was making a large income. My business relations bound me more particularly to Mr. Lumley, the manager of Her Majesty's Theatre, and he had enough confidence in me to entrust me with the work of adapting Balfe's Bohemian Girl to the Italian stage. This was about the time of the gala performances in honour of the marriage of the Crown Prince of Prussia (late Emperor of Germany) to the Princess Victoria of England, when a number of Shakespearian representations were given at Her Majesty's Theatre, with Mr. Phelps in the principal parts.

No Italian version of Balfe's work existed previously, and I received for mine the sum of £50. Operatic translations are often severely judged, but it is no easy matter to adapt the words of a song so that, while other more obvious requirements are duly fulfilled, the accents shall fall in exact accordance with the composer's music.

In the early part of this year (1858) the late E. T. Smith, then lessee of the Theatre Royal, Drury Lane, called upon me at my office, in the Haymarket, requesting me to aid him in the formation of an Italian Opera Company, which he wished to secure for his theatre during the coming summer months. He had so many enterprises on hand that he asked me to undertake the superintendence and management of the Italian Opera season he had in view. I explained to him that the business I was then carrying on required all my care and attention, and that it was far more profitable than any interest he could offer me in his contemplated enterprise.

But won over by his solicitations, and influenced by my love of the divine art, I consented, and found myself at once drawn into the artistic vortex. My knowledge and experience fitted me well enough for the conduct of the undertaking, which, however, I considered rather a hazardous one.

On the one hand would be ranged against me Her Majesty's Theatre, under the late Mr. Lumley's able management, with such artists as Piccolomini, Alboni, Giuglini, and the new and successful Thérèse Titiens, who had already fully captured London; and on the other hand the Royal Italian Opera, Covent Garden, newly rebuilt, under the skilful direction of Mr. Gye, with Grisi, Mario, Costa, and a host of celebrities. I felt the great responsibility of the position I had undertaken. I, however, set to work and engaged the services of Salvini-Donatelli, Viardot, Persiani, Naudin, Badiali, Marini, Rovere, Charles Braham and other tried artists.

My first object was to secure an able conductor. I discovered Signor Vianesi (afterwards of the Royal Italian Opera, and now of the Grand Opera, Paris), and appointed him to the post at a salary of £8 a month. Much trouble was experienced in forming an efficient orchestra on account of the two great Italian Operas, and still more in obtaining a stage military band. This latter difficulty I surmounted when one day in Leicester Square I lighted upon a very excellent one composed of itinerant Italian musicians performing in the open street.

The season opened in due course, and the public gave ample support to the undertaking. I will not fatigue the reader by entering into details with respect to that season, which I began five days before the opening of the new Royal Italian Opera, Covent Garden, just rebuilt, in order that the singers might at all events give two public performances before the whole attention of the town would be centred on the new theatre.

On one occasion I encountered a slight difficulty, when the opera of La Traviata had, in consequence of the illness of one of the singers, to be suddenly substituted for the work originally announced. It was already half-past seven o'clock at night, and we were without a stage band.

I sent the call-boy down all the likely thoroughfares where my Italian wanderers might be playing, and I myself started to look for them in another direction. I ultimately traced them to a small restaurant in Soho, where they were eating macaroni. I gave them orders to come on immediately to the theatre to perform behind the scenes in La

Traviata, and hurried back to the theatre. On arriving there I found the call-boy had brought another street band, which now refused to quit the stage. At one time things looked very serious, as the Italians of the opposing bands, with their stilettos drawn, vowed vengeance on one another. Ultimately all was satisfactorily arranged.

The interest of this first season was kept up until its close, in the latter part of July. The only other incident here worth mentioning was the performance, on the 17th July, of Mozart's Don Giovanni with the following powerful cast:—

"Donna Anna"   Madame Pauline Viardot.
"Donna Elvira"   Madame Rudersdorff.
"Zerlina"   Madame Persiani.
"Don Giovanni"   Signor Badiali.
"Leporello" Signor Rovere.
"Commendatore"   Signor Marini.
"Masetto"   Signor Insom.
"Ottavio"   Signor Naudin.

The evening prior to its performance I met Mr. E. T. Smith, who horrified me by saying that in order to "strengthen up the bill," it being his benefit, he had added The Waterman, in which Charles Braham would play "Tom Tug," and moreover, introduce into the piece a new song dedicated by Mr. E. T. Smith to the Metropolitan Board of Works, who, said Smith, with a knowing wink, were "a most useful body."

I paid no attention to this at the time, thinking it was only a joke; but on looking at the Times newspaper on the day of the performance, I found that the announcement, as communicated to me by Mr. E. T. Smith, had really been made. The performance, too, of the Waterman, with the introduced song, was really given.

I waited with interest to see what the newspapers would say as to my closing representation. Only one paper mentioned the performance; and it confined itself to stating that Don Giovanni had been played the previous evening "by a body of singers whose united ages amounted to nearly 500 years."

Mr. E. T. Smith, the manager, had made money by our season; and he remunerated me very handsomely for my labours. In the meantime, notwithstanding the phenomenal success of Mdlle. Titiens at Her Majesty's Theatre, Mr. Lumley's difficulties had been constantly increasing; and Her Majesty's Theatre now closed, never to open again under his management.

CHAPTER II.

INJUNCTION AGAINST THE BIRDS ON THE TREES—DRURY LANE SEASON OF 1859—DÉBUTS OF VICTOIRE BALFE, MONGINI, AND GUARDUCCI—MY CONTRALTO MARRIES A DUKE—THE DUKE AND DUCHESS AT NAPLES.

EFFORTS were now made to obtain the lease of Her Majesty's theatre, but it was so entangled with legal difficulties that it was resolved, on my advice to remain another year at Drury Lane. I therefore set to work to secure a very powerful company for the London season of 1859.

During the latter part of 1858 the baritone Graziani had called repeatedly upon me, stating that as Mr. Gye had not renewed his engagement, and as there were some arrears outstanding, he was very desirous that I should engage him for the forthcoming season. After lengthy negotiations, some time during the month of March, 1859, I signed with him, and added him to the list of artists in the official programme.

On the prospectus being issued, law proceedings were immediately commenced by Mr. Gye, who asked for an injunction to restrain Graziani from appearing at Drury Lane.

Application was made before Vice-Chancellor Wood, and the most eminent counsel were engaged on both sides. Mr. Gye retained Rolt, Giffard, Martindale, etc., whilst Mr. E. T. Smith was represented by Sir Hugh Cairns, Hawkins, Swanstone, Serjeant Ballantine, Cottrell, Daniel, &c. The case was heard on the 11th and 12th May, 1859, when an injunction was granted. At this I felt somewhat astonished, inasmuch as Graziani's engagement had never been renewed by Mr. Gye, although in a period of more than eight months the eminent baritone had made more than a dozen applications for a renewal; neither had his salary been paid him.

I have repeatedly failed to obtain injunctions against my singers, both here and in America, though the engagements which they had broken were in every respect perfectly in order. I recollect a case in which one of my principal singers was announced to appear at the Crystal Palace in a concert, notwithstanding a written engagement whereby he contracted that I should have his exclusive services, and that he would sing nowhere without my written consent. No salary was owing to him, and I felt perfectly sure of obtaining an injunction, for which I duly applied, in order to restrain him from committing the contemplated breach of engagement.

A formal injunction was, in fact, granted; but the case was immediately afterwards brought before the Lords Justices for a full hearing. As I was very much occupied at the theatre with rehearsals, and felt sure the injunction would be confirmed, and, moreover, that the case would occupy but a few minutes, I did not attend; but at the end of my day's labours, feeling a little curious, I called on my solicitor on my way home, when I was informed by his clerk that he was still in Court and that my case was not concluded. I went there. Sure enough, there were the counsel still arguing. Two attendants were busily employed handing in law-books every minute or two, with pieces of paper between the leaves indicating pages for reference. The counsel on the other side was forcibly explaining the case by supposing a similar one between a vendor and a purchaser of sacks of flour. I could not believe that it was my case they were proceeding with.

Later on "—— v. ——, page ——," was quoted, and now sacks of corn and of linseed were brought in. The candles of the Court were burnt low down in the sockets, and the three Lords Justices were evidently very tired, when one of them spoke thus—

"I cannot conceive how Mr. Mapleson could expect to retain the exclusive services of any vocalist. In my opinion, sweet musical sounds should be for the benefit of everybody, and Mr. Mapleson might just as well apply for an injunction to restrain the birds from singing on the trees."

The other Justices concurred in the view that a singer must be free to sing where he liked.

In the United States I have been invariably unsuccessful in my applications for an injunction, or of even getting the Courts to define the meaning of a singer's engagement. The legal mind cannot grasp the idea. Were it a contract for the erection of buildings or machinery, or the sale of goods, or the exclusive manufacture of a piece of cotton printing, the matter would be clear enough. But no evidence on the part of musical experts is ever by any chance understood by the Court.

The Drury Lane season of 1859 opened on the 25th April with La Sonnambula, when I was fortunate enough to introduce two new singers, who both met with unequivocal success. One was Mdlle. Victoire Balfe (afterwards Lady Crampton, and subsequently Duchess de Frias), who appeared as "Amina;" the other, Signor Mongini, whose triumph was instantaneous in the part of "Elvino." This was his first appearance in England.

For this season two conductors had been engaged, Signor Arditi and Mr. (afterwards Sir Julius) Benedict. Both were excellent, but neither wished to be mistaken for the other. Both, moreover, were bald, and I remember on one occasion, when a grand combined performance was to take place, Benedict going into the prima donna's dressing-room, taking up a brush, and carefully arranging his scanty hair so as to cover as much as possible of his denuded cranium.

"What are you about, Benedict?" I asked.

"Nothing particular," he replied; "only I don't want, whilst wielding the baton, to be mistaken for Arditi."

Soon afterwards Arditi appeared, and with a couple of brushes began operating on his hair so as to leave as much as possible of his bare skull exposed to view. He explained his action by exclaiming—

"I don't want to be mistaken for Benedict."

On the following night I brought forward Mdlle. Guarducci, who appeared as "Leonora" in La Favorita, with Giuglini as "Fernando." Guarducci's success was instantaneous, her lovely voice being the object of universal admiration.

A very strange thing occurred in connection with Guarducci's début. She had arrived in London only two days before, in the belief that she would have two or three weeks to prepare the part which she had undertaken to perform. By a careful process of cramming we got her through; and she made one of the most marked successes London had witnessed for many years. I thereupon announced the opera for repetition four days afterwards, when to my great astonishment Guarducci informed me that she did not know a note of her part, and it took ten days' rehearsals for her to learn it in systematic style.

Later on I produced Mercadante's Giuramento, which, however, met with indifferent success. Mdlle. Titiens shortly afterwards appeared as "Lucrezia Borgia," when her phenomenal voice attracted such a house as had rarely been seen. Her performances throughout the remainder of the season were a series of triumphs never to be forgotten.

Arrangements were afterwards made for an operatic tour in the provinces, which we commenced in Dublin.

About this time the attentions of an Italian nobleman towards Mdlle. Guarducci became rather conspicuous, and at Mdlle. Titiens' suggestion I resolved to ask him what his intentions towards her really were. As no satisfactory answer could be obtained, Mdlle. Titiens took Guarducci entirely under her charge, and all communication with the Italian nobleman was put an end to.

Shortly afterwards he visited me, assuring me his intentions were most honourable, and begging me to intercede so that he might again meet Guarducci. Mdlle. Titiens' reply was—

"Yes, as her husband, not otherwise;" and to this ultimatum he consented.

In the course of a few days preparations were made for the marriage, but many difficulties presented themselves. The duke's father would have to be consulted, together with the Neapolitan Government, the Pope, and a few other powers.

About this time Mr. E. T. Smith appeared on the scene, and he assured the priests that of his certain knowledge the proposed marriage would be most agreeable to the duke's father; whilst I, on my side, induced the Consul of the then King of Naples and of the Two Sicilies to affix the Government stamp to the contract. I also had a marriage settlement drawn, whereby it was stipulated that if Mdlle. Guarducci at any time after the marriage should feel disposed she should have liberty to resume the exercise of her profession, and take the whole of the benefits she might derive therefrom for her own use; the duke engaging, moreover, that on the day he succeeded to his father's property and title he would assign to her £50,000 for her sole and separate use. The marriage was celebrated in the Metropolitan Church of Dublin, with full choral service, in which Piccolomini, Titiens, Aldighieri, Giuglini, and others took part. The scene was most impressive.

Within a week afterwards the marriage had made such a stir in Italy that the new duchess had to leave me, and, accompanied by the duke, take her departure for Italy.

I did not meet them afterwards until the year 1863, when at my hotel in Naples a gorgeous equipage drove up, in which were the Duke and Duchess di Cirilla, with a beautiful little child. It appeared that he had succeeded to his titles and estates, that he had already handed over the large sum of money promised in the settlement, and that they were the happiest couple in the world. They insisted upon my spending several days with them at their palace; and as it was the closing day of the Carnival we amused ourselves from the balcony of the Palazzo by throwing the most gorgeous sweetmeats, dolls, and other things at the heads of the populace. I was afterwards invited by the duke to a wild-boar hunt. He had charge of all the King's preserves at Caserta, and by his hospitable attentions he enabled me to pass the time most pleasantly.

Looking over my papers I find, what had really escaped my memory, that in order to ensure, so far as we could, the execution of the Duke's promise in regard to the settlement on his wife, Mr. E. T. Smith and myself made him sign a bond by which he bound himself, should he fail to fulfil his pledge, to pay to each of us the sum of £5,000.

Here is an exact copy of the deed; the like of which could scarcely be found in the archives of any Opera House in the world:—

"Know all Men by these Presents that I Alfonso Catalano Gonzaga de Duchi de Cirella formerly of Naples but now stopping at Gresham Hotel Dublin am held and firmly bound unto Edward Tyrrel Smith of Pensylvania Castle Dorset England and Lessee of the Theatre Royal Drury Lane London but now stopping at Gresham Hotel Dublin and James Henry Mapleson of 12 Haymarket London Gentleman but now stopping at Gresham Hotel Dublin in the sum of Ten thousand pounds sterling good and lawful money of the United Kingdom of Great Britain and Ireland to be paid to the said Edward Tyrrel Smith and James Henry Mapleson or their lawful Attorney Executors Administrators or assigns to the which payment to be made I do bind myself my heirs executors and administrators firmly by these presents Sealed with my seal and dated the eighth day of August in the year of our Lord one thousand eight hundred and fifty-nine.

The Condition of the above obligation is such that if the above bound Alfonso Catalano Gonzaga de Duchi de Cirella his heirs executors or administrators shall and do well and truly pay or cause to be paid unto the above named Edward Tyrrel Smith and James Henry Mapleson their executors administrators or assigns the just and full sum of Five thousand pounds sterling of good and lawful money of the United Kingdom of Great Britain and Ireland according to the covenant on his part contained in a certain Indenture of Settlement bearing even date herewith and made between Carolina Guarducci of the first part the said Alfonso Catalano Gonzaga de Duchi de Cirella of the second part and the said Edward Tyrrel Smith and James Henry Mapleson of the third part and shall also fully perform all and singular the other covenants and agreements on the part of him the said Alfonso Catalano Gonzaga contained in the aforesaid Settlement without fraud or further delay that then the above obligation is to be void and of none effect or else to stand and remain in full force and virtue in law

ALFONSO CATALANO GONZAGA
DE DUCHI DE CIRELLA

Signed sealed and delivered in the presence of by Alfonso Catalano Gonzaga de Duchi de Cirella the same having been first truly read explained and interpreted to him by J H Mapleson

THOMAS FITZGERALD
Solicitor 20 Saint Andrew St Dublin
THOS SNOWE
Neapolitan Vice Consul

I hereby certify that the within named James Henry Mapleson took a solemn oath administered by me that he had truly read explained and interpreted the true contents of the annexed Bond to the within named Carolina Guarducci and Alfonso Catalano Gonzaga de Duchi de Cirella

Neapolitan Vice Consulate
Dublin 10th August 1859 (nine)
THOS SNOWE
V Consul"
SEAL.
CHAPTER III.

NOCTURNAL NEGOTIATIONS—REOPENING OF HER MAJESTY'S THEATRE—SAYERS AND HEENAN PATRONIZE THE OPERA—ENGLISH AND ITALIAN OPERA COMBINED—SMITH AND HIS SPECULATIONS— DISCOVERY OF ADELINA PATTI—MY MANAGEMENT OF THE LYCEUM.

EARLY in the spring of 1860 I opened negotiations again with Lord Dudley, on behalf of Mr. Smith, to obtain the lease of Her Majesty's Theatre. After spending two days at Witley Court with his lordship I returned to London with the lease, and loaded with game.

The next step was to secure the services of Mdlle. Titiens, Giuglini, and others who still were bound to Mr. Lumley; and for that purpose Mr. Smith and myself started for the Continent. Mr. Lumley met us at Boulogne; the Channel, as in the previous year, being still too breezy for him to cross.

On our arrival we found that Mr. Lumley had prepared a sumptuous banquet. Every kind of expensive wine was on the table, together with the most famous liqueurs. The Bordeaux, the Burgundy, the Champagne, the Chartreuse, the Curaçao, and the Cognac were for us; whilst Mr. Lumley, like a clever diplomatist, confined himself to spring water. After I had made several attempts to broach the subject of our visit, which Lumley pretended not to understand, he showed himself quite astonished when he heard that Mr. Smith contemplated engaging his artists. To me fell the duty of conducting the negotiations between these two wily gentlemen; and it was not until about three or four o'clock the following morning that things began to get into focus. Mr. Lumley, in the meantime, had kept ordering innumerable syphons and fines champagnes for Mr. Smith, before whom the bottles were perpetually empty. As Mr. Smith warmed up, he wanted extensions for the following autumn, to which Lumley, reluctantly, of course, agreed. In the end the transfer was to cost some £16,000—I having obtained a reduction of £3,000 or £4,000 from the original price insisted on by Lumley. I afterwards had to draw an engagement that would prove satisfactory to both parties; a matter which was not finally settled until nearly six o'clock in the morning.

Mr. Smith having observed that he would see to the financial part being promptly carried out, Mr. Lumley replied that he would prefer to have bills drawn and handed over to him at once, payable at different dates, for the whole of the amount. He feared, he said, that some hostile creditor might attach any moneys in Smith's hands payable to him. Smith regretted that in France they could not purchase bill stamps, otherwise he would have been delighted to meet Mr. Lumley's views. Mr. Lumley, however, in getting a brush from his little hand-bag found some papers he could not account for, but which had somehow got in there; and these, to the astonishment of both Lumley and Smith, proved to be bill stamps. The next thing was to draw the various bills; and Smith remarked before leaving the banqueting-room that it would be better to finish the remains of the bottle then before him, lest the hotel servants should do so and get drunk. Mr. Lumley, instead of going to bed, went back to Paris by the early morning train, while Smith and myself returned to London.

The company for the season of 1860 was a marvellously attractive one.

Admirable, too, were the works produced.

Mr. Smith about this time had acquired various restaurants in London, besides the Alhambra, Cremorne Gardens, Drury Lane, and a variety of other establishments. The management of the opera was, therefore, left entirely to me, except that I received occasional visits at the most unseasonable hours from Mr. Smith, who arrived with the strangest suggestions. About this time the celebrated fight for the championship took place between Sayers and Heenan, and as the Covent Garden people were getting rather ahead of us, Mr. Smith, with a view to increased receipts, insisted on my announcing that Messrs. Sayers and Heenan, who had fought the day previously, would attend the opera in their bruised state. It was with the greatest difficulty that I afterwards got the announcement withdrawn from the papers. Both men appeared, nevertheless, that evening—one worse-looking than the other—in a private box which Smith had prepared specially for them on the grand tier; one corner being filled with brandies and sodas, and the other with bottles of champagne. Both men were so fatigued with their business of the previous day that before the end of the first act they went home, much to my relief.

Shortly afterwards Smith proposed that the Champion's belt (which had been divided in two) should be presented on the stage between the acts of the opera. This, too, I overruled, and the ceremony ultimately took place at the Alhambra.

On another occasion Mr. Smith suggested to me an idea that had occurred to him for closing up Covent Garden, by giving a grand double performance of Il Trovatore without any increase of prices. He proposed dividing the stage into two floors, as in the opera of Aida, with the occupants as follows:—

Top floor.		Bottom floor.		
"Manrico" ...	Mongini ...	Giuglini.		
"Conte di Luna"	...	Aldighieri	...	Everardi.
"Azucena" ...	Alboni ...	Borghi-Mamo.		
"Leonora" ...	Grisi	...	Titiens.	

The singers were alarmed, as the matter became serious. This project, however, like previous ones, I ultimately succeeded in setting aside. I pleaded that the preparations for the production of Oberon, now resolved upon, needed all my attention. Benedict, the favourite pupil of Weber, had undertaken to adapt the famous opera for the Italian stage by introducing recitative and excerpts from some of Weber's other works, whilst Planché, the author of the libretto, undertook the mise en scène. A really grand performance took place, with the following cast of characters:—

"Sir Huon," Mongini; "Scerasmin," Everardi; "Oberon,"

Belart; "Fatima," Alboni; "Rezia," Titiens.

Despite the artistic successes of the season, matters, as usual with operatic managers, did not go well in a financial sense. This, in a great measure, was to be accounted for by the drain on our exchequer caused by Mr. Smith's numerous outside speculations; for the receipts from the various establishments were all lumped into one banking account.

On one occasion I recollect having a deal of difficulty with the Sheriff's officers, who had got possession of the wardrobes. We were on the point of producing the Huguenots, and the whole of the dresses for that opera were under ban. One afternoon Smith came in; and after some little time it appeared that the officers had agreed not to take the Huguenots until we had had two performances out of it.

In fact, there was always some trouble going on, and it was with the greatest difficulty that we got through the season.

In the Boulogne contracts Lumley's artists were ceded not only for a summer, but also for an autumn season at Her Majesty's. As, however, they were to sing but three times a week, it occurred to me that English opera might be tried with advantage on the alternate nights. Arrangements were accordingly entered into, through the kindness of Mr. Thomas Chappell, with Mrs. L. Sherrington, Mr. Sims Reeves, and Mr. Santley. Charles Hallé was at the same time engaged as conductor.

Negotiations were also entered into with Macfarren for the production of an English work entitled Robin Hood, the libretto by Oxenford. The opera met with very great success, so much so that the chief attentions of the public were directed to the evenings on which Robin Hood was performed. I then opened negotiations with Vincent Wallace to prepare an opera to follow, entitled the Amber Witch, libretto by Chorley, in which Mr. Sims Reeves, Mrs. L. Sherrington, Santley, Patey, and others appeared.

But again the war cloud seemed to hover over the establishment, and again the Sheriff's officers appeared in force. It was thought advisable to transfer the Amber Witch to Drury Lane, leaving the myrmidons of the law in possession of the theatre and its belongings. The Amber Witch wardrobe (which somehow had fallen off the portico of the theatre early one Sunday morning) found its way to the other theatre. Here the part of the "Amber Witch" was undertaken by Madame Parepa, vice Sherrington.

Mr. Edward Tyrrel Smith, with whom I had business relations for some three or four years, was an extraordinary personage, whose like could only be met with in our own time, and in such capitals as London or Paris, where the population in general has certainly not the faintest idea how some small part of that population lives. Mr. E. T. Smith had made up his mind early in life to be the possessor, or at least the handler, of considerable sums of money; and he at one time found it worth his while, so as never to be without funds, to hire daily, at the rate of £1 a day, a thousand-pound note, which was obligingly entrusted to him by a money-lender of the period, one Sam Genese.

There are not many persons to whom such a loan would be worth the thirty-six and a half per cent. interest which Mr. E. T. Smith paid for it. He was an adept, however, at all kinds of business, and his thousand-pound note enabled him to make purchases on credit, which, without deposit money, he would have been unable to effect. Attending sales he would buy whatever happened to suit him, with a view to immediate resale, offering his thousand-pound note as a deposit, to discover, as a matter of course, that it could not be changed, and have the article for which he had bid marked down to him all the same. Then he would resell it, and pocket the difference.

11

The mere exhibition of the thousand-pound note secured him a certain amount of credit, and he was not likely ever to meet with an auctioneer able to change it. Before offering his (or rather Mr. Genese's) note he took care to write his name on the back of it. Afterwards his usurious friend would replace the note that had been endorsed by a brand new one, and occasions presented themselves in which it was a distinct advantage for E. T. Smith to be known as a gentleman who, in the course of a comparatively short space of time, had inscribed his name on several bank-notes, each for a thousand pounds.

Once, when St. Dunstan's Villa, in the Regent's Park, was knocked down to Smith for ten thousand pounds, the thousand-pound note which he had, as usual, in his waistcoat pocket was just what was wanted to satisfy the auctioneer's immediate demands. Smith handed up the note with the observation that he would turn the place into a second Cremorne Gardens, in which character it could not fail to attract thousands of people and bring in lots of money. At this announcement the auctioneer drew back and informed the apparently eager purchaser that the house could be converted to no such purpose.

One day, when I had run down to Brighton with Mr. Smith, then associated with me in the management of Drury Lane, we missed, by about half a minute, the return train we had intended to catch; and we had now two hours to wait. Smith could not remain idle, and strolling with me along the Parade his attention was attracted by a corner house which was for sale, and which, it at once struck him, might be turned to profitable account as a milliner's shop. He inquired as to the rent and other conditions, bought the house there and then, and at once ordered that the windows on the ground floor should be replaced by much larger ones of plate glass.

That night he started for Paris, and in the Passage du Saumon, where bonnets of almost the latest fashion can be purchased for moderate prices, laid in a stock of millinery for his Brighton "magasin des modes." While making his purchases in Paris he secured the services of two eligible young women, who were brought over to direct the Brighton establishment. This, within a very short time, he duly opened under the name of "Clémentine," and the house of Clémentine did such good business that a few weeks afterwards its spirited proprietor was able to sell it at seven hundred pounds' profit.

On the occasion of a melancholy event which compelled all the London managers to close their theatres, Mr. E. T. Smith saw in this day of national gloom a tempting opportunity for a masked ball. It was to be given at Her Majesty's Theatre, and earnestly as I sought to divert him from his project he insisted on carrying it out. I had no right of veto in the matter, and the masked ball took place. The sum of one guinea entitled a ticket-holder to entrance and supper, and a day or two before the entertainment fires were lighted in the property-room, the painting-room, and the wardrobes, in order to cook some hundreds of fowls which had been purchased in the market, after ordinary market hours, at a very cheap rate.

Wine would be an extra charge. In order to suit the tastes of connoisseurs, Mr. Smith made large purchases of Heidsieck, Pommery Greno, Perrier Jouet, and other favourite brands somewhere in Whitechapel, where they can be secured at a much less cost than at Epernay or Rheims. When the wine came in he showed it to me with a look of pride, and opened a bottle of someone's cuvée réservée in order to have my opinion. I told him frankly that the bottles, labels, and the names branded on the corks seemed all that could be desired, and that I found nothing bad except the wine. This he seemed to look upon as an unimportant detail, and the Whitechapel champagne was sold to infatuated dancers at ten and twelve shillings a bottle.

About this time I chanced to hear of an extraordinary young vocalist, who had been charming the Americans, and, although hardly nineteen, seemed to have obtained a firm hold on the sympathy and admiration of their public. I opened negotiations at once, in order to secure her services for the forthcoming season at Her Majesty's, and a contract was duly entered into on behalf of Mr. Smith, whereby the little lady undertook to sing four nights on approval, when, in case of success, she was to have a salary of £10 a week. I likewise concluded an engagement with Mario, whose term had expired at Covent Garden, and with Madame Grisi; while Costa undertook to join the following year on the expiration of his existing contract with Mr. Gye.

In fact, all looked very promising for the year 1861. But, as the time approached, I found more difficulty than ever in communicating with Mr. Smith, who seemed to be out of the way. I then accidentally learned that owing to the extreme financial difficulty in which he was placed through his numerous outside speculations he had been compelled to accept an offer from Mr. Gye of £4,000 on condition of his not opening.

In accordance with this arrangement Her Majesty's Theatre remained closed.

Some time in the month of April the little lady from America arrived and sent me up her card, bearing the name of Adelina Patti. She was accompanied by Maurice Strakosch, her brother-in-law. They wished to know when Mr. Smith's season was likely to begin. I could give them no information beyond the current report which they had already heard themselves. The little lady, who was then seated on a sofa at the Arundel Hotel, at the bottom of Norfolk Street, Strand, suggested that I should try the speculation myself, as she felt sure she would draw money. I thereupon asked her to let me hear her, that I might judge as to the quality of her voice, to which she responded by singing "Home, Sweet Home." I saw that I had secured a diamond of the first water, and immediately set about endeavouring to get Her Majesty's Theatre. But this was a hopeless business, as Smith, who still held the lease, was nowhere to be found. Shortly afterwards, however, I met Smith by chance, and proposed renting Drury Lane from him, without saying what for.

Two days later he brought me an agreement which he requested me to sign. I said that I should like first to glance over it. He pointed out to me that I might give operas, dramas, pantomimes, ballets, in fact everything; and that I should have no difficulty in making a very fine season. But on the top of the page overleaf my eye caught sight of a parenthesis, within which were the words "Italian Opera excepted." I thereupon put down the pen, raised some question about the deposit, and afterwards kept clear of Mr. Smith.

But many years after he had ceased to be connected with theatres I one day received a letter from him, in which he told me he was in the metal trade, and asked me to send him a couple of stalls for himself and his "old woman." The heading of the letter announced the character of his new business, and he added in a postscript: "Do you ever want any tin?"

Nothing now remained but to secure the Lyceum; the only other theatre available. This I did. It having been occupied but two or three years previously by the Royal Italian Opera, I considered the locale would be perfectly suited for my purpose. I thereupon started off to Paris to find Mr. Lumley, from whom I now wished to secure for myself the singers still engaged to him. Mr. Lumley had unfortunately left for Marseilles. I myself started for Marseilles, but in passing Avignon I thought I saw black whiskers in the passing train resembling those of Mr. Lumley. But I was not sure. I therefore continued my journey.

"Mr. Lumley, est parti," I was told on my arrival. I returned to Paris, and was informed that he had gone to England, which I knew was not possible, except on a Sunday. This being Saturday, I determined to stop at Boulogne and make inquiries; and in the same hotel where I had conducted the negotiations some two or three years previously I found him. I soon completed my arrangements, undertaking to give him half my total gross nightly receipts in exchange for Titiens and Giuglini. I undertook to provide the whole of the expenses, with Alboni, Patti, and others among my other singers. I returned joyfully to London, and at once went to the Arundel Hotel to inform Miss Patti and Strakosch of my good luck. They did not seem overjoyed, or in any way to participate in my exuberant delight.

Maurice Strakosch told me that as their last £5 note had been spent he had been obliged to borrow £50 of Mr. Gye, which intelligence at once reduced my height by at least two inches; and after a deal of difficulty I ascertained that he had signed a receipt for the said loan in a form which really constituted an engagement for the Royal Italian Opera, Covent Garden.

In short, I found myself manager of the Lyceum Theatre, with an expensive Company, and with Mdlle. Patti opposed to me in the immediate vicinity at Covent Garden.

My season opened at the Lyceum on Saturday, the 8th June, 1861, the opera being Il Trovatore, "Manrico," Signor Giuglini; "Il Conte di Luna," Signor delle Sedie, the eminent baritone, who made his first appearance in England; "Ferrando," Signor Gassier; whilst "Azucena" was Mdme. Alboni, and "Leonora," Mdlle. Titiens; Arditi conducting the orchestra, which was composed of the members of the Philharmonic Society and Her Majesty's private band. On the second night I gave Lucrezia Borgia, with Giuglini, Gassier, Alboni, and Titiens in leading parts.

In the meanwhile I placed Verdi's new opera, Un Ballo in Maschera, in rehearsal in order that I might have the honour of representing it for the first time in this country; and by dint of almost superhuman effort on the part of Arditi and the principal artists, I produced it some few days before Covent Garden, although it had been in rehearsal there for over six weeks. I well recollect how, after a fatiguing performance of such an opera as Les Huguenots, Lucrezia Borgia, or Norma, Mdlle. Titiens, Giuglini, and other artists would go in the direction of Eaton Square to take supper with Signor Arditi, and at about half-past one in the morning begin rehearsing. The rehearsals terminated, the full blaze of the sun would accompany us on our way home to bed. This was done night after night.

But our efforts were rewarded by the immense success the opera achieved at its first performance.

During the first weeks of my management I had a strong counter-attraction operating against me in the shape of a large fire raging in Tooley Street, which it seemed to be the fashionable thing to go and see. Thousands attended it every evening.

Before the close of the season I gave a grand combined performance composed of excerpts from various operas—a kind of representation never popular with the British public; but, this being the last night of my season, the house was crowded from top to bottom. During the evening the choristers had banded together, threatening to refuse their services unless I complied with an exorbitant claim which I considered they had no right to make.

Prior to the curtain rising for the final section of the performance—the entire fourth act of the Huguenots—I was sent for. All reasoning with the chorus singers was useless. I therefore left the room, telling them to remain until I returned, which they promised to do. I then instructed Mdlle. Titiens and Giuglini that the "Conspirators' Chorus" ("Bénédiction des Poignards") would be left out, and that the act must commence, as it was now very late, with the entry of "Raoul" and "Valentine" for the grand duet, whereby I dispensed with the services of the chorus altogether.

14

No sooner did they hear that the opera was proceeding than they one and all surrendered. I, however, had the pleasure of telling them that I should never require one of them again—and I never did.

This really was the origin, now common at both Opera-houses, of the introduction of choristers from Italy. I may mention that the members of my refractory chorus were people who had been some thirty or forty years, or even longer, at the Opera-houses and other theatres in London, and it was really an excellent opportunity for dispensing with their services.

At the close of the opera season, on balancing my accounts, I found myself a loser of some £1,800. Thereupon, I resolved to carry on the Opera again in a larger locale next year in order that I might get straight; vowing, as the Monte Carlo gambler constantly does, that as soon as I got quite straight I would stop, and never play again. I have been endeavouring during the last thirty years to get straight, and still hope to do so.

CHAPTER IV.

AT HER MAJESTY'S THEATRE—VERDI'S CANTATA—GIUGLINI AT THE SEASIDE—POLLIO AND THE DRUM-STICK—AN OPERATIC CONSPIRACY—CONFUSION OF THE CONSPIRATORS.

EARLY in the following spring, I succeeded in securing a promise of the lease of Her Majesty's Theatre for 21 years, for which I deposited £4,000 pending its preparation. I hastened to make public announcement of the fact. Lord Dudley, however, kept varying the conditions of payment, which I understood originally to have been a deposit of £4,000 to remain as security for the payment of the rent throughout the tenancy. His lordship contended, however, that the sum deposited was in part payment of the first year's rent, and that another £4,000 must be paid before I could obtain possession.

This was indeed a terrible set-back to me, and I was at my wits' end what to do. However, through the kindness of my friend Mitchell, who subscribed largely, together with various members of the trade, I secured the remainder; and on the first day of April—ominous day!—I passed through the stage door with the key of the Opera in one pocket and £2—my sole remaining balance—in the other. I stood in the middle of the stage contemplating my position. I was encouraged by the celebrated black cat of Her Majesty's; which, whether in good faith or bad, rubbed herself in the most friendly manner against my knees.

Prior to the opening of my season of 1862 I made an increase in the number of stalls from seven to ten rows, my predecessor having increased them from four to seven. This removed the Duke of Wellington, who was an old supporter of the house, much farther from the stage, it having always been his custom to occupy the last number. Thus in Mr. Lumley's time he occupied No. 82, in Mr. Smith's time 163, whilst this increase of mine sent back His Grace to 280. Nothing but the last stall would satisfy him; he did not care where it was.

Prior to my opening the most tempting offers were made by Mr. Gye to my great prima donna Titiens. Her name, which closed my list of artists, was mentioned in my prospectus with the subjoined prefatory remarks: "The Director feels that with the following list of artists nothing more need be said. Of one, however, a special word may not be out of place, since she may without exaggeration be said to constitute the last link of that chain of glorious prime donne commencing with Catalani. It is seldom that Nature lavishes on one person all the gifts which are needed to form a great soprano: a voice whose register entitles it to claim this rank is of the rarest order. Melodious quality and power, which are not less essential than extended register, are equally scarce. Musical knowledge, executive finish, and perfect intonation are indispensable, and to these the prima donna should add dramatic force and adaptability, together with a large amount of personal grace. Even these rare endowments will not suffice unless they are illumined by the fire of genius. By one only of living artists has this high ideal been reached—by Mdlle. Titiens."

The subscriptions began pouring in, and all appeared couleur de rose, when Mr. Gye's envoy, the late Augustus Harris, again appeared, Titiens not having yet signed her contract with me; and he produced a contract signed by Mr. Gye with the amount she was to receive in blank. She was to fill in anything she chose. It was indeed a trying moment, and various members of her family urged her to give consideration to this extraordinary proposal. She, however, replied in few words: "I have given my promise to Mr. Mapleson, which is better than all contracts." My season, therefore, commenced in due course.

I had got together a magnificent company, and as the public found that the performances given merited their support and confidence, the receipts gradually began to justify all expectations, and within a short time I found myself with a very handsome balance at my bankers. This may be accounted for by the very large influx of strangers who came to London to visit the Exhibition of 1862. One day, about this time, in coming from my house at St. John's Wood, I met Verdi, who explained to me that he was very much disappointed at the treatment he had received at the hands of the Royal Commissioners, who had rejected the cantata he had written for the opening of the Exhibition. I at once cheered him up by telling him I would perform it at Her Majesty's Theatre if he would superintend its direction, Mdlle. Titiens undertaking the solo soprano part. The cantata was duly performed, and the composer was called some half-dozen times before the curtain. At the same time the work was purchased by a London publisher, who paid a handsome price for it. Verdi appeared very grateful, and promised me many advantages for the future.

Early in the season I produced the opera of Semiramide, in which the sisters Marchisio appeared with distinction. Afterwards came Weber's romantic opera of Oberon; J. R. Planché, the author of the libretto, and Mr. Benedict, Weber's favourite pupil, taking part in its reproduction.

This was followed by the remounting of Meyerbeer's Robert le Diable, with Titiens in the part of "Alice," the whole of the scenery and dresses being entirely new. Mdlle. (now Mdme.) Trebelli shortly afterwards arrived, and on May 4th appeared with brilliant success as "Maffio Orsini" in Lucrezia Borgia, her second appearance taking place four days afterwards in the part of "Azucena" (Trovatore), when her permanent reputation seemed to be already ensured, as it in fact was.

About this time I had a great deal of difficulty with the tenor, Giuglini, who, like a spoilt child, did not seem to know what he really required. He went down to Brighton accompanied by a certain notorious lady, and all persuasion to induce him to return proved useless. He said he had the "migraine." Thereupon I hit upon a device for making him return, which succeeded perfectly.

On the day of my visit I announced the Trovatore for performance, with Naudin, the tenor whom I had introduced some two years previously to London, in the principal rôle. I spoke to a friendly critic, who promised, in the event of Naudin's meeting with the success which I anticipated, to make a point of recording the fact; and on the following morning at Brighton, as I was accidentally walking with Giuglini, I purchased the paper in which my friend wrote and handed it to the lady who was absorbing all Giuglini's attention. I casually observed that Giuglini might now remain at Brighton for a lengthened period. In the course of an hour the tenor was on his way to London, volunteering to sing the same evening if necessary; adding, however, a condition which really caused me some inconvenience.

He now informed me that he had written a better cantata than Verdi's, and that unless I performed it I could no longer rely upon his services; if, however, his work were given he would remain faithful to me for the future. The work was duly delivered, in which I remember there was a lugubrious character destined for Mdlle. Titiens, called "Una madre Italiana." Giuglini further required 120 windows on the stage, from each of which, at a given signal, the Italian flag was to appear; and no smaller number than 120 would satisfy him. We were at our wits' end. But the difficulty was met by arranging the scene in perspective; grown-up people being at the windows nearest the public, then children at those farther removed, until in the far distance little dolls were used.

At a given signal, when the orchestra struck up the Garibaldi hymn, these were all to appear. I need scarcely say that the cantata was given but for one night. Poor Arthur Bacon, of the Ship Hotel, backed up Giuglini's own opinion when he declared it to be "a fine work."

The business meanwhile kept on increasing. In fact, I kept the theatre open on and off until nearly Christmas time, and always to crowded houses.

During my autumn provincial tour of 1862 I had much trouble in finding a substitute for my contralto, at that time Mdlle. Borchardt, who was suffering from a sudden attack of "grippe;" an illness which, at least in the artistic world, includes influenza, low fever, and other maladies hard to define. The opera announced was Lucrezia Borgia, and my difficulty was to find a lady capable of singing the part of "Maffio Orsini." I improvised a substitute who possessed good will, but was without knowledge of music and had scarcely a voice. In an apology to the public I stated that Mdlle. Borchardt being indisposed, another artist had at a moment's notice kindly consented to sing the part of "Maffio Orsini," but that "with the permission of the audience she would omit the brindisi of the third act."

This seemed little enough to ask, though the part of "Maffio Orsini" without the famous drinking song, "Il segreto per esser felice," was only too much like the celebrated performance of Hamlet with the part of the Crown Prince of Denmark left out.

It being quite understood, however, that the brindisi was to be omitted, the singer left out on her own account and by my special directions (scarcely necessary, it must be admitted) the legend of the opening scene. Cut out the legend and drinking song, and nothing of the part of "Maffio Orsini" remains except the few bars of defiance which this personage has to address to "Lucrezia Borgia" in the finale of the first act. These, however, can be sung by some other artist, and an audience unacquainted with the opera will probably not complain if they are not sung at all. The brindisi of the banqueting scene could not, of course, have been omitted without explanation. But the necessary apology having been frankly made there was nothing more to be said about the matter.

I hoped that Mdlle. Borchardt would be sufficiently recovered to undertake next evening the part of "Azucena" in Il Trovatore. But "la grippe" still held her in its clutches. She would have sung had it been possible to do so, but all power of singing had for the time left her, and it was absolutely necessary to replace her in the part which she was advertised to play.

In the first act of Il Trovatore "Azucena" does not appear, and I had reason to believe, or at least to hope, that before the curtain rose for the second act I should succeed in persuading my seconda donna to assume in the second and succeeding acts— in which "Leonora's" confidant is not wanted—the character of "Azucena."

At the last moment my eloquence prevailed, and the seconda donna declared herself ready to undertake the part of the gipsy. As for singing the music, that was a different question. Already instructed by me, she was to get through the part as well as she could without troubling herself to sing.

Meanwhile I had desired Titiens, Giuglini, and Aldighieri to exert themselves to the utmost in the first act; and it was not until after they had gained a great success in the trio which concludes this act that I ventured to put forward an apology for my new and more than inexperienced "Azucena."

It was necessary first of all to see to her "make up," and as soon as the requisite permission had been given, I myself covered her face—and covered it thickly—with red ochre. Unfortunately, in my haste and anxiety I forgot to paint more than her face and the front part of her neck. The back part of her neck, together with her hands and arms, remained as nearly as possible a pure white. I had told my new "Azucena" to sit on the sofa, resting her head upon her hands, and this, at the risk of bringing into too great contrast the red ochre and the pearl white, she obligingly did.

I had arranged that after the anvil chorus, the opening scene of the second act should terminate; the duet between "Manrico" and "Azucena" being thus left out. We passed at once to the "Count di Luna's" famous solo, "Il balen," and so on to the finale of this act. In the third act "Azucena" was simply brought before the Count and at once condemned to imprisonment. In the fourth act she had been strictly enjoined to go to sleep quietly on the ground, and not to wake up until "Manrico" was decapitated.

Thus treated, the part of "Azucena" is not a difficult one to play; and how else is it to be dealt with when the contralto of the Company is ill, and no adequate substitute for her can possibly be found?

The devices, however, that I have set forth are obviously of a kind that can only be resorted to once in a way under stress of difficulties otherwise insurmountable.

Accordingly, when the third day came and Mdlle. Borchardt was still too unwell to sing, there was nothing left for me but to announce an opera which contained no contralto part. The one I selected was Norma, a work for which our principal tenor, Signor Giuglini, had conceived a special hatred and in which he had sworn by the Holy Virgin and Madame Puzzi never to sing again. I must here break off for a moment to explain the origin of this peculiar detestation.

About a year before Giuglini had been playing the part of "Pollio" to the "Norma" of Mdlle. Titiens; and in the scene where the Druid priestess summons by the sound of the gong an assembly which will have to decide as to the punishment to be inflicted upon a guilty person unnamed, Mdlle. Titiens, on the point of administering to the gong an unusually forcible blow, threw back the drum-stick with such effect, that coming into violent contact with the nose of Signor Giuglini, who was close behind her, it drew from it if not torrents of blood, at least blood in sufficient quantity to make the sensitive tenor tremble for his life. He thought his last hour had come, and even when he found that he was not mortally wounded still nourished such a hatred against the offending drum-stick that he uttered the solemn combination oath already cited, and required, moreover, that the drum-stick should never more be brought into his presence. If not destroyed, it was at least to be kept carefully locked up.

Mdme. Puzzi had been to Giuglini more than a mother. Frequently, indeed, this lady helped him out of scrapes in which a mother would probably not have cared to interfere. She rescued him, for instance, more than once from enterprising young women, who, by dint of personal fascinations, of flattery, and sometimes of downright effrontery, had got the impressionable singer beneath their influence. When things were at their worst,

Giuglini would write or telegraph to "Mamma Puzzi," as he called her; and his adopted mother, to do her justice, always came to his relief, and by ingenuity and strength of will freed him from the tyranny of whatever siren might for the time have got hold of him.

When, therefore, he swore by Madame Puzzi he was serious, and when he pronounced his grand combination oath, "By the Holy Virgin and Madame Puzzi," it was understood that he had spoken his last word, and that nothing could ever move him from the determination arrived at under such holy influences.

Giuglini was in many things a child. So, indeed, are most members of the artistic tribe, and it is only by treating them and humouring them as children that one can get them to work at all.

The only two things Giuglini really delighted in were kites and fireworks. Give him kites to fly by day and rockets, roman candles, or even humble squibs and crackers to let off at night, and he was perfectly happy. Often in the Brompton Road, at the risk of being crushed to death by omnibuses, he has been seen lost in admiration of the kite he was flying, until at last the omnibus men came to know him, and from sympathy, or more probably from pity for the joy he took in childish pleasures, would drive carefully as they came near him.

His fireworks proved to him more than once a source of serious danger. On one occasion, in Dublin, for instance, when he was coming home from the theatre in company with Mademoiselle Titiens, who had just achieved a triumph of more than usual brilliancy, the carriage, already stuffed full of fireworks, was surrounded by a number of enthusiastic persons who, heedless of the mine beneath them, smoked cigars and pipes as they at the same time leaned forward and cheered.

Let us now return to the doings of Signor Giuglini in connection with the opera of Norma, in which he had sworn his great oath never again to appear.

I have said that the artist is often child-like; but with this childishness a good deal of cunning is sometimes mixed up. The one thing he cannot endure is life under regular conditions. Exciting incidents of some kind he must have in order to keep his nerves in a due state of tension, his blood in full circulation. It annoys him even to have his salary paid regularly at the appointed time. He would rather have an extra sum one day and nothing at all another. The gratuity will give him unexpected pleasure, while the non-payment of money justly due to him will give him something to quarrel about.

The artist is often suspicious, and in every Opera Company there are a certain number of conspirators who are always plotting mischief and trying to bring about misunderstandings between the manager on the one hand, and on the other the vocalists, musicians, and even the minor officials of the establishment.

Needless to say that the singer on the night he sings, his nerves vibrating with music, cannot at the end of the performance go to bed and get quietly to sleep; and on one occasion, at Edinburgh, I passed on my way to my bed the room in which Signor Giuglini was reposing, with a cigar in his mouth, between the sheets and listening to the tales, the gossip, the scandal, and the malicious suggestions poured into his ears by the camorristi of whom I have above spoken.

All I heard was, uttered in exciting tones, such words as "extra performance," "almanac," "imposition," "Mapleson," and so on.

I knew that some plot was being hatched against me, but what it could be I was unable to divine; nor, to tell the truth, did I trouble myself much about it.

Meanwhile I had spoken to Mr. Wyndham, manager of the Edinburgh Theatre, about the necessity, should Mademoiselle Borchardt still remain ill, of performing some opera in which there was no part for a contralto. He saw the necessity of what I suggested, and agreed with me that Norma would be the best work to play. I, at the same time, informed him that Giuglini had sworn "by the Holy Virgin and Madame Puzzi" never more to appear in that work, and I had no reason for believing that he had forgotten either his impressive oath or his bruised nose.

It was resolved, therefore, to announce Signor Corsi for the part of "Pollio." This might have suited Giuglini, from the superstitious point of view; but it put him out in the project which, prompted by the camorristi, he had formed for extorting from me a certain sum of money. He was engaged to play sixteen times a month at the rate of sixty pounds a performance. I had wished to have his services four times a week; and in signing for sixteen performances a month it did not occur to me that now and then in the course of the year the tenor might be called upon to give a seventeenth. This was the point which he and his fellow-conspirators had been discussing in his bedroom on the night when it had struck me that some sort of dark scheme was being prepared for my confusion.

It had been pointed out to Giuglini that if he sang on the 31st of the month, as I originally intended him to do, he would be singing once too often—once more than had been stipulated for in his engagement; and thereupon he would be in a position to enforce from me whatever penalty be might choose to impose. This he deigned to fix at the moderate sum of £160; and his claim was sent in to me just before—in consequence of the continued illness of Mdlle. Borchardt—I had decided to change the opera, and out of respect for Signor Giuglini's own feelings, to assign the tenor part in Norma not to him, but to an artist who was not bound to keep clear of this opera either by a peculiarly solemn oath or by painful recollections of a dab on the nose from a vigorously-handled drum-stick.

The opera, then, was announced with Signor Corsi in the part of "Pollio;" and there seemed to be no reason why the performance should not go off successfully. I noticed, however, some ominous signs, and, for one reason or another, it seemed to me that the carefully-laid mine, if it exploded at all, would burst that evening.

Giuglini was in a very excited condition, and I knew that whenever he felt unduly agitated he sent for "Mamma Puzzi" to come and soothe his irritated nerves. I did not know where Mdme. Puzzi was; but I did know that she might at any moment arrive, and I therefore gave orders that she was not, under any circumstances, to be admitted. The stage door was closed absolutely against her. With or without explanations, she was not to be let in.

When the night for the performance arrived I took care to see that Signor Corsi, at the proper time, was fitly attired for the character of "Pollio." He had often played the part before in company with Mdlle. Titiens, and I saw no reason for believing that his performance would not on this, as on previous occasions, be thoroughly satisfactory. The house was crowded. "Oroveso" had sung his air, and was being warmly applauded. I stood at the wing close to the first entrance and waited for Corsi to appear. The music in announcement of "Pollio's" entry was played; but no "Pollio" was to be seen. I motioned to Arditi, and the introductory strains were heard again. Still no "Pollio."

I rushed to Corsi's room in order to find out the meaning of the delay, when, to my consternation and horror, I saw Corsi seated in a chair with Mdme. Puzzi—Mdme. Puzzi, to whom all access to the theatre had been so strictly forbidden!—pulling off his fleshings (she had already divested him of his upper garments) while Giuglini was hurriedly taking off his costume of ordinary life in order to put on the uniform of the Roman soldier.

Giuglini, I found, had some days before telegraphed to Mdme. Puzzi at Turin begging his "mamma" to hurry to Edinburgh, where her child was in a terrible difficulty; and to Edinburgh she had come.

20

Mdme. Puzzi, refused admission at the stage door, had before the raising of the curtain gone round to the pit entrance, paid for her place, climbed over into the stalls, and then clambered from the stalls to the orchestra, and—most difficult of all these gymnastic performances—from the orchestra to the stage. She had then made her way to the dressing-rooms, and, finding Corsi already costumed for the part, had by persuasion or force induced him to change clothes with the excited tenor, who, by the very lady who was now helping him to break his vow, had sworn never to play the part he was on the point of undertaking.

The curtain, meantime, had been lowered, amidst deafening protests from the audience; and it was difficult to know what to do, until Giuglini, having, with due assistance from his "mamma," completed his toilette, declared himself ready to sing the part of "Pollio" provided one hundred pounds were stopped out of the receipts to pay him for his extra performance!

On my afterwards taunting Giuglini with having broken his vow, he declared that Mdme. Puzzi possessed the power to liberate him from it.

When the audience were informed that the part of "Pollio" would be played by Signor Giuglini, they were naturally delighted. The performance was begun again from the beginning. The drum-stick, however, in accordance with Giuglini's earnest prayer, was kept in the property-room under lock and key, and Mdlle. Titiens struck the gong with her hand.

Afterwards Giuglini showed himself a little ashamed of his conduct; and of the hundred pounds paid to him for the extra performance he presented fifty to Mrs. Wyndham, with a request that she would expend the money in the purchase of a shawl. Mrs. Wyndham, however, would do nothing of the kind. She considered that I had been very badly treated, and made over the sum to me.

The remaining fifty pounds had to be shared between Giuglini and the conspirators who had put him up to the trick, each of them having bargained beforehand for a share in such plunder as might be obtained.

Then a claim was put in by Mdme. Puzzi for her travelling expenses from Turin. This her affectionate child was not prepared to allow, and some violent language was exchanged between him and his "mamma." How the delicate matter was ultimately arranged I forget; but in the end, when he had satisfied all demands made upon him, Giuglini could scarcely have gained much by his too elaborate stratagem.

CHAPTER V.

RUNNING OVER A TENOR—TITIENS IN ITALY—CASHING A CHEQUE AT NAPLES—A NEAPOLITAN BALL—APPROACHING A MINISTER—RETURN TO LONDON.

ONE afternoon about four o'clock, during the month of November, 1862, Giuglini sent word that he would be unable to sing the part of "Lionel" in Martha that evening, having had some dispute at home. All my persuasion was useless; nothing would induce him, and as at that period of the year there were no tenors to be found in London, I was at my wits' ends to know what to do, and I ultimately decided to close the theatre, having no alternative. I therefore got into a hansom and drove off to inform Mdme. Trebelli, also Mdlle. Titiens, who was dining at her house, that there would be no need of their coming down.

On turning the corner of the Haymarket, Piccadilly, the horse's head struck a gentleman and forced him back on to the pavement. The cab was stopped, and a policeman came up. The gentleman was not, however, injured, and to my great astonishment he turned out to be an English tenor, who had been lately in Italy. On learning this I politely took him into my cab and inquired what had brought him back to England. He said that he had been performing at various Italian theatres, and that he was now very desirous of obtaining a début in this country.

I at once informed him that nothing could be easier, and that it would be best for him to make his appearance immediately, without any further preparation, for thus he would have no time to reflect and get nervous. I then quite casually, as we were going along, asked him if he knew the opera of Martha, to which he replied that he knew nothing of the music and had never seen the work. This for the moment wrecked all my hopes as to saving my receipts that evening, the booking for which exceeded £600.

My impulse was to stop the cab and put him out; but first I sang to him a few bars of M'appari. This romance he said he knew, having occasionally sung it at concerts, but always with the English words. I thought no more of ejecting him from the cab, and continued my drive up to St. John's Wood.

On my relating to Mdlle. Titiens and Mdme. Trebelli how by good luck I had nearly run over a tenor they both said it was useless to think of attempting any performance.

I assured, however, my newly-caught tenor that if he would only be guided by me and appear forthwith he would make a great success. I at once set to work and showed him the stage business in the drawing-room, requesting Mdme. Trebelli to go through the acting of the part of "Nancy," and Mdlle. Titiens through that of "Martha." I explained to the tenor that on entering he merely had to come on with his friend "Plunkett," go to the inn table, seat himself, drink as much beer as he liked, and at a given signal hand over the shilling to enlist the services of "Martha" at the Richmond Fair, after which he would drive her away in a cart. This would complete Act I.

In Act II. he simply had to enter the cottage leading "Martha," and afterwards to attempt to spin (two drawing-room chairs served as spinning wheels), until at last the wheels would be taken away by the two ladies. When the spinning quartet began he was merely to laugh heartily and appear joyous. In the third act I explained that he might sing his song provided always that he confined himself to Italian words. It did not much matter, in view of the public, what he sang if he only kept clear of English; and I advised him to keep repeating M'appari as often as he felt inclined. This he did, and in consequence of a printed apology which I had previously circulated in the theatre, to the effect that Signor Giuglini had refused his services without assigning any reason, my new tenor was warmly applauded, receiving for his principal air a double encore, and afterwards a recall. In the last act there was, of course, nothing for him to do, and the newspapers of the next morning were unanimous in his praise.

The singer who rendered me these services was Mr. George Bolton, who some years later (his voice having by that time become a baritone) played with great success the part of "Petruchio" to Minnie Hauk's "Katherine" in Goetz's Taming of the Shrew.

In the course of the season, which ended about the 18th December, I had accepted an engagement for Mdlle. Titiens to sing at the San Carlo of Naples. The contract was made direct with the Prefect, at the recommendation of the "Commissione." The leading soprano engaged by the manager had not given satisfaction, and the "Commissione" had the power, before handing over the subvention, of insisting on the engagement of a capable artist so as to restore the fortunes of the establishment.

Naturally, then, on my arrival with the great prima donna every possible difficulty was thrown in our way. At length the début took place, when Titiens appeared as "Lucrezia Borgia." The vast theatre was crowded from floor to ceiling, the first four rows of stalls being occupied by the most critical "cognoscenti," who literally watched every breath and every phrase, ready in case of need to express hostile opinions. At length the boat came on, and "Lucrezia" stepped on to the stage amidst the most solemn silence; and it was not until the close of the cabaletta, of the first aria that the public manifested its approbation, when it seemed as if a revolution were taking place. Mdlle. Titiens' success went on increasing nightly, and the theatre was proportionately crowded.

I recollect on one occasion after I had made four or five applications to the Prefect for the money payable for the lady's services he handed me a cheque the size of a sheet of foolscap paper. The amount was £800 for her first eight nights' services. On presenting myself at the bank I was referred from one desk to another, until I was told that I must see the chief cashier, who had gone out to smoke a cigar, and would not return that day. I went again the following day, and after waiting a considerable time at length saw him, when he told me to go to a certain counter in the bank where I should be paid.

I endorsed the cheque in the presence of the cashier, who told me, however, that he could not hand me the money for it unless my signature was verified by the British Consul. On going to the British Consul I found that he had gone to Rome, and would not be back for a couple of days. At length I obtained the official verification of the signature, and presented myself for the seventh time at the bank, when I was invited by the cashier to go down into the cellars, where a man told me off the amount in bags of silver ducats, which he drew from a large iron grating. He did not count the sacks he was giving me, but only those remaining behind; which left me one bag short. This he did not care for; he only wanted his own remainder to be right.

Eventually the manager of the bank insisted on my having the amount stated in the cheque, and I was then left to myself, surrounded by my bags, with no porters to move them for me.

On my returning to the manager, who was very polite, and telling him that I wished for the money in gold napoleons, he said it would be very difficult, and that in the first place I must hire men to carry the bags of silver up into the gold department. Thereupon I bargained with four ill-looking individuals who were brought in out of the streets, and who moved the bags at my risk to the gold department, when a vast premium had to be paid. On my leaving the bank with the gold I saw my four lazzaroni who had helped to move the silver, with hundreds of others, all extending their hands and following me.

I drove with difficulty to the British Consul, who happened to be a banker, followed by this vast multitude; for such a sum of money had not been seen for a long time in or about Naples. I had now to pay another large premium to get a bill on London for my gold, and this concluded the matter, which had occupied me altogether seven days and a half.

After the next payment had become due I went three or four times to the Prefect, but could never find him. One day, however, about twelve o'clock, I was told he was within, but that he had a headache, and could not see anyone. I nevertheless insisted on the necessity of his receiving me, saying that otherwise the night's performance at the San Carlo might be jeopardized. I was invited upstairs, where his Excellency was eating macaroni in the grand ball-room, lying on a sofa, which had served as a bed, he having returned home too late to mount the stairs, whilst about eighty Bersaglieri were rehearsing a selection from Rigoletto for a ball he was going to give that evening. The sound was deafening.

The Prefect was very polite, and gave me another of those large cheques, which with a little manipulation I induced the British Consul to change, and get me a bill for it. The Prefect invited me very courteously to the ball he was giving, at which over 2,000 persons were present. It was a most magnificent affair, the four angles of the large room being occupied by wild boars roasted whole (with sundry fruits, wines, etc.), to which the guests after every dance or two helped themselves, and then continued their dancing.

At that time I was very anxious to secure the lease of the San Carlo Opera-house, and by the aid of my friend the Prefect so far advanced the matter, that it wanted but the sanction of the Minister at Turin to complete it. The pay-sheet of the orchestra contained over 150 names, but as the salaries varied from six to eight shillings a week I made no objection to this. The heaviest salary was that of the conductor Mercadante (composer of Il Giuramento, &c.), who received £5 a week.

On leaving Naples I went to Turin to present myself to the Marquis Braham, but before I could get my card forwarded, even to the first room, I was obliged to make a monetary advance. On reaching the second room I was referred to another room on the entresol. It was impossible to gain entrance, or even get my card sent further, without the help of a napoleon. On going into the fourth room another tax was laid upon me, and it being evening I thought it better to go home and reserve my money offerings towards meeting the Marquis Braham until the next day. I returned, armed with sundry five-franc pieces and napoleons; but it was not until the fourth day, when I gave an extra douceur, that I could approach him at all. It then appeared that someone had anticipated me, and I was recommended to wait another year. I left for England, and the matter dropped.

CHAPTER VI.

PRODUCTION OF GOUNOD'S "FAUST"—APATHY OF THE BRITISH PUBLIC—A MANAGERIAL DEVICE—DAMASK CRUMB CLOTH AND CHINTZ HANGINGS—HEROIC ATTITUDE OF A DYING TENOR—PRAYERS TO A PORTMANTEAU.

ON my return from Italy I set to work preparing for my grand London season of 1863, and entered into several important engagements. About this time I was told of an opera well worthy of my attention which was being performed at the Théâtre Lyrique of Paris. I started to see it, and at once decided that Gounod's Faust—the work in question—possessed all the qualities necessary for a success in this country. On inquiry I found that Mr. Thomas Chappell, the well-known music publisher, had acquired the opera for England. The late Mr. Frank Chappell, on the part of his brother, but acting in some measure on his own responsibility, had bought the Faust music for reproduction in England from M. Choudens, of Paris; and I have heard not only that he acquired this privilege for the small sum of £40 (1,000 francs), but moreover that he was remonstrated with on his return home for making so poor a purchase.

The music of an opera is worth nothing until the opera itself has become known, and Messrs. Chappell opened negotiations with Mr. Frederick Gye for the production of Faust at the Royal Italian Opera. The work, however, had not made much impression at the Théâtre Lyrique, and Mr. Gye, after going to Paris specially to hear it, assured his stage manager, the late Mr. Augustus Harris, who had formed a better opinion of Gounod's music than was entertained by his chief, that there was nothing in it except the "Chorus of Soldiers." After due consideration Mr. Gye refused to have anything to do with Faust, and the prospect of this opera's being performed in London was not improved by the fact that, in the Italian version, it had failed at Milan.

Meanwhile I had heard Faust at the Théâtre Lyrique, and, much struck by the beauty of the music, felt convinced that the work had only to be fitly presented to achieve forthwith an immense success in London. Mr. Chappell was ready to give £200 towards the cost of its production, and he further agreed to pay me £200 more after four representations, besides a further payment after ten representations.

Certain that I had secured a treasure, I went to Paris and bought from M. Choudens a copy of the score, the orchestral parts, and the right for myself personally of performing the work whenever I might think fit in England. I then visited Gounod, who for £100 agreed to come over and superintend the production of what he justly declared to be his masterpiece.

I was at that time (as indeed I always was when anything important had to be done) my own stage manager. My orchestral conductor was Arditi; Titiens undertook the part of "Margherita;" Giuglini that of "Faust;" Trebelli was "Siebel;" Gassier "Mephistopheles;" and Santley "Valentine."

Far from carrying out his agreement as to superintending the production of the work, Gounod did not arrive in London until nearly seven o'clock on the night of production; and all I heard from him was that he wanted a good pit box in the centre of the house. With this, for reasons which I will at once explain, I had no difficulty whatever in providing him.

One afternoon, a few days before the day fixed for the production of the opera, I looked in upon Mr. Nugent at the box-office and asked how the sale of places was going on.

"Very badly indeed," he replied.

Only thirty pounds' worth of seats had been taken.

This presaged a dismal failure, and I had set my mind upon a brilliant success. I told Mr. Nugent in the first place that I had decided to announce Faust for four nights in succession. He thought I must be mad, and assured me that one night's performance would be more than enough, and that to persist in offering to the public a work in which it took no interest was surely a deplorable mistake.

I told him that not only should the opera be played for four nights in succession, but that for the first three out of these four not one place was to be sold beyond those already disposed of. That there might be no mistake about the matter, I had all the remaining tickets for the three nights in question collected and put away in several carpet bags, which I took home with me that I might distribute them far and wide throughout the Metropolis and the Metropolitan suburbs. At last, after a prodigious outlay in envelopes, and above all postage stamps, nearly the whole mass of tickets for the three nights had been carefully given away.

I at the same time advertised in the Times that in consequence of a death in the family, two stalls secured for the first representation of Faust—the opera which was exciting so much interest that all places for the first three representations had been bought up—could be had at twenty-five shillings each, being but a small advance on the box-office prices. The stalls thus liberally offered were on sale at the shop of Mr. Phillips, the jeweller, in Cockspur Street, and I told Mr. Phillips that if he succeeded in selling them I would present him with three for the use of his own family. Mr. Phillips sold them three times over, and a like success was achieved by Mr. Baxter, the stationer, also in Cockspur Street.

Meanwhile demands had been made at the box-office for places, and when the would-be purchasers were told that "everything had gone," they went away and repeated it to their friends, who, in their turn, came to see whether it was quite impossible to obtain seats for the first performance of an opera which was now beginning to be seriously talked about. As the day of production approached the inquiries became more and more numerous.

"If not for the first night, there must surely be places somewhere for the second," was the cry.

Mr. Nugent and his assistants had, however, but one answer, "Everything had been sold, not only for the first night, but also for the two following ones."

The first representation took place on June 11th, and the work was received with applause, if not with enthusiasm. I had arranged for Gounod to be recalled; and he appeared several times on the stage, much, I think, to the annoyance of Arditi, to whom the credit of a good ensemble and a fine performance generally was justly due. The opinions expressed by several distinguished amateurs as to the merits of Gounod's admirable work were rather amusing. The late Lord Dudley said that the only striking pieces in the opera were the "Old Men's Chorus" and the "Soldiers' March;" which was going a step beyond Mr. Gye, who had seen nothing in the work but the "Soldiers' Chorus."

Another noble lord, when I asked him what he thought of Faust, replied—

"This demand is most premature. How am I to answer you until I have talked to my friends and read the criticisms in the morning papers?"

The paucity of measured tunes in the opera—which is melodious from beginning to end—caused many persons to say that it was wanting in melody.

The second night Faust was received more warmly than on the first, and at each succeeding representation it gained additional favour, until after the third performance the paying public, burning with desire to see a work from which they had hitherto been debarred, filled the theatre night after night. No further device was necessary for stimulating its curiosity; and the work was now to please and delight successive audiences by its own incontestable merit. It was given for ten nights in succession, and was constantly repeated until the termination of the season.

So successful was Faust at Her Majesty's Theatre that Mr. Gye resolved to produce it at once; and he succeeded in getting it out by July 2nd.

The following was the cast of the work at the Royal Italian Opera:—"Margherita," Miolan-Carvalho (the creator of the part at the Théâtre Lyrique); "Siebel," Nantier Didiée; "Mephistopheles," Faure; "Valentine," Graziani; "Faust," Tamberlik.

The success of Faust at the Royal Italian Opera was so great that it enabled the manager to keep his theatre open until long beyond the usual period. On the 15th May of the following year Faust was reproduced with Mdlle. Pauline Lucca and Signor Mario in place of Madame Miolan-Carvalho and Signor Tamberlik. Three weeks afterwards, June 7th, the part of "Margherita" was assumed for the first time by Adelina Patti.

Mr. Gye, who had purchased of M. Gounod "exclusive rights" over the work, sent to inform me that he did not wish to interfere with my arrangements during the season already begun, but that for each performance given at Her Majesty's Theatre he should expect in future to be paid, and that meanwhile he had a claim against me of £800 for performance of the work given in London and the provinces during 1863 and 1864. I, of course, resisted this extraordinary pretention on the part of Mr. Gye; for, as the reader has already been informed, I had, before producing Faust, purchased from the Paris publishers the right of performing it wherever I personally might think fit. Mr. Gye brought his action, of which the result was to establish the fact, painful enough for M. Gounod, that, owing to some defect in regard to registration, no exclusive rights of performance could be secured for Faust in England by anyone.

After the close of the season of 1863 I made a concert tour in the autumn, a recital of Faust being the chief attraction. The company comprised Mdlle. Titiens, Mdme. Trebelli, Mdlle. Volpini, Signor Bettini—who had just married Trebelli—and Signor Volpini. After we had been out about two or three weeks Signor Volpini became very ill, and whilst at Birmingham sent for a leading physician, who, on examining him, said he would require a deal of attention, but that he hoped to bring him round in about a couple of weeks. The patient replied that on no account would he separate himself from his wife, who had to travel to some fresh city daily, but that the doctor must do what he could for him until he left the following morning with the Company. This he insisted upon doing.

From Birmingham we went to Bristol, and on arriving the sick tenor was at once put to bed and the leading physician sent for, who, on examining him, asked who had been attending him. On the name of the Birmingham physician being mentioned, the Bristol physician rejoined: "A very able man. One of the very first in the profession." The patient had been in good hands.

But on seeing the last prescription the doctor was astonished that his predecessor should have written such a thing; in fact, he could scarcely believe it, and it was fortunate for the patient he had left Birmingham and come to place himself under his care.

The patient informed the physician that on no account could he part from his wife, and that he would have to move off with the Company the following morning to Exeter.

From Exeter we went to Plymouth, from Plymouth to Bath, from Bath to Oxford, and so on during a space of some two or three weeks, the sick tenor being carried from the hotel to the railway and from the railway to the hotel, and each medical man of eminence making the same observations with regard to his esteemed colleague in the previous town; each one exclaiming that had Volpini remained in the previous city he must have died. He was carried to London, and there he remained, as all thought, on his death-bed, at the Hôtel Previtali, Panton Square. He was not yet, however, destined to die, and, as I am about to relate, it was a miracle that saved his life.

About this time I had engaged Sims Reeves to sing the rôle of "Faust" on certain evenings at Her Majesty's Theatre, and one day received a telegram from the eminent tenor, dated "Crewe," expressing his astonishment that I had announced him for that evening, when the engagement was for the following one.

I at once went off to Sims Reeves's house, and learned from the butler that his dinner had been ordered for half-past seven o'clock. I thereupon informed the man that the orders had been changed, and that the dinner was to be served at twelve o'clock instead of the time originally fixed. I ascertained that Mr. Reeves was to arrive at Euston Station, and there met him, accompanied by Mrs. Sims Reeves.

While she was busying herself about the general arrangements, I got the tenor to myself and told him the difficulty I was in, to which he replied that it was quite impossible for him to sing that evening, as he had ordered his dinner at home. I at once explained that I had postponed it for a few hours, and that a light dinner was being prepared for him in his dressing-room at the theatre.

The suddenness of my proposition seemed rather to amuse him, as he laughed; and I was delighted to get a kind of half-promise from him that, provided I mentioned the matter to his wife, he would consent.

At this moment she appeared, asking me what I was talking about to her husband. One of us began to state what the object in view was, when she exclaimed—

"It's all nonsense; but I can well understand. Mapleson is an impresario, and wants to ruin you by making you sing."

She then asked me how I could possibly think of such a thing when the chintz and the crumbcloth of his dressing-room had not been fixed?

It was the custom of Mrs. Reeves to hang the walls with new chintz and place a fresh-mangled white damask cloth on the floor the nights her husband sang; and on this occasion the sacred hangings had gone to the wash.

27

I explained that I had provided other chintz, but to no effect. Reeves was hurried to his brougham and driven away, his wife remarking as she looked scornfully at me: "He's only a manager!"

It being now half-past six I was in a nice state of mind as to how I could possibly replace the great tenor in Faust. Signor Bettini, it was true, had on the concert tour sung portions of the garden scene and the duet of the prison scene in the recital of Faust which we had given throughout the provinces. Signor Volpini, moreover—only he was on his death bed—knew the introduction and the trio of the duel scene. Putting all this together I decided on my course of action.

First I called on Signor Bettini, requesting him to oblige me by going to the theatre.

I next presented myself at Volpini's hotel, when I was informed that I must step very quietly and say but few words. On entering I was told by the invalid in a faint whisper that it was very kind of me to call upon him; and he wished to know whether I had really come to spend the evening with him. I told him that I had been informed on entering that my visit must be a short one.

He asked me again and again what could possibly be done to save his life, as he had tried all the doctors, but in vain. I said I would give him my advice if he would only follow it. I then assured him that he had but one chance of recovery. He must first allow me to mix him a pint of Château Lafite and a couple of raw eggs, beaten up with powdered sugar, and come down with me to the theatre, where, after drinking it, if he was to die, he could die like a man before the footlights.

A faint smile came over his pallid countenance. Of course he thought I was joking. But in due course the Château Lafite appeared, and the eggs were beaten up, and I managed to make him swallow the stimulating beverage. I put him on his flannel dressing-gown, took the blankets off the bed, and, wrapping him up in them, carried him myself in a four-wheeler down to the theatre.

I explained to him that he would have very little to do, beginning simply with the few bars of the introduction; after that nothing but the music he had been in the habit of singing on the concert tour. I explained to him that although "Mephistopheles," the Prince of Darkness, would in the eyes of the public transform him from an old man into a young one, there would be no difficulty about this inasmuch as Bettini would continue the part. Later on he could sing the trio in the duel scene, where with his lovely voice a great effect would be produced.

The long and short of it was I induced him to dress; and all now seemed in good order. I explained the matter to Titiens, Trebelli, and Arditi; and as I had not touched a particle of food since nine o'clock that morning, I went next door to Epitaux's, where I ordered a very small repast, pending the commencement of the opera.

I had hardly seated myself at the table when my servant rushed in, stating that there was a general row going on amongst the artists, and that they were all going home. The doors of the theatre had been opened, and the apology for the absence of Sims Reeves, which I had posted on the outer doors, had been accepted by the public. This was evident from the fact that over £650 of money was now in the house. The audience must be already a little irritated by the disappointment, and I knew that any further one might be attended with serious consequences. I believed that there would be a riot unless the representation took place.

On entering the stage-door I met Mdlle. Titiens, who was about to step into her carriage, going home. She told me it was useless to think of performing. This was at ten minutes past eight. I begged her to remain. I gave orders to the hall-keeper not to let anyone out of the place, and to get two policemen to assist him. I then crossed the stage to the dressing-room, where high words were going on—first between the two tenors, and afterwards between their two pretty wives. Mdme. Volpini's voice was uppermost, and I heard her say to Trebelli—

"Of course you will rejoice! My poor sick husband brought out at the risk of his life, and then simply to undertake an old man's part, with grey hair and beard concealing his beauty; whilst your husband is to come on and make all the love in the garden scene, and get all the applause."

Mdme. Trebelli responded by snapping her fingers at Mdme. Volpini, and taking her husband, despite my entreaties, from the theatre. All this excitement tended to work Volpini up; and, like a true artist, he said he would do his best—even if he had to walk through the scenes in which he was unacquainted with the music—rather than let me be disappointed.

It was now half-past eight, and the opera was on the point of commencing. This I had ordered should be done punctually. Meanwhile I had followed Mdme. Trebelli to her apartments in Regent Street. The excitement had made her quite ill, and she was totally unable to appear in consequence. I appealed forcibly to her husband, begging him if he would not sing "Faust" to help me by taking the part of "Siebel." He was a very good musician, and as at this time he never quitted his wife's side I knew that he must be intimately acquainted with the music. I thereupon got him down to the theatre in time for the garden scene, had his moustache taken off, and put him into his wife's clothes. Everything went off brilliantly, the male "Siebel" and the dying "Faust" sharing with the admirable "Margherita" the applause of the evening.

The sudden exertion, the unwonted excitement, had really the effect of saving Volpini's life; and he lived happily for many years afterwards.

During the worst stage of poor Volpini's illness, when, as already set forth, he persisted in being moved from town to town, wherever his charming wife had to go, they were both astonished one night to find that their little girl, a child of three or four years of age, had got out of bed, and apparently was praying to a large travelling trunk which accompanied them on all their journeys. Kneeling before the huge box, the little thing was heard to say: "And make my dear papa well again, or I will believe in you no more."

The explanation of this touching mystery was that the little girl had been in the habit of saying her prayers before an image of the Holy Virgin, which the family carried with them from town to town. The image, or picture, was now enclosed within the travelling trunk which had not yet been unpacked, and the affectionate child addressed it where she knew it to be.

CHAPTER VII.

GARIBALDI VISITS THE OPERA—GIUGLINI'S TROUBLE AT ST PETERSBURG—GIUGLINI VISITED BY TITIENS—ALARM OF FIRE— PRODUCTION OF "MEDEA"—GRISI'S LAST APPEARANCE—AN ENRAGED TENOR.

IN 1864 my season opened brilliantly, and on the fifth night I induced Garibaldi, who was then in this country, to visit the theatre; which filled it to overflowing. On that evening Titiens and Giuglini really surpassed themselves; and at the close of the opera Garibaldi told me he had never witnessed such a spirited performance, and that he had been quite carried away by the admirable singing of the two eminent artists. The opera was Lucrezia Borgia.

Some few nights afterwards I placed Nicolai's opera, the Merry Wives of Windsor, before the public, under the name of Falstaff, introducing a charming contralto named

Bettelheim; who undertook the rôle of "Mrs. Page," whilst Titiens impersonated "Mrs. Ford," Giuglini "Fenton," Bettini "Slender," Gassier "Mr. Page," Santley "Mr. Ford," &c., &c. The magnificent new scenery was by Telbin. The opera met with most unequivocal success, and was repeated for several consecutive nights. But, as with so many other operas, the public were so slow in expressing their approbation that it gradually had to drop out of the répertoire. Shortly afterwards I produced, remounted, Beethoven's Fidelio, with Titiens as the heroine, which was given some seven or eight nights in succession to the most crowded houses. In the winter I gave my usual extra performances in the provinces and in London.

Prior to the close of the London season of 1864 Giuglini signed an engagement for St. Petersburg, receiving a very large honorarium for his services. Regarding himself as the only representative of "Faust," he had not taken the precaution of stipulating for his appearance in this, or, indeed, any other part in his répertoire. On his arrival he was much mortified to find the Covent Garden artists, of whom there were several, always working and intriguing together; and to Giuglini's great dismay the part of "Faust" was assigned to Signor Tamberlik; Patti being the "Margherita" and Nantier Didiée the "Siebel." Now passed some two or three weeks before Giuglini could obtain a début. One afternoon, about three o'clock, he was informed by the intendant that he was called upon to perform the rôle of "Faust," Tamberlik being taken suddenly ill. This was indeed good news, and he set about arranging his costumes and looking over the music. Towards six o'clock he heard it rumoured that Madame Patti would be too indisposed to sing the rôle of "Margherita," and that he would have to appear with some débutante.

This thoroughly unnerved him, and he himself became indisposed, which he at once notified to the intendant. At the advice of some friends he was induced to take a walk, and pay a visit to some acquaintances to spend the evening.

About ten o'clock the door was rudely opened without any warning, and an employé entered, accompanied by two officials, one of whom politely raised his hat and said, "Signor Giuglini, I believe?" to which the Signor replied that he was Giuglini. They thereupon immediately left. Nothing more was heard of this matter until about a fortnight afterwards. It being pay day for the principal artists, that afternoon the Imperial Treasurer called at Giuglini's house with a roll of rouble notes, requesting him to sign the receipt for his month's pay, which Giuglini at once did. But on leaving, the treasurer begged to draw his attention to the notes, as a deduction of £150 had been made from his monthly stipend in consequence of his having left the house on the day he was reported to be indisposed. He got into a towering fit of rage, requesting the balance to be handed to him, as he was allowed certain days of indisposition according to the terms of his contract. The treasurer replied that according to the provisions of that clause he should have remained at home in his house on the day of his reported illness. The arguments became very warm, and Giuglini, in a fit of rage, threw the whole bundle of rouble notes into the stove, which was then burning; and from that moment his reason seemed to have left him.

On the termination of my spring concert tour in 1865 we began a season of opera in the beginning of March at Dublin, Giuglini promising to join us at the conclusion of his St. Petersburg engagement, which ended about that time.

One morning at breakfast I received a telegram from London: "Come on at once. Giuglini arrived." I was indeed delighted, and, having notified the good news to the Dublin press, left immediately for London. On my arrival at Giuglini's house in Welbeck Street I was told that he was very much indisposed in consequence of the fatigues of the journey, and that his mind did not seem quite right. I went upstairs to him at once. He was very pleased to see me, but to my astonishment he had no trousers on. Otherwise he was all right.

I talked with him some time, and advised him to put on the necessary garment, so that we might start that evening for Dublin. By force of persuasion I at last obtained his consent to let me put his trousers on for him, and in the course of an hour succeeded in getting one leg in. I then ordered some oysters for him, and talked to him whilst I was coaxing in the other leg. This I at length managed to do, when to my horror I found the first leg had come out again. After wasting the whole of the day I found myself too late to catch the Irish mail, and the Signor still with one leg only in his pantaloons.

Whilst Giuglini was sleeping I inquired as to the full particulars of his condition, and was informed that he had arrived from St. Petersburg in charge of a hired courier, who simply wanted a receipt for him. At the same time his magnificent fur coats and other costly clothing were all missing. He had made the journey in second-class, wearing a summer suit although it was the depth of winter; and on examining his jewel case I found that the stones had been taken out of everything he possessed, although the articles themselves were there. It was indeed a sad affair. I was advised to place him for a short time under the care of Dr. Tuke, and I had then to hurry back to Ireland.

On my return to London I went to pay Giuglini a visit at Chiswick, Mdlle. Titiens insisting on accompanying me. We waited some time during which we were particularly cautioned not to approach him. At length he entered; he was delighted to see us and talked quite rationally. We persuaded the doctor to allow us to take him for a drive, the signor at the same time expressing a wish to be driven to the Star and Garter, at Richmond, to dine. To this the keeper, who was on the box alongside the coachman, objected, promising Giuglini that if he would return to the doctor's he should have a nice large plate of meat, which seemed greatly to please him. Giuglini had previously complained to me that he was made to drink sherry, a wine which he particularly disliked, his ordinary drink being claret or claret and water. He afterwards sang us "Spirto gentil" from the Favorita, followed by "M'appari" from Martha, singing both airs divinely. The only thing peculiar was that his tongue was drawn very much to the right, and that he had to stop after every ninth or tenth bar to straighten it.

When we got back to the doctor's Mdlle. Titiens and myself stayed to dinner. During the repast Giuglini, who had been looking forward to his plate of meat, came into the room exhibiting on a very small plate a very small piece of meat.

"Look what they have given me, Thérèse," he said to Titiens. "I am afraid to eat it," he added, in a tone of irony; "it might give me an indigestion."

My firm belief is that if I could have got both Giuglini's legs into his trousers the day that he arrived in London I should have saved him. Living something like his ordinary life, among his old companions, he would have had at least a chance of getting well.

Thus matters went on until the London season of 1865 opened, which took place on the Saturday night of the Easter week. I had made a series of improvements throughout the theatre, by reducing considerably the number of the private boxes, and enlarging those I retained. I likewise removed the twelve proscenium boxes, ten each side of the stage, thereby advancing the drop curtain some 16 feet nearer the public. This gave me much more room behind the scenes.

Amongst the new singers I introduced was Miss Laura Harris, who afterwards, as Mdme. Zagury, achieved brilliant success throughout the whole of Europe; also Mdlle. Ilma de Murska, a lady who at once took high rank from her phenomenal vocal qualities. I also presented Signor Foli, a young artist, who was engaged at the Italian Opera in Paris, and who soon became a public favourite; likewise Signor Rokitanski, another eminent basso. Despite the blow I had received in the loss of Giuglini I went to work with renewed energies, and presented to the public Beethoven's Fidelio, with a magnificent cast, including Titiens, the incomparable "Leonora." I, moreover, mounted in great style Mozart's Flauto Magico, Titiens being the "Pamina," Ilma de Murska the "Queen of Night," Sinico the "Papagena," and Santley the "Papageno;" whilst the subordinate parts were all undertaken by principal artists.

During the last act an accident occurred, which might have been very serious, inasmuch as the house was crowded from the stalls right up to the back of the gallery. In preparing for the final scene some of the gauze, which had been used for clouds during the evening, caught fire over the gas battens. Instantly the alarm was given, when one of the flymen, at the risk of his neck, flung himself across the stage, balancing himself on a "batten" (a narrow strip of wood, some forty feet long), while he cut the ropes with his knife, causing the burning gauze to fall down on to the stage, where it was extinguished by the firemen. Mr. Santley, who was undertaking the rôle of the "Bird-catcher," remained on the stage unmoved. He walked forward to the audience, and addressed them in these eloquent words—

"Don't act like a lot of fools. It's nothing."

This speech had an immediate effect; and Santley continued his song as if nothing had happened. But for his presence of mind the loss of life would have been most serious.

I likewise produced Cherubini's tragic opera, Medea; a work considered by musical amateurs one of the finest dramatic compositions ever written. No musician ever exercised more influence on his art than Cherubini. His compositions are of the first authority, so that no musical library, whether of the professor or the amateur, can claim to be considered complete without them. The part of "Medea" was represented by Mdlle. Titiens. In assuming this rôle Mdlle. Titiens certainly added the final touch of lustre to her lyric crown. I need scarcely say the opera was magnificently mounted, even to the smallest detail. It was particularly successful, and still retains its place in the répertoire. I was interested to find in what large numbers the relatives and descendants of Cherubini were attracted to my theatre by the announcement of his Medea. Naturally they all expected free admissions, even to great-grandchildren and third cousins.

The season was a very successful one. In the autumn I started the regular provincial opera tour, Mario being my principal tenor, vice Giuglini. We commenced in Manchester, where Mario's unrivalled performances in Faust, Rigoletto, Martha, Ballo in Maschera, and Don Giovanni attracted crowded houses. We afterwards visited Dublin, proceeding thence to Belfast, Liverpool, etc., terminating, as usual, about Christmas.

In the early part of January, 1866, I made a very successful concert tour, giving no less than one hundred and twenty concerts in some seventy cities in sixty successive days, with two very strong parties: Titiens, Trebelli, Santley, Stagno, and Bossi in one; and Grisi, Lablache, Mario, Foli, and Arditi in the other; ending up with a brilliant series of operas with casts combined from the two parties in the northern capital and at Glasgow, where Mdme. Grisi distinguished herself in the rôles of "Lucrezia Borgia," "Norma," "Donna Anna," etc.

Thus matters went on until the London season. On each occasion when I visited Giuglini I found no improvement, and it was ultimately decided that a sea trip might benefit him. He, therefore, left London in a sailing ship for Italy. I never saw him afterwards. I need scarcely add that his loss was irreparable.

I opened my London season of 1866 early in April, for which I engaged a very powerful Company, including Mdme. Grisi. I announced her engagement in the following terms:—

"Mr. Mapleson has the gratification to announce that he has prevailed on Mdme. Grisi to revisit the scene of her early triumphs, and again to appear at the Theatre, her previous connection with which formed one of the most brilliant epochs in operatic history. Mdme. Grisi will once more undertake some of the parts which she created, and in her impersonations of which will be revived the traditions obtained direct from Rossini, Donizetti, and Bellini. These representations can only extend for a few nights, and they will derive additional interest from the fact that Mdlle. Titiens has consented to take part in them as a mark of respect to one who for so many years reigned absolutely without a rival on the lyric stage."

I was justified in making this announcement in consequence of the magnificent style in which Mdme. Grisi had been singing during our spring opera tour.

Grisi seemed interested and affected by her return to the old house of which she had taken leave twenty years previously. The old habitués came in large numbers to see her, to hear her, and naturally to support her with their applause on her first (which proved also to be her last) appearance. This took place on the evening of May 5, 1866. The Prince and Princess of Wales were both present.

When the gondola came down, from which, in the first act of Lucrezia Borgia, the heroine makes her entry, there was breathless attention throughout the house. The great vocalist had the command of all her resources, and sang the two verses of "Com'è bello" admirably, omitting, according to her custom, the cabaletta, which Titiens and all other "Lucrezias" made a point of giving.

Well as she sang, I noticed some signs of nervousness. She had been visited by misgivings before the performance began. I had done my best, however, to reassure her, and was under the impression, judging from the apparent result, that I had succeeded. But her hands, I remember, just as she was going on, were extremely cold. I took them in my own, and found that they were like stone.

At the end of the first act, on the conclusion of the scene in which "Lucrezia" is taunted and reproached by her victims and their friends, Mdme. Grisi, accustomed to the stage of the Royal Italian Opera, remained too far in front, though at a point where, at Covent Garden, the curtain would have fallen between her and the audience. It was otherwise at Her Majesty's Theatre (I refer, of course, to the old building), where the stage advanced far into the audience department; and when the curtain came down the "Lucrezia" of the evening found herself kneeling on the ground (in which attitude she had defied the conspirators) and cut off by the curtain from the stage behind. This placed the unfortunate singer in a ludicrous and, indeed, painful position; for she had a stiffness in one of her knees, and was unable on this occasion to rise without the help of the stage attendants.

Mdme. Grisi was, of course, much distressed by this contretemps. She had recourse, however, to the homeopathic remedies which she always carried with her, and after a time was herself again. These remedies were for the most part in the form of stimulants, which, however, Mdme. Grisi took only in the smallest quantities. Her medicine-chest contained a dozen half-pint wicker-covered bottles, which held, besides orgeat and other syrups, brandy, whisky, hollands, port-wine, and bottled stout.

In the second act Mdme. Grisi got on very well, especially in the scene with the bass preceding the famous trio. In the passionate duet with the tenor, just when the Duke, after administering the poison to "Gennaro," has gone away, she made an unsuccessful attempt to reach the A natural; and the failure caused her much confusion. She got through the performance; but she ran up to me immediately the curtain fell and exclaimed that it was all over with her, and that she never could appear again.

The notices next morning were sufficiently favourable; but it was evident that the career of the great vocalist was now, indeed, at an end. Let me here say a word about Mdme. Grisi's pecuniary affairs.

After the duel between her husband, M. de Meley, and Lord Castlereagh a separation took place; and the injured spouse made an arrangement by which he was to receive out of his wife's salary the moderate income of two thousand a year. This she was to pay as long as she remained on the stage. In order that the famous singer might enjoy the use of her own earnings, I made an agreement with her by which on my provincial tours she was to sing for me gratuitously, while I at the same time engaged to pay Signor Mario £300 a week. For this salary the two admirable artists were ready to sing as often as I liked. They were most obliging; full of good nature, and without any of the affectation or caprice from which so few singers at the present day are free. They took a pleasure in their performances, and thought nothing of playing three or four times a week. They would have sung every night had I been unreasonable enough to ask them to do so.

Far from insisting that she should never be called upon to do anything that was not expressly set down for her in her written contract, Mdme. Grisi would often volunteer her assistance in cases where it was really very useful. In Don Pasquale, for instance, while Mario was singing the beautiful serenade "Com'e gentil!" she would direct the chorus behind the scenes, singing herself and marking the time on the tambourine.

She was invaluable to Mario in many ways, not only in connection with his art, but also with the occupations of his ordinary life. She was always punctual, and, indeed, a little before the time; whereas Mario was invariably late. He had always his cravat to tie or a fresh cigar to light just when the last moment for catching the train had arrived. He was the most inveterate smoker I ever knew. He had always a cigar in his mouth, except when he was on the stage and actually in the presence of the audience. When he came off, if only for a moment, he would take a puff at his still burning cigar, which he had carefully left in the wings where he would be sure to find it again. "Faust" in the garden scene passes for a few moments behind some bushes at the back of the stage. During those moments Mario had just time to enjoy a few whiffs, after which he returned to continue his love-making.

Mario spent large sums of money on his favourite weed, and thought nothing of giving away a box of cigars to a friend for which he had paid (to some friendly tobacconist who had cheated him) £5 or £6 a hundred.

About this time I charged Mr. Telbin and his talented sons to paint me the whole of the scenery for Meyerbeer's Dinorah, which was brought out in due course, Ilma de Murska appearing as the demented heroine, Gardoni as "Corentino," and Santley as "Hoel." It was a truly magnificent performance, well worthy the reputation of the theatre.

Shortly afterwards I produced another classical opera, which was gladly welcomed by all musical amateurs. The work I refer to was Gluck's Iphigenia in Tauris—a work not less remarkable for its intrinsic merits than for having been the cause of one of the most fierce and prolonged artistic controversies on record. Paris, ever the champ de bataille of such contests, was, figuratively speaking, shaken to its foundations by the antagonistic Gluckists and Piccinists; and the dispute was only ended by Gluck leaving France.

This work was likewise magnificently put upon the stage, Titiens, Santley, and Gardoni really surpassing themselves.

34

I afterwards had the honour of introducing Mozart's comic opera, Il Seraglio, in which Mdlle. Titiens appeared as "Constanza," the remaining personages being entrusted to Dr. Gunz, Signor, Stagno, Rokitanski, &c.

One evening, when the opera of Rigoletto was being performed, with Mongini as the "Duke," feeling tired, as I had been working in the theatre throughout the day, I went home just before the termination of the third act. I had been at home about three-quarters of an hour when my servant hurried up in a cab to inform me that the curtain had not yet risen for the final act, and that a dreadful disturbance was going on in consequence of some question with Mongini, who was brandishing a drawn sword and going to kill everybody. I immediately slipped on my clothes and went down to the theatre.

At the stage door, without her bonnet, I met the tenor's charming wife, the only person, as a rule, who could control him in any way; and she entreated me not to go near him, or there would be bloodshed. I insisted, however, on going to his room without delay, as the curtain was still down and the public was getting tumultuous. I took the precaution of buttoning my overcoat across my chest, and in I went, my first words being—

"This time, Mongini, I hear you are right (Questa volta sento che avete ragione)."

With this preliminary we got into conversation, but he still remained walking up and down the room with nothing but his shirt on and a drawn sword in his hand. I saw that I had to proceed very slowly with him, and began talking on indifferent matters. At last I asked him the details of all the trouble. He thereupon explained to me that the master tailor, who had been requested by him in the morning to widen his overcoat by two inches, had misunderstood, and contracted it by two inches. I wished to have a look at the dress, which, however, was lying on the floor torn to pieces. I assured Mongini that the man should be cruelly punished, and he and his family put upon the streets to starve early the next morning.

He then got calmer, and I casually observed, "By-the-bye, is the opera over yet, Mongini?" to which he replied, "No, it is not."

"Never mind that," I continued; "the public can wait. Everyone, by the way, is talking of the magnificent style in which you have been singing to-night."

His eyes brightened, and he said he should like to go on with the opera.

"Not at all a bad idea!" I remarked.

"But I have no dress," said Mongini, rather sadly; "it is destroyed."

I suggested that he should wear the dress of the second act, putting on the breastplate and the steel gorget with the hat and feathers, and he would then be all right, and "La Donna e Mobile" would make amends for the delay. He dressed and followed me to the stage, when I made the sign for the stage manager to ring up the curtain, greatly to the astonishment of Mongini's wife, who was fully expecting to hear that I had been run through the body.

The next day at twelve o'clock, as per appointment, Mongini came to my office to be present at the punishment of the master tailor. I had taken the precaution to inform the tailor, who was a single man, that he had a wife and four children, and that he was to be sure and recollect this. I called him into my room in the presence of Mongini, and told him gravely that he with his wife and children must now starve. There was no alternative after the treatment Mongini had received the previous evening.

Mongini at once supplicated me not to let the children die in the gutter, as it might injure him with the public, and he ended by promising that if I would retain the tailor in my service he would sing an extra night for nothing.

35

PAYMENT AFTER PERFORMANCE—DISCOVERY OF MADGE ROBERTSON—MARIO AND THE SHERIFF—GENEROSITY OF THE GREAT TENOR—DÉBUT OF CHRISTINE NILSSON—DESTRUCTION OF HER MAJESTY'S THEATRE—A GREAT PHILANTHROPIST.

AT the close of the London season of 1866 we went to Ireland for the usual autumn operatic tour, stopping en route at Liverpool to give a morning concert. The rush was so great that all the metal cheques for the half-crown seats were exhausted and we had to use penny pieces. Numbers of the public found out, therefore, a ready way of getting in without payment. As soon as I observed this, and as there were still many hundreds unable to obtain admission, I conducted them across to another door which led into the orchestra. There being no money-taker, I let some four hundred of them crowd in, impressing upon them that they would have to pay half-a-crown apiece as they came out; and I must add that every one paid up punctually.

We left Liverpool after the concert for Dublin, where we fulfilled a very profitable engagement.

After leaving Dublin we went, early in October, to Leeds, and afterwards to Hull, at which latter place I recollect well that a full rehearsal of Les Huguenots was necessary in consequence of a new "Queen" having joined the company. Both Mario and Titiens complained of the incident and wondered how they were to finish the rehearsal in time to dine by a quarter past three, it being a general rule with artists not to eat later than that hour when they have to sing the same evening. We began the rehearsal early; and it was not until after two that it was concluded. The dinner being nearly ready at the hotel, I went in a carriage to fetch Mario and Titiens back from the theatre without loss of time. At a quarter past three I found them both seated in the stalls, witnessing a morning performance, at which a Miss Madge Robertson was playing in a piece called A Wolf in Sheep's Clothing. So rivetted to the spot were Titiens and Mario—both exclaiming "Do not disturb us, let us wait a little longer"—that it was nearly five o'clock before I got them home, when it was, of course, too late to dine. Not that they regretted this. They both told me that I ought to write to every London manager telling them what a charming actress they had discovered. I need hardly say that the Miss Robertson of those days is now Mrs. Kendal, more perfect in her art than ever.

I again started my concert tour in the early part of January, 1867, with Titiens, Trebelli, and others; and was as usual pre-eminently successful all along the line. Mario joined us about the 7th March in Scotland.

About this time he experienced considerable worry through being served with various writs for bills of exchange, for which he had received no consideration whatever, and which had been accumulating for many years. In more prosperous times preceding the period in question he had frequently assisted young artists, painters, sculptors, and Italians generally, who had come to this country with recommendations to him, and who had nearly all proved most ungrateful. It was computed that over £40,000 had been distributed by the great tenor on various occasions amongst his compatriots and others seeking aid.

I recollect meeting at Fulham one Sunday at dinner a young sculptor who had arrived with a letter of recommendation to Mario, and who on presenting himself exclaimed that he had not come to borrow money, hearing how much victimized Mario had been by others. All he wanted was to bring a piece of sculpture from Rome to London, for which he already had a purchaser in view; and if Mario would but accept a bill at two months, which he then had with him, he would within a month have sold his work and the money could be put to Mario's credit, so that the bill would be punctually met. In fact, every possible device was resorted to by persons well acquainted with his generous nature—which brings me to the case in point.

We had gone through a most arduous tour, and Mario had been singing four times a week throughout the whole time, and with most brilliant voice. As he had sung four nights running during the week I am speaking of, and was to be replaced the following evening (Saturday) by Signor Tasca in the Huguenots, he devoted his last day to the packing of his luggage, intending to leave by an early train for York, whence, after a night's rest, he would go on to London, presenting himself on the Monday for rehearsal at the Royal Italian Opera, Covent Garden, where the season was to commence on Tuesday.

In the hall at the Edinburgh Hotel, where Mario had put up, a Sheriff's officer was waiting for him with a writ or an attachment for £100; and I thought to help him out of the dilemma by the following device, knowing how delicate and sensitive he was. I called to bid him good-bye, taking with me a closed envelope containing a £100 note. I by degrees gave him to understand that I had been looking about the city for some little souvenir, but without success, and as his taste was so superior to mine, if he would select one in memory of the pleasant time we had spent together, I should feel obliged. I at the same time handed him the envelope. I was on the point of leaving the room when a note was brought to me, requesting me to come to the theatre at once, as Tasca, the new tenor, had been taken ill at the rehearsal, and was obliged to go home. Mario, noticing signs of displeasure across my brow, insisted upon knowing the reason; and after some pressure I informed him that the new tenor, who was to replace him, had fallen sick, and that I must be off to see how the matter could be remedied.

My dear friend patted me on the shoulder, and said he knew of a way. The opera to be performed being Les Huguenots, for the benefit of Mdlle. Titiens, he would try, he said, to satisfy the public in the part of "Raoul," and thus help me out of my difficulty. I readily acceded, and asked him to name any terms he liked; but he assured me that he should consider himself amply repaid if I would be present at Covent Garden on the following Tuesday, when he was to appear as the "Duke" in Un Ballo in Maschera, as that would encourage him. I thanked him, and was again leaving when he called me back to express his displeasure at my having offered him the hundred-pound note in the envelope, requesting me at once to take it back. This I, of course, declined to do, until at last he said—

"If no one is to have it, it had better go into the fire; but sing I do not unless you allow me to return it to you at once."

All argument was useless. Then reluctantly I left him.

The following Monday night I started for London, where I attended the opening of the Royal Italian Opera the next evening, and had the pleasure of applauding Mario, and complimenting him in his dressing-room, after the second act. He could not express sufficiently his delight at my being present.

The London season of 1867 was remarkable for the first performance in England of Verdi's Forza del Destino.

Prior to the commencement of this season my attention had been drawn to a young Swedish singer, named Christine Nilsson, who had appeared at the Théâtre Lyrique of Paris, and was attracting a certain amount of attention. I went over and heard her in the Magic Flute, and was delighted with the purity of her voice. She was also singing La Traviata and Martha. I at once concluded an engagement with her.

Before disclosing the fact to Arditi, or any other member of my Company, I invited Mdlle. Titiens and Mdme. Trebelli, with Signor and Mdme. Arditi, over to Paris for a fortnight's holiday prior to the commencement of our laborious London season. Amongst the places of amusement we visited was the Théâtre Lyrique, where the Swedish singer was that night filling the rôle of "Martha." I must say I was not impressed myself, whilst the remainder of the party thought nothing whatever of her. I, therefore, refrained from even hinting that I had already engaged her. As the time approached, the lady insisted on making her début as "Martha." I plainly foresaw that it would be the greatest possible mistake to acquiesce in her desire; and, after a lengthy discussion, Verdi's Traviata was decided upon. I at once instructed a Bond Street dressmaker to make her four of the most elegant toilettes possible, discarding in toto the costume of the 16th century so far as "Violetta" was concerned.

At all times it is a difficult thing for a manager to employ with advantage assistants placed among the audience to support either a new singer or a new piece; for grave mistakes are sure to be made, thus defeating the object for which the supporters were intended. I have often known singers send in friends to applaud; but they invariably begin their uproar on the appearance of the singer, even before he or she has uttered a sound.

On one occasion I recollect at Her Majesty's Theatre a singer appearing in Il Trovatore, and about a dozen bouquets falling at her feet from the top boxes before she had sung a note.

I saw that great judgment was necessary, while convinced in my own mind that I possessed a jewel of the first water. I, therefore, gave the very simplest instructions as to the amount of encouragement necessary for my fair Swede in order to ensure the rapture of London; knowing that when once serious attention had been drawn to her she could do the rest herself on her own merits. Being very fond of rowing in my spare time on the River Thames, I made an arrangement with the head-boatman at Essex Stairs, near where I resided, to supply me with some twenty-five horny-handed watermen, who were merely told that they should receive one shilling apiece provided they did not applaud Mdlle. Nilsson—the lady who would appear on the stage at the beginning of the opera, wearing a pink dress. They were moreover informed that when the first act was over and the curtain down, they would be paid a shilling apiece for each time they could get it up again; and I believe they succeeded some five or six times in their repeated attempts. That was all that was ever done for Mdlle. Nilsson; her extraordinary talent did the rest. At all events, it gave her a fair start, and her début was the talk of London.

Mdlle. Nilsson's performances were continued throughout the season with increasing success, she appearing successively as "Martha," "Donna Elvira," and the "Queen of Night" in the Magic Flute. She repeated the Traviata again and again, bringing the season to a most brilliant termination.

After a short holiday I recommenced my regular autumn tour in Dublin, repeating the usual Liverpool morning concert with the usual success.

After visiting Liverpool and Manchester, I returned to London and opened my season on the 28th October.

In consequence of my having engaged a female harpist I received a round Robin from the orchestra, threatening to leave at the end of the week unless I at once replaced her by a male performer. I insisted on receiving the week's notice to which I was entitled, and, seeing evidence of a conspiracy, took out a summons against every member of my orchestra. On the day fixed for the hearing the musicians excused themselves, through their solicitor, from appearing, their case not being ready. Afterwards I myself was unable through indisposition to appear on the day to which the case had been adjourned. At this there was much groaning among the defendants, and threats were uttered. The Trade Unions were very active just then throughout the country, and the players had been promised unlimited support towards maintaining their menaced strike. At last the case was heard; but on the very day before the one fixed by the Magistrate for giving his decision an occurrence took place which rendered all further proceedings in the matter unnecessary.

Towards the end of November an insurance agent called upon me urging the necessity of effecting an insurance on my properties, scenery and dresses, which had been accumulating since the beginning of my tenancy. I replied that in consequence of the high rate of premium it was better to let things take their chance. Besides, there was no probability, under my management, of the theatre ever being destroyed by fire. Eventually we came to terms as to the rate to be charged.

About this time a proposition was made to let the theatre to Professor Risley for his Japanese performances, to run from Christmas to February. A large sum of money was to be paid to me, and it was verbally agreed that my treasurer should be retained by the new-comers to superintend the front of the house and the monetary arrangements.

On the 7th December, during a rehearsal of Fidelio, my insurance agent called to complete the insurance. I showed him the inventories of the different departments, and agreed to insure for £30,000; but as the costumier's list was not at hand, and the costumier himself was out at dinner, the agent suggested my giving him £10 on account and keeping the matter open until the following Monday, when he would call again. Just as he was leaving the room my treasurer came in, stating that he had just heard that the Japanese people did not intend to avail themselves of his services after he had given them all the information respecting the working of his department.

I asked whom they had engaged. He mentioned the name of Mr. Hingston, at which I started, and said—

"If Hingston is engaged, good-bye to the theatre. It will make the fifteenth that will have been burnt under his management."

On hearing this, the insurance agent stepped across the room and again suggested that I should hand him the £10 to keep me right till Monday.

I jokingly said: "There is no fear;" and he took his departure.

I remained working in my office at Pall Mall until about six o'clock that evening. As I was engaged to dine at Mdlle. Titiens's in St. John's Wood, I had but a few moments to put my head into the box-office, which was just closing, and ask Mr. Nugent for some opera tickets for the following night. I did not, according to my custom, go through his office on to the stage (which I might have done while he was getting out the tickets), fearing I should be too late for the dinner.

About half-past eleven o'clock that evening our party was alarmed by a violent ringing of the bell. Then my servant rushed in with his clothes very much torn, uttered some inarticulate sounds, and fell on a chair, pointing upwards. On looking out of the window we saw that the sky was bright red, although we were four miles from the fire. Mdlle. Titiens and Signor Bevignani exclaimed with one voice: "It's the theatre!"

I hastened down at once, accompanied by Bevignani, only to find impassable barriers of soldiers and populace, and it was not without great difficulty I could approach the building. On my pointing out to the firemen certain doors which they ought to break open in order to recover wardrobes, music, &c., I was told to "mind my own business." They then went to quite another part and began chopping and breaking, whereas had they allowed themselves to be guided by me they might have saved a considerable portion of my property. It was not until three hours afterwards that the fire reached that part of the theatre which I had pointed out as containing things which might have been saved.

Lord Colville was very kind, and with his assistance I reached one portion of the building, to which he accompanied me, enjoining me to save engagements or any important documents in my private rooms at Pall Mall. But I was so bewildered that all I could do was to seize a dress coat and an opera hat, with which I came downstairs, leaving all my papers and documents on the table. I remained until two or three in the morning. Then, my presence being useless, I went home to change my clothes, which were freezing on me, and next hurried to Jarrett, my acting manager.

Jarrett was in bed. But he had already heard of the calamity, and expressed great regret. I desired him at once to go over to Chatterton, the then lessee of Drury Lane, who resided in the neighbourhood of Clapham, and endeavour to secure his theatre from March till the end of July before he could hear of my disaster.

"Go as quickly as possible," I said, "and if the newspaper is lying about be careful he does not see it."

On arriving at Chatterton's the first thing Jarrett saw, lying on the hall table, was the Times newspaper. He threw his top coat over it, and waited quietly downstairs until Chatterton, who was dressing, could receive him. Then, like the able diplomatist he was, without appearing at all anxious, he concluded a short agreement whereby I was to have the use of Drury Lane for the following spring and summer seasons, with a right to renew the occupation for future years. By half-past nine o'clock Mr. Jarrett was able to hand me the agreement, and it was not until half-past ten that Mr. Gye drove up to Mr. Chatterton's to inform him of the disaster Mapleson had met with, and at the same time to offer him £200 per week provided he did not let Drury Lane for Italian Opera.

The day after the fire I received letters of sympathy from all parts of the country; likewise telegrams of condolence, including one from Her Majesty the Queen, which greatly affected me. In fact, my nerves were so unstrung that I was hardly master of myself. In the course of the next day His Royal Highness the Prince of Wales came to see me. I showed him over the ruins of what the day before had been the Opera-house. After his departure I was so unnerved that I took to my bed in the adjoining hotel, and remained there some two weeks.

The Monday after the fire the insurance agent, with whom I had neglected to do business, called upon me to assure me of his deep sympathy, since if I had paid him the £10 on account of the proposed insurance he would now have had to give me a cheque for £30,000. I told him that I was exceedingly glad I had not paid him the £10, as I certainly should have been suspected of having myself caused the fire, and should never afterwards have been able to set myself right with the public.

Prior to my recovery, amongst the numerous callers was one particularly sympathetic gentleman, who came in a carriage and pair, and said he would see that the theatre was rebuilt, asking, as it were, my permission for this. I was deeply touched by his kindness. Some short time afterwards he wrote saying that he thought it better, for my sake, that Covent Garden should be closed, and that he had seen Mr. Gye and made terms for its purchase. On a later occasion he called upon me, and stated that the site of Her Majesty's Theatre, which had then been cleared by Lord Dudley, being such a desirable one, he was in treaty with the Bank of England to lease it to them at a considerable ground rent, they erecting the building. By this means, he explained, the £80,000 then lying in consols for the purpose of re-erecting the theatre could be handed over to me. But he ultimately consented that I should give him half.

Notwithstanding all my troubles, within three weeks after the fire I was already on the road with a strong concert company for the usual spring tour; all my spare time being utilized in the creation of a new wardrobe, music library, etc. Whilst at Manchester Mdlle. Titiens aided me kindly in the purchase of various goods, stuffs, cottons, needles, etc., etc.; all the prime donne of the Company volunteering their services as dressmakers in order to have everything ready for my Opera season, which was to commence early the following month in Glasgow.

Being under the belief that this fire had cancelled the contract I had already made at the Theatre Royal, Glasgow, I got entangled, in my mistake and hurry, into an engagement at another theatre, the Prince of Wales's; and as the time approached for my coming to Scotland both managers threatened me with an attachment if I did not fulfil my engagement. In fact, I found myself announced at both houses, with war to the knife threatened by the two rival managers. At one time they proposed to combine against me and leave me, with my expensive Company, outside in the cold. But about ten days before the date fixed I paid a visit to each, when, out of consideration for me personally, they both agreed to have me alternately at their theatres. This caused great excitement in the city, and as the adherents of each manager mustered in force the receipts at both houses were very great, so that eventually each manager had taken more money in the half number of representations than he would have received had I given him the full number.

Prior to the opening of my London season of 1868 I received another visit from my philanthropic friend, Mr. Wagstaff. He told me that he had purchased Mr. Gye's interest, showing me the agreement, and he considered that it would be more desirable that Covent Garden for the future should be run by a Company, of which I should be the manager, receiving some £20,000 cash as a consideration for my goodwill and for any property I might have in music or other effects, with a salary of £3,000 a year as long as I chose to retain my post, and a fair share in the profits.

I became quite uncomfortable at having so much wealth suddenly thrust upon me, and wished I were back in my old position of trouble and anxiety. In due course all the necessary documents were signed, Mr. Gye at the same time writing a letter to a high personage, in which he stated that his long-sought desire to quit the cares of management had at length been satisfied, and strongly urged that all patronage should now be transferred to me, as the shattered state of his health would preclude him for the future from taking part in operatic affairs. On entering upon my duties I began to reorganize the establishment by, in the first place, relieving myself of some sixty old choristers who had been engaged from time immemorial, and introducing in their stead my fresh, full-voiced young Italians whom I had imported the previous year.

One evening a card was brought to me from a young gentleman, the son of an old musical friend of mine, requesting an interview. He told me that he had been promised the secretaryship of the Grand Opera (meaning Her Majesty's and Covent Garden, united under the new arrangement) for seven years at a salary of £800 a year, provided he lent £200 for a month to my philanthropic friend, who had organized the whole thing. It appeared to me like a dream. I could not understand it; but still, as nothing astonishes me in this world, I took it as a matter of course, and later in the day went over to Wandsworth to call on Mr. Gye, in order to see how matters stood.

On my entering, Mr. Gye said how pleased he was to leave operatic management for ever, and that he wondered how he had found the nerve to continue it so long. Before I could say a word to him, he desired me to be seated and handed me a cigar, when he began to inform me of his plans for the future. He told me he had secured by private treaty a vast estate in Scotland of some 20,000 acres, with the right of shooting and fishing. He was arranging, moreover, to purchase a large estate in Oxfordshire. Various guns had been ordered, with fishing rods and other appurtenances. Steps, too, had been taken for the sale of the house in which he was then living.

I made two or three attempts to get a word in, but without success; and at last I had scarcely the courage to hint that the projected arrangements might, possibly, not be carried out.

I explained, however, that on the following Monday a small payment of £10,000 would be due to me; also that a further deposit on Drury Lane would become payable, and that I should make that deposit, as it was probable, nay, very possible, that I should be called upon to resume my position at Drury Lane, instead of Covent Garden. I at the same time recommended Mr. Gye at all events to be prepared to open Covent Garden, as it wanted but some three or four weeks to the beginning of the season. This he replied he could not do, as the deposit he was to receive would not be payable before some three or four weeks. He still, moreover, doubted all I had been telling him.

On the Monday following I attended at the Egyptian Bank, which had been specially hired for the occasion, and on entering with my order for the payment of £10,000, found one small boy seated on a very high stool, drawing figures on a sheet of blotting paper. On my demanding £10,000 the boy turned deadly pale and was at first inclined to run. I explained to him that it was not his fault if the money was not forthcoming, but I requested him, in the presence of a witness I had brought with me, to present seven letters which I already had in my pocket, each one containing notice to the Directors that, they having failed to pay me my money at the appointed time, my contract as general manager was at an end. I at once informed Gye of what had occurred, recommending him again to get his Company together and re-engage Costa and the orchestra, as my own prospectus was to come out the middle of that week.

From what I afterwards learned, the £200 my musical friend's son was to have advanced prevented some thousands of circulars from being posted for want of stamps, and the printer from delivering the remainder of the circulars he had prepared for want of a deposit. I must add that Mr. Gye repeatedly thanked me for my straightforward conduct in preventing him from being practically ruined.

Considerable changes were necessary in adapting the Theatre Royal, Drury Lane, for Italian Opera. I was obliged to have sundry discussions with the Committee before I could be allowed to alter the floor of the pit and boxes, and to take about twenty feet off the stage, its removal enabling me to add some two or three rows of stalls. I had, moreover, to decorate, clean, and carpet the house from top to bottom, the outlay for which, irrespective of the rent, cost me from £3,000 to £4,000. A further difficulty presented itself, as there were some six or seven hundred renters who were at that time allowed free admission to any part of the theatre, and it was only by temporizing with their representatives that I ultimately made an equitable arrangement satisfactory to all parties.

The season opened in due course, and a magnificent Company I was enabled to introduce: Mdlle. Titiens in the zenith of her powers; Christine Nilsson, who had made such a prodigious success the previous season at Her Majesty's; also Miss Clara Louise Kellogg, Mongini, Fraschini, Santley, etc. The performances were really of the first order, and Mozart's masterpieces were given with such strong combined casts as to attract the whole of London. In fact, the success was such as to paralyze the efforts of the rival manager.

CHAPTER IX.

PROPOSAL FOR AN OPERATIC UNION—TITIENS IN DUBLIN—HER
SERVICES AS A PACIFICATOR—AUTUMN SEASON AT COVENT GARDEN—
THE COMBINATION SEASON—IMMENSE SUCCESS—COSTA'S
DESPOTISM—AN OPERATIC CONSPIRACY—LUCCA AND HER HUSBANDS.

DURING my successful Drury Lane season, in the month of June, 1868, a letter
addressed to me was left by an unknown person in the hall. The superscription on the
envelope was in a disguised hand, but the letter enclosed was in the writing of Mr. Gye.

The manager of the Royal Italian Opera proposed a coalition with the manager of
Her Majesty's Theatre, and Mr. Gye suggested a personal interview on the subject. Here,
however, is his letter:—

[COPY.]
"Springfield House,
"Wandsworth Road,
"June 19th, 1868.
"DEAR MR. MAPLESON,
"The last time you were over here I believe we were pretty well agreed that our
interests lay rather in the combination of the two operas than in fighting one another. As
we shall both of us be making our engagements for the next year, if anything is to be
arranged between us it is time it were thought about. I should be very glad to see you on
the subject if you still remain in the same mind as when I saw you last. It would perhaps
be well if we did not meet either at Drury Lane or at Covent Garden. Would you mind
coming over here, or would you prefer our meeting somewhere in town? This matter, for
obvious reasons, had better remain strictly between ourselves for the present.
"Yours very truly,
"(Signed) FREDERICK GYE.
"James Mapleson, Esq."

When I met Mr. Gye by appointment his first proposition was that we should work
together at either of the two theatres, the other one being kept closed; and that I should
take a quarter of the profits.

I suggested, as a more equitable adjustment, an equal division of profits; and to that
Mr. Gye at last agreed.

Articles of partnership were then drawn up binding us to remain together for three
years on the basis of half profits, and our agreement was to be kept secret for the next six
months.

At the close of my engagement at Dublin, in the beginning of October, 1868, a great
demonstration took place in honour of Mdlle. Titiens, it being the last night of the season.
Weber's opera of Oberon was performed, and after Titiens had sung the exacting air of
the third act, "Ocean, thou Mighty Monster," a most animated scene took place, many
requiring the great air to be repeated, whilst others called out the names of different Irish
songs. The uproar lasted upwards of fifteen minutes before silence could be restored,
when it was decided that "The Last Rose of Summer" should be given.

But the orchestra had no music and the conductor would not venture a performance
without it. Further delay and further uproar took place, until at length Signor Bettini, who
had undertaken the rôle of "Oberon," came from the wing, pulling on a cottage piano,
whilst Titiens helped the conductor to get out of the orchestra in order to accompany her.
As Bettini was turning the piano round, in consequence of the slope of the stage it fell
right over, causing an immense cheer from the gods, when no less than five demons (who
were to appear in the next scene of Oberon) rushed from the wings to raise it up again on

43

its legs. At length order was restored, and such was the silence that when Mdlle. Titiens was on the point of beginning the beautiful air I remember taking a pin from my collar and dropping it on the stage in order to give a practical and effective illustration of the old saying that you "could hear a pin drop."

No sooner had the singer finished the last verse than a roar of admiration was heard, so loud, so overpowering, that I can only compare it to the belching forth of huge pieces of artillery. At the close of the opera a great crowd, composed of the public and the medical students who habitually occupy the gallery (always without their coats, sometimes without their waistcoats, occasionally without their shirts), was awaiting the Queen of Song's departure. They had actually cut the traces of her carriage, and from a ship chandler's opposite had got two long coils of rope which they fastened to the vehicle. Titiens shortly afterwards appeared, amidst deafening cheers, and the procession started. No less than a dozen of the singer's most enthusiastic admirers were on the roof letting off fireworks. All went on in something like order until with our two long strings of volunteer horses we arrived at Dawson Street, when, in consequence of no previous arrangement having been made, one half of the team went up Dawson Street and the other half down Nassau Street, the result being a violent collision against Morrison's Hotel. It was not without considerable difficulty and delay that things could be readjusted.

On our arriving at Shelbourne Hotel the police found themselves powerless to cope with the multitude. But we had been accompanied by a young man, who, standing on the carriage step, had repeatedly addressed Mdlle. Titiens both in German and in French, telling her that she had "nothing to fear." On arriving at the door of the Shelbourne he gave a shrill whistle as a call for volunteer special constables, when a passage was at once cleared. It being a wet night the enthusiasts around us made a carpet for Titiens to walk on by throwing their coats on to the pavement. The crowd remained opposite the hotel for over an hour, during which time repeated calls were made for a song. But the gas of Mdlle. Titiens's sitting-room had been turned low, and the blinds being drawn down she hoped it might appear that she had retired for the night.

Shortly afterwards, however, a deputation came up accompanied by one of the chief constables, stating that if madame could not disperse the crowd the consequences would be very serious, as it refused to move. She at last felt compelled to go to the window of her hotel, when, after entreating for silence, she addressed the crowd in these words: "I will sing you 'The Last Rose of Summer' provided you promise to go home immediately afterwards like mice."

And sure enough they did, for at the conclusion of the song the crowd melted away in dead silence, not one person being left.

The inspector afterwards remarked to Mdlle. Titiens that if ever a revolution broke out in Ireland they would send over for her to quell it.

During the stay of my Opera Company at Dublin I allowed some of the principal artists to sing in various churches for charitable purposes. Mdlle. Titiens's services were sought for far and wide, and she was always ready to devote her Sunday, which was the only day of rest she had during the week, to the cause of charity. On one occasion I recollect her singing in a poor neighbourhood near Thomas Street, when many persons actually stooped to kiss the ground where she had trodden. She was held in the highest esteem by the clergy.

One Saturday evening, after the termination of the opera, several of my Italian choristers were wending their way home when they were accosted by some rowdy, good-natured Irishmen, who insisted upon having a drink with them. They, not comprehending the language, thought the men were robbers, and placed themselves in a position of

44

defence, whereupon they were boldly attacked by the sons of Erin, and a free fight ensued, in which some two or three Irishmen got stabbed. About noon the following day it was notified to me that some four or five of my choristers were in prison on account of this serious affair, and would be kept there until the wounded men, who were then in hospital, were sufficiently recovered to appear against them. I at once sought Mdlle. Titiens's aid, who went with me to one of the priests, with whom we afterwards visited the prison where our choristers were. They insisted that it was only a small affair, and that they had defended themselves against their aggressors.

They seemed also in great distress because the police authorities had taken away their week's salary which they had in their pockets, together with such pieces of jewellery or keys they had about them. By the advice of the priest we afterwards visited the hospital, and I, accompanied by the surgeon, inspected their wounds, which were triangular, as if caused by an Italian stiletto.

My clerical friend was very kind, and after a deal of whispering with the hospital surgeons, and afterwards with the wounded men themselves, he stated that they might have done it in accidentally falling down, but that it was not their intention to appear against the choristers, who were afterwards bailed out by Mdlle. Titiens. They duly appeared the next morning at the police-court and were dismissed, no one appearing against them.

I omitted to inform the reader that on the conclusion of the partnership agreement with Mr. Gye, which was to be kept a secret for the next six months, I rented the Royal Italian Opera for the autumn of 1868 for this double reason: first, that Her Majesty's Theatre was in ashes, and that I had no place wherein to give my autumn performances; and secondly, that my being seen about Covent Garden would in that case cause no surprise, whilst it would enable me occasionally to meet Mr. Gye in order to discuss our coming arrangements.

During my autumn season at Covent Garden I discovered Mdlle. Scalchi, the eminent contralto—then singing at a building which had been a circus. Struck with the lovely quality of her voice I engaged her for five years, events fully confirming my judgment on that occasion. About this time I first brought to this country Miss Minnie Hauk, a young singer about 18 years of age. She made her début at Covent Garden as "Amina" in La Sonnambula, her next part being that of "Cherubino" in Mozart's Nozze di Figaro.

After due discussion with Mr. Gye it was decided that our joint enterprise should be carried on at the Royal Italian Opera pending the rebuilding of my new theatre.

As the time for opening the season approached Mr. Gye suggested that we should ourselves make all engagements with the orchestra, instead of leaving that duty, as heretofore at the Royal Italian Opera, to Mr. Costa. This famous conductor was a despot, not only in the musical direction of his orchestra, but in other ways. He made his own engagements, and, leaving, of course, the manager to pay the appointed salaries, took care to be always present on pay day; when, in the case of any short-coming on the part of a musician, he would stop a portion of the salary payable to him, if not the whole amount. It was his custom to arrive at the theatre half-an-hour before the time fixed for the beginning of the evening's performance. He then took up a position as if of inspection, and, as he sat on the stage, the players passed him one by one as if in order of review. I remember on one occasion a young violinist arriving with mud on his boots, and in a frock coat. Costa pulled him up short, and asked him how he could venture to present himself in such a condition. The musician replied that he had just arrived from the Crystal Palace, and had not had time to make his toilet.

"Go home instantly," said Costa, "and come back with clean boots and in evening dress."

By the time the violinist (who lived in some distant suburb) got back the second act of the opera was nearly over; and when on pay-day the offender presented himself for his monthly salary he was informed that by reason of his absence on the occasion in question one week's salary was stopped. This sort of treatment the musicians had to put up with, or, as the only alternative, to accept their dismissal, which really meant the loss of the provincial festivals and of the Sacred Harmonic Society.

It must be added in favour of Costa's despotic ways that he never allowed any musician that he had engaged to be replaced by a substitute, even at rehearsal; a practice which in orchestras less severely governed has become only too frequent, to the great detriment of the performances.

Costa, meanwhile, by mere force of will, had gained so much authority at the Royal Italian Opera that the manager feared him, and was most anxious to be rid alike of his services and of his tyranny.

When it was intimated to Costa that the joint managers proposed to reserve to themselves the right of making direct engagements with the musicians for the orchestra, he would not hear of such an arrangement, and, much to Mr. Gye's satisfaction, resigned his post.

In view of the new works we proposed to give, and of the large number of rehearsals that would be required, two conductors were now engaged, Arditi and Vianesi.

Long before the theatre opened we had abundant signs of a prosperous season, and as the event drew near money poured in from various sources. We received in private subscriptions as much as £12,000. The booksellers' subscriptions amounted to £29,000 more, and in the course of the season the box-office sales alone brought in another £29,000. Altogether, counting profits from the Floral Hall concerts and sums received for the services of singers at public as well as private concerts, we received during the season of 1869 a grand total of £80,000.

On the other hand, we paid away in artists' salaries £22,000; for working expenses (including chorus), £13,000; orchestra, £7,500; sundry charges, £2,000.

Our whole expenditure came to £44,000, leaving us a clear profit of about £36,000.

Out of my half-share of this profit I had to pay for insurance and poor rates £3,000. Against this Mr. Gye put the use of the theatre, which was his property.

By our articles of partnership Mr. Gye had stipulated that he should "take no part in the management of the theatre unless he wished to do so." This wish came upon him after about a fortnight.

Our success during this season proved that though two rival Italian Operas can scarcely be carried on without loss on both sides, one Italian Opera can be made the source of very considerable profit. Even, however, with a monopoly there are two things essential to success. The operatic manager who would prosper must appeal to the public with a very strong Company, and with new works. Such casts as we secured for some of the recognized masterpieces of dramatic music could not fail to fill the theatre.

Among the new works or revivals produced at the Royal Italian Opera during the season of 1869 may be mentioned: Fidelio, The Magic Flute, Robert le Diable, Cherubini's Medea, Hamlet (first time in England), with Nilsson as "Ophelia," and Don Bucefalo (also first time in England). Medea had before been given at my own establishment with Mdlle. Titiens in the tragic part of the heroine. In Le Prophète, Titiens and Mongini appeared together, Titiens, of course, as "Fidès," Mongini as "John of Leyden." Don Giovanni was played with Titiens as "Donna Anna," Nilsson as "Donna

Elvira," and Patti as "Zerlina;" while the part of the dissolute hero was taken by Faure, and that of "Don Ottavio" by Mario.

About this time the secret oozed out that Mr. Jarrett, who had come with me from Her Majesty's Theatre to the Royal Italian Opera, had made engagements with Mongini, Ilma de Murska, Trebelli, Christine Nilsson, Santley, Foli, Faure, and Arditi. Mr. Jarrett, who in after years became known as the agent of Mdme. Nilsson, and especially of Mdlle. Sarah Bernhardt, held at that time a post with vague duties attached to it at the Royal Italian Opera, as previously at Her Majesty's Theatre, which during the combination season of 1869 was being rebuilt. Jarrett also acted as agent to Mongini, Ilma de Murska, Trebelli, and Bettini—Mdme. Trebelli's husband. Many years before he had been in partnership with Mr. George Wood, representing the firm of Cramer and Co., the well-known music publishers, for the direction of an Opera Company, and had been left by his associate in the lurch, Mr. Jarrett being called upon to meet single-handed liabilities which would have been far too much even for the partners combined.

Nor was Jarrett particularly well disposed towards the manager of the Royal Italian Opera, in whose orchestra he had once played the horn, and who in one of those orchestral strikes so common in the history of Opera-houses had taken a leading part as against the manager. Mr. Gye had thereupon dismissed him; and he now objected to have in his employment an agent receiving percentage on the salaries of his singers.

If, then, in the opposition he proposed to organize against the Royal Italian Opera Jarrett injured Mr. Gye, he would not be sorry; while if as a result of a failure at Drury Lane he injured Mr. Wood, he would be very glad. Naturally, however, he worked chiefly with a view to his own success.

Whether Wood mistrusted Jarrett, or whether after entering into partnership with him he mistrusted the success of the project, can never be decided; but it is certain that after securing Drury Lane Theatre for an operatic campaign, Mr. Wood repented of what he had done, and, unknown to Jarrett, entered into negotiations with Mr. Gye.

The advantages of an operatic monopoly were too obvious for Mr. Gye not to be anxious once more to secure it. This he was prepared to do, even at a considerable sacrifice; only it was I, his associate, not he himself, who was to make it. He proposed to me that Mr. George Wood should be taken into partnership, and that the profits for the season should be thus divided: Half to Gye, one quarter to Mapleson, one quarter to Wood. Mr. Gye was ready at that time to take in any number of partners who seemed in a position to threaten his justly-cherished monopoly, provided always that their share in the profits came to them out of my half, not out of his. For me the smallest fraction was deemed sufficient; he himself, however, could accept nothing less than a clear moiety.

After some amusing negotiations between Mr. Gye and myself, it was arranged that Mr. Wood should be taken into the concern on a basis of equal shares. Each, that is to say, was to receive one-third of the profits. The seceding artists, whose services we could not wish to lose—apart from the effect they might have in creating against us a formidable opposition—had all signed with Mr. Wood; and by the new arrangement these vocalists (Christine Nilsson, Mongini, Ilma de Murska, Trebelli, Faure, Santley, etc., with Arditi) were all to form part of the Royal Italian Opera Company. Our profits would still be large, though both Gye and myself would have to cede a portion of our gains to the new-comer.

Mr. Gye, Mr. Wood, and myself were all seated round a table in Mr. Gye's private room at Covent Garden Theatre, on the point of signing the contract which was to bind us together for the season of 1870, when suddenly a gentle tap at the door was heard, and, like "Edgardo" in the contract scene of Lucia, Jarrett appeared. He had, as he afterwards

47

informed me, entirely lost sight of Mr. Wood, who was supposed to be out of town, gone abroad, anywhere except in London; whence, however, he had not stirred. Jarrett had not traced his slippery partner to the Royal Italian Opera. He assured me that having no indications whatever to act upon he had come there guided simply by instinct. He was a man whose instinct seldom misled him.

While Mr. Gye and myself were a little surprised at the sudden apparition, Mr. Wood was lost in confusion. Jarrett meanwhile was absolutely calm. Standing at the door, he took a pinch of snuff, and for a few moments remained silent. Then, addressing his partner, he simply said: "Mr. Wood, can I have a minute's conversation with you outside?" Mr. Wood rose, and left the room, but returned in less than a minute, when Gye whispered to me: "It is all right; he is sure to sign." But when he was asked to put his name to the document which only awaited his signature to constitute a perfect contract between him, Gye, and myself, he hesitated, spoke of the necessity in which he found himself of first consulting his friends, and finally did not sign.

The conversation which had taken place outside the room, as it was afterwards repeated to me by Jarrett, was short and simple.

"The singers you have engaged," said Jarrett, "are under contract to sing at Drury Lane, and nowhere else. If, then, you join Mapleson and Gye they will not come to you at Covent Garden, and you will have to pay their salaries whether you open at Drury Lane or not."

Wood could only reply that he would not sign with Mapleson and Gye.

There was no money made that season at the Royal Italian Opera; whilst Mr. Wood's season at Drury Lane was simply disastrous. The moneyed partner soon proposed to shut up; but Jarrett, to whom Mr. Wood was bound, would not hear of this.

"I have no more money," said Wood.

"But you have a number of pianofortes," replied Jarrett. "You have music shops here and in Scotland whose contents and goodwill can be sold."

"You wish to ruin me?" asked Wood.

"You did not mind ruining me in 1854," answered Jarrett, "when we carried on Opera together and you left me to bear the burden of your losses."

It is bad enough for a manager to lose money, hoping night after night that by some new and successful stroke, or some change of taste on the part of the capricious public, the tide of luck may at last turn in his favour. But Mr. Wood had no such sanguine delusions to maintain him in his adversity; his losses were irretrievable. They increased as the season went on without any chance of being even arrested; and in the end anyone but a man of Mr. Wood's indomitable energy and courage would have been ruined beyond hope of recovery.

During the Wood season at Drury Lane many interesting performances were given, including Wagner's Flying Dutchman, with Ilma de Murska as the heroine and Santley as the hero; Mignon, with Mdme. Christine Nilsson; also Weber's Abu Hassan, each for the first time in England. But the enterprise could not stand against the superior attractions of the Royal Italian Opera, while the Royal Italian Opera, on its side, suffered in its receipts from the counter attraction presented by Drury Lane.

Towards the end of the season, war having been declared between France and Germany, Mdme. Pauline Lucca became anxious about her husband, who was an officer in a Prussian cavalry regiment, and now under campaigning orders. She was anxious, therefore, to see him before his departure with the army moving towards the French frontier. Some weeks afterwards, at the battle of Mars la Tour, a portion of the Prussian cavalry was sacrificed in order to hold in check the French, who were seeking to leave

Metz in order to march towards Paris. Mdme. Lucca's husband, Baron von Rhaden, was dangerously wounded in the charge; and the Baroness received special permission to visit him in the field hospital, where he was lying, outside Metz. Another officer of the same regiment, also wounded, came in for a good share of her attentions; and afterwards, being at that time in the United States, she applied in the New York Courts for a divorce from Baron von Rhaden in order to marry Baron von Wallhofen, the officer, who—as just mentioned—had, like Von Rhaden, been severely wounded at Mars la Tour. The New York Tribunal granted the divorce on Mdme. Lucca's simple affidavit; and before her husband (No. 1) had had time to reply by a counter affidavit from Berlin the second marriage had been celebrated. Such being the case the decree of divorce, so hastily pronounced, could not well be interfered with. So, at least, said the judges to whom the matter was referred; and Mdme. Pauline Lucca remained as she is now, Baroness von Wallhofen.

CHAPTER X.

GYE'S FRATERNAL EMBRACE—LAW-SUITS INTERMINABLE—DISSOLUTION OF PARTNERSHIP—RETURN TO DRURY LANE—ARRIVAL OF ALBANI—DÉBUT OF CAMPANINI—THE ANNUAL ONSLAUGHTS OF MR. GYE.

I SOON found that Mr. Gye, on the principle of embracing pour mieux étrangler, had taken me into partnership in order to stifle me at his ease.

In the early part of June, 1869, Mr. Gye suggested to me that it would be very desirable to renew my lease of Her Majesty's Theatre in order to get rid of a provision in the existing one, under which the Earl of Dudley had the power to determine it in the month of February in any year. Gye expressed his intention of seeing the Earl of Dudley on the subject, and at this interview it was agreed that the Earl should grant a new lease for seven, fourteen, or twenty-one years, Mr. Gye requesting that it should be granted either to himself alone or to Gye and Mapleson conjointly. The Earl decided the latter to be more desirable, requesting that the new lease should be signed on or before the 1st September. In due course we were informed that the lease was ready for signature.

As the duration of my partnership with Mr. Gye was only for three years (one of which had already nearly expired), I naturally desired to know what my position would be at the expiration of the partnership if we were joint managers of Her Majesty's Theatre for twenty-one years; as it appeared to me that it would leave him in command of a monopoly at the Royal Italian Opera, whilst I on my side, unable to perform Opera at Her Majesty's Theatre, would be called upon to pay half the rent of the building, which meantime would remain closed. I, therefore, took the precaution, when the day arrived for approving the draft lease, to append the following words:—"I am willing to execute the enclosed lease in conjunction with Mr. Gye upon the understanding as between him and me that our acceptance of the lease is not to affect in any way our relative rights under the articles of partnership. We shall respectively have the same rights under the proposed new lease as we now have or are subject to in respect of the subsisting lease under the articles of partnership, and on determination of our partnership this lease shall be exclusively vested in me for the residue of the term, I indemnifying Mr. Gye and his estate against any future liability for rent and covenants, or obtaining his release from the same."

This gave great umbrage to Mr. Gye, who thereupon refused to affix his signature to the lease.

In the meantime, the 1st of September (the date stipulated by the Earl for signature) having passed, Mr. Gye contended that by attaching a condition to my signing of the lease I had not accepted the lease at all. Besides, therefore, refusing to sign the joint lease, he insisted upon having a lease of Her Majesty's Theatre for himself alone. A deal of correspondence and trouble took place about this time, which I will not weary the reader with, and hundreds of letters passed between us and our solicitors. It was threatened, in short, that the lease would be granted by the Earl of Dudley to Mr. Gye alone, to my exclusion. I was, therefore, compelled in my own defence to file a bill in Chancery, making Mr. Gye and the Earl of Dudley defendants, to restrain them from carrying out their plan.

I ultimately, however, terminated our joint relations with more haste than I perhaps should have shown in consequence of the abject despondency, together with absolute physical prostration, into which Mr. Gye had been thrown through the turn lately taken by operatic affairs. As he lay exhausted on the sofa there seemed, indeed, but little chance of his ever rising again to take part in the active business of life. He could scarcely speak. He was pale, agitated, and such was his feverish condition that it was necessary from time to time to apply wet bandages to his forehead. In his state of exhaustion, combined with a certain nervous irritability, it seemed cruel to delay the signature he so much desired; and the effect of my putting pen to paper was, indeed, to cause him instantaneous relief. Never before did I see such a change. His despondency left him. He rose from the sofa, walked about with an elastic step, a cheerful air, and had he been anything of a vocalist would, I feel sure, have sung.

By the terms now agreed to between Mr. Gye and myself I was freed from all outstanding claims upon the theatre, and received a payment in money. I at the same time agreed to withdraw the Chancery proceedings against Dudley and Gye.

Immediately afterwards I set about forming a Company for my provincial operatic tour of 1870; also renting Covent Garden from Mr. Gye for the autumn, as I found it impossible to obtain Her Majesty's, being informed by Lord Dudley's solicitors that it had been let to Mr. Gye. The ensuing spring I returned to my old quarters at Drury Lane, my first act being to secure the services of Sir Michael Costa, who forthwith began forming his orchestra, whilst I went to the Continent in quest of vocal talent. I will not trouble the reader about my provincial opera tour, which, as usual, was very successful indeed; nor with my spring concert tour of 1871, with Titiens, Trebelli, Santley, Foli, and other eminent artists.

I opened my London season of 1871 under brilliant auspices, the Prince of Wales having taken a box as well as all the leading supporters from the old house. About this time I secured the services of Mdlle. Marimon, who drew enormous receipts, but unfortunately fell sick after the third night. It was only on rare intervals that she appeared again during the season. I, however, got safely through; producing several standard works, under the able direction of Sir Michael Costa, in addition to a revival of Robert the Devil, also Semiramide, with Titiens and Trebelli, who in this work always drew crowded houses. I also produced Anna Bolena. The season finished up satisfactorily, and I was glad to get a fortnight's well-earned rest prior to my autumn tour of opera, which was pre-eminently successful. I returned to London to take up my autumn season afterwards at the Royal Italian Opera, Covent Garden, which terminated early in December, after which I gave a few concluding operatic performances at Brighton.

Early the following year I again started on my spring concert tour; during which I gave 48 concerts in 48 cities in 48 days, followed by a spring opera season at Edinburgh.

50

I have omitted to state that prior to the opening of my successful Drury Lane season of 1871, the Earl of Dudley became the plaintiff and Mr. Gye the defendant with regard to Her Majesty's Theatre. Finding I was at Drury Lane, and in open opposition to the Royal Italian Opera, Mr. Gye did not seem to think it desirable that he should execute the lease; whereupon Lord Dudley took proceedings against Gye for £7,500, as arrears of rent for Her Majesty's Theatre.

About this time Jarrett, in reply to my constant applications, informed me that Mdlle. Nilsson was about to be married, and, in fact, that her future husband had already arrived in America, but that he, Jarrett, had succeeded in inducing her to give four performances the next season prior to the marriage, which was to be postponed until the following year. He explained in his letter that as her performances were to be limited to four I was not to complain of the only terms he could get the lady to assent to; namely, £200 for each representation. He explained that £800 would be the total sum; "and what," he asked, "is that where thousands are concerned, in addition to the prestige it will give to your house, as well as the influence on the subscription list?" I thereupon authorized him to close the matter for the season of 1872.

About this time my attention was drawn by my friend Zimelli, the manager of the theatre at Malta, to a most charming young soprano, who he assured me was destined to take a very high rank; and about the same time I received a letter from a regular subscriber to the house, a distinguished officer, pointing out the excellence of this young lady. I at once opened negotiations which ultimately led to favourable results. Colonel McCray, I may add, had written to me from Florence on the same subject. The name of the young singer was Emma Albani; and having, as I thought, secured her services— positively promised in a letter written to me by the lady—I found myself deprived of them by Mr. Gye; who I find, now that I look back on the past, paid me an attention of this kind—sometimes greater, sometimes less—regularly every year.

On her arrival Mdlle. Albani was to sign the contract; and as soon as she got to London she, with perfect good faith, drove to what she believed to be my theatre. She had told the cab-man to take her to the manager's office at the Italian Opera. She was conveyed to the Royal Italian Opera, and, sending in her card to Mr. Gye, who had doubtless heard of her, was at once received. On Mdlle. Albani's saying that she had come to sign the contract which I had offered her, Mr. Gye, knowing that I never made engagements but with artists of merit, gave her at once the agreement she desired.

To do Mr. Gye justice I must here mention that after the contract had been signed he, in the frankest manner, avowed to Mdlle. Albani that he was not Mr. Mapleson, for whom she had hitherto mistaken him. He explained to her that there was a manager named Mapleson who rented an establishment somewhere round the corner where operas and other things were from time to time played; but the opera, the permanent institution known as such, was the one he had the honour of directing. If, he concluded, Mdlle. Albani was sorry to have dealt with him she might still consider herself free, and he would at once tear up the contract.

Mdlle. Albani, however, was so impressed by the emphatic manner in which Mr. Gye dwelt on the superiority of his theatre to mine that she declared herself satisfied, and kept to the contract she had signed. Colonel McCray called on me soon afterwards to beg that out of consideration for the lady I would give up the letter in which she declared herself ready to sign with me. I assured him that I had no intention of making any legal use of it, but that I should like to keep it as a souvenir of the charming vocalist who had at one time shown herself willing to be introduced to the London public under my auspices.

51

Why, it may be asked, as a simple matter of business—indeed, as an act of justice to myself—did I not take proceedings for an enforcement of the agreement which Mdlle. Albani had virtually contracted? I, of course, considered the advisability of doing so, and one reason for which I took no steps in the matter was that Titiens, Nilsson, Murska, and Marimon were members of my Company, and that even if Mdlle. Albani had come to me I should have found it difficult to furnish her with appropriate parts.

The young lady duly appeared at Covent Garden about the beginning of April in La Sonnambula, and at once achieved a remarkable success, which caused me very much to regret the loss of her. She afterwards appeared as "Elsa" in Lohengrin in an Italian version, which had been made for me by Signor Marchesi, husband of the well-known teacher of operatic singing, and himself an accomplished musician.

I had ordered from Signor Marchesi as long before as 1864 an Italian version of Tannhäuser, which I duly announced in my prospectus for that year, but which I was dissuaded by some critical friends, who did not believe in Wagner, from presenting to the public. I had been advised, and there was certainly reason in the advice, that if I had quite decided to run such a risk as would be necessarily incurred through the production of an opera by Wagner (whose Tannhäuser had three years previously been hissed and hooted from the stage of the Paris Opera-house) I should at least begin with his most interesting and most attractive work, the poetical Lohengrin. Accordingly, reserving Tannhäuser for a future occasion, I determined to begin my Wagnerian operations with the beautiful legend of Elsa and the Knight of the Swan; and I commissioned Signor Marchesi to execute such a version of Lohengrin as he had previously given me of Tannhäuser—a version, that is to say, in which, without any departure from the meaning of the words or from the forms of the original versification, the musical accents should be uniformly observed.

But in England the laws relating to dramatic property seem to have been made for the advantage only of pirates and smugglers. I had printed the Italian translation of Lohengrin which Signor Marchesi had executed for me, and for which I had paid him the sum of £150. But I had not secured rights of representation in the work by going through the necessary farce of a mock performance before a sham public; and anyone, therefore, was at liberty to perform a translation which in any country but England would have been regarded as my property. How Signor Marchesi's translation of Lohengrin got into Mr. Gye's hands I do not know. But the version prepared for me at my cost was the one which Mr. Gye produced, and which somehow found its way to all the Italian theatres.

It has amused me in glancing through the history of my operatic seasons since 1861 to see how persistently Mr. Gye endeavoured by some stroke—let us say of policy—to bring my career as operatic manager to an abrupt end.

In 1861, when at Adelina Patti's own suggestion I was engaging a Company and taking a theatre with a view to her first appearance in England, he entangled her in an engagement by means of a fifty-pound loan.

In 1862, just when I was on the point of opening Her Majesty's Theatre, the late Mr. Augustus Harris, Mr. Gye's stage manager and adviser on many points, approached Mdlle. Titiens with an offer of a blank engagement.

In 1863 Mr. Gye's insidious but unsuccessful advances towards Mdlle. Titiens were repeated.

In 1864 Mr. Gye having, as he pretended, bought exclusive rights in Faust over my head, tried by means of an injunction, impossible under the circumstances (since the right of representing Faust at my own theatre had been duly purchased by me from the Paris publishers), to prevent me from performing the most successful opera I had yet secured.

52

In 1865 Mr. Gye did not renew his annual attack until my season was almost at an end. But on the last night, or nearly so, just when I had been promising good things for the ensuing season, he attempted to spring a mine upon me in my own house. I was sitting calmly in my box watching a particularly good performance of Faust, with Titiens, Trebelli, Gardoni, Junca, and Santley in the principal parts, when the old Duke of Leinster came in and said—

"Look here, Mapleson; what is the meaning of this?"

He handed me a printed announcement which I found had been placed in every seat in my theatre, and which I here reproduce with all possible precision, not excepting the typographical peculiarities by which the name of the "Right Hon. the Earl of Dudley" is made to appear in large capitals, and that of Mr. Gye in larger capitals still. Here is the astonishing document which if, on reflection, it filled me with mirth, did also, I freely admit, cause me for a few moments considerable surprise:—

Mr. GYE has the honour to announce that he has transferred the proprietorship of THE ROYAL ITALIAN OPERA, COVENT GARDEN, to a Public Company.

Mr. GYE will occupy the position of General Manager.

The Company has now made arrangements for purchasing of THE RIGHT HON. THE EARL OF DUDLEY his Lordship's interest in HER MAJESTY'S THEATRE, HAYMARKET.

The Prospectus of the Company will be issued in a few days.

ROYAL ITALIAN OPERA,
COVENT GARDEN,
JULY 29TH, 1865.

On inquiry I found that an emissary from Covent Garden had bribed one of my box keepers, who, for the small sum of one sovereign, had betrayed his trust, and deluged my theatre with daring and mendacious announcements from the opposition house.

In 1866 Mr. Gye tried to carry out the arrangement with which he had audaciously threatened me in my own theatre just as the season of 1865 was terminating. I happened to hold a twenty-one years' lease of Her Majesty's Theatre; and to purchase Lord Dudley's interest in the establishment was a very different thing from purchasing mine. But what at once put a stop to Mr. Gye's action in the matter was an injunction obtained by Colonel Brownlow Knox to restrain Mr. Gye from dealing with the Royal Italian Opera as his property until the seemingly interminable case of Knox v. Gye had been decided.

In 1867 Mr. Gye may have been nurturing I know not what deadly scheme against my theatre. But this year a fatal accident came to his aid, and he was spared the trouble of executing any hostile design. It was in 1867 that Her Majesty's Theatre was destroyed by fire.

In 1868 came the proposition for partnership. Mr. Gye wished to grapple with me at closer quarters.

In 1869 Mr. Gye was intriguing with Lord Dudley to get Her Majesty's Theatre into his hands.

In 1870 Mr. Gye made his droll proposal to the effect that I should go equal shares with him in paying the rent of Her Majesty's Theatre, I binding myself not to open it.

In 1872 Mr. Gye engaged Mdlle. Albani, already under contract to me, and helped himself to my version of Lohengrin.

In 1873 he offered an engagement to one of my two leading stars, Mdlle. Nilsson; and I had myself to write explaining to him very clearly that she was engaged to me.

For two whole years Mr. Gye remained quiet as towards me. But in 1876, when I was on the point of completing the capital necessary for carrying out my grand National

Opera project on the Thames Embankment, he wrote a letter which somehow found its way into the Times, denouncing the whole affair, and proving by an extraordinary manipulation of figures that my rent would be something like £40,000 a year.

In 1877 Mr. Gye, knowing that I had engaged Gayarré, and well assured that I should not have done so had not Gayarré been a good artist, offered him double what I was to pay him. Gayarré, with all the innocence of a tenor, explained to me that the temptation presented to him was irresistible. I brought an action against him all the same, and obtained in the Italian Courts a judgment for £8,000, which I have not yet been able to enforce by reason of his having no property in Italy.

CHAPTER XI.

ADELINA'S SUCCESSOR—A PRIMA DONNA'S MARRIAGE NEGOTIATIONS—POUNDS V. GUINEAS—NILSSON AND THE SHAH—PRODUCTION OF "LOHENGRIN"—SALVINI'S PERFORMANCES AND PROFITS—MARGUERITE CHAPUY—IRONY OF AN EARL.

HAVING relied upon Mdme. Nilsson's services for my Drury Lane season of 1871, I felt in a position of great difficulty. I thereupon set about inquiring for a capable prima donna to supply her place. About two days afterwards I received a letter from America informing me of a most extraordinary singer, the writer further setting forth that his father had, some twenty years previously, recommended me Adelina Patti, and that he could equally endorse all that was now said of this coming star. Without one moment's hesitation I accepted, feeling sure the "tip" must be a good one, and in due course the lady arrived. She was of short stature and remarkably stout, which I considered at once a drawback; but so unbounded was my confidence in the recommendation that I persuaded myself these defects would be of no consequence whatever in the general result.

At the conclusion of the first rehearsal Sir Michael Costa came down in a most mysterious way, asking me if I was sure as to the prima donna's talents. I told him he need be under no apprehension whatever on the subject.

At length the general rehearsal arrived, and a message came from Sir Michael, begging me to ask the little lady to sing out, as up to the present time nobody had heard her voice at any of the rehearsals. I came on to the stage, but as our new Diva was conducting herself with great importance, and moreover seemed to be busy with the preparation of her music, I told Sir Michael that he need labour under no misapprehension, as she was guaranteed to take the town by storm.

Evening came, and a more dismal fiasco I do not recollect. Such unbounded faith had I placed in my American friend's recommendation, together with the laudatory notices which had appeared in the numerous journals he had sent, that I confess I was on this occasion taken in.

This is the only instance in the course of my lengthened career in which an artist introduced by me has not been forthwith accepted by the public, and I admit that the result in this particular case was entirely due to my own neglect in not hearing her beforehand.

It was rather hard lines on the "Faust" of the evening, M. Capoul, who made his first appearance in England on this occasion; likewise on Moriami, the favourite baritone, and Rives, a young French artist, who sustained the rôle of "Mephistopheles" with great credit.

The following evening I produced Robert le Diable, in which Signor Nicolini made his first appearance in England, enacting the rôle of "Roberto" to perfection. Belval, the first bass of the Paris opera, was the "Bertramo," Mdme. Ilma de Murska the "Isabella," and Titiens the "Alice." In the excellence of this performance my "Margherita" of the previous evening was soon forgotten, and I booked her an early passage back to America, where, strange to say, she still retained a first-class position, and did so for many years afterwards.

As matters were still unsettled between Lord Dudley and his would-be tenant, Gye, I again secured Drury Lane for my season of 1872. Prior to concluding Mdlle. Nilsson's engagement, as she was still unmarried, her Paris agent, who advised her, called upon me, stating that in the event of my requiring her services I had better notify to him that the marriage must be postponed until the close of my proposed opera season. To this I consented, and I attended at a meeting where I met the future husband and the agent, when it was explained to the former that Mdlle. Nilsson was ready and willing to perform her agreement to marry him, but that in that case she would lose her London engagement, and would be very angry; whereupon it was agreed the marriage should be further postponed. Papers were drawn up, and the proper stamps affixed, whereby Mdlle. Nilsson was to return to me for my season of 1872.

On the 28th May she made her reappearance, after an absence of two years, renewing her success as "La Traviata," followed by Faust, Trovatore, etc.

During this season I produced Cherubini's Water-carrier, in which Titiens sang; also Lucia di Lammermoor, with Nilsson for the first time as the heroine, which drew enormous houses; followed by the Marriage of Figaro, in which Titiens and Kellogg appeared, Nilsson acting the "saucy page" to perfection. A most successful season was the result, and in lieu of appearing only four times Mdlle. Nilsson sang never less than twice a week until the close. The terms I was paying her caused a deal of trouble between Patti and Gye; for la Diva had heard of Nilsson's enormous salary. Gye had ultimately to give in; but £200 a night would not satisfy Mdme. Patti, although previously she had been contented with £80; and it was ultimately arranged that she should have more than Nilsson. Gye managed this by paying her 200 guineas nightly, whilst Nilsson had only 200 pounds.

Some two or three weeks after the opening of the season I heard of a desirable tenor in Italy, named Campanini, and at once endeavoured to add him to my already strong Company. My agent reached Rome before Mr. Gye, and secured the prize. I thereupon set to work to create all the excitement I possibly could, knowing that unless this were done no curiosity would be felt by the public as to his first appearance. I said so much of him that general expectation was fully aroused. In the meantime I was anxiously awaiting his arrival. One evening, about nine o'clock, the hall-keeper brought me word that there was someone "from Campini, or some such name." I immediately brightened up, and said, "Send the messenger in," who accordingly entered. He had a coloured flannel shirt on, no shirt collar, a beard of two or three days' growth, and a little pot-hat. He, in fact, looked rather a rough customer. In reply to my interrogation he informed me that Campanini had arrived, and was in London. I replied, "Are you sure?" Thereupon he burst out laughing, and said that he was Campanini. I felt as if I should go through the floor.

However, the night arrived for his first performance, which took place on May 4th, when he appeared as "Gennaro" in Lucrezia Borgia, with Titiens and Trebelli, and with Agnesi as the "Duke." The house was crowded from floor to ceiling, and I must say the tenor fulfilled every anticipation, and, in fact, surpassed my expectations. The salary I paid him was not a large one, and I had engaged him for five years. After ten or twelve days an agent arrived from America who had heard of his success, and offered him £1,000 a month, which was five times what I was to pay him. I need hardly say that this offer, coupled with his great success, completely turned his head, and he became partially unmanageable. Marie Roze, I may add, made her first appearance in England during this season.

At its close Mdlle. Christine Nilsson was married to M. Rouzaud at Westminster Abbey, surrounded by a numerous circle of friends, the ceremony being performed by Dean Stanley. The wedding party were afterwards entertained by the Cavendish Bentincks at their splendid mansion in Grafton Street, where a sumptuous déjeuner was served.

After two or three weeks' holiday at Aix-les-Bains, I started my autumn tour, as usual, at Dublin, for which I engaged Titiens, Marimon, de Murska, Trebelli, Scalchi, Agnesi, Campanini, Fancelli, Foli, etc. This season of fourteen weeks, which carried us up to Christmas, was an unbroken series of triumphs, the receipts being simply enormous; whilst on the spare days when certain of my singers were not required I filled in sometimes as much as £1,000 a week from concerts, without the regular service of the tour being disturbed. We visited Dublin, Cork, Belfast, Glasgow, Edinburgh, Manchester, Liverpool, Birmingham, Bristol, and Brighton. This was followed by the usual spring concert tour of 1873, when we did, as usual, our 60 or 70 towns, concluding with a spring opera tour in the north.

For my season of 1873, which again took place at Drury Lane—Her Majesty's Theatre, although built, being still without furniture or scenery—I re-engaged Mdme. Nilsson, paying her £200 per night, in addition to my regular company, which, of course, included Titiens; also Ilma de Murska, Marie Roze, Trebelli, etc., etc. I, moreover, introduced Mdlle. Valleria, Mdlle. Macvitz, an excellent contralto; Aramburo, a tenor possessing a marvellous voice, who has since achieved European fame; Signor Del Puente, the eminent baritone, and many others.

I likewise engaged Mdme. Ristori, who appeared in several of her favourite characters alternately with the operatic performances. Her success was striking, notably in the parts of "Medea," "Mary Stuart," "Elizabeth," and "Marie Antoinette." In the latter impersonation she moved the audience to tears nightly by her pathetic acting.

During this season, early in the month of July, it was intimated to me that His Majesty the Shah of Persia would honour the theatre with his presence. I thereupon set about organizing a performance that would give satisfaction both to my principal artists and to the Lord Chamberlain, who had charge of the arrangements, and decided that the performance should consist of the third act of La Favorita, Mdlle. Titiens enacting the rôle of "Leonora," the first act of La Traviata, and, after a short ballet, the first act of Mignon, Mdme. Nilsson taking the title rôle in the two latter operas. Mdlle. Titiens, who rarely created difficulties, took rather an exception to commencing the evening, and said that it would be better to divide the two appearances of Nilsson by placing the act of La Favorita between them; Mdme. Nilsson, on the other hand, objected to this arrangement. Two days before the performance Mdme. Nilsson suddenly expressed her willingness to commence the evening with the act of La Traviata, she having ascertained from the Lord Chamberlain, or some other high personage (as I afterwards discovered), that His Majesty the Shah could only be present from half-past eight until half-past nine, being due at the grand ball given by the Goldsmiths in the City at about ten o'clock.

Mdme. Nilsson had ordered, at considerable expense, one of the most sumptuous dresses I have ever seen, from Worth, in Paris, in order to portray "Violetta" in the most appropriate style. On the evening of the performance His Royal Highness the Prince of Wales arrived punctually at half-past eight to assist in receiving the Shah, who did not put in an appearance; and it was ten minutes to nine when Sir Michael Costa led off the opera. I shall never forget the look the fair Swede cast upon the empty royal box, and it was not until half-past nine, when the act of La Favorita had commenced, that His Majesty arrived. He was particularly pleased with the ballet I had introduced in the Favorita. The Prince of Wales, with his usual consideration and foresight, suggested to me that it might smooth over the difficulty in which he saw clearly I should be placed on the morrow in connection with Mdme. Nilsson, if she were presented to the Shah prior to his departure.

I thereupon crossed the stage and went to Mdme. Nilsson's room, informing her of this. She at once objected, having already removed her magnificent Traviata toilette and attired herself for the character of "Mignon," which consists of a torn old dress almost in rags, with hair hanging dishevelled down the back, and naked feet. After explaining that it was a command with which she must comply, I persuaded her to put a bold face on the matter and follow me. I accompanied her to the ante-room of the royal box, and before I could notify her arrival to His Royal Highness, to the astonishment of all she had walked straight to the farther end of the room, where His Majesty was then busily employed eating peaches out of the palms of his hands.

The look of astonishment on every Eastern face was worthy of the now well-known picture on the Nabob pickles. Without a moment's delay Mdme. Nilsson made straight for His Majesty, saying—

"Vous êtes un très mauvais Shah," gesticulating with her right hand. "Tout à l'heure j'étais très riche, avec des costumes superbes, exprès pour votre Majesté; à present je me trouve très pauvre et sans souliers," at the same time raising her right foot within half an inch of His Majesty's nose; who, with his spectacles, was looking to see what she was pointing to. He was so struck with the originality of the fair prima donna that he at once notified his attendants that he would not go to the Goldsmiths' Ball for the present, but would remain to see this extraordinary woman.

His Majesty did not consequently reach the Goldsmiths' Hall until past midnight. The Lord Mayor, the Prime Warden, the authorities, and guards of honour had all been waiting since half-past nine.

On the close of my London season of 1873 I had considerable difficulty in obtaining a renewal of Mdme. Nilsson's contract for the ensuing year; in fact, she declined altogether to discuss the matter with me. I was fully aware that she was very jealous of the firm position which Mdlle. Titiens enjoyed in the good opinion of the British public. This had manifested itself on the occasion of Titiens's benefit, when Nozze di Figaro had been selected for the closing night of the season. Much correspondence took place, in the course of which it was asserted that M. Rouzand would not allow his wife to put on "Cherubino's" trunks, he having decided that her legs should never again be seen by the public. I, therefore, had to substitute Mdme. Trebelli, who, as an experienced contralto, could make no objection on such points.

Mdme. Nilsson's agent, Mr. Jarrett, succeeded at last in inducing her to sign a contract, and he then explained to me that Mr. Gye had been repeatedly making offers to her during the previous week, which, in spite of his notorious friendship for Mr. Gye, he had the greatest difficulty in making her refuse.

Ultimately an engagement had been prepared, and Jarrett asked me to sign it at the station just as Mdme. Nilsson was about to start for Paris. Before doing so I requested permission at all events to glance it over, when Mdme. Nilsson replied—

"The train is going. Either sign or leave it alone. I can make no possible alteration." I mechanically appended my signature; the train started.

On perusing the engagement I discovered that she had reserved for herself the exclusive right of playing "Norma," "Lucrezia," "Fidelio," "Donna Anna," "Semiramide," and "Valentine" in Les Huguenots. But having omitted the words "during the season," and inasmuch as her engagement for 1874 did not commence until the 29th day of May, I had a clear period of eleven weeks during which another prima donna could play the parts Mdme. Nilsson claimed without overstepping her stringent condition.

I, moreover, felt placed in great difficulty with regard to Mdlle. Titiens, who was then at the Worcester Festival, and to whom it was, of course, necessary to mention the matter. I decided to go to Worcester at once and unbosom myself.

The great prima donna, on hearing what I had to tell her, smiled and said—

"By all means let her play the parts she wants; and, if the public prefers her rendering of them to mine, by all means let her keep them. But during the first eleven weeks they are open to other singers, and I will repeat them one by one so that the public may have a fair opportunity of judging between us."

The great artist was, therefore, on her mettle during the early performances of 1874, prior to Nilsson's arrival.

The season opened with Semiramide, followed immediately by Fidelio, Norma, Huguenots, Lucrezia, etc., which were played one after the other until the arrival of Nilsson, who sang first in Faust, and immediately afterwards in Balfe's Talismano, after which I called on her to appear as "Lucrezia."

The next morning I had a visit from her agent requesting me not to press the matter, as she was not quite prepared. I thereupon said "Semiramide" would do as well; to this he offered some objection; but at length, on my urging "Fidelio," he explained to me that if I insisted upon her playing any of those characters which she had expressly stipulated for I should mortally offend her. I could not even induce her to appear as "Donna Anna." Not one of those parts which she had reserved for her exclusive use was she able to undertake. We, therefore, had to fall back on Faust, alternated with La Traviata.

Finally a compromise was made whereby Mdme. Nilsson undertook the rôle of "Donna Elvira" in Don Giovanni, Mdlle. Titiens retaining her great impersonation of "Donna Anna," in which she was acknowledged throughout the world of music to be unrivalled. This happy combination having been brought about, the season concluded with my benefit, when Don Giovanni was given to some £1,200 receipts.

During the autumn of 1873 I made my usual operatic tour, commencing in Dublin about the middle of September, where we remained three weeks, afterwards visiting Belfast, Glasgow, Edinburgh, Newcastle, Liverpool, Manchester, Birmingham, Bristol, Bath, and Brighton, where we concluded on the 20th December.

Early in January, 1874, I again gave my usual forty-eight concerts in the various cities, opening the Edinburgh opera season about the middle of February. We afterwards visited other places, which brought us on to the London season, when I again occupied Drury Lane Theatre.

During this year I produced Auber's Crown Diamonds, and afterwards Balfe's Talismano, in which Mdlle. Nilsson undertook the principal rôle, Marie Roze appearing as the "Queen." Balfe's opera was very successful, and this, coupled with the alternate appearances of Titiens and Nilsson in other characters, followed by the revival of the Magic Flute, in which the whole Company took part, brought the season to a successful conclusion.

In the autumn of 1874 I opened, as usual, at Dublin, with a very powerful company, and continued out in the provinces until the latter part of December. I then went on the Continent in search of talent for the ensuing year, and returned in time to be present at my first concert, which took place in Liverpool early in January, 1875. We afterwards went through Ireland and the English provinces, commencing in the beginning of March the regular Italian Opera season in the northern capital, followed by Glasgow, Liverpool, &c.

Ilma de Murska was punctual with a punctuality which put one out quite as much as utter inability to keep an appointment would have done. She was sure to turn up on the very evening, and at the very hour when she was wanted for a representation. But she had a horror of rehearsals, and never thought it worth while, when she was travelling from some distant place on the Continent, to announce that she had started, or to give any idea as to when she might really be expected. Her geographical knowledge, too, was often at fault, and some of the routes—"short cuts" she called them—by which she reached London from Vienna, were of the most extraordinary kind. She had taken a dislike to the Railway Station at Cologne, where she declared that a German officer had once spoken to her without being introduced; and on one occasion, partly to avoid the station of which she preserved so painful a recollection, partly in order to get to London by a new and expeditious route, she travelled from Vienna to St. Petersburg, and from St. Petersburg took boat to Hull, where she arrived just in time to join my Opera Company at the representations that I was then giving in Edinburgh. We had not heard of her for weeks, and she came into the dressing-room to find Madame Van Zandt already attired for the part Mdlle. de Murska was to have played, that of "Lucia." She argued, with some truth, that she was in time for the performance, and declared, moreover, that in entrusting the part of "Lucia" to another singer she could see a desire on my part to get rid of her.

The prima donna has generally a parrot, a pet dog, or an ape, which she loves to distraction, and carries with her wherever she goes. Ilma de Murska, however, travelled with an entire menagerie. Her immense Newfoundland, Pluto, dined with her every day. A cover was laid for him as for her, and he had learned to eat a fowl from a plate without dropping any of the meat or bones on the floor or even on the table cloth.

Pluto was a good-natured dog, or he would have made short work of the monkey, the two parrots, and the Angora cat, who were his constant associates. The intelligent animal hated travelling in the dog-truck, and he would resort to any sort of device in order to join his mistress in her first-class carriage, where he would, in spite of his immense bulk, squeeze himself beneath the seat. Once I remember he sprang through the closed window, cutting himself severely about the nose in his daring leap.

The other animals were simple nuisances. But I must do the monkey the justice to say that he did his best to kill the cat, and a bare place on Minette's back showed how badly she had once been clawed by her mischievous tormentor.

The most expensive of Mdlle. de Murska's pets were probably the parrots. They flew about the room, perching everywhere and pecking at everything. Once at the Queen's Hotel, Birmingham, they tore with their beaks the kid off a valuable set of chairs, for which the hotel-keeper charged £30. The hotel bill of this reckless prima donna was always of the most alarming kind. She had the most extraordinary whims, and when Signor Sinico, Mdme. Sinico's first husband, in order to show the effect of parsley upon parrots, gave to one of Mdme. de Murska's birds enough parsley to kill it, nothing would satisfy the disconsolate lady but to have a post-mortem examination of the bird's remains. This was at Glasgow, and the post-mortem was made by two very grave, and I have no doubt very learned, Scotch practitioners. Finding in the parrot's maw some green matter for which they could not satisfactorily account, they came, after long deliberation, to the conclusion that the bird had been eating the green wall-paper of the sitting room, and that the arsenic contained in the colouring matter had caused its death. The cost of this opinion was three guineas, which Mdlle. de Murska paid without a murmur.

I again returned to Drury Lane for my London season of 1875. After lengthy negotiations with a great Italian tragedian, engagements were signed, and he duly arrived in London, and appeared the second night of my season in the character of "Otello." I need scarcely say that this tragedian was Salvini, who at once struck the public by his magnificent delineation of Shakespeare's hero. I was now compelled to open my theatre seven times every week (four for opera, three for tragedy), from the early part of March until the latter end of July. I produced various works, notably Wagner's Lohengrin, in which Mdlle. Titiens, who very kindly undertook the rôle of "Ortruda," really excelled herself. This, with Mdlle. Christine Nilsson as "Elsa," Campanini as the "Knight of the Swan," and Galassi as "Telramund," with an increased orchestra under Sir Michael Costa's able direction, caused me to increase the prices of admission; and even then it was impossible to get a seat during the remainder of the season.

About this time the usual annual proposals were made for Mdlle. Titiens's services at a series of concerts to be given in the United States of America, by which she was to receive £160 a night guaranteed, and half the receipts beyond a certain amount. After some time I consented to this arrangement.

At the close of Salvini's engagement I handed him £8,000 for his half-share of the profits, retaining a like amount for myself.

In July, 1875, one of the most charming vocalists that it has been my pleasure to know, a lady who as regards voice, talent, grace, and style was alike perfect, and who was as estimable by her womanly qualities as by her purely artistic ones, made her first appearance at my temporary Operatic home, Drury Lane, as "Rosina," in Il Barbiere. This was Mdlle. Marguerite Chapuy, and no sooner had the news of her success been proclaimed than Adelina Patti came, not once, but twice running to hear her.

At the first performance Mdlle. Chapuy made such an impression on the public that in the scene of the music lesson she was encored no less than four times; particularly successful among the various pieces she introduced being the "Aragonese" from Auber's Domino Noir, and the waltz from Gounod's Romeo and Juliet. Sir Michael Costa hated encores, but on this occasion he departed willingly from his usual rule.

Marguerite Chapuy charmed everyone she came near; among others a young French sergeant, a gentleman, that is to say, who had enlisted in the French army, and was now a non-commissioned officer. Her parents, however, did not look upon the young man as a fit husband for such a prima donna as their daughter, and it was true that no vocalist on the stage seemed to have a brighter future before her. Mdlle. Chapuy remained meanwhile at Drury Lane, and the success of her first season was fully renewed when in the second she appeared as "Violetta" in La Traviata. A more refined impersonation of a character which requires very delicate treatment, had never been seen.

It struck me after a time that my new "Violetta" was not wasting away in the fourth act of La Traviata alone. She seemed to be really perishing of some malady hard to understand; and when the most eminent physicians in London were called in they all regarded the case as a difficult one to deal with since there was nothing definite the matter with the patient. Gradually, however, she was fading away.

There could be no thought of her appearing now on the stage; and at her own desire, as well as that of her father and mother, who were naturally most anxious about her, she was removed to France. No signs of improvement, however, manifested themselves. She got weaker and weaker, and when she was seemingly on the point of death her hard-hearted parents consented to her marriage with the young sergeant. My consent had also to be given, and I naturally did not withhold it.

Mdlle. Chapuy had signed an engagement with me for several years. But everyone said that the unhappy vocalist was doomed; and such was beyond doubt the belief of her parents, or they never would have consented to her throwing herself away on an honourable young man who was serving his country for something less than a franc a day, when she might so easily have captured an aged banker or a ruined Count.

Shortly afterwards I met her in Paris looking remarkably well. She told me that her husband had received his commission soon after their marriage, and that he now held some local command at Angoulême. As I had not released her from her engagement, I suggested to her, and even entreated, that she should fulfil it. Her husband, however, would not hear of such a thing. He preferred that they should live quietly on the £120 a year which he was now receiving from the Government. I offered as much as £200 a night, but without effect.

All I could get was a promise from Mdlle. Chapuy that in the event of her returning to the stage she would give me her services in accordance with the terms of the contract she had previously signed. Later on she told me that she still sang once a year for charitable purposes; and I still hope for her return to the lyric stage.

I here append the letter she addressed to me just after her marriage:—

"Angoulême, 8 Decembre, 1876.

"CHER MONSIEUR MAPLESON,

"Je vous remercie de votre bonne lettre et je m'empresse d'y répondre pour vous assurer que je m'engage aussi formellement que vous pouvez le désirer à ce que l'engagement que nous avions ensemble soit remis en vigueur si jamais je reprends la carrière théâtrale: je vous promets aussi que vous pourriez compter sur moi pour la grande saison de Londres qui suivrait ma rentrée sur la scène. Vous avez été trop bon et trop aimable pour moi, pour que j'hésite un instant à vous faire cette promesse. Du reste, il me serait bien agréable, si je reprenais le théâtre, de reparaître sur la scène de Londres, car je n'ai pas oublié combien le public Anglais a été bienveillant pour moi.

"En attendant votre réponse veuillez agréer cher Monsieur Mapleson l'assurance de mes sentiments dévoués.

"MARGUERITE ANDRÉ-CHAPUY,

"Rue St. Gelais, 34.

"Mon mari, ma grande-mère, et ma mère sont bien sensibles à votre aimable souvenir et vous font tous leurs compliments."

There are two ways of judging a singer—by the vocalist's artistic merits, and by the effect of his or her singing on the receipts. In the first place I judge for myself by the former process. But when an appearance has once been made I fall back, as every manager is bound to do, on the commercial method of judgment, and calculate whether the amount of money drawn by the singer is enough to justify the outlay I am making for that singer's services. The latter was the favourite system of the illustrious Barbaja, who, when he was asked his private opinion as to this or that member of his Company, would say—

"I have not yet consulted my books. I must see what the receipts were, and I will answer your question to-morrow."

Referring to my books, I find with great satisfaction that the charming artist, whom I admired quite as much before she had sung a note at my theatre as I did afterwards, when she had fairly captivated the public, drew at her first performance £488, and at her second £538; this in addition to an average nightly subscription of £600.

Thus Mdlle. Chapuy made her mark from the first.

Other vocalists, even of the highest merit, have been less fortunate. Thus Mdlle. Marimon, when she appeared at my theatre in 1871, drew at her first performance (that of "Amina," in La Sonnambula) £73, at her second £280, at her third £358, at her fourth £428. To these sums, as in the case of Mdlle. Chapuy, the nightly proportion of the subscription has, of course, to be added.

As with singers, so with operas. I choose a work which, according to my judgment, ought to succeed, and cast it as well as I possibly can. It will not in any case please the public the first night; and I have afterwards to decide whether I shall make sacrifices, as with Faust, and run it at a loss in the hope of an ultimate success, or whether I shall cut the matter short by dropping it, even after a vast outlay in scenery, dresses, and properties, and after much time and energy expended at rehearsals.

When I brought out Cherubini's admirable Deux Journées (otherwise The Water Carrier) I was complimented by the very best judges on the beauty of the work, and also (how little they knew!) on its success. I received congratulations from Jenny Lind, from Benedict, from Hallé, from Millais, from the Baroness Burdett-Coutts. But there was not more than £97 that night in the treasury. Thereupon I made my calculation. It would have cost me £1,200 to make the work go, and I could not at that moment afford it. I was obliged, then, to drop it, and that after five weeks' rehearsals!

Some time afterwards I produced Rossini's Otello with a magnificent cast. Tamberlik was the "Otello," Faure the "Iago," Nilsson the "Desdemona." The other parts were played by Foli, Carrion (an excellent tenor from Spain), and others. All my friends were delighted to find that I had made another great success. I listened to their flattering words. But the treasury contained only £167 3s., for which reason Otello was not repeated.

In rebuilding Her Majesty's Theatre Lord Dudley did not think it worth while to consult me or any other operatic manager. He had the opportunity of erecting the only isolated theatre in London, and the most magnificent Opera-house in the world, for the shops in the Opera Colonnade and the adjoining hotel in Charles Street might at that time have been purchased for comparatively small sums. The Earl, however, as he himself told me, cared only to comply with the terms of his lease, which bound him to replace the theatre which had been destroyed by another of no matter what description, provided only that it had four long scenes and four short ones.

Messrs. Lee and Paine, the architects entrusted with the duty of covering the vacant site, acted after their own lights, and they succeeded in replacing two good theatres by a single bad one. The old Opera-house, despite its narrow stage, had a magnificent auditorium, and the Bijou theatre, enclosed within its walls, possessed a value of its own. It was let to Charles Mathews, when theatrical property possessed less value than now, for £100 a week; and Jenny Lind sang in it to houses of £1,400.

When the new theatre had been quite finished Lord Dudley was shown over it by the delighted architects. His lordship was a tall man, and his hat suffered, I remember, by coming into collision with the ceiling of one of the corridors. Turning to the senior partner, who was dying to catch from his aristocratic patron some word of satisfaction, if not of downright praise, the Earl thus addressed him—

"If narrow corridors and low ceilings constitute a fine theatre you have erected one which is indeed magnificent."

The architect, lost in confusion at being addressed in terms which he thought from his lordship's finely ironical demeanour must be in the highest degree complimentary, did nothing but bow his acknowledgments, and it was not until a little later that some good-natured friends took the trouble to explain to him what the Earl had really said.

CHAPTER XII.

THE NATIONAL OPERA-HOUSE—FOUNDATION DIFFICULTIES—
PRIMÆVAL REMAINS—TITIENS LAYS THE FIRST BRICK—THE DUKE OF
EDINBURGH THE FIRST STONE—THE OPERA AND PARLIAMENT—OUR
RECREATION ROOMS.

DURING all this time I was busily engaged selecting plans for the construction of
my new National Opera-house, which I then considered a most desirable investment,
inasmuch as Her Majesty's Theatre, which had been hastily built, was ill-adapted for the
requirements of Italian Opera, whilst Covent Garden was heavily encumbered with
liabilities. Indeed, more than one negotiation had already taken place with the Duke of
Bedford with a view to its purchase and demolition. I, therefore, saw that sooner or later
London would be without a suitable Opera-house. In order to expedite the works it was
considered desirable that the foundations should be proceeded with pending the final
settlement of the drawings, taking out the quantities, etc., and deciding who the
contractors should be.

Mr. Webster, who constructed the best part of the Thames Embankment, was
deemed to be the fitting man, and I therefore had an interview with him on the subject. In
this interview he told me he would execute the whole of the foundations up to the datum
level for the sum of £5,000.

On consulting with my architect he advised that it would be more economical that
this preliminary work should be paid for by measurement, which Mr. Webster ultimately
agreed to. No sooner had they dug to a certain depth than it was discovered that no
foundation could be obtained. Afterwards screw piles were attempted and all other kinds
of contrivances to obviate the expense with which we were threatened in the prosecution
of the works. The digging proceeded to a depth of some 40 or 50 feet without discovering
anything but running springs and quicksands, covered by a large overlying mass of
rubbish, being the accumulation of several ages in the history of Westminster. Many relics
of olden times came to light, including the skulls and bones of wild elks and other
primitive animals that once roamed about the Thames Valley and were hunted by ancient
Britons in the days of the Druids. Various swords, gold and inlaid, often richly-fashioned,
told of the feuds of York and Lancaster; while many other objects, concealed for
centuries, now came forth to throw a light on the faded scroll of the past.

As the builders had got considerably below the depth of the Thames and
consequently that of the District Railway, the water began to pour in, which necessitated
some fifteen or twenty steam-pumping machines being kept at work for several months.
At length the London Clay was reached, which necessitated various cuttings, some 16ft.
wide, down which had to be placed some 40ft. of concrete.

At length the foundations were completed, and the sum I had to pay, according to
measurement, was not £5,000, but £33,000. This was really one of the first blows to my
enterprise.

Early in September the first brick of my new National Opera-house, prior to the
commencement of the substructure, was laid. A number of friends were on the ground at
one o'clock, and in a short time a great throng of spectators had assembled around the
spot. Punctually at 1.30 Mdlle. Titiens arrived, under the escort of Lord Alfred Paget, Mr.
Fowler, the Architect, and myself. The party passed along the wooden platform, and
descended a handsomely-carpeted staircase, which led to the foundation of concrete upon
which the "brick" was to rest. On reaching the bottom, Mdlle. Titiens, as she leaned on
the arm of Mr. Fowler, was presented with an elaborately-engraved silver trowel by Mr.

Webster, the Contractor. The fair singer was then conducted to the spot, where a thin, smooth layer of white mortar had been spread on the concrete. The foreman of the masons placed a brick in the midst of this, and Mdlle. Titiens then in a formal manner laid the first brick, using the plumb-line to ascertain that the work had been properly done. Second, third, and fourth bricks were afterwards laid by Mr. Fowler, Lord Alfred Paget, and myself. Hearty cheers were then given for Mdlle. Titiens by the 600 workmen congregated around, who wished the Queen of Song success and happiness on her approaching Atlantic voyage.

Prior to her departure, Mdlle. Titiens gave four farewell concerts in Ireland; and it was with great difficulty after the last one, at Cork, that she escaped from the concert room at all, so numerous were the encores. The steamer having been signalled, she had to rush straight from the concert room, in her concert dress, with all her jewellery on, to catch the train leaving for Queenstown.

In the autumn of 1875 Mdlle. Titiens was replaced on the provincial tour by Madame Christine Nilsson; and the business again was highly successful. The tour continued until Christmas. I came up to London on the 16th December, to be present at the laying of the first stone of the new Opera-house by H.R.H. the Duke of Edinburgh.

The following was the programme of the ceremonial, which was duly carried out:—
CEREMONY OF LAYING THE FIRST STONE
OF THE
GRAND NATIONAL OPERA-HOUSE,
VICTORIA EMBANKMENT.
Holders of Cards of Invitation will not be admitted after 1.15.
"The bands of the Coldstream Guards and Honourable Artillery Company will be in attendance, and a Guard of Honour will line the entrance.
"His Royal Highness the Duke of Edinburgh and suite will arrive at the entrance on the Victoria Embankment at half-past one o'clock.
"His Royal Highness will be received by Mr. W. H. Smith, M.P., Sir James Hogg, Chairman of the Metropolitan Board of Works, Mr. F. H. Fowler, the Architect, and Mr. J. H. Mapleson, the Director of the National Opera.
"On arrival at the platform an address will be read to the Duke of Edinburgh in the name of the founders of the Grand National Opera-house.
"His Royal Highness the Duke of Edinburgh will then proceed to lay the first stone.
"The trowel will be handed to His Royal Highness by Mr. Mapleson, the Director; the plumb-rule and level by Mr. F. H. Fowler, the Architect; and the mallet by Mr. W. Webster, the Builder.
"On the completion of the ceremony His Royal Highness will make a brief reply to the address.
"The Duke of Edinburgh will then be conducted to his carriage at the entrance by which His Royal Highness arrived, and will drive to the St. Stephen's Club.
"16th December, 1875."
The following address was then read by Sir James McGarel Hogg:—

YOUR ROYAL HIGHNESS,—
"On behalf of the founders of the Grand National Opera-house, I have the honour to present to your Royal Highness the following address in which the objects of the undertaking are set forth:—
"The establishment of a National Opera-house in London has long been contemplated, the obstacle to which, however, was the impossibility of finding a suitable

site, and it was not until that vast undertaking was carried out by the Metropolitan Board of Works, which has resulted in reclaiming from the Thames large tracts of land, and in throwing open the great thoroughfare of the Victoria Embankment, that a site sufficient to meet the requirements of a National Opera-house could be obtained; and it is this building that your Royal Highness is graciously pleased to inaugurate to-day.

"The National Opera-house is to be devoted firstly to the representation of Italian Opera, which will be confined as heretofore to the spring and summer months; and, secondly, to the production of the works of English composers, represented by English performers, both vocal and instrumental.

"It is intended, as far as possible, to connect the Grand National Opera-house with the Royal Academy of Music, the National Training School for Music, and other kindred institutions in the United Kingdom, by affording to duly qualified students a field for the exercise of their profession in all its branches.

"The privilege, which it is the intention of the Director to grant to the most promising of these students, of being allowed to hear the works of the greatest masters performed by the most celebrated artists, will, in itself, form an invaluable accessory to their general training.

"Instead of being compelled to seek abroad further instruction when their prescribed course at the various establishments is finished, they will thus be able to obtain this at home, and more quickly and efficiently profit by example.

"In Paris, when sufficiently advanced, the students can make a short step from the Conservatoire to the Grand Opera; so it is hoped that English students will use the legitimate means now offered and afforded for the first time in this country of perfecting their general training, whether as singers, instrumentalists, or composers, according to their just claims.

"In conclusion I beg leave to invite your Royal Highness to proceed with the ceremony of laying the first stone of the new Grand National Opera-house.

"Grand National Opera house,

Victoria Embankment,

16th December, 1875."

In designing this, I intended it to be the leading Opera-house of the world; every provision had been made. The building was entirely isolated; and a station had been built beneath the house in connection with the District Railway, so that the audience on leaving had merely to descend the stairs and enter the train. In the sub-basement dressing-rooms, containing lockers, were provided for suburban visitors who might wish to attend the opera. A subterranean passage, moreover, led into the Houses of Parliament; and I had made arrangements by which silent members, after listening to beautiful music instead of dull debates, might return to the House on hearing the division-bell. The Parliamentary support thus secured would alone have given an ample source of revenue.

Having plenty of surplus land, I had arranged with the Lyric Club to lease one corner, whilst the Royal Academy of Music had agreed to take another. The buildings, moreover, were to include a new concert room, together with a large gallery for pictures not accepted by the Hanging Committee of the Royal Academy, to be called the "Rejected Gallery."

There were recreation rooms, too, for the principal artists, including billiard tables, etc., besides two very large Turkish baths, which, it was hoped, would be of service to the manager in cases of sore throat and sudden indisposition generally.

The throat doctors appointed to the establishment were Dr. Morell Mackenzie and Mr. Lennox Brown.

65

Sir John Humphreys had arranged for the purchase of a small steamer to act as tug to a large house-boat which would, from time to time, take the members of the Company down the river for rehearsals or recreation. The steamer was being built by the Thorneycrofts. The house-boat was of unusually large dimensions, and contained a magnificent concert-room.

The nautical arrangements had been confided to Admiral Sir George Middleton, a member of my acting committee; or, in his absence, to Lord Alfred Paget.

When about £103,000 had been laid out on the building another £10,000 was wanted for the roofing; after which a sum of £50,000, as already arranged, could have been obtained on mortgage. For want of £10,000, however, the building had to remain roofless. For backing or laying against a horse, for starting a new sporting club or a new music-hall, the money could have been found in a few hours. But for such an enterprise as the National Opera-house it was impossible to obtain it; and, after a time, in the interest of my stockholders (for there was a ground rent to pay of £3,000), I consented to a sale.

The purchasers were Messrs. Quilter, Morris, and Tod-Heatly, to whom the building was made over, as it stood, for £29,000.

Later on it was resold for £500; and the new buyers had to pay no less than £3,000 in order to get the walls pulled down and broken up into building materials.

The site of what, with a little public spirit usefully applied, would have been the finest theatre in the world, is now to serve for a new police-station. With such solid foundations, the cells, if not comfortable, will at least be dry.

CHAPTER XIII.

FIRST VISIT TO AMERICA—MAKING MONEY OUT OF SHAKESPEARE—CHATTERTON'S SECRET AGENTS—BIDDING FOR HER MAJESTY'S THEATRE—ILLNESS OF TITIENS—GERSTER'S SUCCESS—PRODUCTION OF "CARMEN."

AT the close of the year 1875 I was invited to spend the evening with some friends to see the old year out and the new year in. Amongst the visitors at the house I met an American gentleman who had seen many of my performances; and he assured me that if I would but go to America I should do a very fine business, but that prior to making arrangements I either ought to send over a trusted agent or go myself. So fully did he impress me by his conversation, that, although I had never contemplated such a thing, I went home late that night, or rather early the next morning, put a lot of traps together, and started the same afternoon for America, reaching Queenstown early on the morning of the 2nd January in time to catch the steamer.

I shall never forget my first voyage. I knew no one on board: we were six or seven passengers in all. Few care to leave for a long voyage on New Year's Day. The vessel was not only small, although a Cunarder, but very unsteady. She was known amongst nautical men as the "Jumping Java." Our passage occupied 14 days, and we had to weather several very severe gales. One day we only made 16 knots.

However, I arrived on the other side in due course, and was forcibly struck with the grand country I had entered. As I could remain there only nine or ten days I hastened to visit Chicago, Philadelphia, Boston, Cincinnati, and other places, in addition to New York. I, however, "prospected" by carefully noting all I saw; and afterwards returned to England to join my touring concert party during the latter part of the month. It was then in the provinces. I felt myself fully master of what I intended the following year to undertake; namely, a tour of Her Majesty's Opera Company in America, which later on in these memoirs I shall have occasion to describe. I also organized another tour in the English provinces, with Salvini, who appeared afterwards in all the principal provincial towns with immense success.

In the middle of October, 1875, I had the honour of being invited by the Duke of Edinburgh to Eastwell Park. Thinking the invitation was only for the day, I took nothing with me but a small bag containing an evening suit and a single shirt. When I arrived at Ashford station I was met by two six-foot men in scarlet liveries, who had arrived with a fourgon, drawn by two splendid horses, into which they proposed to put my luggage. I noticed their efforts to restrain a smile when I handed to them my little hand-bag. Another magnificent equipage had been sent for me personally.

I was received with the greatest possible kindness; and it will interest many of my readers to know that just before dinner the Duchess took me to a buffet on which was laid out caviare, smoked salmon, salt herring (cut into small pieces), dried mushrooms, pickled cucumbers, and the various appetizing delicacies which, with spirits or liqueurs, form the preliminary repast known to the Russians as zakuska.

I had the honour of taking the Duchess in to dinner, where we formed a party of four: the Duke, the Duchess, the equerry in attendance, and myself. After dinner we adjourned to the music-room, where I noticed piles upon piles of music-books. I soon saw that the Duchess was an excellent musician. The Duke, too, received evidence of this; for in difficult passages he was pulled up and corrected again and again. Smoking being permitted and even enjoined, I lighted a cigar and smoked in silence on the sofa, listening with interest to the musical performances, which were in the form of duets for violin and piano, or violin solos with pianoforte accompaniment.

The next morning we were up early, and I was taken over the estate. The Duchess pointed out to me her own particular fish-pond, in which she sometimes angles with a view to the table.

Then I went out shooting with the Duke; a rather trying business, for I had neither shooting-clothes nor, far worse, shooting-boots. Of course it began to rain, and I was soon wet through to the skin, my ordinary walking boots being soaked in such a manner that when I got back to the house, by which time the leather had partially dried and contracted, I had considerable difficulty in getting them off. The Duke was kind enough to lend me an overcoat.

At luncheon the Duchess asked for the key of the wine cellar, at which the Duke expressed surprise and curiosity. He was reproached for his inquisitiveness, but was not at the time enlightened as to the object for which the keys were wanted.

It appeared later on at dinner that the Duchess had been visiting a curate at some eight miles distance, who was ill, and had been recommended port wine. This, out of his meagre income, he would be unable, she said, to afford.

"With eighty pounds a year and five children, how," she asked, "can he drink port wine and eat new-laid eggs?"—which the doctor had also recommended. She had herself, therefore, driven over in the afternoon through the pouring rain to take them to him.

After lunch we had more shooting, the weather being now a trifle better. We got home in good time for dinner, and in the evening played at billiards. The Duke is an infinitely better player than I am; but by a series of flukes I got ahead of him, and at last found myself within two points of the game, and with the balls so left that it was most difficult for me to avoid making a final cannon. I saw, however, from the expression of the Duchess's countenance, that she had set her heart upon her husband's defeating me; and I must now confess that if I succeeded in not making that cannon, so difficult to miss, I did so simply out of regard for Her Royal Highness's feelings. The Duchess during the game acted as marker.

It was the Duchess's birthday, and in the course of the evening a courier from Russia, who had been anxiously expected all day, arrived with innumerable presents of jewellery. To these offerings the Duchess paid little or no attention. All she cared for was a letter she was awaiting from her father, and, on receiving it, she was soon absorbed in the perusal of its contents.

A few months afterwards, when the Duchess was present at a performance of Fidelio given at Her Majesty's Opera, I had a new proof of Her Royal Highness's musical knowledge and of her delicate ear. She arrived before the beginning of the overture, and brought with her two huge orchestral scores. The Duchess sat on the floor of the box reading one of them, and turning of course very rapidly over the leaves during the stretto of the "Leonora" overture. Suddenly she noticed an uncertain note from the second horn, and exclaimed, as if to set the musician right, "B flat!" After the act I asked Sir Michael Costa whether something did not go wrong with one of the horns. "Yes," he said, "but only a person with a very fine ear could have perceived it." I repeated to Her Royal Highness Costa's remark precisely as he had made it.

I opened my season again at Drury Lane early in 1876; but the lessee, Mr. Chatterton, who had been secretly treating with Salvini, did not think it right that in the great national theatre under his control I should be making so much money out of Shakespeare. The only contract I could now get from him had practically the effect of excluding Salvini, and this was really the beginning of Chatterton's ruin. Although I was to pay him the same amount of rental he insisted on retaining the Wednesday and Friday evenings and Saturday mornings for himself. I had therefore to rent another theatre wherein to place Salvini. Mr. Chatterton brought over another Italian tragedian, Signor Rossi, and put him to perform at Drury Lane in opposition to Salvini, whom I had to present at the Queen's Theatre in Long Acre. The consequence was that both of us dropped money, and Mr. Chatterton's losses during that time were, I believe, considerable.

To my Opera Company I had added M. Faure, while retaining all the favourites of the previous year, including Titiens, Trebelli, Nilsson, &c.; Sir Michael Costa remaining as conductor.

At the close of 1876 I again visited the provinces, beginning my usual Italian Opera season at Dublin, with Mdlle. Titiens, who had returned fresh from her American triumphs, supported by Marie Roze, Valleria, Ilma de Murska, Emma Abbot, Trebelli, etc., etc. The tour was indeed a most prosperous one, and it terminated towards the latter part of the December of that year.

Early in 1877, when I applied for the renewal of my lease of the Theatre Royal, Drury Lane, Mr. Chatterton showed much ill-will, which I attributed to his jealousy at my previous success with Salvini, and to my having declined to allow him to engage the Italian tragedian on his own account. He insisted that I should have the theatre but three days a week, and then only from ten in the morning till twelve at night. Not only was I precluded from using the theatre on the other days, but I was to finish my performance always by midnight and then hand him the key. As my rehearsals invariably have to take place on the "off days," when there is no opera, I should have been prevented by this arrangement from rehearsing at all. In fact, I found nothing but impossible clauses and conditions in the contract now offered.

At this time Mr. Chatterton was very anxious to find out whether or not the Earl of Dudley was prepared to let me Her Majesty's Theatre; and to ascertain this the good offices of some highly attractive young ladies performing in the pantomime were employed. Lord Dudley gave Mr. Chatterton to understand that though he was willing to sell the theatre, of which he saw no probability, he would not under any circumstances let it to Mapleson or any other man. Hence Chatterton continued to insist on his stringent conditions, although I had been his tenant for some eight or nine years, paying a very large amount of rent in addition to cleaning and carpeting his theatre every year, which was very much required after the pantomime.

On learning, in a direct manner, Lord Dudley's decision, I saw that it was hopeless to approach him in the character of a tenant. A purchaser I did not wish to be, as my new Opera-house, it was anticipated, would be ready for opening the following spring. All I, for the present, desired was a theatre where I could, unmolested, continue my season. I therefore made offers to Lord Dudley with a view to purchase, at the same time explaining to him my inability to pay the whole of the amount he then demanded, namely, £30,000. All I could do was to give him a deposit of £6,000 on account, and a further £6,000 in the following November, leaving £18,000 still due, with a clause, in case of any default being made in regard to the second instalment, by which the first was to be forfeited. To this his lordship assented. I had been ready to pay him £7,000 as rent for a single year, but this he would have refused. By paying an instalment of £6,000 I saved £1,000, and equally obtained the use of the theatre. In due course the matter was completed.

During the month of February I entered into possession. There was not a single seat in the house, not a particle of paper on the walls; neither a bit of carpet, nor a chair, nor a table anywhere. I therefore had to go and see Blundell Maple, the well-known upholsterer, who, out of regard for me and the advertisement I promised him, consented to give me a few things I required for the sum of £6,000. It involved the furnishing of the whole of the dressing-rooms, the auditorium, and corridors.

About four miles of carpeting were required, there being so many staircases and passages, all of which were luxuriously covered. New amber satin curtains, the traditional colour of the house, had to be manufactured specially. Stall chairs, appointments, fittings, and looking-glasses were also, of course, required. A room had to be built through solid masonry for the Prince of Wales, as a retiring-room. In fact, it was a very heavy affair; and on my inviting a few friends and members of the Press to a dinner I gave at my club some two days before the opening, they confessed to having believed that the theatre could not be opened for two months. Maple, in order to show what he could do in a short space of time, had purposely left all to the last day, when he sent in some 200 workmen and upholsterers, together with about 300 girls and carpet-sewers, so that the effect was really like the magic of Aladdin's Palace. The theatre, I need scarcely say, was finished in time, and gave great satisfaction.

The new theatre opened on 28th April, Titiens appearing as "Norma;" and a grand performance it was. Sir Michael Costa directed the orchestra, which went à merveille.

The day following it became evident that the great prima donna was suffering from a complaint which caused her the most serious inconvenience. The next evening Mdlle. Salla appeared with some success in Il Trovatore. On the succeeding Saturday, Mdme. Christine Nilsson made her rentrée in La Traviata; but immediately afterwards she too fell ill.

It seemed as if the new theatre was to bring nothing but bad luck, as it since has done to all connected with it. Mdlle. Titiens, however, had to make an effort, and she appeared again the next night as "Norma," and the Saturday afterwards in the Trovatore. Meantime Mdme. Nilsson recovered and reappeared on the following Thursday. Mdlle.

Titiens was sufficiently well to appear at St. James's Hall, for Mr. Austin's benefit, at which she sang superbly, Mr. Austin, after the performance, assuring me that he had never before heard such magnificent singing. Mdlle. Titiens now informed me that she felt considerably better, and would appear on the following Saturday, 19th May, as "Lucrezia Borgia," which she in fact did. But, as the evening progressed she felt she could hardly get through the opera. Her voice was in its fullest perfection; but her bodily ailments caused her acute agony, and it was not until some time after the conclusion of the opera that she was able to leave the theatre.

The best advice was sought for, and it was decided by the lady herself that the operation, which ultimately caused her death, should be performed. At the end of three weeks, having recovered from the effects of the operation, as she thought, she expressed a wish to return to her duties at the theatre. But, alas! that wish was never to be fulfilled, and I had to go through the season with a loss, as it were, of my right hand.

She lived on in hopes of being able to recover, and she was even announced to appear at the usual period in the following September. But as time drew on it was clear that she was not long for this world. I last saw her on the 29th day of September. Early on the morning of the following Wednesday, October 3rd, she passed away.

I continued the London season of 1877 as best I could without the invaluable services of Mdlle. Titiens, although from time to time we had formed hopes of her reappearing. I again brought Mdme. Nilsson to the front, but found it incumbent on me to discover a new planet, as Mdme. Nilsson, finding she was alone in the field, became somewhat exacting. At last I found one; but, unfortunately, she was just on the point of being married, and nothing could induce her future husband to defer the ceremony. However, by dint of perseverance I succeeded in persuading him, for a consideration, to postpone the honeymoon; and in addition to this I was to pay a very large extra sum per night, while his wife's appearances were strictly limited to two each week.

About this time a great deal of intrigue was going on in order to prevent the success of the new star. I, however, discovered the authors of it, and worked accordingly. Thus I induced several members of the Press to attend after they had been positively assured that she was not worth listening to. Mdme. Gerster's success was really instantaneous, and before her three or four nights were over I had succeeded in again postponing the honeymoon—still for a consideration. Her success went on increasing until the very close of the season, by which time her receipts fairly balanced those of Mdme. Nilsson.

The charges for postponing the honeymoon were put down under a separate heading lest they should by any mistake be regarded as a portion of the prima donna's salary and be used as a precedent in connection with future engagements. At last, when several large payments had been made, the season came to a close, and the young couple, after several months' marriage, were at liberty to begin their honeymoon.

After a journey through Italy and Germany in search of talent I returned to England, when I found the great prima donna's case was hopeless. Although it had been fully anticipated that she would make her reappearance in Dublin, she being in fact announced to sing there, it was, unhappily, decreed otherwise; and on the third night of our opening I had to substitute Mdlle. Salla in Il Trovatore, in which Titiens had been originally announced. I received early that day (October 3, 1887) a telegram stating that she was no more. The Irish public on hearing the sad news at once left the theatre. It cast a gloom over the entire city, as it did throughout the musical world generally. A grand and gifted artist, an estimable woman, had disappeared never to be replaced.

After visiting several of the principal towns I returned to London and reopened Her Majesty's Theatre, reviving various operas of repute, and producing for the first time in this country Ruy Blas, which met with considerable success. My season terminated on the 22nd of December.

At Christmas time I reopened the theatre with an admirable ballet, composed expressly by Mdme. Katti Lanner, in which none but the children of my National Training School for Dancing took part. I afterwards performed a series of English operas, which were successful, Sir Julius Benedict conducting. Concurrently with this I continued my regular spring concert tour, which did not terminate until the middle of March.

The London season of 1878 opened inauspiciously, the loss of the great prima donna causing a cloud to hang over the theatre. However, Mdme. Nilsson duly arrived, likewise Mdme. Gerster, and each sang so as to enhance her reputation.

Prior to the commencement of the season I had heard Bizet's Carmen in Paris, which I contemplated giving; and my decision was at once taken on hearing from Miss Minnie Hauk of the success she was then making in that opera at Brussels.

I therefore resolved upon engaging her to appear as "Carmen." In distributing the parts I well recollect the difficulties I had to encounter. On sending Campanini the rôle of "Don José" (in which he afterwards became so celebrated), he returned it to me stating he would do anything to oblige, but could not think of undertaking a part in an opera of that description where he had no romance and no love duet except with the seconda donna. Shortly afterwards Del Puente, the baritone, entered, informing me that the part of "Escamillo," which I had sent him, must have been intended for one of the chorus, and that he begged to decline it.

In vain did Sir Michael Costa order the rehearsals. There was always some trouble with the singers on account of the small parts I had given them. Mdlle. Valleria suggested that I should entrust the part of "Michaela" either to Bauermeister or to one of the chorus; as on no account would she undertake it.

This went on for some time, and I saw but little prospect of launching my projected opera. At length, by force of persuasion, coupled with threats, I induced the various singers, whether they accepted their parts or not, to attend a general rehearsal, when they all began to take a great fancy to the rôles I had given them; and in due course the opera was announced for the first representation, which took place on the 22nd June.

The receipts for the first two or three performances were most miserable. It was, in fact, a repetition of what I had experienced on the production of Faust in 1863, and I frankly confess that I was forced to resort to the same sort of expedients for securing an enthusiastic reception and thus getting the music into the heads of the British public, knowing that after a few nights the opera would be sure to please. In this I was not mistaken, and I closed my season with flying colours.

CHAPTER XIV.

FIRST AMERICAN CAMPAIGN—DIFFICULTIES OF EMBARKATION— CONCERT ON BOARD—DANGEROUS ILLNESS OF GERSTER—OPERA ON WHEELS—"THE DRESSING-ROOM ROW"—A LEARNED THROAT DOCTOR—GERSTER SINGS BEFORE HER JUDGE—THE PIANOFORTE WAR—OUR HURRIED DEPARTURE.

AT the end of the season I went abroad to complete my Company for the first American tour, which was to begin about the middle of October. I started my Opera Company from London on the 31st August on its way to America, numbering some 140 persons, including Gerster, Minnie Hauk, Trebelli, Valleria, Campanini, Frapolli, Galassi, Del Puente, Foli, etc., with Arditi as conductor. This also comprised a magnificent chorus of some 60 selected voices, together with the whole of the corps de ballet and principal dancers; and I had decided to give some three or four weeks' performances in Ireland prior to sailing, in order to get things in working order, as well as to recruit the exchequer for my costly enterprise. Although immense success attended the appearance of my new singers in the Irish capital, they were not sufficiently known to draw the great houses more famous artists would have done. Etelka Gerster almost drove the gods crazy with her magnificent singing; but as she was totally unknown, never having been in Ireland before, the receipts were not commensurate with her artistic success. Minnie Hauk, again, had never appeared in that country; nor had the opera of Carmen been heard, its very name seeming to be unknown. However, the artistic success was beyond measure, and the representations, moreover, served as a kind of general rehearsal for my coming performances in America. On reaching Cork I found the receipts were again below what they ought to have been, and I began to realize that in lieu of increasing my exchequer prior to starting for America I ran the chance of totally exhausting it.

I therefore telegraphed to my representative in New York for £2,000, in order that I might straighten up my position, and pay the balance of our passage money, the boat being then off Queenstown.

I was really anxious on this occasion, and it was not until late in the day that my cable arrived, notifying to me that the money was at my credit in the Bank of Cork. With some difficulty, it being after banking hours, I obtained admittance, when lo! the money was all payable in Irish notes. These the singers pronounced to be useless for their purpose in America. They absolutely refused to embark, and it was not until towards evening that I was enabled with great difficulty to find gold at the various hotels and shops in exchange for my Irish notes.

At length we departed from Queenstown; though it was late in the evening before I succeeded in getting the last squad on board. Some of the Italian choristers had been assured by Irish humorists that the streets of New York were infested by crocodiles and wild Indians; and these they were most unwilling to encounter. We had a splendid passage across. The day before our arrival in New York it was suggested to give a grand concert in aid of the sufferers by the yellow fever then raging in New Orleans. I recollect on the occasion of the concert the collection made amongst the passengers amounted to some £3 or £4. One Western gentleman asked me particularly, in the presence of the purser, if the money would really be devoted to the relief of the sufferers. He, moreover, demanded that Captain Brooks, the officer in command, should guarantee that the money would reach them. The collection was made by those two charming young pianists, Mdlles. Louise and Jeanne Douste, and by the equally charming young dancer, Mdlle. Marie Muller; and at the conclusion of the concert, in which he had encored every one of the pieces, the careful amateur from the West gave the sum of sixpence. Gerster, Minnie Hauk, Campanini, and the others were irate, at the result of their united labours; and as they thought it might injure them on their arrival in New York, were the public to know of it, they privately subscribed £20 apiece all round to make the return look a little decent.

On our arrival in New York we were met by thousands of people, accompanied by military bands, etc., and although I had left, as it were, a winter behind me, we landed in the midst of a glorious Indian summer.

I set about making my preparations for the opening of my season, which was to commence on the 16th October, and to prepare the way for the début of Madame Etelka Gerster, who since our arrival had scarcely been her usual self. This I attributed to the sea voyage. Two days before the opening I gave a dinner, to which I invited several influential friends including members of the New York Press. As I was just about responding to the toast of the evening, wishing health to Madame Gerster and success to the Opera, the waiter beckoned me to the door, whispering that a gentleman wanted to speak to me for one moment. I went out, when Dr. Jacobi, the New York physician, called me into an adjoining room, where the eminent specialist, Dr. Lincoln, was waiting. They had just visited Madame Gerster, and regretted to inform me that a very bad attack of typhoid fever had developed itself, and that consequently there would be no probability of her appearing the following Wednesday, while it was even doubtful in their minds if she would survive. She was in a very bad state.

This was indeed a great blow to me; but I returned to the room, continued my speech, and then went on with my dinner as if nothing had happened.

Making it a point never to think of business when I am not in my office, I decided to turn matters over the following morning, which was the day preceding the opening of the house. Being so far away, it would be impossible to replace Mdme. Gerster. I thereupon persuaded Miss Minnie Hauk to undertake her part in La Traviata, which she did with success. Del Puente, our principal baritone, refused, however, to sing the part of the father, in consequence, I presume, of this change.

This was a most fortunate thing for the other baritone, Galassi, who replaced Del Puente. It virtually made his fortune. He possessed the ringing quality of voice the Americans are so fond of. He literally brought down the house that evening. I cannot recall a greater success at any time, and henceforth Galassi became one, as it were, of the idols of the American public.

I opened my theatre in London the following night with a very powerful Company, Mdme. Pappenheim making her début as "Fidelio"; for I was now working concurrently the London and the New York Operas. This I did for the whole of that season, closing Her Majesty's Theatre on the 21st December, though the American "Academy" was kept open beyond.

Costumes, properties, and even singers, were moved to and fro across the ocean in accordance with my New York and London requirements. Franceso, who was ballet-master on both sides of the Atlantic, made again and again the voyage from New York to Liverpool, and from Liverpool to New York. On one occasion the telegraph played me false. I had wired to my acting-manager at Her Majesty's Theatre, with whom I was in daily telegraphic communication, desiring him to send me over at once a "2nd tenor." The message was inaccurately deciphered, and out came "2 tenors;" one of whom was kneeling on the quay at New York returning thanks for his safe arrival, when I requested him to re-embark at once, as otherwise he would not be back at Her Majesty's Theatre by Monday week in time to sing the part of "Arturo" in the Lucia, for which he was already announced.

I afterwards produced Carmen at the Academy of Music, which met with very great success, as likewise did Faust, Don Giovanni, etc. It was not till the 8th November that Mdme. Gerster was declared out of danger, and I was in constant attendance upon her until the 18th November, when she appeared as "Amina" in La Sonnambula. Her success was really electric, the public going quite wild about her.

I afterwards produced all the great operas I had been giving in London, including the Magic Flute, Talismano, Robert le Diable, etc., etc., my season continuing without intermission some six months, during which time I visited Boston, where public breakfasts and other entertainments were given to my singers. A special train was fitted up expressly for my large Company, and all the carriages elegantly decorated. I had also placed at my disposal by the Railroad Company a carriage containing writing-room, drawing-room, bedrooms, and kitchen stocked with wines and provisions, under the direction of a chef.

Whilst at Boston I had the honour of making the acquaintance of Longfellow, who, being anxious to hear Mdme. Gerster, occupied my box one evening, the attention of the audience being very much divided between its occupant and Mdme. Gerster, who on that occasion was singing "Elvira" in I Puritani. He likewise attended the final morning performance, which took place on the last Saturday of our engagement, when Gerster's receipts for "Lucia" reached no less than £1,400. We left that evening for Chicago, a distance of some 1,100 miles, arriving in that city just in time to commence the opera the following Monday, when Gerster appeared and created an excitement only equalled by that of Jenny Lind. I recollect, by-the-bye, an amusing incident that occurred the second night, on the occasion of the performance of Le Nozze di Figaro.

On the right and left-hand sides of the proscenium were two dressing-rooms alike in every respect. Madame Gerster, however, selected the one on the right-hand side, which at once gave the room the appellation of the prima donna's room. On the following evening Le Nozze di Figaro was to be performed, in which Marie Roze was to take the part of "Susanna," and Minnie Hauk that of "Cherubino." In order to secure the prima donna's room Minnie Hauk went to the theatre with her maid as early as three o'clock in the afternoon and placed her dresses in it, also her theatrical trunk.

At four o'clock Marie Roze's maid, thinking to be the first in the field, arrived for the purpose of placing Marie Roze's dresses and theatre trunks in the coveted apartment. Finding the room already occupied, she mentioned it to Marie's husband, who with a couple of stage men speedily removed the trunks and dresses, put them in the room opposite, and replaced them by Marie's. He then went back to his hotel, desiring Marie to be at the theatre as early as six o'clock.

At about 5.30 Minnie Hauk's agent passed by to see if all was in order and found Marie Roze's theatrical box and costumes where Minnie Hauk's were supposed to be. He consequently ordered the removal of Marie Roze's dresses and trunk, replaced those of Minnie Hauk, and affixed to the door a padlock which he had brought with him.

Punctually at six o'clock Marie Roze arrived, and found the door locked. By the aid of a locksmith the door was again opened, and Minnie Hauk's things again removed to the opposite room, whilst Marie Roze proceeded to dress herself in the "prima donna's room."

At 6.30 Minnie Hauk, wishing to steal a march on her rival, came to dress, and found the room occupied. She immediately returned to Palmer House, where she resided, declaring she would not sing that evening.

All persuasion was useless. I therefore had to commence the opera minus "Cherubino;" and it was not until the middle of the second act, after considerable persuasion by my lawyers, that Minnie Hauk appeared on the stage. This incident was taken up throughout the whole of America, and correspondence about it extended over several weeks. Pictures were published, also diagrams, setting forth fully the position of the trunks and the dressing-rooms. The affair is known to this day as "The great dressing-room disturbance."

During all this visit to Chicago there was one unbroken line of intending buyers waiting to secure tickets at the box office; and frequently I had to pay as much as twenty dollars for wood consumed during the night to keep the purchasers warm.

About the middle of the second week I produced Bellini's Puritani, with Gerster as "Elvira," Campanini as "Arturo," Galassi as "Riccardo," and Foli as "Giorgio." On this occasion the house was so crowded that the outer walls began to crack, and in the managerial room, in which I was working, I could put my hand through one of the corners where the two walls met. I communicated with Carter Harrison, who was then

Mayor. He at once proceeded to the theatre, and, without creating any alarm, and under the pretext that the house was too full, caused upwards of a thousand people to leave the building. So pleased were they with the performance that they all refused to have their money returned.

We terminated one of the most successful Chicago seasons on record, and the Company started the following morning for St. Louis. As I was suffering from a sharp attack of gout I had to be left behind, and but for the kindness of Lord Algernon Lennox (who had acted as my aide-de-camp at one of our Easter sham-fights) and Colonel Vivian I do not know what I should have done. Both these gentlemen remained in the hotel with me, interrupting their journey to do me this act of kindness, for which I felt very grateful.

On the Company's arriving at St. Louis, Mdme. Gerster declared her inability to sing the opera of Lucia that evening. My son Henry, who had charge of the Company until I could rejoin it, explained to madame that it would be necessary to have a medical certificate to place before the public. Mdme. Gerster replied she was too honourable an artist to require such a thing, and that when she said she was ill, she was ill. My son, however, brought in a doctor, who insisted upon seeing her tongue. She merely, in derision, said, "There!"—rapidly putting it out as she left the room. The doctor immediately put on his spectacles, and proceeded to write his certificate, saying that there was a little irritation in the epiglottis, that the uvula was contracted, together with the muscles of the throat, and that the tonsils were inflamed. On Mdme. Gerster's husband showing the certificate to his wife she got so angry that she insisted upon singing—just to show what an "ass" the doctor was. Of course, this answered my purpose very well, and my large receipts were saved.

On leaving the hotel at the end of that week the eminent physician presented Mdme. Gerster with a bill of $60 for medical attendance. This, of course, she resisted; and she gave bonds for her appearance when called upon, in order to save her trunks from seizure, which the M.D. had threatened.

Whilst I am on this subject, I may as well inform the reader that two years afterwards when we visited St. Louis the matter was brought before the Court. Feeling sure that this attempt at extortion would not be allowed, and that the Court proceedings would be of very short duration, I attended at nine o'clock, the hour set down for trial, leaving word that I should be home at about half-past ten to breakfast. It was not until eleven that I was called up to the witness-stand. On my mentioning to my counsel that I felt very faint, as I had not yet eaten anything, he repeated it to the judge, who at once adjourned the Court in order that I might have my breakfast. He enjoined me not to lose too much time in "mastication," and ordered the reassembly of the Court at half-past eleven. On my return my evidence was duly given; but when the defendant, Etelka Gerster, was summoned, the call-boy from the theatre appeared, stating to the judge that as she had to sing "Lucia" that night, and was not very well, it would jeopardize the whole performance if she left the hotel.

His honour, thereupon, considerately ordered the Court to adjourn to Mdme. Gerster's rooms at the Lindell House, where the trial could be resumed. On our arrival there counsel and others amused themselves by looking at various pictures until the prima donna appeared, accompanied by her two dogs, her birds, etc., when the judge entered into conversation with her on musical matters. Later on his honour solicited Mdme. Gerster to kindly sing him a song, especially the "Last Rose of Summer," which he was very partial to, being from the Emerald Isle. At the close of the performance he thought it was useless troubling Mdme. Gerster to go further into the case, which was at once decided in her favour.

Talking of law, I may mention another lawsuit in which I was concerned.

Whilst in Boston in January, 1879, Mdme. Parodi, who lived in an hotel close by the theatre, had need of medical attendance, and the theatrical doctor, who had the entrée to the house, was naturally selected to see what the matter was. He prescribed a gargle for Mdme. Parodi; and Mdlle. Lido, who had been attending on the patient, having shown the doctor her tongue as he went out, he merely said "You want a little Friedrichshall," and left the room.

Nothing more was heard of the matter until January, 1880, when, as I was seated at the breakfast table in the hotel with my wife and family, two Deputy-Sheriffs forced their way unannounced into the room to arrest me for the sum of 30 dollars, which the doctor claimed as his fee. This was the first intimation I had had of any kind, and it was afterwards shown in evidence that the doctor had debited Parodi and Lido in his day-book separately with the amount which he also charged to them collectively. Finding that both ladies had left the city he thought it better to charge the attendance to me. Rather than be arrested, I of course paid the money, but under protest.

The next day I commenced proceedings against the doctor, as well as the Sheriff, for the return of my money, which I contended had been handed over under duress, and was not a voluntary payment on my part. The doctor's counsel contended on the other hand—first, that I had derived benefit from the treatment he had given these ladies; secondly, that I was liable. In due course the matter went to trial, and was heard by Judge Parmenter in the Municipal Civil Court at Boston. It was proved that the doctor was the regular physician to the Boston Theatre, and that in consideration of free entrance he attended without fee members of the Company who played there. The Judge, after commenting on the testimony, decided the matter in my favour. I was, however, baulked of both money and costs; for the same afternoon the doctor went home and died.

On my return to New York for the spring opera season I produced Dinorah, in which Mdme. Gerster again achieved a triumph. The business went on increasing. About this time a meeting of the stockholders of the Academy of Music was convened, and I ultimately signed a new lease for three more years, commencing October 20th following.

During my first sojourn in America I gave 164 performances of opera, likewise 47 concerts. Concurrently with this I gave 135 operatic performances and 48 concerts in England. The season in New York extended from October 16th to December 28th, 1878, also from February 29th to April 5th, 1879. At Boston the season lasted from December 30th, 1878, to January 11th, 1879; at Chicago from January 13th to 25th; at St. Louis from January 27th to February 1st; at Cincinnati from February 3rd to 8th; at Philadelphia 10th to 18th, at Baltimore and Washington 19th to 25th. During this period Lucia was performed twenty times, Sonnambula nineteen times, Carmen twenty-six times, Faust sixteen times, Trovatore nine times, Flauto Magico eight times, Puritani eight times, Nozze di Figaro seven times, Rigoletto five times, Don Giovanni five times, Traviata four times, Lohengrin ten times, Barbiere twice, Ruy Blas twice, Dinorah twice, Talismano ten times, Robert le Diable twice, Huguenots six times, Freischutz three times; making altogether twenty-four morning performances and one hundred and forty evening performances.

About this time the disastrous floods took place at Szegedin, in Hungary. This being Mdme. Gerster's birth-place I proposed a grand benefit concert for the sufferers, in which my prima donna at once joined. By our united efforts we raised about £800, which was remitted by cable to the place of disaster within five days of its occurrence, much (I need scarcely add) to the relief of many of the sufferers.

76

My benefit, which was fixed for the last night of the season, took place on Friday, April 4th. At quite an early hour crowds collected right down Fourteenth Street and Irving Place, and within a very short time every square inch of available room in the house was occupied. The enthusiasm of the auditors was immeasurable, and they began to show it as soon as the performance opened. The representation consisted of the third act of the Talisman, with Mdme. Gerster as "Edith Plantaganet," and Campanini as "Sir Kenneth;" followed by the fourth act of Favorita, in which Mdme. Marie Roze undertook the rôle of "Leonora;" and concluding with an act of La Traviata, with Mdme. Gerster as "Violetta." Mdme. Gerster's performance was listened to with the deepest attention, and rewarded at the end with enthusiastic cheers. Mdme. Gerster afterwards came out three times, but her courtesies were of no avail in quieting the multitude. It was necessary, at the demand of the public, to raise the curtain and repeat the entire act. Then nothing would satisfy the audience but my appearance on the stage; when I thanked the ladies and gentlemen present for their support, notifying, moreover, that, encouraged by my success, I should return to them the next autumn. This little speech was vehemently applauded, especially the references I made to the singers and to the conductor, who, I promised, would come back with me.

During our stay in New York we were supplied with pianos both for the artists individually as well as for use at the theatre by Messrs. Steinway and Sons; and before we left the following flattering but just letter of compliment and of thanks was addressed to the firm:—

"Academy of Music, New York,

"December 28, 1878.

"GENTLEMEN,

"Having used your pianos in public and private during the present Opera season we desire to express our unqualified admiration of their sonority, evenness, richness, and astonishing duration of tone, most beautifully blending with and supporting the voice. These matchless qualities, together with the precision of action, in our opinion, render the Steinway pianos, above all others, the most desirable instruments for the public generally.

"(Signed) ETELKA GERSTER, MARIE ROZE,

MINNIE HAUK, C. SINICO, CAMPANINI,

FRAPOLLI, GALASSI, FOLI,

DEL PUENTE, ARDITI."

Messrs. Steinway now offered and undertook to supply each leading member of the Company with pianos in whatever town we might visit throughout the United States.

On our arrival in Philadelphia I was surprised to find that every artist in the Company had had a magnificent Steinway placed in his or her bedroom; this in addition to the pianos required at the theatre. But while the Company were dining, a rival pianoforte maker, who had shown himself keenly desirous of the honour of supplying us with instruments, invaded the different bedrooms and placed the Steinway pianos outside the doors, substituting for them pianos made by his own firm—that of Weber and Co. The Webers, however, were ultimately put outside and the Steinways replaced.

Shortly afterwards a pitched battle took place in the corridors between the men employed by the rival firms, when the Weber men, being a more sturdy lot, entirely defeated the Steinway men and ejected them bodily from the hotel. The weapons used on this occasion were piano legs, unscrewed from the bodies of the instruments.

Not only did physical force triumph, but the superior strength exhibited by the Weber side was afterwards supplemented by cunning. That very night Weber gave a grand supper to the whole of my Company, and I was at once astonished and amused the next day to find that a new certificate had been signed by them all stating that Weber's pianos were the best they had ever known. A paper to that effect had been passed round after sundry bottles of "Extra Dry," and signatures appended as a matter of course.

Such was the impartiality of my singers that they afterwards signed on behalf of yet a third pianoforte maker, named Haines.

In accordance with numerous solicitations, I agreed to give a Farewell matinée the next day. But the steamer had to sail for Europe at two o'clock in the afternoon; and this rendered it necessary that my morning performance should commence at half-past eleven, the box-office opening at eight. In the course of a couple of hours every seat was sold. Towards the close of the performance, Arditi, the conductor, got very anxious, and kept looking up at my box. It was now half-past one, Madame Gerster's rondo finale in La Sonnambula had absolutely to be repeated, or there would have been a riot; and we were some three miles distant from the steamer which was to convey us all to Europe.

At length, to my relief, the curtain fell; but the noise increased, and I had again to show myself, while Arditi and the principal singers and chorus took their departure, Signor Foli, with his long strides, arriving first. I afterwards hastened down in a carriage I had expressly retained. As the chorus had scarcely time to change their dresses, many of them rushed down as best they could in their theatrical attire, followed by a good portion of the audience, who were anxious to get a last glimpse of us all.

Arriving on board the Inman steamer City of Chester, I found it crowded with personal friends, many of whom had been there at least an hour. Hearty embraces were exchanged by the men as well as the women, and numerous bottles of champagne were emptied to fill the parting cups. The cabins of the steamer were literally piled up with flowers. Trunks and boxes containing the wardrobe of the morning performance were lugged on board.

"All ashore!" shouted the captain. Prior to my arrival, the bell had rung for the seventh and positively last time. The steamer's officers now urged all but passengers to get on shore, and hinted at the probability of some of them being inadvertently carried over to Europe. The women hurried back to escape that dreadful fate.

Ole Bull, whom I had invited to go to Europe with me, darted across the gang-plank carrying his fiddle in a box. The whistle then blew, and the bell rang for the eighth and now absolutely last time. At length the steamer took her departure. A band of music on the wharf had been playing lively airs, to which my chorus responded by singing the grand prayer from I Lombardi.

To my dismay, I discovered that the prima donna had been left behind; also the property-master, the ladies' costumier, one of the ballet, and five of the chorus. The latter had nothing with them but the theatrical costumes they carried on their bodies. They had previously sent all their worldly belongings on board the ship, and we now saw them gesticulating wildly on the quay as we passed down the bay. They were treated very kindly after our departure; ordinary day clothes were provided for them, and they were sent over by the next steamer.

On entering my cabin I found a silver épergne, a diamond collar-stud, any quantity of literature, several boxes of cigars, bottles of brandy, etc., which had been left anonymously; also an immense basket of fruit. There were, moreover, two large set-pieces of flowers in the form of horse-shoes that had been sent me from Boston, likewise a basket of rose-buds, lilies, and violets, and an embroidered table-cover.

A few minutes later, a tug carrying a large American flag at the side of an English one steamed up to the pier and took on board a number of ladies and gentlemen who, accompanied by an orchestra, followed the steamer down the bay, giving the Company a farewell ovation of cheering as the vessel passed the Narrows and got out to sea.

CHAPTER XV.

RECEPTION OF A TENOR—BELOCCA AND LADY SPENCER—MARIMON'S SUPERSTITIONS—HER LOVESICK MAID—AN ENCOURAGING TELEGRAM—MARIMON IN THE CATHEDRAL—DISAPPEARANCE OF A TENOR

FOR my London season of 1879, in addition to Gerster, who was already a prime favourite, Marie van Zandt, Clara Louise Kellogg, Minnie Hauk, Ambré, Marie Roze, Caroline Salla, Hélène Crosmond, Trebelli, Nilsson, etc., I engaged Fancelli, Brignoli, Frapolli, and Campanini. I moreover concluded an engagement with Signor Masini, the renowned tenor, who shortly afterwards arrived in London. I was informed the following morning by his agent that he felt very much hurt that I myself, Sir Michael Costa, and some of the leading artists of the theatre had not met him at the station; the agent kindly adding that "If I would come round to his hotel with Costa he might put the thing straight."

I told him we were too busy to do anything of the kind, but that I should expect Signor Masini to call on me, when I would present him to Sir Michael Costa.

We were within two days of his announced appearance, and I had not yet seen him. That afternoon the agent, who was very anxious to keep things pleasant, rushed in to tell me that Masini was passing along the colonnade outside the theatre smoking a cigar, and that if I went out quickly with Costa we might meet him, and so put an end to all difficulties. I told him I was too busy, and that he had better bring Masini into my office. The signor at length appeared, and in very few words asked me in what opera he was to make his début. I told him he had already been announced to appear as "Faust," in accordance with his engagement; to which he replied that he should like to know who the other singers were to be. I told him that Christine Nilsson would be "Margherita," Trebelli "Siebel," and Faure "Mephistopheles," and that I trusted this distribution of parts would suit him. He was good enough to say that he would have no objection to sing with the artists I had named. He then left.

A few minutes afterwards Sir Michael Costa entered the room, and I told him what had happened. He ordered a rehearsal for the following morning at twelve o'clock for all the artists. Nilsson, Faure, and Trebelli were punctually at the theatre, but not Masini; and just as the rehearsal was being dismissed in consequence of the tenor's non-attendance his agent appeared with the suggestion that a rehearsal was not necessary. If Sir Michael Costa would step round to the hotel Masini, said the envoy, would show him the tempi he wished to be observed in his performance of the part of "Faust." Sir Michael Costa left the room, and never afterwards made the least reference to this audacious proposition.

On going round to Masini's hotel the next morning to see how he was getting on—for he was to perform that evening—I was informed that the previous night he had taken flight, and that he was now on his way back to Italy.

I afterwards heard that an influential friend of Masini's at the Italian Embassy had frightened him by saying that Sir Michael Costa was a man of considerable importance, who was not to be trifled with, and who would probably resent such liberties as Masini had attempted to take with him.

Masini's flight put me to considerable inconvenience. I followed him up on the Continent, harassing him in every city where he attempted to play; though I ultimately let him off on his paying my costs, which came to some £200.

The fact of Signor Masini's asking Sir Michael Costa to come round to his hotel in order to hear the tempi at which the arrogant tenor liked his airs to be accompanied, must have taken my readers by surprise. But in Italy, I regret to say, the practice is only too common for singers to treat conductors as though they were not their directors, but their subordinates. A popular tenor or prima donna receives a much larger salary than an ordinary conductor—or for that matter a first-rate one; and a favourite vocalist at the end of the season often makes a present to the maestro to reward him for not having objected to some effective note or cadenza which is out of place, but which the "artist" is in the habit of introducing with a view to some special effect. In his own country it would have been nothing extraordinary for a tenor so eminent as Signor Masini to ask the conductor to step in and learn from him how the different tempi should be taken.

On one occasion a renowned prima donna about to make her first appearance in England took the liberty of enclosing to Sir Michael Costa with her compliments a hundred-pound note. The meaning of this was that she wished to be on good terms with the conductor in order that he might not cut her short in any little embellishments, any slackening or hastening of the time, in which she might think fit to indulge. On receiving the note Sir Michael Costa requested the manager to return it to the singer, and at the same time declared that he or the offending vocalist must leave the Company. Needless to say that it was not the conductor who left.

Another remark as to Signor Masini's having expected that Sir Michael Costa, myself, and all the leading members of the Company would meet him at the railway station on his arrival in London. This sort of thing is not uncommon with artists of rank, and when Mdme. Patti comes to London a regular "call" is sent to the various members of the Company directing them, as a matter of duty, to be at the station at such an hour.

A good many artists, on the other hand, have a strong preference for not being met at the station. They travel third-class and in costumes by no means fair to see.

Costa would have been horrified at the way in which operatic enterprises are now too frequently conducted—especially, I mean, in a musical point of view; works hurriedly produced, and in some cases without a single complete rehearsal. Often, no doubt, the prima donna (if sufficiently distinguished to be allowed to give herself airs) is in fault for the insufficient rehearsals or for rehearsals being altogether dispensed with. When such singers as Mdme. Patti and Mdme. Nilsson stipulate that "the utility of rehearsing" shall be left to their judgment—which means that they shall never be called to any sort of rehearsal—all idea of a perfect ensemble must, in their case, be abandoned. Sir Michael would, I am sure, have protested against the acceptance of such conditions. Nothing would satisfy him but to go on rehearsing a work until everything, and especially until the ensemble pieces, were perfect. Then he would have one final rehearsal in order to assure himself that this perfection was maintained; and the opera could be played the night afterwards. Costa was born with the spirit of discipline strong within him. As a singer he would never have made his mark. In his original occupation, that of second tenor, his remarkable qualities were lost. As a conductor, on the other hand, his love of order, punctuality, regularity in everything, stood him in excellent part.

At many operatic theatres the performance begins some five or ten minutes after the time announced; at no theatre where Sir Michael Costa conducted did it ever begin a minute late. The model orchestral chief arrived with a chronometer in each of his waistcoat pockets; and when, after consulting his timepieces, he saw that the moment for beginning had arrived, he raised his bâton, and the performance began. He did not even take the trouble to see that the musicians were all in their places. He knew that, with the discipline he maintained, they must be there.

Among other difficulties which an operatic manager has often to deal with is one arising from questions of precedence between the singers. Who is to have the best dressing-room at the theatre? Who the best suite of apartments at the hotel? Naturally the prima donna. But suppose there is more than one prima donna in the Company, or that the contralto claims to be an artist of greater eminence than the principal soprano?

I remember once arriving at Dublin with a Company which included among its members Mdlle. Salla, who played leading soprano parts, and Mdlle. Anna de Belocca, a Russian lady, who played and sang with distinction the most important parts written for the contralto voice. Mdlle. Belocca and Mdlle. Salla entered at the same time the best suite of apartments in the hotel; upon which each of them exclaimed: "These rooms will do for me."

"For you?" said Mdlle. Salla. "The prima donna has, surely, the right of choice, and I have said that I wish to have them."

"Prima donna!" exclaimed Belocca, with a laugh. "There are but two prime donne: moi et Patti."

"You will not have these rooms all the same," continued the soprano.

"We will see about that," returned the contralto. I was in despair, for it was now a matter of personal dignity. Neither lady would give way to the other. Leaving them for a time together I went downstairs to the hotel-keeper, Mr. Maple, and said to him—

"Have you not another suite of rooms as good, or nearly so, as the one for which these ladies are disputing?"

"I have a very good suite of rooms on the second floor," said Maple; "quite as good, I think, as those on the first floor." These rooms had already been pointed out to Mdlle. de Belocca through the window. But nothing, she said, would induce her to go upstairs, were it only a step.

"Come with me, then," I said to Maple. "Mind you don't contradict me; and to begin with, it must be understood that these rooms on the second floor have been specially retained by Lady Spencer"—Lord Spencer was at that time Viceroy of Ireland—"and cannot on any account, or under any circumstances, be assigned even for a brief time to anyone else."

Maple seized my idea, and followed me upstairs.

"What is the meaning of this?" I said to him, when we were together, in the presence of the two excited vocalists. "Are these the only rooms you have to offer us? They will do for one of these ladies; but whichever accepts them the other must be provided with a set of apartments at least as good."

"I simply have not got them," replied Maple. "There is a charming set of apartments on the floor above, but they are specially retained for the Countess Spencer, and it would be more than my business is worth to let anyone else take possession of them."

At these words Belocca opened her beautiful eyes, and seemed to be struck with an idea.

"At least we could see them?" I suggested.

"You could see them," returned Maple, "but that is all."

"Let us go and have a look at them," I said.

Maple and myself walked upstairs. Belocca silently followed us. We pretended not to see her, but as soon as the door of the apartments reserved for the Countess Spencer was thrown open the passionate young Muscovite rushed into them, shut the door, and locked it, declaring that Lady Spencer must be provided for elsewhere.

On the conclusion of my London season of 1879 I immediately started for the Continent in search of talent for my next New York and London seasons, which both commenced on the 18th October.

On the issue of my New York prospectus, every box, together with three-fourths of the parquet, likewise the first two rows of balcony, were sold out for the season; so good an impression had my performances left the previous spring.

I must here mention a circumstance which greatly inconvenienced me. On the day of sailing from Liverpool I received notice that Mdme. Gerster was in a delicate condition, which was confirmed afterwards by a cable which reached me on my arrival in New York. I replied, entreating the lady to come over, if only for a couple of months, when she could afterwards return. All my proposals failed, though it was not until I received five doctors' certificates from Italy sealed by the Prefetto and viséd by the Consuls that I gave up begging her to appear.

I was really at my wits' ends, for there was no possibility of replacing the favourite artist. I, however, engaged Mdlle. Valleria, also Mdlle. Ambré, a Moorish prima donna of some ability and possessing great personal charms.

Despite all I could do, the Press and the public became excited about the absence of Gerster; and either she or Lucca or Nilsson, or someone of equal calibre, was urgently wanted. It was too late for either of these distinguished ladies to entertain my proposals. I, therefore, addressed Mdlle. Marimon, who was then in Paris.

About this time the members of my orchestra, who all belonged to the Musical Union, struck for a ten per cent. increase of pay in consequence of the success I had met with the previous year. I flatly refused to comply with their demand, whereupon the main body of the players informed me that they would not enter the orchestra on my opening night, unless their terms were conceded. I explained that the previous year I had paid them no less than 50,000 dollars, being more than double the price of my London orchestra, but it was all to no avail. However, I induced them to play at my opening performance, leaving the matter to be decided at a conference to be held in the course of a few days.

To return to Mdlle. Marimon; time being of importance, all our correspondence had to be carried on by cable, I having to pay the answers. As at the time I speak of the price was some fifty cents or two shillings a word, and as the correspondence went on for over a fortnight, I found at last that I had spent over £160 in cables alone. The lady insisting that the money should be deposited beforehand at Rothschild's, in Paris, this, too, had to be transmitted by cable.

At length a day was fixed for her departure, and I awaited with impatience her arrival. Some four days later I received a cable from my agent, Jarrett, who had gone over at my request to Paris, informing me that Marimon had not started and that a new element of trouble had arisen.

Mdlle. Marimon having lost her mother some time before in the foundering of the Pacific steamship was nervous about going to sea, and would not start unless accompanied by her maid. The maid, however, objected to go with her mistress to America on a visit which might last some months. She was attached at the time to an actor at the Gymnase, and preferred remaining in Paris. She knew her mistress to be very superstitious, and, in order to avoid starting, resolved to play on her weak point. Pretending, therefore, to be ignorant of Marimon's intentions, she imparted to that lady the secret of a terrible dream with which she had been visited three nights in succession, to the effect that she and her mistress had embarked in a big ship for a long voyage, and that upon the third day at sea the vessel had collided with another and both had gone to

82

the bottom. This fable had the desired effect. With blanched cheeks the frightened Marimon, who was still in Paris, informed Jarrett that it was impossible for her to go, and that she wished to have her engagement cancelled. To this I refused to accede, the engagement being complete and the money having been paid.

Volumes of cable messages were now again commenced. Here is a copy of one of my replies:—

"Tranquil sea. Charming public. Elegant city. Luxurious living. For Heaven's sake come, and duplicate your Drury Lane triumphs.—MAPLESON."

At length tact and diplomacy overcame her terrors, and she started in the City of Richmond the following day.

I was expecting her with the greatest anxiety, for several days had now passed beyond the ordinary time, when on the morning of November 24th I read in the morning papers the following telegram from Halifax:—

"The steamer Circassia of the Anchor Line, with the American mail, came into port this morning, having picked up the disabled ship the City of Richmond, encountering heavy weather, with a broken shaft, off Sable Island, 180 miles from Halifax, the second officer having been washed overboard and lost. Amongst the saloon passengers were Mdlle. Marimon and her maid."

I thereupon despatched messengers to Halifax, and in due course Mdlle. Marimon reached New York.

On her arrival she immediately insisted on going to the Catholic Cathedral, in Fiftieth Street, to offer up thanks and a candle for her narrow escape. Despite all my entreaty to cease praying, in consequence of the extreme cold in the vast Cathedral—it was now near the close of November—madame remained prostrate for another half-hour, during which time my rehearsal was waiting. I had hoped to get her to attend by inviting her to have a look at the interior of the theatre where she was to perform.

The result, meanwhile, of her devotions was that she caught a violent cold and was obliged to lie in bed for a week afterwards.

I was next much troubled by a renewed outbreak in the orchestra, the occasion being the first performance of Linda di Chamouni, when to my astonishment more than half the musicians were absent. I was too perplexed with other matters to worry beyond appealing to the public, who sympathized with me.

A kind of operatic duel was now going on betwixt my two tenors, Campanini and Aramburo. The latter, with his magnificent voice, had quite conquered New York. Being a Spaniard, his own countrymen supported him nightly by their presence in large numbers. But the tenor was displeased at sundry hisses which came from unknown quarters of the gallery, whilst two or three newspapers attacked him without any reason. It was the eve of his performance in Rigoletto when I was informed that Senor Aramburo and the Gilda, Mdme. Adini (at that time his wife), had suddenly sailed for Europe. The last I could trace of them was that that very day they had both been seen in the city at five o'clock. Early that morning Aramburo had come to me wanting to borrow 300 dollars. At first I refused, but he pressed me, saying that he had property "in Spain," and that he really needed money to close up certain business transactions. I gave him the sum, and this was the last I saw of him. At 5.30, however, in the afternoon, I received a note from him, in which he said that he would like five nice seats for that evening's performance, as he wished to oblige some friends. I sent him the tickets, but by the time they reached his address he must have packed up and gone.

At length the day for Mdlle. Marimon's appearance arrived. It was not until Wednesday, 3rd December, that she made her début in La Sonnambula, when she was supported by Campanini as "Elvino," Del Puente as "Conte Rodolfo," and Mdme. Lablache as the mother. Mdlle. Marimon scored a positive success, and the ovations she received were something unprecedented. I at once forgot all my troubles, for I now plainly foresaw that she would replace Mdme. Gerster until the following year. Anything like her success had not been witnessed since Gerster's. At one bound, as it were, she leaped into the highest favour and esteem of the music lovers of New York. I announced her reappearance for the following Monday.

But the reaction consequent on the agitation caused to her by the perils of the sea voyage now began to manifest itself. The nervousness from which she had suffered at sea, in the belief that her maid's dream was about to be verified, had caused such a disturbance to her nervous system that this, coupled with the subsequent excitement due to her brilliant success, caused the fingers of both her hands to be drawn up as if with cramp. She found it impossible to reappear for several days; and it was not until the 15th, some twelve days later, that she was able to give her second performance. She afterwards sang the part of the "Queen of Night," in Flauto Magico, which terminated the New York season.

We afterwards left for Boston, where on the opening night Mdlle. Marimon's success was again most marked; and from the beginning until the end of the engagement there her receipts equalled those of Mdme. Gerster. During the tour we visited Philadelphia, Chicago, St. Louis, Detroit, and Cleveland. We afterwards made a second visit to Philadelphia, the season concluding about the middle of March, 1880, when we returned to Europe.

During our stay in Philadelphia Mdlle. Marimon, who had met with such great success two evenings previously, was announced to appear as "Dinorah." About six o'clock in the afternoon she sent word that she would be unable to sing. All persuasion on my part was useless. However, as I was descending the staircase of the hotel I met Brignoli, who on hearing of my trouble declared that he had a remedy and that he felt sure he could induce Mdlle. Marimon to sing. He made it a condition, however, that in case of success I should re-engage him for the approaching London season. To this I readily consented, and I was greatly surprised at hearing within half an hour that Mdlle. Marimon and her maid had gone on to the theatre. This was indeed a relief to me, as nearly every seat in the theatre had been sold, Meyerbeer's romantic opera not having been performed in Philadelphia for some twenty years.

On the rising of the curtain Mdlle. Marimon's voice was inaudible. She was very warmly greeted, and went through all the gestures of the part; played it, in short, pantomimically. At the close of the act I went before the curtain, and announced that Mdlle. Marimon's voice, instead of recovering itself, was going gradually from bad to worse; and that the shadow scene in the second act would have to be omitted; but that, to compensate the public for the disappointment, Signor Campanini, who was then present in one of the boxes, had kindly consented, together with Miss Cary, to give the concluding acts of Il Trovatore. This at once restored the depressed spirits of the audience.

Miss Cary surprised everyone by the dramatic force of her "Azucena." Galassi was equally effective in the rôle of the "Count di Luna." But Campanini, in Di quella pira, met with more than a success: it was a triumph. The house broke into rapturous applause, and cheered the singer to the echo. At the conclusion he was loaded with flowers. Thus I avoided the misfortune of having to close the theatre.

On returning home to supper I discovered the "remedy" Brignoli had employed, which was this: He presented himself on leaving me to Mdlle. Marimon, and informed her that he understood Mapleson meant to close up the Opera-house that evening, and charge her the value of the receipts, then estimated at nearly £1,000. He, therefore, advised her to go to the theatre, even if she walked through the part.

One or two newspapers the following morning insisted on regarding my speech of the previous evening as a melancholy joke. I had announced that Mdlle. Marimon was physically unable to fulfil the demands of her rôle, and that she would omit the shadow song. But, said the papers, her efforts throughout the evening had all been shadow songs, the little lady having been absolutely voiceless.

Mdlle. Marimon, however, in settling up the account some weeks afterwards, charged me £120 for this performance, arguing that she had appeared and done her best under the circumstances.

CHAPTER XVI.

SIR MICHAEL AND HIS CHEQUE—SIX MINUTES' BANKRUPTCY—SUCCESS OF "LOHENGRIN"—PRODUCTION OF "MEFISTOFELE"—RETURN TO NEW YORK—"LOHENGRIN" UNDER DIFFICULTIES—ELSA'S TAILS—CINCINNATI OPERA FESTIVAL.

I BEGAN my London season of 1880 a few days after my return from the United States, Mdme. Christine Nilsson appearing as "Margherita" in Faust on the opening night, followed by La Sonnambula, Carmen, Aida, etc., also Lohengrin, for which I had specially entered into an engagement with Richter, who after some fifteen rehearsals declared the work ready for presentation. He at the same time informed me that on looking through the orchestral parts he had discovered no less than 430 mistakes which had been passed over by his predecessor, Sir Michael Costa, and which he had corrected.

About this time law proceedings were pretty hot between myself and Sir Michael Costa, and as they led to my becoming a bankrupt for about six minutes, I may as well explain to the reader how this occurred.

My engagement with Sir Michael Costa was for a season of three months in each year, for which I was to give him £1,500—£500 each month, payable in advance. My season of 1875 was fixed to open on the 24th April, and to terminate on the 24th July, which it actually did; but having at that time secured the services of the great tragedian Salvini, I thought it desirable to open the theatre about a fortnight earlier, giving opera only twice or three times a week, and utilizing the other nights for the appearances of Salvini. I mentioned my idea to Costa, who said I had better pay him his regular cheque as from the commencement of the season, and that the few extra nights could be settled for apart.

On the 10th July Sir Michael Costa asked for his usual monthly cheque in advance. I reminded him of our conversation on the subject, and pointed out to him that I had already made him the three payments as agreed. He told me that he wanted particularly to have the cheque, as he desired to show it to H.R.H.; adding with a mysterious air: "You will be pleased!" From his manner he led me to believe that he would return me the cheque after it had been shown. I, therefore, gave it to him; and, hearing no more of it for five years, thought he had destroyed it. However, prior to my announcing my season of 1880, application was made for the payment of this cheque. Sir Michael declined, in fact, to wield the bâton unless the old cheque were paid. He seemed quite determined on the subject; and I, on my part, was equally determined to resist the demand. I made various propositions for an equitable adjustment, as also did several influential friends; but all to no purpose. Sir Michael Costa, like Shylock, insisted on his bond; and the law was allowed to take its course. In the end the "blue paper" was signed by Mr. Registrar Hazlitt constituting me a bankrupt, and I left the Court in a state of depression quite unusual to me.

We had scarcely got outside when a happy thought struck my solicitor, who, hurrying back with me to the Registrar, addressed him as follows:—

"Pending the appointment of a trustee, which may take some eight or nine days, your honour is, in fact, the manager of Her Majesty's Theatre, and my client thinks it only right to take your honour's orders as to the production of Lohengrin on Saturday. Some new skirts, moreover, which might be of calico, but which your honour would, perhaps, prefer of silk, are wanted for the ballet in Il Trovatore next Monday. But the Lohengrin matter is the more pressing of the two, and we should be glad if you would meet Herr Richter, who, though unwilling to tamper with the score of so great a composer as Wagner, thinks some cuts, already on another occasion authorized by the master, might be ventured upon in the long duet between "Elsa" and "Ortrud." There is an obstinate tenor, moreover, whom your honour, by adopting a decided tone towards him, might perhaps bring to reason."

Mr. Registrar Hazlitt was amazed, and in tones of something like dismay declared that he had trouble enough where he was, and could not undertake the management of an Opera-house. He had not considered that, he continued, when he signed the paper. He rang for a messenger, caused the paper to be brought to him, and at once tore it up; thus putting an end to my six minutes of bankruptcy.

Lohengrin met with very great success, and we ran it alternately with Carmen, Don Giovanni, Faust, and several other operas, in which Mdlle. Gerster maintained her pre-eminence. During all this time we were busily rehearsing Boito's Mefistofele, which I was unable to produce until the early part of July. The following was the cast:—

"Margherita" and "Helen of Troy" ...	Mdme. Christine Nilsson.
"Martha" and "Pantalis" ...	Mdme. Trebelli.
"Mefistofele" ...	Signor Nannetti.
"Faust" ...	Signor Campanini.

The rehearsals were under the immediate personal superintendence of the composer Boito, and the scenic department under that of the celebrated scene-painter Magnani. The greatest pains were taken to give such a representation of this opera as would be worthy of the composer's high reputation.

At last the day arrived, the 6th July; but not the properties, which were expected in large cases from Italy, but could not be heard of and were nowhere to be found. I went to all the likely places in London, telegraphed to Boulogne and to Calais, but in vain. Finally, however, at half-past six in the evening, they were brought to the stage door.

The reader cannot, of course, understand the enormous difficulty which arose in unpacking these hundreds of various properties, each one done up in separate paper. At last shields, armour, spears, serpents, goblets, torches, demon's wigs, etc., etc., were all piled up on the stage. The supernumeraries and chorus were ready dressed, and were left to help themselves, the supers, who were all guardsmen, picking out the prettiest properties they could find; and it was with immense difficulty that, with Boito's aid, we could distribute the most necessary for the performance. The success of this opera is doubtless fresh in the minds of most lovers of music. I look upon it as one of the most memorable on record. It went without a hitch. Madame Nilsson as "Margherita" impressed me by her singing and acting in the prison scene as she had never done before. The opera was repeated every other night until the close of the season, the receipts continually increasing.

At the close of my London season I again went to the Continent in quest of talent, and paid a visit to Mdme. Gerster at her elegant villa near Bologna. She received me with every expression of delight, and we concluded forthwith our arrangements for her return to America, she making it a condition that the baby should accompany her. I now made great preparations to ensure a brilliant season. Great improvements were made by the Directors in the auditorium of the Academy of Music in New York, and new carpet was everywhere laid down. At my suggestion, too, a few feet were cut from the front of the stage, which improved the proscenium boxes, and gave me two extra rows of stalls or parquet seats, numbering sixty in all. These were immediately let at high premiums for the whole of my season. Preparations were afterwards made for the production of Boito's Mefistofele, which had been such a great success during my past London season.

As I found it desirable not to leave myself entirely in the hands of one principal tenor, I concluded arrangements whereby Signor Ravelli was to form part of my Company. Ravelli made his début as "Edgardo" in Lucia di Lammermoor on the opening night, when Mdme. Gerster made her rentrée, after an absence of a year, as "Lucia." The house was crowded from floor to ceiling, Mdme. Gerster receiving more than her usual ovations.

The following night Campanini made his re-appearance as "Fernando" in La Favorita, Miss Annie Louise Cary undertaking her unrivalled impersonation of "Leonora."

Wishing to do all in my power to make the production of Mefistofele a representation of the first class in every respect, I caused to be removed from each end of the orchestra some five-and-twenty parquet seats in order that it might be enlarged, and I engaged some twenty-five extra musicians of ability so that the ensemble of my orchestra might be equal to that of London. Arditi was indefatigable with his rehearsals, of which he had several, in order to obtain every possible perfection in the execution of the music, to secure even the minutest nuances in the necessary light and shade. The cast included Signor Campanini as "Faust," Annie Louise Gary as "Martha" and "Pantalis," a new-comer, Signor Novara, as "Mefistofele," whilst Alwina Valleria undertook the rôle of "Margherita"—and right well did the little lady fulfil the task she had undertaken. She had moments at which she showed herself quite equal to Mdme. Nilsson, especially in the prison scene.

In the newspapers the following morning no mention whatever was made either of the increase in my orchestra or of its performance; the critics at that time being less discerning than they are now. This greatly mortified Arditi, who had been working like a slave for so long a time before the production.

We shortly afterwards produced Mignon, when Arditi said one rehearsal would do, as sure enough it did; and this time we met with great praise. On my returning for the following spring season I dispensed with the services of my twenty-five extra musicians; and the excellence of the orchestra was now fully commented upon.

About this time I remounted Aida in grand style, with new properties, scenery, and dresses, Mdme. Gerster shortly afterwards appearing as "Elsa" in Lohengrin. This reminds me of an interesting occurrence.

The fatigues incident to the continued rehearsals of Lohengrin had rather unnerved Mdme. Gerster, who, however, made her appearance in the rôle of "Elsa" on the night for which the opera had been originally announced. Her success, though great, was not what she desired, and the next day she complained of indisposition, though she at the same time insisted upon further rehearsals. I therefore closed the theatre at great loss, in order that her desires might be complied with.

At length the time for the second performance arrived. I had spent a fatiguing day, and had finished up with directing the difficult machinery of the scene in which the swan disappears to be replaced by the missing child, while the dove comes down from heaven to draw the boat which, as "Elsa" embraces her long-lost brother, bears "Lohengrin" away.

Feeling sure that all was in order, I went home for a short time, not having tasted anything since early morn. I sat down to my dinner, and ordered my servant to bring me a pint of champagne. I had hardly taken the knife and fork into my hand when Dr. Gardini, Mdme. Gerster's husband, put his head through the door, beckoning to me, and saying that he wanted me for one "second" only. On my getting into the vestibule he entreated me to come over a moment to the Everett House, where his wife was residing, it being then about a quarter to seven (my opera was to commence at eight). On my reaching the Everett House her maid, her brother, and her sister-in-law desired me to step a moment into her bedroom. On entering I smelt a powerful odour of chloroform, and on inquiry found that her brother, who was a medical man of some standing in New York, had been prescribing chloroform to allay a tooth-ache, or some other ailment she was suffering from; but in the nervous condition she was in it had acted rather too violently upon her general system, and there she lay speechless.

I was beside myself, and I am afraid rather rude at the moment to those in attendance. However, I insisted upon taking the matter entirely into my own hands. I commenced by opening the tops of the windows so as to let the odour out, and dispatched the sister to get me a bottle of soda-water, together with some sal-volatile, also a bottle of strong smelling salts. By raising Mdme. Gerster's head I got her to take the soda-water and sal-volatile, and at each respiration I took good care to place the smelling-bottle to her nose, but all to no effect. She was in a state of semi-unconsciousness.

I, however, insisted upon raising her (it being then a quarter past seven), and by the aid of the maid I put a large shawl over her, and carried her off in my arms to the carriage, which I had ordered to be at the door, and took her over to the Academy, where I seated her on a chair. She now swooned on to the dressing-table.

Whilst I continued to apply the smelling-bottle I gave directions to the theatrical hair-dresser to be careful to come gently in and comb out her back hair and plait in the little tails which are sometimes added by prime donne. It was about twenty minutes to eight when Arditi came into the room, accompanied by the call-boy, and both looked upon the matter as hopeless. I, however, begged the maestro to go into the orchestra, and to leave the rest to me.

I got her to stand upright; but when I suggested the idea of singing "Elsa" she sighed, and said—

"It is utterly useless. It is just eight o'clock, and the tails are not in my hair."

I thereupon informed her that during her unconscious state I had carefully had the tails combed in. This brought a faint smile to her face, and I at once saw that there was still a chance of my opera going. I led her to the entrance, when she went on accompanied by her attendant maidens. I then drew a long breath and went back to finish my dinner, knowing now that the opera would continue.

Long before the first act was completed Mdme. Gerster's energies had returned. She was in full possession of her marvellous vocal powers, and a triumphant evening was the result of my labours.

About this time I commenced autumn Sunday evening concerts, in which the whole of my singers took part, the first portion of the evening beginning, as a rule, with a fine performance of Rossini's Stabat Mater, Valleria, Cary, Campanini, Galassi, and Novara singing the music very effectively. The houses were invariably crowded to the roof.

About this time, I settled a grand opera festival for Cincinnati the ensuing spring, in conjunction with the College of Music, and for that purpose organized a chorus of some 400 extra voices, and an orchestra of some 150 musicians; after which I left for Chicago to confer with Colonel George Nichols as to the arrangements.

We afterwards visited Boston, where our performances met with the greatest possible success, each week's receipts averaging no less than 35,000 dollars, the reappearance of Mdme. Etelka Gerster creating immense excitement. At the matinée given on January 1st, at which she appeared, upwards of 100 ladies' odd india-rubber overshoes were picked up on the family circle staircase lost in the rush after the opening of the doors, there being a heavy snowstorm raging at the time. The receipts were over £1,200 notwithstanding. Aida, Mefistofele, Carmen, Don Giovanni, and Puritani completed the week's répertoire. We afterwards left for Philadelphia, followed by Baltimore, Washington, Pittsburg, Indianapolis, Chicago, and St. Louis, the Opera being a signal success all along the line. We closed up on the Saturday night at St. Louis, leaving by special train at 1 a.m., shortly after the conclusion of the night's representation, for Cincinnati. The soloists, choristers, and orchestra arrived at about three o'clock on the Sunday afternoon, rather tired; and they spent this afternoon in hunting up hotels and boarding-houses. In the evening we had a stage rehearsal of Lohengrin, with chorus and part of the orchestra. My own chorus was on hand, together with the Cincinnati contingent some 350 strong—all present without a single absentee. But large as the stage was there was plenty of room for all and to spare. The beautiful Lohengrin choruses were finely rendered, and the volume of tone resounding through the vast building was truly grand. The rehearsal was afterwards dismissed, and everyone retired to rest.

Early the following morning the final rehearsal was called, which terminated at twelve o'clock; and that same evening the first great Opera Festival was inaugurated— undoubtedly the most daring musical enterprise ever attempted in America or any other country. The sight of the audience from the private boxes was worth a journey to see. It was one sea of faces. Everything looked auspicious for the success of the festival. The weather was pleasant, the crowds were large and enthusiastic, and the singers were en rapport with the audience, whilst the chorus did its very best.

The orchestra, also, was the finest ever heard in Cincinnati, composed of 150 first-class musicians, who did their work splendidly. In fact, the ensemble was complete.

The scene outside the hall was one of bewildering confusion. Myriads of elegant carriages darting round corners, pedestrians jostling against each other to arrive before the doors were closed, an immense rabble outside, who had gone to catch only a glimpse of the handsomely-dressed ladies as they went in; such was the scene, which, I must add, was illuminated by the newly-invented electric light. In spite of the most stringent police regulations the streets were blocked, and it is not surprising that there were several horrible accidents. Notwithstanding four wide exits it was an hour and a half after the performance was over before the last carriage could get off.

The toilettes of the ladies, for which Cincinnati is so famous, were most elegant. Our grand performance of Lohengrin was followed by Mozart's Magic Flute, Mdme. Gerster singing the rôle of the "Queen of Night." The third opera was Boito's Mefistofele, for which 8,000 reserved seats were sold. The fourth night we had Lucia di Lammermoor, followed by an act from Moses in Egypt; the extreme back of the stage representing a burning sun, and the whole 400 choristers joining together with the principals in the grand prayer, "Dal tuo stellato soglio," which terminates the opera. On the fifth night Verdi's Aida was given with entirely new scenery, painted for the occasion, together with new dresses and properties.

A morning performance, La Sonnambula, was given next day, with Gerster. The audience, like all the previous ones, was immense. Every seat was occupied, whilst 2,000 people who had paid two dollars apiece were standing up. The toilettes of the ladies were simply magnificent, baffling all description. The audience went wild over Gerster, encores were demanded and re-demanded, people hurrahed and waved their handkerchiefs, whilst the most expensive bouquets and flowers were pelted on the prima donna, who at last was embowered in roses.

On the last evening Gounod's Faust was performed. The end was as glorious as the beginning. By seven o'clock the big hall was again filled, and at half-past seven, when Arditi took up the bâton, the house was packed and jammed from the top-most part of the gallery.

The audiences throughout the week were most brilliant. Before separating a Committee meeting was held; and it was resolved that the festival should be renewed the following year, when Mdme. Patti and Mdme. Albani should, if possible, be added to the list of vocalists.

This was followed by a grand banquet at the club, where amongst others I had the honour of making the acquaintance of Mr. Reuben Springer, the donor of the magnificent hall in which the festival had been held.

The profits of the week reached 50,000 dollars. We afterwards visited Detroit, Syracuse, and Albany, returning to New York in the early part of March.

On the 25th March a morning performance was given of Lucia di Lammermoor, when the Academy was fairly packed from parquet to gallery by a most fashionable audience, not so much to hear Lucia as to hear Mdme. Gerster. At the rush at the opening of the doors the ticket-taker discovered a forged free pass purporting to bear my name. On his own responsibility he handed over to the police the two men who had come in with the ticket, and they were taken off to the police-station, where I was immediately sent for.

The forgery being proved they were both committed for trial, the magistrate at the same time notifying that if we took them up at once in an elevated train to Ninety-second Street the assizes would be on, and their case could be at once decided.

They were duly taken on, and the matter gone into. One of the men was committed to prison for a year, and the other one was placed under the care of the Commissioners of Charities and Corrections for two years on Randall's Island.

I got back to the Academy in time to hear the mad scene.

On returning the following year I made inquiry as to the man who had been sent to the Reformatory, and was informed that he had died only the day before. So also had the judge of the Assize Court: a remarkable coincidence.

We remained in New York until the 9th April, when we were again called to Boston to give six performances, each of which averaged $5,000. After a matinée on the Saturday we returned to New York by special train, in order to give a Sunday concert, when over 4,000 dollars were taken at the doors. We then gave six more extra farewell performances in New York, sailing for Europe immediately on the conclusion of the last one, and arriving in London about six days prior to the opening of my season.

Early in the spring of 1881 I received a communication from Messrs. Ricordi, of Milan, the publishers and proprietors of Boito's Mefistofele, in which they solicited me to allow Signor Nannetti, the basso, who was then performing the title rôle at the Scala, to delay his engagement with me for the period of a fortnight, in order that the successful run of the work might not be interrupted; in exchange for which they offered me the services of the musical director, Signor Faccio. To this I consented, and the eminent conductor was duly announced in my prospectus. But instead of keeping Nannetti two weeks in Milan they kept him five, during which time my season had opened and Mdme. Nilsson had arrived in London in order that I might take up the successful run of Mefistofele which had been interrupted only by the close of the previous season. Mdme. Nilsson, however, refused to appear until Nannetti came; and it was not until the 23rd June that I could reproduce Boito's Mefistofele. Faccio never turned up at all.

CHAPTER XVII.

PRODUCTION OF "IL RINNEGATO"—RAVELLI'S OPERATIC THEORY— NEGOTIATIONS WITH COVENT GARDEN "LIMITED"—A SEARCH FOR A PRIMA DONNA—FAILURE OF PATTI'S CONCERTS—CINCINNATI OPERA FESTIVAL OF '82—PATTI'S INDISPOSITION.

MY London season of 1881 commenced at Her Majesty's Theatre, on the 7th May. Nothing of note took place prior to the arrival of Mdme. Christine Nilsson, who appeared on the 28th as "Margherita" in Faust, which character she repeated, together with "Mignon," until the 23rd June, when, after two postponements, we were enabled to reproduce Boito's Mefistofele. The attraction of this opera had, however, considerably diminished, possibly on account of its having been produced so late in the previous season, when a few performances were given, and afterwards interrupted for a period of nearly ten months. During this time negotiations were entered into between Baron Bodog Orczy and myself for the production of an opera composed by the Baron on a Hungarian subject, and entitled The Renegade; in Italian Il Rinnegato.

Baron Orczy, friend and pupil of Liszt, and a fervent admirer of Wagner's works, had been the Intendant of the Royal Theatre at Pesth, where he at once gave a proof of keen musical discernment by engaging Richter as his orchestral conductor. Report said that he had given up his important post by reason of representations made to him on the subject of his excessive devotion to Wagnerian music. However that may be, the Baron had shown himself by several excerpts from his opera, performed at St. James's Hall and at the Crystal Palace, to be a composer of no mean ability. He handled the orchestra with skill and power, and if his opera did not prove so successful with the general public as his friends must have desired, that result may partly be accounted for by the over-elaboration of the score, and the importance attached by the composer to the instrumental portions of his work.

Composed to a Hungarian libretto, The Renegade, of which the subject was derived from an historical romance by a popular Hungarian novelist, had, with a view to production at my theatre, been translated into Italian; and two of the leading parts had been assigned to Ravelli the tenor, and Galassi the baritone.

Ravelli had not long been a member of my Company; he was one of my chance discoveries. One evening, as so often happened, I was at the last moment in want of a tenor. The hall porter, finding that I was sending about London in quest of a possibly suitable vocalist, told me that a dark little man with a tenor voice had been hanging about the stage-door, and the Colonnade in front of the theatre, for some ten days past, and that he was sure to be somewhere in the neighbourhood. The artist in question was found. I asked him whether he could really sing. His answer may be guessed; and when I further questioned him as to whether he knew the part of "Edgardo" he replied that he did, and in some measure verified his assertion by singing portions of it. He showed himself the possessor of a fine, clear, resonant voice; and if he sometimes sang without true dramatic expression, and without the grace which springs from perfect art, he at least knew how to thrill the public with a high note effectively thrown in.

It is not my purpose, however, for good or ill, to criticize the singing of Signor Ravelli. I am now dealing with him only in so far as he was connected with the opera of Il Rinnegato. In the second act of that work the tenor and baritone fight a duel. In this there was no novelty. But instead of the tenor killing the baritone, the baritone puts the tenor to death, and this struck Signor Ravelli as far too new. He appealed to operatic traditions and asked in an excited manner whether such a thing was heard of before. "No!" he exclaimed, answering with vigour his own question; and he added that though he was quite ready to take part in the duel, he would do so on condition that not he but his antagonist should be slain. It was useless to explain to him that in the story upon which the opera was based the character represented by the tenor perished, while the baritone lived on. This, he said, was just what he complained of. "Why," he indignantly demanded, "should the tenor's part in the opera be thus cut short? But why, above all, should the habitual impersonator of heroes fall beneath the sword of one who was accustomed only to play a villain's part?"

It was impossible to get the infatuated man to hear reason on the subject. He cried, screamed, uttered oaths, and at one time threatened to kill with his dagger, not only his natural enemy, the baritone, but everyone around him. "I will kill them all!" he shrieked.

After a time, by humouring him and agreeing with him that in a well-ordered operatic duel the tenor ought, of course, to kill the baritone, I got him to listen to me; and I at last contrived to make him understand that there were exceptions to all rules, and that it would be generous on his part to overlook the species of indignity to which he was asked to submit, the affront offered to him not having been intended as such, either by the librettist or, above all, by the amiable composer. It was settled then that Ravelli was to be killed. But what, he wished to know, was to be done with his body after death? The proper thing would be, he said, for six attendants to enter, raise the corpse, and carry it solemnly away to a place of repose.

It mattered little to me whether the body of Ravelli was borne from off the stage by six, eight, or a dozen attendants. But according to the plan of the opera he had to lie where he had fallen while the soprano, whom in his character of tenor he had passionately loved, sang a lament over his much-loved form. I told Ravelli that it was a great compliment thus to be treated by a despondent prima donna. But he could not see it, and he calculated that the soprano's air, with the orchestral strains introducing it, would keep him in what he considered an ignominious position for something like ten minutes. It was absolutely necessary to promise Ravelli that his mortal remains should be removed from the stage to some quieter resting-place by six corpse bearers, the number on which he had set his heart; and he was honoured, if I remember rightly, with the funeral he had stipulated for at the last rehearsal. Baron Orczy had protested against this arrangement; but I assured him that there was nothing else to be done, and that everything should take place according to book at the public representation.

On the night of performance Ravelli was, of course, left recumbent on the stage. He must have thought more than once, as he lay writhing with shame and anger on the boards, of rising and rushing off. But he feared too much the laughter and derision of the public, and he had to remain passive while the orchestral introduction was being played, and while the prima donna's soliloquy was being sung. Many of us thought the strain would be too much for him, and that he would go raving mad. But when he found himself once more a free agent behind the scenes he stabbed no one, struck no one, and, strange to say, seemed perfectly quiet. The humiliation to which he had been subjected had somehow calmed him down.

If Ravelli was wild and passionate, Galassi, his associate, was a reasonable man whose presence of mind had possibly the effect of saving my theatre from being burned a second time. There was a good deal of fire in Il Rinnegato, and in one scene the green lights surrounding an apparition starting from a well caught some gauze, so that the well itself burst into flames, the result being such a blaze that but for Galassi's promptitude in dealing with it the conflagration might have proved fatal to the building.

While the baritone was smothering the fire with his cloak and with some canvas on which the grass was painted—at the same time trampling the burning embers under foot—a portion of the audience had taken alarm and was already hurrying to the doors. At this critical moment I could not but admire the calm air of dignity with which Baron Orczy, who was conducting his work, continued to mark the time and to direct the performance generally as though nothing at all extraordinary were taking place. I feel sure that this determined attitude of the composer in the presence of what, for a few seconds, seemed likely to lead to a terrible calamity, had a considerable effect in allaying the general excitement. "How can there be danger," many must have asked themselves, "when that gentleman who is conducting the orchestra, and who is so much nearer the supposed fire than we are, does not evince the least alarm?"

Towards the close of this season, negotiations were again opened by the Messrs. Gye towards purchasing my lease, goodwill, and interest, together with a certain portion of my costumes and scenery, with a view to an operatic monopoly. Ultimately terms were arranged, and an agreement concluded, which was not to come into force until the shares of the projected Company had been taken up; and it was only in August, 1882, that I was notified that sufficient shares had been placed to justify the Company starting, and my agreement coming into force. In the meantime I had been left to sustain the burden of the current expenses, rates, taxes, etc., of my own theatre, until the transfer could be made. The arrangement entered into was that I should have so much cash, and so many shares, together with an engagement for a period of three years, at a salary of £1,000 per annum, besides 50 per cent. of the profits made in America, where I was to have sole control of the business.

In the early part of October, 1881, I started with my party for New York. The season opened on October 17th, with a performance of Lohengrin by Campanini, Galassi, Novara, Anna de Belocca, and Minnie Hauk, which gave great satisfaction. This was followed by a performance of Carmen, in which Minnie Hauk, Campanini, Del Puente, and Valleria resumed their original parts.

A few days prior to the sailing of the Company for America I visited Paris, where I heard a young vocalist, Mdlle. Vachot, sing; and at once negotiated with her for an engagement. She did not like the idea of crossing the ocean; but she was overruled by her father, a small farmer at Varreds.

Being in a hurry to conclude the engagement I called upon her the next day, with a contract in my pocket, when the servant informed me that she and her father had gone to Varreds to consult some relatives. On learning the name of the place I went to the station, and there heard the manager of the Grand Opera asking the ticket-seller how to get to Varreds. Luckily, he decided not to take that train. Thereupon I entered it; though being desperately hungry I was sorely tempted to lunch before doing so.

The nearest place on the railroad was Meaux. I got there in a pelting rain-storm to find that I had to travel nine miles across country to Varreds. I managed to get a trap, but we had not gone more than half way before one of the traces broke, which, after some delay, I got repaired.

Finally I reached a clump of mud hovels; and this, I was told, was Varreds. I asked a cowboy whom I met if he had seen Mdlle. Vachot. He replied that he did not know her. He had seen two strangers, a lady and a gentleman, walking towards the "hotel," which I found to be a mud hut, with accommodation for men, women, and chickens, more especially the latter, which were walking all over the parlour floor. Nothing was known at this hotel, except that two strangers who had recently arrived, after leaving a bundle of shawls, had been seen going towards the cemetery.

On arriving at the cemetery I found the gate locked. I then went to the curé, who said he knew nothing of Mdlle. Vachot. Finally I met a blacksmith who knew her, and he pointed out where she was. I found her at table with six or seven country cousins. As I was hungry, I was glad to take pot-luck with them.

With some difficulty I afterwards got my contract signed, and started back for Paris. On my way to Meaux Station I met the manager of the Grand Opera driving over towards Varreds.

I afterwards secured a tenor of the name of Prévost, who had a phenomenal voice, and was then singing with success at the Théâtre du Château d'Eau. He seemed especially adapted to the rôle of "Arnold" in William Tell. After signing with him I left for Italy, where I ordered new and magnificent costumes, including enough for an extra chorus of 90 male voices which I afterwards employed for the Gathering of the Cantons in Rossini's masterpiece.

From there I went to Parma, where the eminent scenografo of the theatre, with some persuasion, undertook to paint the scenery, which on its arrival in New York was pronounced by all connoisseurs simply superb.

About this time the director of the Leipsic State Theatre proposed the production of Wagner's Ring des Nibelungen at Her Majesty's Theatre, with a very powerful cast of characters and a magnificent orchestra under the direction of Richter, the great master himself to superintend personally its production. But of this "more anon."

Mdlle. Vachot duly appeared in the early part of November as "Rosina" in Il Barbiere di Siviglia. The house was crowded in every part, and Vachot was found to have a charming personality, a beautiful voice with a good method, together with no little dramatic talent. She was warmly received for her pretty appearance, and heartily applauded at frequent intervals for her delightful singing. From a good beginning she went on to a gratifying success, fairly establishing herself before the evening was over in the favour of her new public.

Things were progressing favourably when about this time Mdme. Adelina Patti arrived in New York on a speculation of her own, after an absence of some 22 years. A great deal of excitement was thereby created, and as Mdme. Patti's concerts were to take place within three doors of the Academy of Music, I began to fear as to the results of my season then progressing. Mdme. Patti's visit, however, turned out to be a most ill-advised one. Her concerts had not been properly announced, and she came with a very weak Company, believing that the magical name of Patti would alone crowd the hall. Her first concert realized scarcely 3,000 dollars, whilst the second dropped down to 1,000 only. Few people went to see her, and she at once understood what a mistake had been made. The charge, moreover, she demanded was ten dollars per seat! The public, therefore, universally agreed to stay away. The paltry receipts of the second concert proved conclusively to Patti's manager, and to herself as well, that something had to be done to lift the sinking enterprise.

94

I may mention that I gave a gentle hint to Patti that her removal to the Academy would be most desirable by sending her a bouquet which cost some £30, with these words on it: "To Adelina Patti, Queen of the Lyric Stage." Two days afterwards I called to see la Diva at the Fifth Avenue Hotel, and after some negotiation was on the point of concluding arrangements which would have been a fortune to me as well as to Mdme. Patti herself, when at this critical moment Mr. Abbey came between us, offering her a concert tour in which, beyond receiving a fixed salary, she was to participate in his profits.

Abbey's admirable handling of Bernhardt being fresh in everyone's recollection, Patti had no reason to suppose that he would fail in her case to obtain similar results.

During my season at the Academy the production of Rossini's chef d'œuvre, Guillaume Tell, made a prodigious success, and crowded the theatre nightly. The tenor Prévost possessed the voice of exceptional quality necessary for the difficult rôle of "Arnoldo." Signor Galassi's "Tell" was a noble impersonation, marked by great dignity of action, and sung in the broad and grand style of which he is so complete a master; whilst the part of "Mathilde" was undertaken with success by Mdlle. Dotti, who displayed remarkable ability.

Shortly afterwards I reproduced Verdi's Aida, for which I discovered a most capable soprano in the person of Mdlle. Paolina Rossini, whose success went on increasing nightly; and who later on appeared in the difficult rôle of "Valentina" in Les Huguenots, at once taking a firm hold on the public.

We were now approaching the second great Cincinnati Opera Festival. I will, therefore, take the reader once more with me to that city.

The Opera Festival of 1882 opened on February 13th with immense success by a grand performance of Meyerbeer's Huguenots, the audience, an immense and distinguished gathering, numbering over 5,000 persons, the representatives of the wealth, the beauty, and the culture of the city.

As early as six o'clock people began to assemble outside the Music Hall, the scene of so many previous triumphs, and long before the commencement of the opera every seat was occupied, and every available inch of standing room likewise.

At a quarter to eight the opera began, a band composed of 150 selected professors occupying the orchestra under the veteran Arditi. The opera was a signal success, and went smoothly throughout; the grand "Bénédiction des Poignards" being executed marvellously by a chorus composed of 400 trained voices. The acoustic properties of the hall were simply perfect. Even in the extreme rear of the gallery, from where the artists on the stage appeared the size of Liliputians, the softest tones could be distinctly heard.

At the close of the performance, however, an unfortunate accident occurred, which deprived me of my prima donna for the remainder of my tour.

Just as the curtain fell, when "Marcel," "Raoul," and "Valentine" were shot by the Catholic Guards, the guns were pointed too near Mdlle. Rossini, who got touched in the face, and was further hurt whilst falling. She had, therefore, to be carried home.

I omitted to tell the reader that some weeks before I had succeeded in engaging Mdme. Patti to take part in this Festival, for which I paid her £1,600 a night, being the largest amount this invaluable lady has ever received in the shape of salary.

She was announced to appear on the second evening of the festival in a concert, followed by the fourth act of Il Trovatore. On arriving home, flushed with the success of the opening night, but deeply concerned about Mdlle. Rossini, whom I had just left, I received a letter from Mdme. Patti's agent, informing me that she was suffering from a severe cold, so that it was feared she would be unable to appear the following evening.

I at once sought Colonel Nichols, and informed him of this, desiring him kindly to accompany me to Mdme. Patti's with the leading physician of the city, who found the unwelcome tidings to be perfectly true. No alternative was left but to issue an explicit announcement to the public, postponing Mdme. Patti's appearance until the following Thursday afternoon at two o'clock. I therefore substituted the opera Faust the following evening, refunding their money to purchasers, or exchanging their tickets for the night on which Mdme. Patti was to appear. This, of course, needed a great deal of care and attention, and occupied me the greater portion of the night on account of the vast number of tickets to be provided for in the exchanges. I am happy to say that there was no confusion; and the public eventually became satisfied with the arrangement made.

On the Wednesday afternoon the opera of Carmen was given, with Campanini, Del Puente, Dotti, and Minnie Hauk in the principal characters. In the evening Fidelio was produced with a powerful cast, and with 300 extra voices added for the celebrated Chorus of Prisoners, the receipts reaching their maximum on that occasion.

Mdme. Patti, unfortunately, made but slow progress towards recovery, and it was consequently decided to further postpone her appearance until the following Saturday night, it being again necessary to inform the public as to the cause.

Various conflicting rumours at once got into circulation as to the Patti trouble. After it had been announced that the capricious Diva could not sing many refused flatly to believe in the reason assigned, namely, that she had a sore throat. Others declared that Patti was a little stubborn, self-willed person, and had done this expressly "to spite Mapleson." Inquiries were set about in all directions.

Newspapers sent their reporters hundreds of miles to discover the state of Patti's health before she had quitted Detroit to come on to the Festival. Malicious people even went so far as to say that Patti, like Rip Van Winkle, was fond of "schnapps," on the insufficient ground that, prior to starting, she had purchased a bottle of Mumm's "extra dry." Even this turned out to be a mistake, for, in reply to an inquiry made, a special despatch was received from Detroit by the Cincinnati Gazette, stating that "the bills of Patti at the Detroit Hotel show that during her entire stay in that city only two quarts of wine were consumed, and the hotel waiters state they think Nicolini drank the most of it. Further, the landlord stated that none of the party were noticeably intoxicated during their stay in his hotel, showing there could be no truth whatever in the statement that Patti was under the influence of liquor."

An evening paper published the following:—"The explanation that Patti caught cold whilst driving in this city is strengthened by the fact that she at least had a good opportunity for doing so, as she was driving most of the time during the previous day. On our reporter inquiring at the stables, he ascertained that her carriage bill for her drive amounted to 55 dollars." Dr. J. D. Buck, who attended her, informed the newspaper reporter that "Mdme. Patti was undoubtedly ill of a cold, but she was rapidly improving."

Meanwhile Dr. F. Forchheimer, physician to the College of Music, was also sent to inspect the larynx of the prima donna, and he confirmed what the previous doctor had said.

The ticket speculators, however, lost nothing by the affair, the city being very famous for matinée performances, and as the ladies came forward in great numbers at five dollars apiece for the purpose of showing their new toilettes, very few returned after once entering the doors. Each of the audiences for Carmen and Fidelio numbered 8,000 people.

On Friday evening I produced Mozart's Magic Flute; and on Saturday a magnificent representation with complete scenic effects was given of William Tell, where again my increased chorus of 400 did very effective work, the voices coming out with full freshness and vigour. So good a chorus had never been heard on the operatic stage before. The orchestra, too, particularly distinguished itself. The overture, which musically embodies the whole opera, was given with such precision, correctness of tempo, and delicacy of colour that it called forth at once an encore.

On the Saturday morning a grand performance of Lohengrin was given, and in the evening Mdme. Patti was enabled to appear, the first part being devoted to a concert, while the second was composed of the fourth act of Trovatore.

As the success of the Festival kept on increasing we resolved to give an extra performance, for which purpose an engagement was entered into with Mdme. Patti for the following Monday, when she appeared as "Margherita" in Faust.

I afterwards visited Detroit, Buffalo, Cleveland, Syracuse, and Albany, returning to New York for the usual spring season, and there performing Fidelio, Huguenots, Lohengrin, Carmen, William Tell, and Faust.

In the meanwhile I had put in rehearsal Meyerbeer's Africaine, which was placed on the stage at considerable expense, all the costumes, scenery, dresses, and armour being entirely new, and the stage being occupied by some 400 persons. The gorgeous revival of l'Africaine proved an extraordinary success. The audience fairly packed the large house nightly, the fine spectacle presented in the third and fourth acts causing great enthusiasm. Miss Hauk undertook the part of "Selika," and was particularly successful from a dramatic point of view, whilst Signor Galassi and Campanini found great opportunities for the display of their vocal abilities. The great ship scene of the third act created a perfect furore. So anxious was I that the acting of the Indians on boarding the ship should create a sensation, that I went to Union Square and from the various agencies engaged some 12 or 15 actors, who were then out of employment, and whose make-up with the tattoo marks and their realistic fighting made such an impression that on the conclusion of the scene the curtain had to be raised.

The grand march, too, in the fourth act created a sensation, equally with the magnificent spectacle and the gorgeous palanquin in which "Selika" enters accompanied by "Nelusko." I had requested Bradwell to design for me a full-sized elephant with a palanquin on its back, in which people were seated, the interior of the elephant being occupied and kept firm by two stalwart policemen.

The scenery was of the most gorgeous description, specially painted for me by Magnani, who surpassed even his previous efforts. L'Africaine was repeated for five or six consecutive nights to crowded houses.

On one occasion we had to perform L'Africaine on consecutive nights in New York and Philadelphia, which entailed the removal of the whole of the scenery and dresses, likewise the transport of the whole of the supernumeraries, ballet, etc., numbering altogether 400 persons; and we had, moreover, to return the same evening after the performance to New York, in which city the work was to be repeated the following night.

The supernumeraries, with their blackened faces, and the Indians with their tattoo marks, caused a great sensation at the railway station on the return journey, as there was no time to think of washing them. We only reached New York the next morning at six o'clock, when again the early morning public were startled by the arrival of these sable gentry under a blazing sun.

We remained in New York for further representations, when I revived Verdi's Ernani, Don Giovanni, Huguenots, etc.

CHAPTER XVIII.

I ENGAGE PATTI—MY MILITARY EXPERIENCE—INFLUENCING
ELECTORS—OPERATIC JOINT STOCK COMPANY—OBJECTIONS TO
ENGLISH MONOPOLY—PATTI IN NEW YORK.

ABOUT this time I set to work for the purpose of engaging Adelina Patti for my
ensuing season, and sent a letter to all the 200 stockholders of the Academy (who
occupied free seats) to know what amount they would contribute towards the
accomplishment of my object. Mr. Pierre Lorillard wrote to me that in case I should be
short he would donate 1,000 dollars beyond the amount he then contributed should Patti
sing at the Academy the next winter. I replied that I simply required each stockholder to
contribute three dollars a seat for the Patti nights in order to aid me in carrying out this
much-desired engagement.

I regret to say that many of the stockholders sent me no response whatever. Others
destroyed the value of their consent by adding that it was only to be given if all the other
shareholders agreed to do the same.

Another great difficulty presented itself. I was called upon to deposit no less than
£11,000 at Belmont's bank as caution money on the signing of the contract. This
difficulty I ultimately got over through the kindness of August Belmont, who guaranteed
Mdme. Patti's deposit, I at the same time assigning to Mr. Belmont the whole of my
subscriptions. The agreement with Mdme. Patti was, therefore, duly signed.

The conclusion of this contract made a great sensation. When it became known that
Mdme. Patti was to return the following season, numbers of applications were made for
subscriptions, although it was six months before the opening.

About this time the building of the new Metropolitan Opera-house had been
resumed in earnest, in order that it might be completed by the following spring.

The season shortly afterwards closed with the benefits of the various singers, I
taking the last night, when I gave acts of four different operas, namely, Faust, Daughter of
the Regiment, Ruy Blas, and Africaine, with a new ballet.

Having secured Mdme. Patti for the ensuing season, I endeavoured to effect an
engagement also with Mdme. Gerster, who was then in New York, having returned from
New Orleans, and being now on her way to England. I only succeeded, however, in
securing her services for the following morning, when an early matinée had to be given
prior to the departure of the Company for Europe in the afternoon, the receipts on that
occasion reaching no less than 9,000 dollars.

This year the Americans paid me the compliment of making me an honorary
member of the 22nd Regiment, with rank corresponding to my own actual rank in the
English volunteers. But beyond attending a couple of balls and some competition drills in
the uniform of the regiment I had never time enough to profit by the privileges extended
to me in so friendly a manner.

I must not forget among my volunteering reminiscences a rather dramatic incident
which occurred at Her Majesty's Theatre in the year 1860, when I had just joined the
Honorable Artillery Company, and, as yet but little instructed in the mysteries of drill, was
anxious to qualify myself as soon as possible for admission into line. With this view I
spent every spare moment in practice, sometimes with the Scots Guards at St. George's
Barracks, Trafalgar Square, and often in the evening, when some operatic representation
was actually going on, at Her Majesty's Theatre, where I utilized the services of the guard
of honour in attendance. The first time I carried out what had struck me as rather a happy
idea I was putting the squad of guardsmen through the bayonet exercise in the Ballet
practice room. I had just given the orders, "Advance, advance, point!" when the door
opened, and Lewis, the treasurer, appeared, bearing in his hand a bag which held the

receipts of the evening. The word "point!" brought the bayonets of the guardsmen almost into contact with the breast of the startled official, who, uttering a shriek and dropping the money-bags, turned and fled.

So scared was he that not until some time afterwards did he quite recover himself. Had he fancied in his terror that the guard had suddenly invaded the theatre and prepared an ambuscade in order to rob the treasurer of the night's receipts? He could give no explanation on the subject. The sight of the red-coats, the authoritative cry of "Point!" and the rapid presentation of the bayonets, which all but pierced him, had the effect of depriving him for a time of his wits. No other account could poor Lewis give of the matter.

In these degenerate times it is considered enough at one of the Royal Theatres to station outside during the performance a sergeant's guard; and Mr. Augustus Harris is modest enough to consider a corporal's guard sufficient. In former days, however, Her Majesty's Theatre was almost always during a performance under the care of a captain's guard, the officers being provided for inside, where the captain, the lieutenant, and the ensign occupied stalls one, two, and three, specially reserved for them.

Three other stalls used, at this time, to be reserved for the Captain of the Body-Guard, the Exon in Waiting, and the Clerk of the Cheque.

To show that my military studies and military labours of the last twenty-eight years have not been altogether in vain, I may here append a few letters from various commanding officers and adjutants with whom I have at various times done duty.

During my English provincial tours I have for many years, thanks to the kindness of H.R.H. the Commander-in-Chief, been enabled to do duty with a number of different regular regiments, whose officers have done me, moreover, the honour of making me free of their mess. Sometimes, too, the Colonel of the regiment has been good enough to place his troops under my command. I have the pleasantest recollections of having, in the course of my various provincial tours, worked and dined with the officers of, I can scarcely say how many regiments. Here are some of the letters which, on my taking leave, I received from the commanding officers or adjutants of those corps:—

"Richmond Barracks, Dublin,
"Dec. 14, 1869.
"I certify that Lieutenant-Colonel Mapleson, 6th Tower Hamlets Rifles, has drilled regularly under my supervision from the 4th of September, 1869, until the 9th of October, 1869. During this period he went regularly through company drill, and for the last fortnight took command of the Battalion; he on joining being well up to his work and thoroughly acquainted with the theory of drill. On leaving I considered him well qualified to take command of a regiment in the field. He took the greatest interest in his work, and went in for mastering the minutiæ of drill with great perseverance.
"C. J. BURNETT,
"Captain and Adjutant 2/15 Regiment."
"Salford Barracks, Manchester,
"May 6, 1870.
"I hereby testify to the capabilities of Lieutenant-Colonel Mapleson in drill during the time I had command of the 100th Regiment at Manchester. He drilled the Battalion several times, and from the report of the Adjutant I have no hesitation in stating that few officers are superior to him in the knowledge of battalion manœuvres.
"H. COOKE,
"Major Commanding 100th Regiment."
"Gallowgate Barracks, Glasgow,

"May 26, 1870.

"I certify that Colonel J. H. Mapleson, Honble. Artillery Company, was drilling with the 2nd Battalion 5th Fusiliers, then under my command, and that he showed considerable proficiency in company and battalion drill.

"GEORGE CARDEN,
"Major 2nd Battalion 5th Fusiliers."

"Junior United Service Club,
"November 1, 1871.

"I have much pleasure in testifying as to Colonel Mapleson's thorough knowledge of the 'Field Exercise Book,' etc., etc., and I feel convinced from what I saw of him whilst attached to my regiment that he could handle it under any circumstances.

"J. CLOWES HINDS,
"Major 40th Regiment."

"Beggars' Bush Barracks, Dublin,
"January 13, 1871.

"Lieutenant-Colonel Mapleson drilled with the 1st Battalion Scots Fusilier Guards during the autumn of 1870. He was thoroughly up in company and battalion drill, more especially the latter, and is perfectly able to drill the Battalion.

"J. W. WALKER,
"Captain and Adjutant
"1st Battalion Scots Fusilier Guards."

"Glasgow, October 30, 1871.

"Lieutenant-Colonel Mapleson has during the last month frequently attended the parades of my regiment. He has both taken command of a company at battalion drill and has also manœuvred the Battalion himself, in both situations, showing a thorough knowledge of the Infantry Field Exercise.

"J. C. RATTRAY,
"Colonel Commanding 90th Light Infantry."

"Edinburgh Castle,
"May 21, 1873.

"Certified that Colonel James H. Mapleson was attached to the 93rd Highlanders for drill. I consider him able to drill a squad, company, or battalion according to the Field Exercise, and fully impart instruction therein.

"FITZROY MACPHERSON,
"Adjutant 93rd Sutherland Highlanders."

"Infantry Barracks, Windsor,
"July 7, 1873.

"This is to certify that Colonel Mapleson was attached for drill to the 1st Battalion Scots Guards during the winter months; that he is thoroughly acquainted with battalion drill, and perfectly competent to drill the Battalion either singly or in brigade.

"J. W. WALKER,
"Captain and Adjutant 1st Battalion Scots Guards."

"Edinburgh Castle, N.B.,
"April 10, 1875.

"I certify that during the stay of Colonel Mapleson at Edinburgh he attended regularly all parades of the 90th Light Infantry, and manifested thorough knowledge of company and battalion drill. He has a good 'word of command,' and nothing could exceed his zeal for military information, which he is fully in possession of.

"H. W. PALMER,

"Major Commanding 90th Light Infantry."

"Wellington Barracks,

"January 10, 1874.

"We certify that Lieutenant-Colonel Mapleson, of the Tower Hamlets Rifle Brigade, is conversant with the drill of a company and of a battalion, and able to give instruction in the same.

"That he can command a battalion in brigade.

"That he is competent to superintend instruction in aiming and position drill, and to superintend blank firing and ball practice.

"That he is acquainted with the proper mode of route marching and the duties of guards.

"Also that he can ride.

"Also that he is acquainted with the mode of posting picquets and their sentries and the duties of orderly officer.

"L. E. PHILLIPS,

"Colonel 2nd Battalion Grenadier Guards.

"E. ANTROBUS,

"Captain and Adjutant 2nd Battalion Grenadier Guards.

"Approved

"EDWARD SAXE WEIMAR,

"Major-General Commanding Home District."

Among my experiences of exercise and drill I remember an incident in connection with a Scottish regiment which, though I cannot very well narrate it in minute detail, I can say enough to make the whole story intelligible to those who have worn a kilt. At Edinburgh, in 1873, the 93rd Highlanders were one morning placed under my orders in the Queen's Park by the Commanding Officer, at that time Colonel Burroughs. The regiment was on the slope of a hill looking downwards. I gave the word to fire a volley at a distance of 500 yards, and my military readers are aware that at a distance beyond 200 yards the position for firing is the kneeling one.

A great number of persons were looking on. Suddenly an adjutant rode up to me, and pointing to the crowd exclaimed—

"For heaven's sake give the word, 'As you were!'"

Friends have often asked me how, occupied, absorbed, distracted as I must have been by the affairs of a great operatic establishment, I could nevertheless find time, leisure, and even strong inclination for military pursuits. The simple explanation is that I needed diversion from my ordinary labours, and that I found this in the active duties of a volunteer officer. Frequently at the end of a long rehearsal I have, without finding time to dine, had to put on my uniform, get on horseback, and hurry to take the command of my regiment in the Regent's or in Hyde Park. The entire change of occupation was, I am convinced, the best possible relaxation I could have. I never could have recruited my energies by simple idleness, which, besides being in my case intolerable, is apt to lead one into scrapes.

Many years ago, at the beginning of the volunteer movement, at which time I was still associated with Mr. E. T. Smith, I qualified myself for the duties of sergeant, and used to receive half-a-guinea a time from the corps for drilling recruits, who came to us, naturally under the circumstances, in the rawest condition. My reflection (not, perhaps, a particularly new one) as to the perils of idleness was forcibly illustrated when, a short time afterwards, I found myself at Walton-on-the-Naze doing duty with a battery. Anything

101

more hopelessly dull than that place when drill was once at an end, can scarcely be imagined. At last I could stand it no longer, and was obliged to devise some means of diversion, which if culpable was, I hope, original.

The people of the place told me that, though Walton was dull and desolate, there were plenty of farmers in the neighbourhood who had buxom wives and pretty daughters, and that when anything really worth seeing was going on whole families would flock in, and render the place quite lively with their presence.

What would attract them? I put the question to myself as an impresario just beginning his career, but already accustomed to consider such questions. Our artillery drill was evidently not enough. The great sensation of the moment with the British public was Blondin and his tight-rope performances.

Would Blondin fetch them? I asked myself; and, Blondin himself being out of the question, would public announcements to the effect that Blondin would appear on a certain day have the desired result?

A day or two afterwards the walls of Walton-on-the-Naze as well as Colchester were covered with placards setting forth that on a fixed day Blondin would appear and walk on the tight-rope from the end of the pier to the top of the hotel in which we were staying.

On the day appointed the sun shone brightly, and long before the time at which Blondin was expected an army of holiday folks from the surrounding country came in with as many pretty girls as one could wish to see in the somewhat similar scene of the "statute fair" in the opera of Martha.

There was no room for the carts in the stables of the place, and they had to be packed close together on the beach.

The regimental band played on the pier, and the holiday folk had, I am sure, an agreeable time. Some disappointment may have been caused when telegrams in fac-simile were posted on the walls with the information that Blondin from indisposition would be unable to appear. But this was atoned for by an announcement that in lieu of the tight-rope performance there would be a grand display of fireworks; and the pyrotechnics, which the organizers of the hoax paid for, went off most brilliantly.

At one time, moreover, I used to find solace from my managerial cares in the pursuit of politics, and, with or without justification, I nourish the hope that I did something towards securing the return of Mr. W. H. Smith for Westminster. I was an active member of his committee, both in connection with the elections which went against him and the subsequent one which brought him triumphantly in. After his second failure I remember the late Mr. Lionel Lawson saying to me—

"The thing is impossible; I would not mind giving you a written promise to pay you £10,000 if ever he gets in."

Lists were at that time in the hands of the registration committees, showing on which side each elector gave his vote. It seemed useless to interfere with those who were marked "L," as voting firmly on the Liberal side. But among the Westminster shop-keepers there were numbers who were marked "LC," who apparently did not care on which side they voted, and who generally divided their vote between a Liberal and a Conservative candidate. With these undecided men there was evidently something to be done; and I gave them to understand that, having strong Conservative sympathies, I should feel it my duty to place on my free list those of the undecided who could bring themselves to support that side.

As the ballot system had just been introduced when Mr. W. H. Smith was for the first time returned, I cannot, of course, say to what extent my advocacy and aid may have benefited him. But I hope, as before observed, that I did something towards securing his presence in Parliament.

On my arrival in London I was notified that the Royal Italian Opera, Covent Garden, Limited, had not yet been floated. But this result was daily expected. I was precluded then from taking further steps towards opening my London season of 1882, fearing that the Company might be floated just as I started, in which case I should have to close up again.

In the meantime, fire insurances, poor rates, and taxes generally kept on accumulating, and although I notified that I was ready to hand over possession of the theatre, I still could get no reply. The consequence was that I had to pay all sorts of arrears whilst an action for ejectment was brought against me for having been a few days late in paying the fire insurance. My landlord, in order to keep his superior lease straight with the Woods and Forests, had also paid it, so that the Company received the money twice over. Considerable battles hereupon commenced in the law courts with a view of ejecting me from my theatre, and it was not till late in the season that the long-expected notification came that the Company had been floated.

The consideration I was to receive consisted of a payment of £2,500 in cash and 1,000 fully paid up £10 shares in the new Company. I need hardly inform the reader that I never saw one of the shares, and could never get them; whilst all the cash that I received was consumed in paying off the arrears of ground rent of Her Majesty's Theatre, insurance, etc., whilst I was waiting for the Company to be floated.

The main object of the Gyes and of the new Royal Italian Opera, Covent Garden, Limited, was to obtain possession of the new Metropolitan Opera-house, New York, which was then approaching completion. By the terms of my agreement with the Academy of Music in New York I was prohibited from parting with or assigning my interest or any part thereof in that building during the remaining portion of my tenancy, which still had two years to run. The agreement in reference to my services for the next season at the Academy had to be drawn so as to make it appear that I had not in any way parted with my interest or any portion thereof; although by another agreement it was stipulated that I ran no pecuniary risks whatever in connection with the approaching season, simply receiving my personal expenses, my salary of £1,000 a year, and my 50 per cent. of the profits, while retaining, as hitherto, the sole direction of the whole concern.

On starting from Europe, the Royal Italian Opera Company, Limited, gave me a financial secretary to accompany me; and I was also assisted by Commander Gye as treasurer. I formed, as I considered, a most brilliant Company, which included Mdme. Adelina Patti, Mdlle. Savio, a new singer whom I had heard in Italy, Mdlle. Rossini, Mdlle. Minnie Hauk, Mdme. Fursch-Madi, Mdlle. Dotti, Mdlle. Valleria, Mdlle. Zagury, Mdme. Scalchi, Signori Mierzwinski, Ravelli, Campanini, Nicolini, Galassi, Del Puente, and Durat, a Parisian baritone of some note. I augmented the strength of the chorus, and when on the point of publishing my prospectus I found that the general manager in London had added a Mdlle. Berghi, without my knowledge, who on her appearance later on made probably the greatest fiasco ever known in America. He also, however, added his wife, Mdme. Albani, whose brilliant talents added lustre to the season. We began, therefore, in grand style, and had an enormous subscription.

The opera troupe arrived in New York early in October, and was met in the usual way by steamers and bands of music up the bay. These accompanied us to the wharf, where the party landed amidst great cheering.

Whilst on board I organized a grand opera concert, in which the whole of the principal singers and chorus took part, under the direction of Arditi, in aid of the

Liverpool Sailors' Orphanage. The saloon was elegantly decorated for the occasion, and, without exception, every passenger aided the scheme by attendance and contributions. I directed the musical arrangements, whilst the prince of American orators, the Hon. Daniel Dogherty, presided. Over £50 was realized for the charity.

It was now announced by the Royal Italian Opera Company, Limited, that on the completion of the new Metropolitan Opera-house, which Gye felt so sure of obtaining, the Academy would be closed, so that a monopoly of Italian Opera would thus be established in New York.

The papers took the idea up warmly, but in a hostile spirit; the Herald declaring in a leading article that if the Royal Italian Opera, Covent Garden, Limited, of London, ever expected to monopolize opera in America it was very much mistaken. The people in America, it stated, would heartily encourage them in all efforts to establish and maintain a first-class Opera in New York; but when they talked of repeating the London proceeding by closing up either one of the existing Opera-houses for the purpose of monopolizing the business, they might as well understand that they were proposing a scheme which the American public would readily defeat. It was contended that New York was large enough for two Italian Opera-houses, and, if the performances in both were meritorious, both would be well supported.

Of course all the attention of the public was concentrated on the expected arrival of Patti, which in due course took place. There was the usual crowd on the wharf all night awaiting the ship's arrival. I had left orders for a telegram to be sent to me as soon as the vessel passed Fire Island in order that I might be in time to dress and go down to one of the specially chartered steamers with Signor Franchi, Patti's agent, Commander Herbert Gye, and a party of artists and reporters, accompanied by military bands, fireworks, etc. The Servia was out in the middle of the stream, and we steamed up alongside, when we saw Patti, who had been up since half-past four in the morning, in feverish anxiety to reach terra firma.

Our band struck up "God Save the Queen" and everyone bared his head; the Englishmen partly from traditional reverence, but most of those present from admiration of the lyric queen who had come for another reign to the delighted people of New York. Handshaking and greetings followed.

After we had got the Patti through the Custom House she was placed in a carriage and taken to the Windsor Hotel, the room being piled up with telegrams, cards, and bouquets. There was also a large set piece with the word "Welcome!" embroidered on it in roses. In the evening there was a midnight serenade in front of the Windsor Hotel, and ultimately la Diva had to appear at the window, when orchestra and chorus, who were outside, performed the grand prayer from I Lombardi. After three hearty cheers for Adelina Patti people went home, and she was left in peace.

Mdme. Patti made her début a few days afterwards as "Lucia di Lammermoor," followed by the Traviata, etc. To describe in detail her success would be to repeat an oft-told tale.

Amongst the numberless inquiries at the box-office several were made as to how long Mdme. Patti remained on the stage in each of the different operas; and the newspapers busied themselves as to the number of notes she sang in each particular work; larger demands for seats being made on those evenings when she sang more notes. La Traviata generally carried off the palm, perhaps because one journal had calculated the interest of the money accruing on her diamonds, whilst she was singing in that work.

A party of amateurs would buy a ticket between them, each one taking 20 minutes of the ticket and returning with the pass-out check to the next. Lots were drawn to decide who was to go in first; and in the event of anyone overstaying his 20 minutes he had to pay for the whole ticket; correctness of time being the essence of the arrangement.

CHAPTER XIX.

NON-ARRIVAL OF SCALCHI—GENERAL INDISPOSITION—KING KALAKAUA ENNOBLES PATTI—RAVELLI CONSULTS HIS DOG—THE COMPANY VACCINATED—PATTI EATEN BY MICE—ARRIVAL OF ALBANI—CINCINNATI OPERA FESTIVAL OF '83—FREEDOM OF THE CITY.

I was getting very anxious about the arrival of Scalchi, who had never yet appeared in New York, and who had lately been singing in Rio Janeiro and at Buenos Ayres. It was not until the 20th November that I received notice of the sighting of her ship, the Plato, from Rio Janeiro, which at length arrived on the 24th, after a tempestuous voyage of twenty-two days. The vessel had been laden with coffee, hundreds of boxes of which had been thrown overboard to lighten it. Provisions running short, the passengers had mostly to live on biscuit and coffee, so that Mdme. Scalchi on her arrival was in a very feeble state; and in lieu of going down to the Academy to rehearsal, as I proposed, took to her bed and remained there for nearly a month. I was almost daily in attendance upon her.

Early in December I was within a very close shave of closing the theatre. The opera announced for the evening in question was William Tell. At about four o'clock I received a doctor's certificate from Mdlle. Dotti, who performed the principal female character, notifying me that she had been attacked with diphtheria. I therefore had to set about to find a substitute, having decided to give the opera anyhow. Shortly after a notification came from Mierzwinski, the tenor, who was also indisposed, though after a deal of trouble he promised to go on and do his best.

I was, however, compelled to change the opera to Lucia di Lammermoor, as the lady who had undertaken to replace the prima donna in William Tell was in such a nervous state. There was no time for a rehearsal; I therefore decided to give Lucia instead. On the notice being sent to Mdlle. Laura Zagury, the soprano, she informed me that although Lucia was in the répertoire she furnished me on her engagement she had never sung that rôle. The opera therefore had to be changed to Aida. Orders had just been given to the various departments as to the scenery, dresses, music, etc., when the news came that Mdlle. Rossini, whom I had counted upon for the principal part, was lying ill at her house in Fifth Avenue.

I now changed the opera to Rigoletto; but Mdme. Zagury was not ready with the part of "Gilda," and absolutely refused to appear. Les Huguenots was next announced, it being now half-past five. Everything was set in motion for the production of that opera, when Mdme. Fursch-Madi declared her inability to assume the part of the heroine, as she had taken some medicine, believing that her services would not be required until the early part of the following week. Thereupon an attack was made on Mdme. Savio, who, however, regretted that she was unable to appear as "Valentine."

Nothing was left but to try La Favorita; but Signor Ravelli, who had just finished a Carmen rehearsal, declared it would be utterly impossible for him to sing the rôle of "Fernando." Then Minnie Hauk was sought for; but she was saving herself for her appearance in Brooklyn on the morrow, and distinctly declined.

I now took a decision either to perform La Favorita, or to close up, as it was already 6.30 p.m. I at length persuaded Signor Clodio, one of the tenors, to assume the part of "Fernando." But a new difficulty arose, as, being a very portly gentleman, there were no costumes in the house to fit him. The tailors were then set to work, who promised to have the dress ready in time. At this juncture word came from Mdme. Galassi, who was to have taken the part of "Leonora," that she was in bed suffering, and that it would be impossible for her to appear. I immediately went off to Mdme. Galassi myself. She assured me of her willingness to do her best; but she had two large boils under her right arm which caused her acute agony. At that moment she nearly swooned from the pain. To fetch Dr. Mott, our talented theatrical surgeon, was the work of a moment. We raised her up and the boils were lanced, which at once gave her relief, and I got her down to the theatre just at five minutes to eight. She had time to dress, as "Leonora" does not appear until the second act. The performance went off successfully; I had got out of another serious difficulty after changing the opera seven times.

In the midst of my trouble a deputation arrived from Kalakaua I., King of the Sandwich Islands, informing me that they were commanded by his Majesty the King of Hawaii to confer on Mdme. Patti the Royal Order of Kapirlani. They had the diploma and jewels with them, and they were accompanied by the King's Chamberlain. I had to entreat them to wait "a moment" while I got through my troubles. That moment must have been nearly two hours.

At length we all went off to Patti's hotel, when the Order was conferred upon her in the presence of some intimate friends. The Order consisted of a jewelled star, suspended by a red and white striped ribbon, accompanied by the following parchment document:—

"Kalakaua I., King of the Hawaiian Islands, to all who shall see these presents greeting, know that we have appointed and commissioned, and by these presents we appoint and commission, Mdme. Patti to be a Knight Companion of our Royal Order of Kapirlani, to exercise and enjoy all the rights, pre-eminences, and privileges to the same of right appertaining, and to wear the insignia as by decree created.

"In testimony whereof we have caused these letters to be made patent, and the seal of the Order to be hereunto affixed.

"Given under our hand, at our palace at Honolulu, this 8th day of November, in the year of our Lord 1882.

"KALAKAUA REX.

"By the King, the Chancellor of the Royal Order of Kapirlani.

"(Signed)   CHARLES H. JUDD."

The season continued, and Lohengrin, Africaine, Huguenots and other important operas were produced. The unfortunate illness of Scalchi had long delayed me from producing Semiramide, which, however, was at length brought out on the 20th December, being the last night but two of the season. Never shall I forget the enthusiasm of the crowded and fashionable audience of that evening. Mdme. Patti's exquisite purity of intonation and her breadth of phrasing filled the large audience assembled with delight. At length Mdme. Scalchi appeared, and she at once proved herself an artist of extraordinary excellence, and a true dramatic singer, with a contralto of unusual richness, volume, and compass. The enormous success achieved by Scalchi inspired la Diva, and it was generally pronounced that her singing on this occasion was the best she had ever given in America, being, indeed, the perfection of vocal art. The whole performance was beyond criticism.

For the morning of the following Saturday, the 23rd, I announced the opera of Carmen. This was to be the closing matinée of the regular winter season, and the announcement drew one of the largest assemblages of ladies, there being very few gentlemen, to the doors of the Academy.

It was about three-quarters of an hour before the opening of the doors when Ravelli sent word that he could not sing. It was then too late to change the opera. I therefore rushed off to his hotel, leaving word that the doors were on no account to be opened until I returned.

I found him in bed. Hearing me enter he slunk under the clothes, and I could not get him to answer my questions. I approached the bed to remove the sheets, when a dog sprang out at me, Ravelli's favourite dog Niagara.

"Laissez moi dormir!" muttered the sluggard, as he turned over on the other side.

"Get up," I exclaimed; "don't you understand that you are imperilling my enterprise by lying in bed and refusing to sing when there is nothing the matter with you?"

He told me that he was very tired, that he was quite out of sorts, that his voice was not in good order, and so on.

With the aid of his wife, I succeeded in making him get up. He dressed himself. Then taking him to the piano I tried his voice, and found that there was nothing whatever the matter with it. He could sing perfectly well.

Ravelli, however, for some minutes still hesitated. In his difficulty he determined to consult Niagara. Appealing to an animal whose superior intelligence he recognized, Ravelli said in the French language—

"Est ce que ton mâître doit chanter?"

The dog growled, and Ravelli interpreted this oracular response as an order not to sing. He tore his clothes off, sprang hurriedly into bed, and left me to my own resources.

In London I had raised poor Volpini almost from the dead to make him sing the part of Faust, when but for his services I should have had to close my theatre. I had induced George Bolton (of whom I knew nothing at the time, except that he had a tenor voice, and that I had nearly run over him in a cab) to undertake literally at a moment's notice the part of "Lionel" in Martha, of which he knew nothing until I coached him, except one air. But neither a Bolton nor a Volpini was now to be found, and thanks to my lazy, superstitious, dog-ridden tenor, I had to close my theatre and send away one of the most brilliant audiences that New York could produce.

I wrote a hurried notice which was put up in manuscript just as I had scribbled it down, to the effect that in consequence of Ravelli's refusing without explanation to sing, the theatre was closed for that morning.

The excitement outside was prodigious. Everyone, of course, said that it was through my fault the doors were shut.

"It is all that Mapleson," one charming lady was heard to exclaim. "Wouldn't I scratch his face if I had him here!"

Worst of all, the "scalpers" went off with the money they had received for tickets sold outside the theatre.

Let me here explain what "scalper" means. I am afraid that in America our excellent librarians who do so much for the support of the Opera would be called "scalpers;" a scalper meaning simply one who buys tickets at the theatre to sell them at an advance elsewhere. The ferocious name bestowed upon these gentry shows, however, that their dealings are not quite so honourable as those of our "booksellers." For when they had disposed of their tickets, and the performance changed, or the theatre by some accident closed, they would walk off without any thought of restoring the money they had received for tickets now unavailable. At times, too, I have caught them exhibiting a gallery diagram, and selling gallery places as orchestra stalls. They are now obliged, by a just law, to take out licenses, and register their places of abode. Nor do managers allow any one of them to buy more than four tickets for each representation.

Meanwhile the New York fall season of 1882 finished up grandly with Semiramide, the receipts reaching 14,000 dollars, and the public mad with enthusiasm.

I afterwards started with the Company for Baltimore, where we opened with rather less than our usual success, on account of the small-pox which was raging all over the city. Very few notices were given of the opera in consequence of three and four columns a day being occupied with the crusade undertaken against the small-pox by Mayor White, who had telegraphed for a large number of vaccination physicians from various States, determined as he was to stamp out the disease.

The whole of the twenty wards of the city had been placed under properly constituted medical authorities, and there everyone had to be vaccinated, including the whole of my Company. Prima donnas had to be vaccinated on the legs, whilst ballet-girls were vaccinated on the arms; in fact the theatre at one time became quite a hospital.

However, we managed to get through our engagement with success, though Mdme. Patti remained over at Philadelphia, being afraid to enter the city of Baltimore.

The production of L'Africaine, which was new to Baltimore, was a marked success. On terminating our engagement we went over to Philadelphia, where Patti made a splendid opening in La Traviata, the vast theatre being crowded from floor to ceiling.

The next night we produced Aida, the Directors of the Academy of Music having caused to be painted specially for the occasion some of the most gorgeous Egyptian scenery I have ever seen.

At five o'clock Mdme. Scalchi sent me word that she was very ill, and unable to sing. I thereupon went for the physician, whom I conducted forthwith to her hotel. On our arriving at the door of her apartment I saw a waiter going in with some lobsters, salad, and roast duck. I immediately asked for whom he was catering, and he replied: "Mdme. Scalchi." I waited a few minutes in order to give her time to begin operations on the duck and the lobsters; and she was recounting some amusing story which ended in loud laughter, when I took this as my cue for entering.

Mdme. Scalchi could no longer plead indisposition, and in due time she came to the theatre.

Aida was a great success. At two o'clock the following afternoon we performed Lucia with Adelina Patti to a house containing over 14,000 dollars. In the evening we gave L'Africaine, magnificently placed on the vast stage, to receipts not far inferior to those of the morning.

Prior to the close of our very successful engagement sad alarm was created all over the city by a report in some of the leading morning papers that Mdme. Patti the preceding night had been devoured by mice. Several persons had already applied at the box office for the return of their money on the ground that la Diva had ceased to breathe.

On inquiry it turned out that Mdme. Patti had been bitten by a mouse on the left ear. I had better tell the story in the Diva's own words, as given to the reporter of the Philadelphia Press.

"'So you were bitten by rats last evening?' the reporter said.

"'Oh, no, it was not so bad as that,' replied Patti, laughing heartily as she recalled the adventure. 'I hardly, however, like to mention it at all, for I am really so comfortable in this hotel. They do all they can to please me. When I went to bed last evening my maid turned the clothes over for me to get in, when out jumped six mice—a complete family, in fact; nice fat little fellows. I was not frightened; at least, I was only astonished. I took my bon-bon box and scattered some sweetmeats on the carpet so that the tiny intruders should have some supper, and I went to sleep without any apprehension. In the middle of the night, however, something disagreeable occurred, and I was awakened by a sharp pain in my ear. I put my hand to my head when a mouse jumped to the floor, and I felt blood trickling on the side of my cheek. I got up and called my maid, and examination showed a bite on my left ear. It bled a good deal, and to-day my ear is much swollen. I shall not put any bon-bons down to-night,' continued Mdme. Patti, 'and when I sleep in the day time I shall place my maid to act as sentry.'"

The reporter, feeling that he had passed one of the most delightful quarters of an hour in his life, now left the apartment.

When the news got about that Patti had been bitten by a mouse, enterprising makers and patentees of mousetraps approached her from all sides with specimens of their various mouse-catching contrivances. Some of these were very curious. One was prompt and severe in its action, despatching the mouse at the moment of capture by a single cutting blow. Another was apparently the work of some member of the Society for the Prevention of Cruelty to Animals. Far from killing the mouse, it provided the little creature with a wheel, which, as long as it was allowed to live, it could amuse itself by turning.

About this time two "sensations" occurred. One was connected with Commander Gye, who was leaving the city at an early hour, when he was robbed of his black leather travelling-bag, containing money, pins, rings, Roman coins, cigarette boxes, a cheque book, a cheque for 4,400 dollars, which I had signed for Mdme. Patti's previous night's salary, with other documents of less value, including Nilsson's broken contract.

The reports of this robbery, as usual, were considerably enlarged, and it afterwards got into circulation that amongst the things lost were Mdme. Albani's jewels, worth several thousands of pounds. This cost Captain Gye a deal of inconvenience, for it brought down the Inland Revenue authorities on him. He was accused of having smuggled in the diamonds from abroad, and some considerable time passed before all the excitement subsided.

The other "sensation" was the invasion of the basso Monti's room while he was in bed and the theft of 400 dollars worth of jewellery belonging to him. This, too, caused a deal of talk in the papers.

Our last night was, indeed, a gala night. The most brilliant audience of the whole season filled every corner of the theatre, so great was the curiosity of the public to see Mdme. Patti and Mdme. Scalchi together in the same opera. About five o'clock the crowd outside the Academy was already immense, and it was not until seven that we opened the doors.

The rush was great, and a sad incident now took place. A lady in the crowd who had purchased her ticket beforehand was taken up from the bottom of the staircase to the top, though she died before reaching the first landing from disease of the heart, rendered fatal by the excitement. Borne upwards by the dense crowd she did not fall till she reached the gallery. Fearing the alarm this occurrence might cause, the servants, in order that I should not hear of it, had placed the lady on the floor of a little top private box, where she remained during the whole of the performance; her body not being removed by her friends until the next morning.

After leaving Philadelphia we visited Chicago, where the advance sale of seats prior to our opening reached the enormous sum of 16,000 dollars.

On the evening of our arrival I received a telegram from Mdme. Albani stating that she would arrive early the following morning. I met her at the station. She was accompanied by her husband, Mr. Ernest Gye, and his brother, Commander Gye. She had just returned from some concerts which I had arranged in Albany and in New York, where she had met with the most enthusiastic reception.

She appeared on the fifth evening of my first week in I Puritani, when the cold weather did not deter the holders of tickets from claiming their places in the theatre. At an early hour, and long before the curtain ran up for the first act, there was absolutely not a vacant spot in the theatre. Albani was welcomed with an enthusiasm that even Patti might have been proud of. She was queen in the hearts of all who were present that evening.

On leaving Chicago we went to St. Louis, where our triumphs were again repeated; Mdme. Albani, Mdme. Patti, and Scalchi all contributing to the immense success.

About this time several of my songbirds began to take cold, the weather having suddenly changed. Mdme. Patti had to remain at home, Mdme. Scalchi took to her bed, as also did Mdme. Fursch-Madi and Mdme. Albani. The duty, therefore, of singing fell to Mdlle. Dotti, who for three nights in succession sustained the prima donna duties, giving much satisfaction under the circumstances.

Patti, however, was able to resume work the following night in La Traviata; Mdme. Albani singing "Lohengrin" at the morning performance of the next day, whilst Mdlle. Dotti closed the season by singing "Margherita" in Faust the same evening.

I was naturally very anxious about my singers. We had to leave by special train at one o'clock in the morning in order to reach Cincinnati; and as it was now some 40 degrees below freezing point, I left the ballet, chorus, and orchestra to sleep in the railway carriages, which were shunted up a siding. Those who went to the hotel had the greatest difficulty in reaching it.

On ascertaining that nearly every place had been sold for the whole of the Festival week, I entered at once into arrangements for giving two additional nights in the succeeding week, on which I arranged that Patti should sing "Aida" and Albani "Margherita" in Faust.

The first performance at the great Festival was La Traviata, followed by L'Africaine, magnificently placed upon the stage. On the Wednesday afternoon Mdme. Albani appeared as "Amina" in La Sonnambula, and in the evening William Tell was given, with Mierzwinski, Galassi, and Dotti. This drew the largest number of people of any night during the week, the great choruses of the Gathering of the Cantons eliciting the loudest expressions of admiration. On the Thursday evening we performed Rossini's Semiramide, Patti and Scalchi surpassing themselves. On the following evening Wagner's Flying Dutchman was produced, with Ravelli, Galassi, and Albani. The next morning came Don Giovanni; with Fursch-Madi as "Donna Anna;" Dotti as "Elvira;" and Patti as "Zerlina." The first week was brought to a fitting close by a splendid performance of Lohengrin; Mierzwinski performing the "Knight of the Swan;" Galassi, "Telramund;" Monti, the "King;" Scalchi, "Ortruda;" and Albani, "Elsa."

This Festival, without going into details, surpassed the two preceding ones.

Everyone, I believe, made money. All the spring fashions were introduced in the leading stores of the city, whilst visitors came in from many hundreds of miles. The hotels were crowded, and people were sleeping even in the corridors. The railways were making money, and the cabmen making fortunes, from the high charges they taxed the public with.

The Music Hall was nightly crowded to its utmost limit, there being never less than 7,000 people present; and one representation surpassed the other till all ended in one great excitement. The newspapers in the city were taken up almost exclusively with the Festival. Nothing was thought of but the Festival, and all business appeared to be suspended. The toilettes of the ladies were something to be remembered.

On February 18, 1882, prior to my leaving Cincinnati, a meeting was held at the Mayor's Office, when my attendance was requested. To my astonishment and delight the highest possible compliment was now paid me; for I was presented with the freedom of the city, which was given to me in a valuable casket, Mayor Means explaining that since the history of the city no similar compliment had been paid even to one of their own citizens, much less to an Englishman. This was followed by a grand banquet at the Club, where, amongst others, I had the honour of making the acquaintance of Mr. Reuben Springer, the donor of the magnificent hall in which the Festival had been held.

I omitted, however, to mention that my friend Abbey was determined, if possible, to injure this Festival, for which purpose he brought Madame Nilsson into the town, and kept her there during the whole of the week, with a Company of artists, who sang at some small theatre. I need hardly say that no harm whatever was done to the receipts, which totalled up to 40,000 dollars more than any of the preceding Festivals had brought.

CHAPTER XX.

GALASSI DISTINGUISHES HIMSELF—POLITENESS OF PRIME
DONNE—ENGLISH WELCOME IN CANADA—CONCERT AT THE WHITE
HOUSE—VALUE OF PATTI'S NOTES—PHANTOM SHIP WRECKED—
NILSSON'S CONTRACT—PATTI'S CONTRACT—RETURN TO ENGLAND.

THE Company now left for Detroit. Our season opened with Albani as "Lucia;" and for the following night Semiramide was announced, with Adelina Patti and Scalchi. Unfortunately Mdme. Patti had taken cold, and was unable to sing. It appeared that on arriving at the station she had had to walk through piles of snow for some distance in order to reach her carriage.

At one time the public threatened to demolish the building, so disappointed were they; especially as Mdme. Patti had also failed to appear in that same city the previous year.

It was at once put down (as these things generally are) to caprice on the part of the prima donna, or a trick on that of the operatic manager. I, therefore, at once sought Dr. Brodie, an eminent physician of Detroit, and he furnished a certificate as to the Diva' illness.

Despite the change of the bill, a good-sized audience remained for Verdi's tragic opera of Il Trovatore.

On the closing night we performed Guillaume Tell, in which Signor Galassi particularly distinguished himself. According to one of the journals, which appeared the following morning, so dexterously did he shoot the apple off his son's head that he might always be sure of a warm welcome whenever he returned to that city.

Rival prime donne—those, at least, who have the habits of polite society—are very particular in calling on one another, though these visits are sometimes of a highly formal kind. During my American season of 1883 I was associated with Mr. Gye; and it so happened that Nicolini and Patti, Ernest Gye and Albani (Mrs. Ernest Gye) were staying at Detroit in the same hotel where I also had put up. Patti and Nicolini having just gone for a drive, Madame Albani, seeing them pass beneath her window, called out to her husband—

"Ernest, they have gone out. We had better leave cards on them at once."

On returning home Madame Patti duly received the cards; and an hour or two afterwards, when Albani and Mr. Gye had just gone to the theatre, where there was to be a rehearsal, said to Nicolini—

"Ernest" (his name, also, was Ernest), "they have gone to the theatre. Now is the time for returning their visit."

As Madame Patti was still suffering from a very severe cold, I thought it prudent to leave her behind at Detroit, for the purpose not only of re-establishing herself, but of assuring the public that she was really ill. She remained there some four or five days after we had left.

The whole Company, except Madame Patti, had to muster at the station about 2 a.m. to start for Canada. By some mismanagement on the part of the railway company, there being two competing lines, with but one set of rails running into the joint station, the artists were kept waiting at this station for over a couple of hours, the wind bitterly cold, and the thermometer some fifty degrees below freezing point. At length, to the joy of all, our special was drawn up alongside the platform, and we were enabled to make a start, arriving at Toronto the following afternoon.

The next morning the musicians all came to me in great despair, the Canadian Custom House authorities having seized the whole of their instruments as liable to duty. The same difficulty occurred with the wardrobes and properties; and it was not until very late in the day, by going through a course of red-tape, which reminded one of the old country, that they could be released, I giving an undertaking that the troupe should leave Canada within two days.

A right royal English welcome did our Company receive there. Prior to the performance I requested Arditi to play the National Anthem. The whole of the audience stood up, and, on its conclusion, gave three hearty cheers. Nearly all the private box, dress circle, and stall ticket-holders arrived in open sleighs, the snow being very thick.

The opening performance was Il Trovatore, in which Mierzwinski, Galassi, Scalchi, and Fursch-Madi appeared, giving great satisfaction. The excellence of the representation was quite a revelation to the public, as it were.

On the following night Madame Albani appeared as "Lucia," when the parquette, balconies, and boxes were crowded with the élite of the city, the Lieutenant-Governor occupying the gubernatorial box.

The galleries were likewise crowded to their fullest capacity, standing room even being at a premium. Albani was welcomed with vociferous cheers, and her performance throughout received the warmest approbation.

Immediately after the conclusion of our grand two-night season in Canada our special train was put in motion towards Buffalo, where we performed the following evening, leaving again after the performance at 2 a.m. for Pittsburg, at which place Mdme. Patti had arrived the previous day.

At Pittsburg the season opened most auspiciously with La Traviata. The theatre itself was not only crowded to the ceiling, but we charged five dollars a head for standing room on the window sills.

The following night Mdme. Albani appeared as "Margherita" in Faust, supported by Ravelli, Scalchi, etc.

A matinée was given the next day of Il Trovatore, followed by a splendid performance the same evening of William Tell. On each occasion the house was crammed.

The Company had again to muster at 2 a.m. after the performance to start for Washington, at which place we arrived the following evening, Mdme. Albani opening the next day as "Margherita" in Faust.

The next evening I had to change the performance, la Diva having contracted a sore throat during the journey. I substituted William Tell, postponing Mdme. Patti's début until the following night, when she and Scalchi captivated the audience with Semiramide. In a letter to the papers the following morning a mathematician stated that by carefully counting the notes in the part of Semiramide, and dividing the result by the sum paid nightly to Patti for singing that part, he discovered that she received exactly 42 5/8 cents for each of the notes that issued from her throat. This was found to be just 7 1/10 cents per note more than Rossini got for writing the whole opera.

On the following Friday President Arthur gave a private concert at the White House. I here append the programme:—

PART I.
Duetto—"Sull'aria" (Nozze di Figaro)   Mozart.
Mdme. Fursch-Madi and Mdlle. Dotti.
Romanza—"Angelo Casto" (Duca d'Alba) posthumous opera by Donizetti.
Signor Frapolli.
Cavatina—Tacca la notte (Trovatore)   Verdi.
Mdme. Fursch-Madi.
Aria Buffa—Miei rampolli (Cenerentola) Rossini.
Signor Corsini.
Air—Voi che sapete (Nozze di Figaro)   Mozart.
Mdlle. Dotti.

———

An Interval of Half an Hour.

———

PART II.
Trio—Qual Volutta (Lombardi)   Verdi.
Mdme. Fursch-Madi, Signor Frapolli, and Signor Galassi.
Cavatina—"Nobil Signor" (Huguenots) Meyerbeer.
Mdme. Scalchi.
Romanza—O tu bel astro (Tannhäuser) Wagner.
Signor Galassi.
a{Air—"Pur dicesti" Lotti.
b{Song—"Robin Adair"   ———
Madame Albani.
The White House.
February 28, 1883.

At the conclusion of the concert a splendid supper was served in the banqueting hall. As I had to attend upon no less than five ladies, the President observed at the close of the feast that I had had nothing to eat myself. He, therefore, gave orders that on the departure of the guests another supper should be served, at which he occupied the chair. The repast was really of the first order. It was interspersed with excellent Veuve Clicquot, and the President afterwards ordered in cigars and related to me some most interesting anecdotes of his earlier career. He also gave me an account of the alarm felt at New York when one Sunday the Merrimac was expected to come up the bay in order to levy contributions on the city; there being no powder in the forts and but few cannon balls, all of the wrong calibre. Fortunately she met the Monitor, who soon gave a good account of her.

We gave a grand matinée the following day, with Patti as "La Traviata," when people paid even for standing in the passages, where they could only occasionally hear sounds.

113

At the close of the morning performance our special train started for Boston, where we arrived late the next day.

Here further calculations were made in the daily papers as to the value of Patti's notes, Semiramide showing 30 cents. for every note she sang, whilst in "Lucia" the rate of 42 1/2 cents. per note was reached.

We afterwards performed Faust with Albani, and some of the grand operas, such as L'Africaine, Les Huguenots, Lohengrin, and Aida. Towards the close of our engagement Wagner's Flying Dutchman was given for the first time on the Italian stage at Boston.

A rather startling event occurred during the first act on the arrival of the Phantom Ship, which, after sweeping gracefully round, broadside to the audience, suddenly capsized, casting the Dutchman and his crew promiscuously on to the stage, the masts going straight across the occupants of the stalls and the sails covering Arditi, who was then at the desk.

At this juncture loud screams were heard. They came from the wife of the principal baritone, who, witnessing the accident, had fears for her husband's safety. The choristers, who were thrown pell-mell into the water, and on to their stomachs, began with a great deal of tact to strike out as if swimming, until—as soon as possible—the curtain was lowered. The ship was soon set on its keel again, but nothing could induce Galassi to board the vessel.

At the close of the Boston engagement, which was highly successful, we returned to New York, where we remained some five weeks, performing a different opera almost nightly.

About this time I learned that the Washington and Lee University for promoting higher education in the South was in great need of funds. I, therefore, notified General Lilly, of Virginia, who had been interested in that institution for years, my willingness to assist by giving a miscellaneous performance for that purpose. A committee of distinguished ladies was formed to superintend the distribution of the tickets, including Mrs. General Dix, Mrs. Franklin Edson, Mrs. August Belmont, Mrs. G. Rives, Mrs. Livingstone, Mrs. Jay, Mrs. Pierre Lorillard, Mrs. Frederick Kernochan, Mrs. Henry Clewes, Mrs. Pryor, Mrs. General Hancock, Mrs. Barton French, Mrs. W. C. Whitney, Mrs. Vanderbilt, Baroness de Thomsen, Mrs. Bowdoin, Mrs. Alonzo B. Cornell, Mrs. Benjamin Willis, Mrs. F. B. Thurber, etc., etc.

The appearance of the Academy, on this occasion filled by a most brilliant audience, was a thing long to be remembered. The evening commenced with an act of Trovatore, which was followed by the appearance of Mdme. Albani in the first act of Norma. A more beautiful rendering of the lovely cavatina "Casta Diva" could not have been heard, Mdme. Albani's vocalization being really the perfection of art. She was recalled several times, and covered with flowers. An act from Meyerbeer's Dinorah came next, with Mdme. Patti and Scalchi. Both left the stage loaded with flowers, Patti coming forward at the close and afterwards good-naturedly singing in front of the drop curtain "Home, Sweet Home."

A scene then followed not put down in the programme, in the shape of a presentation to myself of two large and handsome silk flags, one English and the other American, the gift of the ladies of the committee; each of the white stars on the blue ground of the American flag having been inserted by a member of this committee.

I thanked the ladies in a grateful speech, shouldered my lofty flags, and left the stage amidst loud cheering. The receipts amounted to some £1,800. About a fortnight afterwards I was informed by General Lilley that a chair of English literature had been established at the University bearing my name.

The following Saturday morning La Traviata was again given, the house being even more crowded than usual. The bank having closed prior to the termination of the performance, the monies were all placed in the iron safe.

Early the following morning I was informed that one of the doors leading to the treasury had been forced open, the floor of which was strewn with tickets and furniture. Worse still, the iron safe had been opened and rifled of its contents; over 21,500 dollars having been carried off. Fortunately this amount was for the most part in cheques, which I succeeded in stopping at the bank; but the loss in hard cash exceeded £1,600.

About this time further rumours were in circulation as to Mr. Abbey trying to take away several of my best singers, notably both Patti and Galassi.

During the New York season I sent Mdme. Albani to sing in a concert at Montreal, the railway directors providing a special car for her. On her arrival she was received by the Mayor and Aldermen of the city; also by a guard of honour of 200 men in uniform, besides the members of four snow-shoe clubs in their beautiful and picturesque costumes.

A reception was afterwards held at the Hôtel de Ville, when a formal address was handed to Mdme. Albani on a beautifully illuminated scroll. All the tickets being instantly sold out, two more concerts had to be given; and Mdme. Albani returned to New York in time to sing the following Friday, having netted for the treasury 16,000 dollars by her three days' visit to Montreal.

Shortly afterwards I gave a combined performance for the benefit of the New York Exchange for Woman's Work. Again I had a ladies' committee to work with, including the charming Mrs. F. B. Thurber, who acted as secretary, the president being Mrs. W. G. Choate, while the vice-presidents consisted of some forty leading ladies of New York. The entertainment consisted of a concert in which Mdme. Adelina Patti, Mdme. Albani, Mdme. Scalchi, Nicolini, and others of the Company appeared.

I append the programme, in which will be found several features of interest, including, in particular, the singing of Mozart's delightful duet by Patti and Albani.

PART I.
Overture—"Egmont" Beethoven
Orchestra.
Romanza—"O lieti, di" (Etoile du Nord)   Meyerbeer
Monsieur Durat.
Aria—"Nobil Signor" (Huguenots)   Meyerbeer
Madame Scalchi.
Ballade et Polonaise   Vieuxtemps
Herr Brandt.
Cavatina—"Qui la voce" (Puritani)   Bellini
Madame Albani.
Romanza—"Vien, vien m'e noto" (Velleda)   Lenepreu
Signor Nicolini.
Valse—"Nell' ebrezza" (Romeo e Giulietta)   Gounod
Madame Adelina Patti.
Ballet, Silvia Delibes
Orchestra.

PART II.
L'invitation a la Valse Weber
Orchestra.

Ballade—"Ouvre ta porte"   Grieg
Signor Ravelli.
Hungarian Fantaisie   Liszt
(With orchestra)
Herr Rafael Joseffy.
Duetto, "Sull aria" (Nozze di Figaro)   Mozart
Madame Adelina Patti and Madame Albani.
Gavotte—"In veder l'amata stanza" (Mignon)   Thomas
Madame Scalchi.
Romanza—"M'appari" (Martha)   Flotow
Signor Ravelli.
Rakoczy March   Berlioz
Orchestra.

After the concert the ladies presented me on the stage with a magnificent gold badge, bearing the English arms on one side, surmounted with diamonds and rubies, and the American arms on the other; also an elegant walking cane with a massive gold top, crowned by a very large uncut sapphire of great value.

The next morning Mr. Gye came to me with the alarming intelligence that the lease of the new Metropolitan Opera-house had been given to Mr. Abbey. He complained bitterly of the treatment he had received at the hands of its Directors after the trouble he had taken in furnishing them with the interior plans and workings of Covent Garden Theatre, in order to assist the architect to get as complete a building as possible. He had been negotiating with the Directors on behalf of the Royal Italian Opera Company, Covent Garden, Limited, and, in fact, those negotiations had never been broken off. He was still awaiting an answer from the Committee, to whom the matter had been referred.

Mr. Abbey having announced that he would open the New Metropolitan Opera-house with Madame Nilsson, Mr. Gye informed me that she was under contract to sing with our Company, and showed me the following engagement:—

"London, 2nd May, 1882.
"Madame Christine Nilsson agrees to accept an engagement with Mr. Gye to sing either for him or for the Royal Italian Opera Company, Limited, in London, during the season of 1883, at a salary of £200 per night. Madame Nilsson also agrees to accept an engagement for America for the season of 1883-1884, for fifty or sixty representations, operas, concerts, or oratorios, at a salary of £300 per night, this to include all hotel expenses, but not travelling. Madame Nilsson agrees also to sing for five or six nights at Covent Garden during next July, the répertoire for Madame Nilsson being Mignon, Lohengrin, Don Giovanni, Mefistofele, and Faust if possible, which Mr. Gye agrees to do his best to obtain for her in London, 1883, and in America, her répertoire to be the same, and other operas by common consent. No opera is to belong to Madame Nilsson exclusively, except one opera that she may create, and that for one season. Should Madame Nilsson wish to remain in America in the summer of 1884 she is to be at liberty to do so, and should she wish to return to England, Mr. Gye engages himself for her to sing in London during the London season on the same conditions. Mr. Gye binds himself to accept the engagement now in preparation.
"(Signed)   CHRISTINE NILSSON ROUZAUD."
Despite this, however, Madame Nilsson signed with Mr. Abbey, receiving a sum considerably in excess of the one stipulated for in the Gye engagement.

116

In the meantime further rumours were getting circulated with regard to Mr. Abbey's razzia on my singers, and the daily papers were full of our disputes and recriminations; with which I will not trouble the reader just now. On the conclusion of our New York season we again returned to Philadelphia, in consequence of the success of our previous visit, opening there with the Flying Dutchman. The next night l'Etoile du Nord was performed with the peerless Adelina, followed by Lohengrin with the charming "Elsa" of Albani. Thus we continued our triumphant career.

Mr. Abbey had begun his intrigues with Campanini, to whom he offered 1,000 dollars (£200) a night. He now proposed a similar amount to Scalchi and a considerable sum to Valleria, whilst his employés were hard at work round the stage-door taking away my choruses, wardrobe keepers, and even the stage-manager. All my people, in short, were offered three or four times their usual salaries, merely for the sake of injuring me, without Mr. Abbey's benefiting himself in any way. I described him, to an interviewer, as a guastomestiere; a word which sorely puzzled him, and caused him to consult his solicitor.

I now endeavoured to make sure of Patti, and she eventually consented to make a small reduction in her terms and to accept 4,000 dollars a night.

In due course her contract had been prepared by her agent and a day fixed for executing it, which happened to be a Thursday. Being much occupied that day at the theatre in consequence of troubles of various sorts I found it too late to get up to Mdme. Patti's hotel, but went the following morning early. Nicolini explained to me that Mdme. Patti never did anything on a Friday, and that I had better call the next day. The day afterwards he informed me that, soon after I had left, Mr. Abbey had come to Mdme. Patti saying that he could offer her a minimum of 5,000 dollars (£1,000) a night, payment to be made on the morning of each performance, and 50,000 deposited in the bank as payment for the last ten nights of the engagement, and that Mr. W. H. Vanderbilt would sign the contract and give her the requisite guarantees.

This was not the only inducement he offered her if she would link her fortunes with the new Metropolitan Opera-house the following season. She was further to have a special private drawing-room and sleeping car, the like of which had never yet been run on rails, to be specially built for her, fitted with a conservatory, fernery, &c.

There was no reason, however, why these propositions should interfere with the formal acceptance of a contract already drawn up and verbally agreed to. The next day, then, about 11 o'clock, I was going in joyously to sign my contract when I was met by Signor Nicolini at the door, who told me that a very dreadful thing had happened since he last saw me. On my inquiring what it was he informed me that Mr. Abbey's visit had quite upset Mdme. Patti, who was ill in her room. She had not even spoken to the parrot, which was a sad sign. He then communicated to me Mr. Abbey's proposition, as above.

Nicolini, however, assured me that Mdme. Patti held me in the highest esteem, and would on no account throw me over, considering that my engagement with her would be just as good as Mr. Vanderbilt's. If I would call later in the day, after luncheon, he hoped to get the matter concluded. He, at the same time, gave me to understand that no reduction could be made in the terms which had been offered by Vanderbilt through Abbey.

On leaving I at once consulted with Mr. Gye, the General Manager of the Royal Italian Opera Company, Covent Garden, Limited, and he fully agreed with me that there was no alternative but to accede to the terms, the sum demanded being but a trifle more than Patti had been receiving throughout the season then about to close. Gye telegraphed the particulars to his London Directors.

117

I accordingly went round in the afternoon and signed the contract. The visit of Mr. Abbey to Mdme. Patti on the previous day had meanwhile caused a rise of no less than 50,000 dollars (£10,000) in her demands.

Next day Mdme. Patti sailed for Europe on the Arizona, Signor Franchi, her agent, remaining behind to complete the details of the new engagement.

About this time Mdme. Cavalazzi, my daughter-in-law, informed me that she had had an offer from Abbey's agent of double the amount I was paying her. I at once told her to accept it, and that I would keep her place open for her, when she could return the following season, by which time Abbey would be closed up. The following season she duly returned, Mr. Abbey, as I shall afterwards relate, having duly come to grief.

Prior to my departure I was entertained by a number of my friends and supporters at the Manhattan Club. The dinner was arranged partly as a farewell to me and partly in acknowledgment of the aid I had given to young American artists essaying an operatic career. Judge J. R. Brady presided, and the company included the Mayor Edson, the Reverend Dr. Hoffman, Recorder Smyth, Judge Abraham R. Lawrence, Chief Justice Noah Davis, Judge W. H. Arnoux, the British Consul General Booker, Chief Justice C. P. Daly, General de Cesnola, Chief Justice Shea, General Stewart L. Woodford, General Hancock, Commissioner J. S. Coleman, Mr. John H. Starin, Mr. F. B. Thurber, Mr. Aaron Vanderpoel, Professor Henry Drisler, Mr. Wm. Steinway, the Reverend Professor Seabury, Professor A. Charlier, Mr. Oscar S. Strauss, and many others.

On the removal of the cloth Judge Brady gave the toast, "The guest of the evening," to which I replied. Other toasts followed, and the entertainment passed off merrily enough. Signor Clodio, Signor Ravelli, and Signor Ronconi came in with the cigars, and pleasantly varied the latter portion of the evening by a choice selection of operatic arias.

At the close of the entertainment it was unanimously resolved to charter a special steamer to accompany me the following morning down the bay conveying those who were present at the dinner. Mr. Starin, who was sitting at the table, offered to place one of his magnificent steamers at their disposal, which was to leave Pier 41, North River, at a quarter to nine the following morning. After singing "Auld Lang Syne" and "He's a jolly good fellow" the company separated. Just prior to my departure the following morning my friends appeared on the chartered steamer, which followed us down the bay with a band of music, accompanied by hearty cheers until we were out of sight.

END OF VOL. I.

CHAPTER I

MY CONNECTION SEVERED—MUSICAL PROTECTION UNION— AMERICAN ORCHESTRAS—RIVAL OPERA-HOUSES—OPERATIC TRIAL BY JURY—ST. CECILIA'S DAY—THE FEAST OF FATHER FLATTERY.

SHORTLY after my return to London I had various meetings with the Directors of the Royal Italian Opera Company, Limited, when, to my astonishment, they informed me they would not ratify the contract I had made with Mdme. Patti. In fact, they repudiated the engagement altogether, although it had been concluded by me conjointly with Mr.

Ernest Gye, the General Manager of the Company. I was therefore left with about £15,000 worth of authorized contracts which the Company had made with other artists, in addition to Mdme. Patti's contract for 250,000 dollars (£50,000).

I represented to the Directors that the only way to get out of the difficulty was to release me entirely from all connection with the Company, as I could then carry out the contracts I had made in the name of myself and of their representative with Mdme. Patti and with several other artists.

The matter, however, ended by the Directors giving me my congé, refusing at the same time to pay me any of the money that was then owing to me.

I had now seriously to consider my position, which was this: I had parted with my lease of Her Majesty's Theatre to the Royal Italian Opera Company, Ltd., a lease for which I had paid Lord Dudley £30,000. I had parted with a large quantity of scenery and dresses, of which a full inventory was attached to my agreement, and which were valued at many thousands of pounds. In addition to this, during my absence in America, Her Majesty's Theatre had been entirely dismantled and many thousand pounds worth of property not in the inventory taken and removed to Covent Garden. The amount of salary owing to me was absolutely refused. My £10,000 worth of shares (being the consideration for the purchase) I could not obtain; and the Company further gave me notice that I owed them some £10,000 for losses incurred whilst in America.

In fact, all I had left to me was my liability for the £50,000 payable to Mdme. Patti, and for over £15,000 on the authorized contracts made with other artists on behalf of the Company; whilst on the other side of the ocean I should have to face Abbey's new Metropolitan Opera-house, for which all the seats had been sold, and the following artists engaged—all with but one or two exceptions taken from me:—Mdme. Christine Nilsson, Mdlle. Valleria, Mdme. Sembrich, Mdme. Scalchi, Mdme. Trebelli, Signor Campanini, etc., etc. My scene painter had been tampered with and taken away, together with many of the leading orchestral performers and the chorus—indeed, the whole Company, even to the call-boy.

[FROM THE Times OF NEW YORK, JULY 4, 1883.]

"MR. MAPLESON'S PARTNERS.

"HIS TROUBLE WITH THE ROYAL ITALIAN OPERA COMPANY.

"THE ACADEMY STOCKHOLDERS PREPARING FOR HIM, HOWEVER, AND CONFIDENT OF A BRILLIANT SEASON.

"Every mail from England brings papers containing some discussion of the trouble in the operatic camp; and it is evident that a serious misunderstanding has arisen between the Royal Italian Opera Company (Limited)—principally Mr. Gye—and Col. Mapleson. The substance of this misunderstanding appears to be that Mr. Gye and his Company have decided to repudiate certain contracts made by Col. Mapleson as their accredited agent. The principal trouble is in regard to the contract by which the Colonel agrees to pay Mdme. Patti 5,000 dollars per night. It will be readily remembered by readers of the Times that a great struggle took place at the close of last season between Mr. Abbey and Col. Mapleson for the possession of the great singer's services. For a long time it was impossible to tell to which house she was going, and public curiosity was aroused to such an extent that everyone felt like addressing her in the language of Ancient Pistol: 'Under which King, Bezonian? Speak, or die!' Mr. Abbey offered her more money than any singer had ever before received, whereupon Mr. Mapleson, knowing that he must have Patti to fight the strong attraction of a new Opera-house, saw Mr. Abbey and went him a few hundreds better. Then Mr. Abbey threw down his hand and Mr. Mapleson gathered in the prima donna. It will also be remembered that subsequently the stockholders of the

Academy met in secret conclave and generously voted to support the manager who established Italian Opera in this country as a permanent source of amusement and art-cultivation by assessing themselves. They decided to raise a subsidy of 40,000 dollars to guarantee the Patti contract and secure the coming season at the Academy. Mdme. Patti subsequently ratified the contract made by Signor Franchi, her agent, with Col. Mapleson, and the Colonel wrote to the stockholders here thanking them for their generous support, and saying that he would return their kindness by bringing to America next Fall a Company of superior strength. An early evidence of the earnestness of his purpose was the engagement of Mdme. Gerster, an artist who is a firm favourite with this public, and whose great merits are unquestionable. Mr. Gye was in this city, it will also be remembered, during the latter part of last season, and was fully aware of Mr. Mapleson's movement. Therefore the stockholders of the Academy have learned with surprise, not to say disgust, the action of the Royal Italian Opera Company (Limited). It has transpired that the principal cause of dissatisfaction was a belief that there could be little or no profit in an American Opera season with Patti at 5,000 dollars per night. The Times, in an article published just after the close of the last season, showed that Col. Mapleson had been unfortunate. While the good people of the West, who are popularly supposed to possess but a tithe of the culture that animates the East, flocked to the Opera as if they really knew that they were not likely, as the Boston Theatre stage carpenter expressed it, to hear any better singing than that of Patti and Scalchi this side of heaven, the people of New York and Philadelphia failed to regard the entertainment in the same light. The result was serious for Col. Mapleson, and he left this country financially embarrassed. The Royal Italian Opera Company (Limited) knew this, and decided that it did not care to embark in another American season, especially with increased salaries and an opposition of respectable strength. The London World, in a long article on the condition of these operatic affairs, has said that another cause of dissatisfaction was Mr. Gye's earnest conviction that, if Mdme. Patti's salary was to be increased, the salary of his wife, Mdme. Albani, ought also to be raised.

"However all these things may be, it is certain that the great question now is whether Col. Mapleson will come over next season as a representative, or rather a part, of the Royal Italian Opera Company (Limited)."

Despite obstacles of all kinds, I felt happy at being rid of the Royal Italian Opera, Covent Garden, and I set vigorously to work to complete the company with a view to the operatic battle which was to be fought the following autumn in New York.

During the month of June I was fortunate enough to conclude an engagement with Mdme. Etelka Gerster, also with Mdme. Pappenheim, who was a great favourite in America. For my contraltos I engaged Miss Josephine Yorke, and also Mdlle. Vianelli. Galassi, my principal baritone of the previous years, remained with me, despite the large offers that had been made to him by Abbey.

Prior to the commencement of my season, I found on perusing Mr. Abbey's list the names of Signor Del Puente, of Mdme. Lablache, of my stage-manager, Mr. Parry, and a good many of the choristers, all of whom were under formal engagement to me.

It is true I did not care much for the services of these people, but I could not allow them to defy me by breaking their contracts. I consequently applied for an injunction against each, which was duly granted, restraining them from giving their services in any other place than where by writing I directed. Arguments were heard the following day before Judge O'Gorman, on my motion to confirm the injunction which I had obtained against Signor Del Puente and Mdme. Lablache, who were announced to sing the opening night at the new Metropolitan Opera House. The injunction, as in the case of all operatic injunctions, was ultimately dissolved by the Court, and I agreed to accept a payment from Del Puente of 15,000 francs, Mr. Parry and the choristers being at the same time handed over to me.

Shortly after my arrival in New York I was honoured with a serenade in which no less than five hundred musicians took part. The sight alone was a remarkable one. I was at my hotel, on the point of going to bed, when suddenly I heard beneath my window a loud burst of music. The immense orchestra had taken possession of the street. The musicians were all in evening dress; they had brought their music stands with them, also electric or calcium lights; and, as I have before said, they occupied the road in front of the hotel.

I was extremely gratified, and when after the performance I went down into the street to thank the conductor, I begged that he would allow me to make a donation of £100 towards the funds of the Musical Protective Union. But he would not hear of such a thing, and was so earnest on the subject that I felt sorry at having in a moment of impulse ventured upon such an offer.

The Musical Protective Union is an association extending over the whole of the United States, to which all the capable instrumental players of the country belong. There may be, and probably are, a very few who stand outside it; and I remember that Mr. Abbey, unwilling to be bound by its rules, resolved to do without it altogether, and to import his musicians from abroad. Soon, however, this determination placed him in a very awkward predicament: his first oboe fell ill, and for some time it was found impossible to replace him.

I have nothing but good to say of the Musical Union. The very slight disagreement which I once had with those of its members who played in my orchestra was arranged as soon as we had an opportunity of talking the matter over. If I have every reason to be satisfied with the Musical Union, I can equally say that this Association showed itself well content with me.

While on the subject of American orchestras, I may add that their excellence is scarcely suspected by English amateurs. In England we have certainly an abundance of good orchestral players, but we have not so many musical centres; and, above all, we have not in London what New York has long possessed, a permanent orchestra of high merit under a first-rate conductor. Our orchestras in London are nearly always "scratch" affairs. The players are brought together anyhow, and not one of our concert societies gives more than eight concerts in the course of the year. Being paid so much a performance, our piece-work musicians make a great fuss about attending rehearsals; and they are always ready, if they can make a few shillings profit by it, to have themselves replaced by substitutes.

All really good orchestras must from the nature of the case be permanent ones, composed of players in receipt of regular salaries. Attendance at rehearsals is then taken as a matter of course, and no question of replacement by substitutes can be raised. The only English orchestra in which the conditions essential to a perfect ensemble are to be found is the Manchester orchestra conducted by Sir Charles Hallé.

A larger and better orchestra than the excellent one of Sir Charles Hallé is that of M. Lamoureux.

Better even than the orchestra of M. Lamoureux is that of M. Colonne. But I have no hesitation in saying that M. Colonne's orchestra is surpassed in fineness and fulness of tone, as also in force and delicacy of expression, by the American orchestra of 150 players conducted by Mr. Theodore Thomas. The members of this orchestra are for the most part Germans, and the eminent conductor is himself, by race at least, a German. Putting aside, however, all question of nationality, I simply say that the orchestra directed by Mr.

Theodore Thomas is the best I am acquainted with; and its high merit is due in a great measure to the permanence of the body. Its members work together habitually and constantly; they take rehearsals as part of their regular work; and they look to their occupation as players in the Theodore Thomas orchestra as their sole source of income. As for substitutes, Mr. Thomas would no more accept one than a military commander would accept substitutes among his officers.

There has from time to time been some talk of Mr. Theodore Thomas's unrivalled orchestra paying a visit to London, where its presence, apart from all question of the musical delight it would afford, would show our public what a good orchestra is, and our musical societies how a good orchestra ought to be formed and maintained.

Before taking leave of Mr. Theodore Thomas and of American orchestras generally, let me mention one remarkable peculiarity in connection with them. So penetrated are they with the spirit of equality that no one player in an orchestra is allowed to receive more than another; the first violin and the big drum are, in this respect, on precisely the same footing. In England we give so much to a first clarinet and something less to a second clarinet, and a leader will always receive extra terms. In America one player is held to be, in a pecuniary point of view, as good as another.

My season at the Academy commenced on the 22nd October—the same night as my rival's at the New Metropolitan Opera, to which subscriptions had been extended on a most liberal scale. In fact the whole of New York flocked there, as much to see the new building as to hear the performance.

On my opening night I presented La Sonnambula, when Mdme. Etelka Gerster, after an absence of two years, renewed her triumphs in America. The rival house presented Gounod's Faust, with Christine Nilsson as "Margherita," Scalchi as "Siebel," Novara as "Mephistopheles," Del Puente as "Valentine," and Campanini as "Faust;" a fine cast and perfectly trained, since all these artists had played under my direction and did not even require a rehearsal. After a few nights I began to discover that the counter attraction of the new house was telling considerably against me, and I informed the Academy Directors of my inability to contend against my rival with any degree of success, unless I could have a small amount of backing.

After consultation, several stockholders signed a paper, each for a different amount, which totalled up to something like £4,500, which I had previously calculated would be about the amount required to defeat the enemy. This was guaranteed by them to the Bank of the Metropolis on the understanding that I should never draw more than £600 a week from it, and then only in case of need.

The Manager of the rival Opera-house had fired off all his guns the first night; and after a few evenings, as soon as the public had seen the interior of the new building, the receipts gradually began to decline. In the meanwhile, I was anxiously expecting notice of Adelina Patti's approaching arrival. I, therefore, arranged to charter sixteen large tug boats, covered with bunting, to meet the Diva; eight of them to steam up the bay on each side of the arriving steamer, and to toot off their steam whistles all the way along, accompanied by military bands. All was in readiness, and I was only waiting for a telegraphic notification. Some of the pilots at Sandy Hook, moreover, had promised to improvise a salute of twenty-one guns; and Arditi had written a Cantata for the occasion, which the chorus were to sing immediately on Patti's arrival.

By some unfortunate mistake, either from fog or otherwise, the steamer passed Fire Island and landed la Diva unobserved at the dock, where there was not even a carriage to meet her. She got hustled by the crowd, and eventually reached her hotel with difficulty in a four-wheeler. The military bands had passed the night awaiting the signal which I was to give them to board the tugs.

On learning of Mdme. Patti's arrival, I hurried up to the Windsor Hotel, when I was at once received.

"Is it not too bad?" she exclaimed, with a comical expression of annoyance. "It is a wonder that I was not left till now on the steamer. As it was, by the merest chance one of my friends happened to come down to the dock and luckily espied me as I was wandering about trying to keep my feet warm, and assisted me into a four-wheeler. However, here I am. It is all over now, and I am quite comfortable and as happy as though twenty boats had come down to meet me."

She then agreed to make her début three days afterwards in La Gazza Ladra.

On the second night of the opera we had a brilliant audience for Rigoletto, Mdme. Gerster undertaking the part of "Gilda," which she sang with rare delicacy and brilliancy of vocalization, so that "Brava's!" rang throughout the entire audience.

My new tenor, Bertini, who likewise made his début on this occasion, produced but little effect, either vocally or dramatically. In the "La Donna è Mobile" he cracked on each of the high notes, whilst in the "Bella Figlia" quartet his voice broke in a most distressing manner when ascending to the B flat, causing loud laughter amongst the audience.

I was therefore under the necessity of sending him the following letter the next morning:—

"TO SIGNOR BERTINI.

"In consequence of the lamentable failure you met with on Wednesday evening last, the 24th inst., it is my painful duty to notify you that by reason of your inability to perform your contract, I hereby put an end to it. At the same time I request that you will return me the balance of the money that I advanced to you, amounting to 1,000 dollars.

"Yours, truly,

"(Signed) J. H. MAPLESON."

Of course he did not return my thousand dollars, but fell into the hands of some attorneys, who at once issued process against me for 50,000 dollars damages!

While admitting that at the time I engaged him he was a good singer, I maintained that latterly, from some cause or other, his voice had utterly gone. I had engaged him to perform certain duties which he was unable to fulfil.

His lawyers insisted upon his having another opportunity. This I at once agreed to; but not before the public, for whom I had too much respect to inflict another dose of Bertini upon them. I therefore offered him the empty house, full orchestra and chorus, and a jury half of his own selection and half of mine, with the Judge of one of the Superior Courts as umpire; but this he refused. The matter, therefore, went into the usual groove of protracted law proceedings and consequent annoyances and attachments. The very next day all my banking account was attached, and it was two days before I could get bondsmen in order that it might be released, so that I could continue to pay my salaries to the other artists.

On the following night we performed Norma at Brooklyn, with Mdme. Pappenheim as the Druid priestess; the night afterwards being reserved for the début of Mdme. Patti at New York in La Gazza Ladra. The occasion naturally drew together an immense audience, which displayed much enthusiasm for the singer. The pleasure of hearing Mdme. Patti again was increased by the fact that the work in which she was to appear was not a hackneyed one.

The opera, however, failed to make the effect I expected, being generally pronounced by the Press and the public to be too antiquated. The contralto who undertook the rôle of "Pippo" was excessively nervous, having had no rehearsals and never having met Patti before.

One daily paper said that the lesser rôles were well taken, down to the stuffed magpie, who flew down and seized the spoon, and sailed away into the flies with prodigious success, adding: "La Gazza Ladra will soon be laid permanently on the shelf. It is many years since it was done here before, and from a judgment of last evening, it will be many years before the experiment will be repeated."

Some time before this, a gentleman called on me. I was about to put him off, saying I was too busy; but he seemed so earnest for a few moments' conversation that I turned round, and on his raising his hat and loosening his overcoat, discovered him to be a priest. On his mentioning to me that Mdlle. Titiens had done service formerly for a church in Ireland with which he was connected, I at once gave him every attention. He explained that the small parish then under his charge was in great want, whilst the church had a debt of some £700 or £800. All he solicited was one of my singers, for whom he would pay the sum I might demand.

I at once told him that I would aid his charity to the best of my ability, and further, that on the appointed day, which happened to be St. Cecilia's Day, the 24th November, I would place some of my leading singers at his disposal for the high mass, and would, moreover, hold the plate myself at the church door to receive any offerings that might be made. After meeting him once or twice, I promised to take still further interest in relieving the Church of its difficulties by giving an evening concert in addition at the Steinway Hall, placing my best artists at his disposal, together with the whole of my chorus, and full orchestra under Arditi's direction, likewise my wonderful child pianist, Mdlle. Jeanne Douste.

In due course the following announcement was made regarding the concerts I had promised:—

"ST. CECILIA'S DAY.

"The greatest musical treat ever offered the people of Harlem will be given on Sunday (to-morrow) in the Church of St. Cecilia, Corner of 105th Street and 2nd Avenue. It will be the feast of the day of the 'Divine Cecilia'—patroness of music. Colonel Mapleson, of the Royal Opera Company, London, takes a personal interest in the celebration of the day, and has kindly consented to send a number of his best artists to delight the people and do honour to the beautiful 'Queen of Melody.' Our music-loving people will have at their own doors a genuine artistic treat—such a one as has never been given in Harlem before—and we doubt not they will appreciate it and fill St. Cecilia's Church to overflowing. The gallant Colonel has promised to hold the plate at the door and receive the offerings of the congregation—the only charge for a rushing torrent of the most delicious music. No doubt his noble and handsome presence will secure for his friend, Father Flattery, quite a big collection—a very essential element in such uncommon events.

"Our readers are referred to our advertising columns for the extensive and varied programme of the great Cecilian Concert at Steinway Hall on the same day. The famous Mapleson Opera Company will be at their best, supported by a superb chorus and a full and powerful orchestra. This will, indeed, be a Cecilian Concert in the best sense of the word."

In due course the day of the Feast of St. Cecilia arrived, which was most appropriately celebrated at St. Cecilia's Church, Harlem, some considerable distance "up town." There was no charge for admission, but I held the plate at the door, and everyone who entered gave something according to his means or inclination, a most handsome sum being thus collected. Father Flattery occasionally showed himself near my plate exhorting the incoming congregation to give liberally.

The service was conducted by Father Peyten, of St. Agnes' Church. Father Flattery did not preach a regular sermon, but confined his remarks to the life and character of St. Cecilia. "In venerating this saint," said he, "we intensify our love of God. St. Cecilia stands conspicuous in the noble choir as one of the typical saints. In studying her life we are carried back to the dark days of the Cæsars. More than St. Peter himself this noble lady sacrificed when she left all and devoted herself to God. Peter was but a poor fisherman, and left but his nets and boats; she was a noble lady of conspicuous distinction. Hers was no common origin, hers no ordinary name; but she relinquished all this social prestige for her religion. What wonder that she should be so popular among Christians when she is everywhere recognized as the patroness of the loveliest of arts, an art which lives beyond the bounds of time and can never die! Like the immortal souls of men, there is nothing destructive about music. It is music which illustrates the relation between art and religion. How much the art of music adds to the profound mystery of religion! How in the hour of exalted triumph it chants its pæans! The Festival of St. Cecilia is a festival of music; and music becomes more beautiful still when it is emblemized through such a life as that of this saint. Enviable is that professional art which has such a saint for its patron." At the close of his sermon Father Flattery expressed his own and the sincere thanks of the congregation to the manager and his artists who in their generosity had done so much for the cause of religion; and he expressed the hope that "when Colonel Mapleson ends his days St. Cecilia may come down to bear him up to Heaven."

At the conclusion of the service a sumptuous breakfast was served at Father Flattery's, to which some 200 guests were invited. Afterwards some speeches were made and thanks tendered to me for what I had done. The ladies present handed me, moreover, a set of studs and sleeve-links.

We afterwards drove down to the Steinway Hall to attend the evening concert (for the breakfast had lasted some time), which was crowded to the very doors. The receipts taken in the morning at the Church, coupled with those of the Steinway concert completely extinguished the debt which had weighed so heavily on St. Cecilia's Church.

About a year afterwards I was in New York, and having one afternoon (strangely enough) a little leisure, I determined to pay a visit to my excellent friend, Father Flattery. It was a Sunday afternoon, and when I got to his house, at some little distance from the central quarters of New York, I found him teaching a number of school children. As soon, however, as he saw me he struck work and his young pupils were dismissed to their homes.

I told Father Flattery that I had come to pay him a short visit.

"Nothing of the kind," he replied, in his frank, genial manner; "you have come to dine with me, and you are just in the nick of time. Dinner will be ready very soon; and I hope you have brought a good appetite with you."

My hospitable friend left me for a minute to give some orders; and while he was away one of his servants whispered to me that dinner was just over, and that there was nothing in the house.

I was too discreet to take any notice of this communication, and when the good priest returned I saw from his manner that he would take no refusal, and that whether there was anything in the house or not, whether he had already dined or not, I was to stay that afternoon to dinner.

After a certain delay, guests arrived, including some very charming ladies; and in due time dinner was served. It was quite an Homeric feast. Three roast turkeys were followed

125

by two legs of mutton, and these, again, by four roast ducks. The wines were of the finest quality, and among those of French growth the vintages of Heidsieck and of Pommery Greno were not forgotten.

No one but Father Flattery could have improvised such a banquet at a moment's notice; and I afterwards found that in order to be agreeable to me, and to express his gratitude for a slight service which I had most willingly rendered him, he had requisitioned viands, wines, and guests from the houses of his neighbours.

"I want that turkey, Pat; I should like to have that leg of mutton, Mike; Murphy, send me round those ducks you have on the table." In this summary fashion my amiable and generous host had furnished the feast; or it may be that in summoning his guests he recommended them to bring their dinner with them. I can only speak with absolute certainty as to the result, and I must add that the banquet was thoroughly successful. After the dinner was at an end we had whisky-toddy and Irish songs.

CHAPTER II.

PATTI AND HER SHOES—PATTI SEIZED FOR DEBT—FLIGHT OF GERSTER—CONFLICT AT CHICAGO—BOUQUETS OUT OF SEASON— CINCINNATI FLOODS—ABBEY'S COLLAPSE—RESOLVE TO GO WEST.

NOTWITHSTANDING the successful performances, which I continued to give, the receipts never reached the amount of the expenditure—as is invariably the case when two Opera-houses are contending in the same city.

So bent was Mr. Abbey on my total annihilation that in each town I intended visiting during the tour at the close of the season I found his company announced. I, therefore, resolved as far as possible to steal a march upon him. I altered most of my arrangements, anticipating my Philadelphia engagement by five weeks, and opening on the 18th December. Mdme. Patti appeared in Ernani to a 10,000-dollar house, Mdme. Gerster performing "Linda" the following night to almost equally large receipts. Semiramide likewise brought a very large house. From Philadelphia we went to Boston, where, unfortunately, the booking was not at all great, it not being our usual time for visiting that city. Moreover, I had to go to the Globe Theatre. On the second night of our engagement we performed La Traviata. That afternoon, about two o'clock, Patti's agent called upon me to receive the 5,000 dollars for her services that evening. I was at low water just then, and inquiring at the booking-office found that I was £200 short. All I could offer Signor Franchi was the trifle of £800 as a payment on account.

The agent declined the money, and formally announced to me that my contract with Mdme. Patti was at an end. I accepted the inevitable, consoling myself with the reflection that, besides other good artists in my company, I had now £800 to go on with.

Two hours afterwards Signor Franchi reappeared.

"I cannot understand," he said, "how it is you get on so well with prime donne, and especially with Mdme. Patti. You are a marvellous man, and a fortunate one, too, I may add. Mdme. Patti does not wish to break her engagement with you, as she certainly would have done with anyone else under the circumstances. Give me the £800 and she will make every preparation for going on to the stage. She empowers me to tell you that she will be at the theatre in good time for the beginning of the opera, and that she will be ready dressed in the costume of "Violetta," with the exception only of the shoes. You can let her have the balance when the doors open and the money comes in from the outside public; and directly she receives it she will put her shoes on and at the proper moment make her appearance on the stage." I thereupon handed him the £800 I had already in hand as the result of subscriptions in advance. "I congratulate you on your good luck," said Signor Franchi as he departed with the money in his pocket.

After the opening of the doors I had another visit from Signor Franchi. By this time an extra sum of £160 had come in. I handed it to my benevolent friend, and begged him to carry it without delay to the obliging prima donna, who, having received £960, might, I thought, be induced to complete her toilette pending the arrival of the £40 balance.

Nor was I altogether wrong in my hopeful anticipations. With a beaming face Signor Franchi came back and communicated to me the joyful intelligence that Mdme. Patti had got one shoe on. "Send her the £40," he added, "and she will put on the other."

Ultimately the other shoe was got on; but not, of course, until the last £40 had been paid. Then Mdme. Patti, her face radiant with benignant smiles, went on to the stage; and the opera already begun was continued brilliantly until the end.

Mdme. Adelina Patti is beyond doubt the most successful singer who ever lived. Vocalists as gifted, as accomplished as she might be named, but no one ever approached her in the art of obtaining from a manager the greatest possible sum he could by any possibility contrive to pay. Mdlle. Titiens was comparatively careless on points of this kind; Signor Mario equally so.

I am certainly saying very little when I advance the proposition that Mdme. Patti has frequently exacted what I will content myself with describing as extreme terms. She has, indeed, gone beyond this, for I find from my tables of expenditure for the New York season of 1883 that, after paying Mdme. Patti her thousand pounds, and distributing a few hundreds among the other members of the company, I had only from 22 to 23 dollars per night left on the average for myself.

Mdme. Patti's fees—just twenty times what was thought ample by Signor Mario and by Mdlle. Titiens, than whom no greater artists have lived in our time—was payable to Mdme. Patti at two o'clock on the day of representation.

From Boston we went to Montreal, opening there on Christmas Eve, operatically the worst day in the year; when Mdme. Gerster's receipts for La Sonnambula were very light. We afterwards performed Elisir d'Amore, and on Friday, the 4th January, Mdme. Patti made her début before as bad a house as Gerster's.

Soon afterwards the most money-making of prime donne was, without being aware of it at the time, seized for debt. It happened in this manner. From Boston we had travelled to Montreal, where, by the way, through the mistake of an agent, gallery seats were charged at the rate of five dollars instead of one. On reaching the Montreal railway station we were met by a demand on the part of the railway company for 300 dollars. The train had been already paid for; but this was a special charge for sending the Patti travelling car along the line. I, of course, resisted the claim, and the more energetically inasmuch as I had not 300 dollars in hand. I could only get the money by going up to the theatre and taking it from the receipts.

Meanwhile the sheriffs were upon me; and the Patti travelling car, with Adelina asleep inside, was attached, seized, and ultimately shunted into a stable, of which the iron gates were firmly closed.

There was no room for argument or delay. All I had to do was to get the money; and hurrying to the theatre I at once procured it. Unconscious of her imprisoned condition, Mdme. Patti was still asleep when I took the necessary steps for rescuing from bondage the car which held her.

The public of Montreal, more gracious than the railway authorities, received us with enthusiasm. An immense ice palace was erected just opposite the hotel at which we were staying; and the architecture of the building, and especially the manner in which the blocks of ice were placed one above the other and then soldered together, interested me much. The ice blocks were consolidated by the agency of heat. Hot water was applied to the points of contact, and the ice thus liquefied left to freeze.

We afterwards returned to New York, performing there the first three weeks of January, business still being very light indeed; and it was not until my benefit night, on the 18th, that a fine house was secured, when over 11,000 dollars were taken. After giving a Sunday concert we left for Philadelphia, where I arranged for three special performances, it being three days before Mr. Abbey's arrival there with his Opera troupe. The three performances were extremely successful. We afterwards left for Baltimore.

On arriving there Mdme. Gerster accidentally saw a playbill in which Mdme. Patti's name was larger than hers; further, that they were charging only five dollars for her appearance, whilst they demanded seven dollars for the Patti nights. Without one moment's warning, and unbeknown even to her husband, the lady went to the station and entered the train for New York. When dinner-time arrived Dr. Gardini was in a great state, as his wife was nowhere to be found, and it was by mere accident one of the chorus told me that he had seen her going in the direction of the railway station.

I thereupon telegraphed to Wilmington—the first station at which her train would stop—requesting her to return, as all matters had been arranged. There was no train by which she could get back. But through the kindness of the manager of the road, who happened to be in Baltimore, a telegraphic despatch was sent to Wilmington to detain the express—in which unfortunately Patti happened to be seated—until the arrival of Gerster's train, so that she could return immediately in time for the performance. I afterwards learned that Mdme. Patti, on inquiring the cause of the delay, was excessively angry at being detained for upwards of three-quarters of an hour on account of Mdme. Gerster. Nicolini was enraged for a different reason. He had ordered a sumptuous dinner at our hotel, where there was a new chef; and he knew that, having to wait for Mdme. Patti, his terrapin and his canvas-back duck would be spoiled.

All endeavours to induce Mdme. Gerster to enter a train in which the state-room was occupied by Mdme. Patti were useless, and I afterwards received a telegram that she had gone on to New York.

I thereupon put up the following announcement at the opening of the doors, not wishing to make a scandal:—"Owing to the non-arrival of Mdme. Gerster from New York she will be unable to appear this evening. The opera of Ernani will be substituted. Money will be returned to those desiring it."

In a short time the entire Opera was closely packed with ladies in full evening dress. All were in a high state of excitement, and seemed unable to decide what to do, whether to go into the theatre or take their carriages and return home. The ladies shrugged their shoulders, and the gentlemen gesticulated indignantly, looking at me as if they would like to say something forcible but impolite. "Outrage!" "disgrace!" "shameful!" and other excited utterances born of polite anger were heard on all sides. About one-third of the indignant ones left the theatre, whilst the balance remained to hear Ernani, which was exceedingly well played. Two minutes after the curtain rose on Ernani I hurried down to the railway station and entered the train for New York in quest of the fugitive prima donna. As I had eaten nothing from early morn I was placed in a very disagreeable position. I could not get even a glass of water or a piece of bread until some six or seven o'clock the next morning.

On reaching New York I went in quest of Mdme. Gerster at all the likely places, and at length discovered her at her brother's. It took the whole of the day to get things into shape, and I succeeded towards night in bringing back the truant, and inducing her to appear the following day, at a matinée, in L'Elisir d'Amore, when she attracted an enormous audience.

I was placed in great difficulty with regard to the public and the press, knowing that the reports would be greatly exaggerated, and injure the business in all the other cities to which we were going. I thereupon circulated the news that Mdme. Gerster's baby in New York had taken a cold in its stomach, and that she had been hurriedly sent for. This got repeated during the next four or five weeks in the papers at all the cities we visited, and afterwards gradually died out.

Before leaving Baltimore I had a bill presented to me for return of money in consequence of the Gerster disappointment as follows:—

Two opera tickets at five dollars		$10.00
Carriage	5.00	
Gloves	2.50	
Necktie	0.25	
Overlooking and pressing a dress suit	3.00	
Flowers for her corsage	3.00	
Two return tickets	14.00	
Total	$37.75	

Legal proceedings were resorted to, but I ultimately settled the matter by giving a private box for our next visit.

On arriving at Chicago we found ourselves not only in the same town with our rivals, but also in the same hotel.

Such a galaxy of talent had never before been congregated together under one roof. The ladies consisted of Adelina Patti, Etelka Gerster, Christine Nilsson, Fursch-Madi, Sembrich, Trebelli, and Scalchi, whose rooms were all along the same corridor.

It was here that our great battle began; and I have much satisfaction in quoting the following account of the conflict from a leading journal:—

"The Mapleson season opened with a brilliant house on Monday evening. The opera and cast were not very strong for an opening night, but Patti's name proves a drawing card on all occasions, and she was given a flattering reception as she once more presented herself to Chicago. Crispino is not a strong opera, the music being of the lightest order. She was finely supported by the other artists. Mdme. Etelka Gerster as 'Adina' was very charming; she appeared the following evening in Elisir d'Amore. At the rival house Ponchielli's La Gioconda attracted a large but not a crowded audience on the opening night. Both Opera Companies continued vigorously throughout the week, giving a series of the finest performances. The palm must readily be awarded to Mr. Mapleson's able management, as Mr. Abbey closed probably the worst-managed opera season Chicago had ever had. It opened amidst a flourish of trumpets, which heralded great conquests, but the results did not justify the reports."

I must now mention that when I organized the first Cincinnati Festival I stipulated with the Directors, in case of any repetitions, that the terms should be the same, and that I should have the sole control. The three preceding Festivals had been given under my direction, with distinguished success, and with large profits. But I now found that here, too, Mr. Abbey had stepped in and secured the great Festival for himself. It was useless going to law with a body of directors. I, therefore, trusted to injustice meeting with its own reward, as it inevitably does. I could illustrate this by many hundreds of cases.

I now hastened to conclude engagements for another Opera Festival at Mr. Fennessy's elegant theatre—one of the most beautiful in Cincinnati—in order that Mr. Abbey might not have the whole affair to himself.

The sale of seats for my contemplated performances at Cincinnati the following week opened grandly, no less than 235 seats being sold for the whole series quite early in the day. The number had increased before the close of the office to 653, the total sale realizing £6,000 (30,000 dollars). Bills were duly posted announcing for the opening night Meyerbeer's Huguenots, with Nicolini as "Raoul," Galassi as "St. Bris," Sivori as "Nevers," Cherubini as "Marcel," Josephine Yorke as "The Page," Etelka Gerster as "The Queen," and Patti as "Valentine." This, it seemed to me, was presenting a bold front against anything Mr. Abbey might produce.

About this time grave rumours got into circulation with regard to Mr. Abbey's losses. It oozed out that prior to the entry of his Company into Cincinnati he had dropped on the road some 53,000 dollars.

The Abbey Company opened their season at Chicago with Gioconda. But the tenor was bad, and the principal female part quite unsuited to Mdme. Christine Nilsson, so that little or no effect was made. I opened with Crispino, Adelina Patti appearing in the principal rôle; which was followed by L'Elisir d'Amore, with Gerster. On the third night Les Huguenots was performed, with Mdme. Patti as "Valentine," and Mdme. Gerster as the "Queen," when the following scene occurred:—

Prior to the commencement of the opera numbers of very costly bouquets and lofty set pieces had been sent into the vestibule according to custom for Mdme. Patti, whilst only a small basket of flowers had been received for presentation to Mdme. Gerster. Under ordinary circumstances it is the duty of the prima donna's agent to notify to the stall-keepers, or ushers, as they are called in America, the right moment for handing up the bouquets on to the stage. That evening Mdme. Patti's agent was absent, and at the close of the first act, during which "Valentine" has scarcely a note to sing, whilst the "Queen" has much brilliant music to execute, he was nowhere to be found. There was a general call at the close of the act for the seven principal artists. At that moment the stall-ushers, having no one to direct their movements, rushed frantically down the leading aisles with their innumerable bouquets and set pieces, passing them across to Arditi, who sometimes could scarcely lift them. Reading the address on the card attached to each offering, he continued passing the flowers to Mdme. Patti. This lasted several minutes, the public meanwhile getting impatient.

At length, when these elaborate presentations to Mdme. Patti had been brought to an end, a humble little basket addressed to Mdme. Gerster was passed up, upon which the whole house broke out into ringing cheers, which continued some minutes. This contretemps had the effect of seriously annoying Mdme. Patti, who, at the termination of the opera, made a vow that she would never again perform in the same work with Mdme. Gerster.

Mdme. Patti had braced herself up sufficiently to go through the performance in very dramatic style. But after the fall of the curtain, when she had time to think of the ludicrous position in which she had been placed, she became hysterical.

On returning to her hotel she threw herself on to the ground and kicked and struggled in such a manner that it was only with the greatest difficulty she could be got to bed. The stupidity of the "ushers" seemed to her so outrageous that she could scarcely accept it as sufficient explanation of the folly committed in sending up her bouquets, her baskets, and her floral devices of various kinds at the wrong moment. At one time when she was in a comedy vein, she would exclaim: "It is all that Mapleson;" and she actually did me the honour to say that I had arranged the scene in order to lower her value in the eyes of the public, and secure her for future performances at reduced rates.

Then she would take a serious, not to say tragic view of the matter, and attribute the misadventure to the maleficent influence of Gerster. The amiable Etelka possessed, according to her brilliant but superstitious rival, the evil eye; and after the affair of the bouquets no misfortune great or small happened, but it was attributed by Mdme. Patti to the malignant spirit animating Mdme. Gerster. If anything went wrong, from a false note in the orchestra to an earthquake, it was always, according to the divine Adelina, caused by Gerster and her "evil eye." "Gerster!" was her first exclamation when she found the earth shaking beneath her at San Francisco.

Far from endeavouring to cure her of her childish superstitions, Nicolini encouraged her, and, in all probability, took part himself in her quaint delusions.

Whenever Gerster's name was mentioned, whenever her presence was in any way suggested, Mdme. Patti made with her fingers the horn which is supposed to counteract or avert the effect of the evil eye; and once, when the two rivals were staying at the same hotel, Mdme. Patti, passing in the dark the room occupied by Mdme. Gerster, extended her first and fourth fingers in the direction of the supposed sorceress; when she found herself nearly tapping upon the forehead of Mdme. Gerster's husband, Dr. Gardini, who, at that moment, was putting his boots out before going to bed.

Two days before the close of the Chicago engagement grave rumours reached me from Cincinnati, where we were due the following Monday. Great floods had set in, and the water was still rising daily, and, indeed, hourly.

I received frequent telegraphic reports as to the sad effects of the flood, and I at last found it necessary to postpone our departure until the following day, hoping the water might then begin to recede.

On learning the state of things Mdme. Patti refused absolutely to enter the train now in readiness, and several of the other artists followed her example. The water still kept rising, and it at last reached the extraordinary height of 64 feet.

Cincinnati, I learned, was placed in total darkness through the gas works being submerged. The inhabitants were compelled to burn candles and oil lamps in order to obtain light, whilst the city was isolated from every other part of America. I was, moreover, informed by the railway authorities there was great uncertainty as to the train ever being able to reach the city at all. No Festival could possibly be given where such utter desolation existed; where the public was so far removed from everything festive.

I therefore telegraphed Manager Fennessy to postpone my week's visit until the 31st of the following month, and I now saw no alternative but to stay at Chicago, though I had no engagements whatever, and had all the people on my hands. On conversing with Mdme. Patti and Mdme. Gerster I found that they both sympathized with the sufferers from this sad calamity. I therefore decided that in lieu of attempting to get money out of the ill-fated city, it was our duty to raise funds and transmit them to the sufferers as speedily as possible. With that view I organized a morning performance in all haste at Chicago, in which both Mdme. Patti and Mdme. Gerster took part. The public accorded the most generous support. Henry Irving, who was staying in our hotel, gave £20 for a box with his usual characteristic liberality; and I had the pleasure of remitting the very next day to the Mayor of Cincinnati upwards of £1,200.

In order to keep the band and chorus employed, I arranged to perform for three nights at Minneapolis, which, although a considerable distance off, I determined to try. I therefore ordered my special train to be in readiness for our departure.

We opened at Minneapolis during the latter part of the week, giving the three performances to excellent business. Whilst there I heard fresh reports as to Abbey's losses, both at the Metropolitan Opera-house, and likewise on his tour.

131

On taking up the newspapers I found it stated that Mr. Abbey had lost nearly 239,000 dollars, and that he was, in fact, compelled to retire from his management.

Although Mr. Abbey had treated me anything but handsomely, I felt some regret at hearing of the downfall of this not very clever showman. It was a struggle between money and ability, his object being to put me out of the way, so that his new enterprise might have no opposition to encounter. My singers, musicians, and employés had been hired away from me at double, treble, and quadruple salaries. From Nilsson down to the call-boy, all had been tempted, and many led away. When my people came in to me and said: "What shall I do? he is offering me four times my salary," I replied: "My dear people, go by all means; you are sure to come back to me next season."

I had myself run very close to the wind throughout all this business, and but for great care and some judgment should have been ruined.

After the morning performance which closed our engagement at Minneapolis, our special train had to travel for 36 hours to reach St. Louis, where we opened on the following Monday.

There was great excitement at St. Louis about the performance of Les Huguenots, announced for the Thursday following, in which Patti and Gerster were to appear together in their respective parts. But in consequence of Mdme. Patti's declaration that she would never sing with Gerster again in any opera, I had to change the bill, much to the annoyance of the public and to my own loss.

I will now mention something that occurred during the latter part of my visit to St. Louis.

Finding business not so flourishing as it would have been but for this irritating rivalry of Abbey's, also that Mdme. Patti's engagement included only fifty guaranteed nights during the five months over which the engagement extended, I concluded to give her a rest of some three or four weeks, inasmuch as she had already sung nearly two-thirds of the guaranteed number of times, and I had ample time to work out the remainder. I also resolved to start the Company far away out of the reach of Mr. Abbey to the wealthy San Francisco. Our exchequer was sadly in need of replenishment. Mdme. Gerster consented to remain with me, but only on condition that Mdme. Patti kept away. Finding this suited my purpose, I agreed to it.

CHAPTER III.

GERSTER REFUSES—PATTI VOLUNTEERS—ARRIVAL AT CHEYENNE—PATTI DINES THE PROPHET—THREATS OF AN INTERVIEWER—ARRIVAL AT SAN FRANCISCO.

AT the conclusion of the farewell morning performance of Martha, in which Gerster took part, at St. Louis, she went home to prepare for the journey to San Francisco. I performed La Favorita that evening, and gave orders for the Company to start at 2 a.m. for the Far West. At about a quarter to one my agent called me, stating that Mdme. Gerster had gone to bed and refused to allow her boxes to leave the hotel. Feeling now that she was free from Patti, she thought she could do as she liked. All arguments were useless, and in lieu of packing the boxes she gave calm directions to her maids to hang her dresses up. During this time the special train was waiting in the station ready to take its departure. In the midst of my trouble a little card was brought in enclosed in an envelope, stating that Mdme. Patti would like to see me. She, too, had been on the point of going to bed. But on learning the strait in which I was placed she at once rang the bell, mustered her maids, requested them to pack up all her worldly effects, and now assured me that she would sing for me day and night rather than let me be the victim of Gerster's caprices.

Whilst I was thanking Mdme. Patti another little card was slipped in my hand from the adjoining room requesting a word with me. On entering Mdme. Gerster's apartments I found her dressed, and she now declared her willingness to accompany me to the Far West.

The long and short of it was that I found myself in the train with both my prime donne. I thereupon telegraphed to my agent in advance to call in at Denver and arrange for a performance of Mdme. Patti in La Traviata on the following Saturday morning on our way through. We duly arrived in Denver, when on reaching the hotel Mdme. Gerster accidentally saw that Patti had been announced for one of the performances.

Without a moment's warning she left the hotel, presented herself at the station, and ordered a special train to take her back to the East on her way to Europe. It was, indeed, a sore trial to bring matters to an amicable conclusion; but in this I eventually succeeded. I assured Mdme. Gerster that Mdme. Patti would have nothing further to do for some length of time. If Patti sang again Mdme. Gerster declared she would leave the Company.

At the conclusion of my Denver engagement we left for Cheyenne. The opera train consisted of eleven elegant carriages; and prior to our arrival at Cheyenne we were met on the road by two special cars, having on board Councillors Holliday, Dater, Babbitt, Warren, Irvine, and Homer, likewise the Hon. Jones, Ford, and Miller, and some forty other representatives of the Upper and Lower Houses of the great territory of the West. We were agreeably surprised when the train pulled up. To my great astonishment both Houses had been adjourned in honour of our visit. There was, in fact, a general holiday. One carriage contained dry Pommery and Mumm champagne, intersected with blocks of ice, whilst another compartment was full of cigars. Both trains pulled up on the plains, when an interchange of civilities took place and several speeches were made.

Shortly afterwards we started the train again in the direction of Cheyenne, where the band of the 9th Regiment, brought from a considerable distance from one of the military stations, was waiting to receive us. Mdme. Patti, who was in her own car, insisted upon having it detached from the train in order not to interfere with the welcome she considered due to Mdme. Gerster, who was to perform that evening in La Sonnambula, which was the only opera to be given during our visit. At the conclusion of the reception Gerster was accompanied to the hotel. Two hours later there was to be a serenade to Mdme. Patti, who at a given time was drawn into the station. The brass band, being placed in a circle with the bandmaster in the centre, commenced performing music which was rather mixed. Mdme. Patti requested me to ask the bandmaster what they were playing; but on my attempting to enter the circle the bandmaster rushed at me, telling me with expressive gestures that if I touched one of his musicians the whole circle would fall down. They had been on duty during the last thirty-six hours waiting our arrival, and as they had taken "considerable refreshment," he had had great difficulty in placing them on their feet. We dispensed with all ceremony, and the night serenade was struck out of the programme, the men being sent home.

The opera of Sonnambula was performed that evening, and although ten dollars a seat were charged, the house was crowded. To my great astonishment, although Cheyenne is but a little town, consisting of about two streets, it possesses a most refined society, composed, it is true, of cowboys; yet one might have imagined one's self at the London Opera when the curtain rose—the ladies in brilliant toilettes and covered with diamonds; the gentlemen all in evening dress.

133

The entire little town was lighted by electricity. The club house is one of the pleasantest I have ever visited; and the people are most hospitable.

When the performance was over we all returned to the train, and started for Salt Lake City.

On our arrival there Mdme. Gerster drove to the theatre. Mdme. Patti and Nicolini amused themselves by visiting the great Tabernacle, I accompanying them. On entering this superb building, excellent in an acoustic point of view, and capable of seating 12,000 persons, the idea immediately crossed my mind of giving, if possible, a concert there on our return from San Francisco; but I was unsuccessful in my endeavours to obtain the use of it. I thereupon resolved that Mdme. Patti should invite the Mormon Prophet himself, together with as many of the twelve apostles as we could obtain, to visit her private car, then outside the station; and a splendid déjeuner was prepared by the cooks.

The next morning the Prophet Taylor came, accompanied by several of his apostles. Mdme. Patti took great care to praise the magnificent building she had visited the day previously, expressing a strong desire that she might be allowed to try her voice there, which led on to my observing that a regular concert would be more desirable. To this a strong objection was made by several apostles, who stated that the building was not intended for any such purpose, but was simply a place of worship.

Mdme. Patti, however, launched into enthusiastic praise of the Mormon doctrines, and, in fact, expressed a strong wish to join the Mormon Church. After hearing her sing two or three of her dainty little songs the Prophet was so impressed that he actually consented to a concert being given in the Tabernacle the following month. On my suggesting three dollars for the best seats an objection was instantly made by one of the apostles, who, having five wives, thought it would be rather a heavy call upon his purse. It was ultimately settled that the prices should be only two dollars and one dollar.

We performed the opera of Lucia that evening in Salt Lake Theatre in presence of all the prominent inhabitants of the lovely city, the receipts reaching some £750. The Prophet attended.

Starting for the West immediately after the opera, we about thirty hours afterwards reached Reno, where we stopped to water the engine; and, although still some 250 miles from San Francisco, the train was boarded by a lot of reporters, who had been waiting a couple of days to meet the party, determined if possible to secure an interview with the Diva. In the meantime they busied themselves writing a description of the magnificent train of boudoir state-rooms until we reached Truckee, where a considerable portion of the line had been washed away. There had, moreover, been a snow-slide from some of the great mountains, which caused a stoppage of nearly twelve hours.

Suddenly, as if by magic, some 1,500 Chinamen arrived and commenced repairing the road. During this time the reporters had ample time to interview everybody, as the railway carriages one by one had to be conveyed over a temporary road which the Chinamen had built.

The whole of Truckee's population came out to meet us, composed of cowboys, miners, and Indians. Patti was much charmed with a little papoose carried on one of the Indian women's backs. She placed herself at the piano and commenced singing nursery rhymes. She likewise whistled a polka very cleverly to her own accompaniment; which made the papoose laugh. She thereupon expressed a strong wish to purchase it and adopt it, having no children of her own. It was only in compliance with Nicolini's persuasive powers that she ultimately desisted.

On our leaving Truckee a wild shout went up from the Indians, resembling a kind of war-whoop, in which the whole of the Truckee population joined.

134

Ultimately we reached Sacramento. Again all the inhabitants came out, many crying, "God bless her Majesty!" "God bless Colonel Mapleson!" the crowd, as usual, being largely composed of Indians and Chinese. An attempt was made to surround Patti's car in order to make her get out and sing.

Prior to leaving Sacramento other reporters got in, insisting upon interviewing Patti. I replied—

"Do you think I pay Patti £1,000 a night and spend all my profits buying these magnificent cars for her and Nicolini to have her interviewed by newspaper reporters? No, sir, you cannot interview Patti. We have a lot of beautifully-written interviews already in type in my ante-room, and you can go and select those you like best. You can see the car, moreover, with Count Zacharoff. In the hind car you will find some Apollinaris and rye whisky, and there is a box of cigars in the corner."

"Look here, Colonel," replied one of the reporters, very firmly, placing his right hand in his hip pocket, "I am no London reporter to be put off in that kind of way. I have come several hundreds of miles to interview Patti, and see her I must. Refuse me, and I shall simply telegraph two lines to San Francisco that Patti has caught a severe cold in the mountains, and that Gerster's old throat complaint is coming on again. Do you understand?"

I replied, "Cannot you interview me instead?" feeling appalled at his threat.

"No, sir," replied he; "Patti or perdition!"

I now saw Nicolini, who ultimately consented to the reporter's seeing the Diva. Summoning a swarthy valet, he ordered him to conduct the journalist to Mdme. Patti's apartments, Nicolini following him.

A few seconds later the reporter was face to face with Patti in her gorgeous palace car. Nicolini performed the ceremony of introduction, while the parrot muttered a few "cusses" in French. Patti smilingly motioned the reporter to be seated, and the long-expected interview was about to take place, when Nicolini suddenly returned and commenced ringing the electric bells. In an instant all was confusion. Valets rushed hither and thither, Nicolini declaring in the choicest Italian that he had discovered a small draught coming through a ventilator; and it was not until this had been closed and his adored madame had been wrapped in shawls that the interview could proceed.

Patti had evidently been interviewed before, for she took the lead in the conversation from the start. Her first inquiry was about the weather in California, of which she had heard. She asked whether it was warm and sunny like her native Spain. She said she was tired of ice and snow, of Colorado and Montana, and that she was very pleased at being able to reach San Francisco. At the conclusion of the interview the reporter left the room, went to the end of the train, and dropped a small parcel overboard on passing one of the signal boxes. I afterwards learned that it contained a page of matter which we found in print on our arrival at San Francisco. He had given a detailed report of all that had occurred in the train.

In due course we reached San Francisco, where my agent informed me that the engagement was going to be a great success, two-thirds of the tickets having been sold for the entire season.

On our arriving at Oakland, opposite San Francisco, the morning papers were eagerly purchased, and the announcements scanned by Signor Nicolini and Patti, both of whom expressed amazement at having been brought some 3,000 miles to do nothing. In fact, I myself felt rather for the moment nonplussed. I nevertheless immediately took the matter up, whispering to Nicolini to be quiet, and to tell Mdme. Patti to be quiet, as I had prepared a scheme which I thought she would be pleased with.

I then set to work to think what could be done. On reaching my hotel, it being Sunday, of course no printing could be attempted. I, therefore, inserted an advertisement in the paper for the following morning notifying that, profiting by Mdme. Patti's and Signor Nicolini's presence on a voyage of pleasure to the Far West, I had persuaded them to give a performance. I had selected the ensuing Thursday—the only blank night I had. At the same time, in justice to those who had subscribed so liberally for the season, I notified that the original subscribers should have the first choice of the Patti tickets in priority to the general public, with a discount of 10 per cent. besides. This contented them, and, in fact, augmented still further the subscription for the whole season, many joining in simply for the chance of being able to obtain a ticket for Patti.

When this arrangement had been carried out I met Messrs. Sherman and Clay, the well-known music sellers, and begged them kindly to dispose of the few remaining tickets at their shop, on the following Tuesday, so as not to have any confusion with my regular box-office lettings at the theatre.

CHAPTER IV.

THE PATTI EPIDEMIC—GERSTER FURORE—TICKETS 400% PREMIUM—MY ARREST—CAPTURE OF "SCALPERS"—OPERA TICKET AUCTION—DEATH OF MY FIRST "BASSO."

ONE of the most extraordinary spectacles ever witnessed in San Francisco was that which presented itself on the evening of our arrival as soon as it got buzzed about that some Patti tickets were to be sold the following Tuesday at Sherman and Clay's.

Shortly after ten o'clock that night the first young man took up his position, and was soon joined by another and another. Then came ladies, until shortly after midnight the line extended as far as the district telegraph office. Some brought chairs, and seated themselves with a pipe or a cigar, prepared for a prolonged siege. Others had solid as well as liquid solace in their pockets to pass away the hours. Telegraph boys were numerous. So were many other shrewd young men who were ready the following morning to sell their places in line to the highest bidder; a position in line costing as much as £2 when within thirty from the door of the office in which the tickets were to be disposed of.

The Adelina Patti epidemic gradually disseminated itself from the moment of her arrival, and began to rage throughout the city from early the following morning.

Many ladies joined the line during the night, and had to take equal chances with the men. Towards morning bargains for good positions in the line reached as high as £4, a sum which was actually paid by one person for permission to take another person's place. Numbers of those in the van of the procession were there solely for the purpose of selling their positions.

The next morning I rose early and took a stroll to admire the city. I observed a vast crowd down Montgomery Street. In fact, the passage within hundreds of yards was impassable, vehicles, omnibuses, etc., all being at a standstill. On inquiring the reason of this commotion I was informed by a policeman that they were trying to buy Patti tickets, which Messrs. Sherman and Clay had for disposal.

On forcing my way gradually down the street and approaching Sherman and Clay's establishment, I saw, to my great astonishment, that there was not a single pane of glass in any of the windows, whilst the tops of the best pianos and harmoniums were occupied by dozens of people standing upon them in their nailed boots, all clamouring for Patti tickets. Messrs. Sherman and Clay solicited me earnestly either to remove Patti from the town, or, at least, not to entrust them with the sale of any more tickets, the crowd having done over £600 of damage to their stock.

136

I had no further difficulty at the moment with Gerster, who believed Patti was going to sing but one night. Besides, the sale of tickets had been very great on her account before Patti's presence in the city had become known.

About eight o'clock that evening a serenade was tendered to Patti by a large orchestra under Professor Wetterman; the court-yard of the Palace Hotel where she was staying being brilliantly illuminated. The six tiers of magnificent galleries surrounding it were crowded with visitors and illuminated a giorno. As soon as the first strains of the music were heard Mdme. Patti came from her room with a circle of friends, and was an attentive listener. After remaining some time she deputed Signor Arditi to congratulate the orchestra on their brilliant performance, the favourite conductor receiving quite an ovation as he delivered the message.

The preparations at the Grand Opera were most elaborate, and the decorations particularly so. The theatre and passages had been repapered, flags festooned, and in the centre facing the main door was a huge crystal fountain, having ten smaller jets throwing streams of eau de Cologne into glass basins hung with crystal pendants. All over the vestibule were the rarest tree orchids, violets in blossom and roses in full bloom; while the corner of the vestibule was draped with the flags of every nation, among which England, America, Italy, and Hungary predominated.

On the opening night the Grand Opera-house presented a spectacle of magnificence which I may say without exaggeration can never have been surpassed in any city. The auditorium was quite dazzling with a bewildering mass of laces, jewels, and fair faces. Every available place was taken. Outside in the street there must have been thousands of people all clamouring for tickets, whilst the broad steps of the church opposite were occupied by persons anxious to catch a glimpse of the toilettes of the ladies as they sprang out of their carriages into the vestibule.

The season opened with Lucia di Lammermoor, in which Mdme. Etelka Gerster appeared as the ill-fated heroine. I will not go into details of the performance, further than to say that the stage was loaded after every act with the most gorgeous set pieces of flowers, several being so cumbersome that they had to be left on the stage at the sides in sight of the audience during the remainder of the opera. The next evening was devoted to rest after the long and fatiguing journey that we had all undergone, Mdme. Gerster remaining in her apartments to prepare for her second appearance the following night.

The next evening was devoted to a performance of L'Elisir d'Amore, when Mdme. Gerster drew another 10,000 dollar house—the floral picturesqueness of the auditorium of the previous Monday being repeated.

Mdme. Patti was now to appear as "La Traviata." On the day of the performance it took the whole of the police force to protect the theatre from the overwhelming crowds pressing for tickets, although it had been announced that no more were to be had. Long before daylight the would-be purchasers of Patti tickets had collected and formed into line, reaching the length of some three or four streets; and from this time until the close of the engagement, some four weeks afterwards, that line was never broken at any period of the day or night. A brisk trade was done in the hiring of camp stools, for which the modest sum of 4s. was charged. A similar amount was levied for a cup of coffee or a slice of bread and butter. As the line got hungry dinners were served, also suppers. High prices were paid to obtain a place in the line, as the head of it approached the box-office; resulting only in disappointment to the intending buyer, who was, of course, unable to procure a ticket. Large squads of police were on duty the whole time, and they were busily employed in keeping the line in its place, and in defeating outsiders in their attempts to make a gap in it. Later on it was announced that a limited number of gallery tickets would be sold, when a rush was made, carrying away the whole of the windows, glass, statuary, plants, etc.

Ticket speculators were now offering seats at from £4 to £10 each, places in the fifth row of the dress circle fetching as much as £4, being 400 per cent. above the box-office price. They found buyers at rates which would have shamed Shylock. Later in the day fulminations were launched upon my head, and I was accused of taking part in the plunder. I therefore determined, as far as possible, to set this right.

At length evening approached, and hundreds of tickets had been sold for standing room only.

Meanwhile Chief Crowley and Captain Short of the police, on seeing the aisles leading to the orchestra stalls and dress-circle blocked by the vast crowd, many of whom were seated on camp-stools which they had secretly brought with them, procured a warrant for my arrest the following morning. Several hot disputes occurred about this time in the main vestibule in consequence of numbers of duplicate tickets having been issued; and several seatholders were unable to reach their places. One gentleman challenged another to come and fight it out on the side walk with revolvers.

To describe the appearance of the house would be impossible. The toilettes of the ladies were charming. Many were in white, and nearly all were sparkling with diamonds. In the top gallery people were literally on the heads of one another, and on sending up to ascertain the cause, as the numbers were still increasing, the inspector ascertained that boards had been placed from the top of an adjoining house on to the roof of the Opera-house, from which the slates had been taken off; and numbers were dropping one by one through the ceiling on to the heads of those who were seated in the gallery.

Patti, of course, was smothered with bouquets, and the Italian residents of the city sent a huge globe of violets, supported on two ladders, with the Italian and American flags hanging over each side. At the end of each act huge stands and forms of flowers were sent up over the footlights and placed on the stage. To name the fashionable people in the audience would be to go over the invitation lists of the balls given in the very best houses in the city. It would be useless to describe a performance of la Diva, with which everyone is already familiar. Galassi, the baritone, made a great success; and in the gambling scene an elegant ballet was introduced, led by little Mdlle. Bettina de Sortis. Chief Crowley reported that it would require 200 extra police to keep order the next day. On going through the tickets in the treasury, we discovered upwards of 200 bogus ones taken at the door. These counterfeits were so good, even to the shade of colour, that it was almost impossible to detect the difference from the real ones; the public having smashed into the opera as if shot from howitzers. Several ladies declared that their feet had never even touched the ground from the time they got out of their carriages; and it was with difficulty that the tickets were snatched from them as they passed. Many who had paid for standing room brought little camp stools concealed under their clothes, and afterwards opened them out, placing them in the main passage ways. Had any panic occurred, or any alarm of fire, many lives must have been sacrificed.

Of course the blame for all this was put upon me. The next day there were low mutterings of discontent all over the city against my management, whilst the newspapers were unanimous in attacking me, some of their articles being headed "The Opera Swindle."

The following day I was arrested at half-past two o'clock by Detective Bowen, on a sworn warrant from Captain Short, for violating Section 49 of the Fire Ordinance of the city and county, in allowing the passage ways to be blocked up by the use of camp stools and overcrowding, the penalty for such violation being a fine of not less than 500 dollars, together with imprisonment for not less than six months.

In obedience to the warrant issued, I entered the police court the next day, accompanied by General W. H. L. Barnes, the eminent counsel who had charge of the famous Sharon case, and Judge Oliver P. Evans. On Barnes asking to see the order for arrest he found that I was described as "John Doe Mapleson," the explanation being that my Christian name was unknown. I was charged with a misdemeanour in violating the ordinance of the fire department, which declares that it is unlawful to obstruct the passage-ways or aisles of theatres during a performance. After some consultation a bond was drawn up in due form of law, General Barnes and Judge Evans being my bondsmen.

A meeting was afterwards held in the court, when the licensing collector suggested that for the protection of the public, ticket pedlars on the pavement should be made to take out a licence at an extra charge of 100 dollars each.

Notwithstanding this enormous tax, more licences were issued that afternoon at the increased rate.

At the next matinée Mdme. Gerster appeared in La Sonnambula, when the house was again crowded.

I now announced a second performance by Mdme. Patti, for the following Tuesday, in Il Trovatore, stating that the box-office would open for the sale of any surplus tickets on the following Monday at 10. Early on the morning of the sale, the line, formed between four and five o'clock in the morning, was gradually increased by new comers, all anxious to secure tickets; and by 10 o'clock, without exaggeration, it had swelled to thousands.

I herewith quote the following spirited and characteristic description of the scene from the Morning Call of March 15th, 1884:—

"To one who has stood on Mission Street, opposite the Grand Opera-house, yesterday forenoon, and 'viewed the battle from afar,' as it might be said, it seemed that a large number of people had run completely mad over the desire to hear Patti sing. Such an excited, turbulent, and, in fact, desperate crowd never massed in front of a theatre for the purpose of purchasing tickets. It absolutely fought for tickets, and it is questionable whether, if it had been an actual riot by a fierce and determined mob, the scene could have been more exciting or the wreck of the entrance of the theatre more complete. After the throng had melted away the approaches to the box-office looked as if they had been visited by a first-class Kansas cyclone in one of its worst moods. The fact that tickets were on sale for several performances had much to do with it. It was a sort of clean-up for last evening and to-day's matinée, but above all for the Patti night on Tuesday. A line began to form as early as five o'clock in the morning, and it grew and multiplied until at ten o'clock it had turned the corner on Third Street, while the main entrance was packed solid with a writhing and twisting mass of humanity, which pressed close to the glass doors which form the first barrier, and which were guarded by a lone policeman. He did his best to reduce the pressure upon himself and upon the doors, but as the time passed and the box-office did not open the crowd became more noisy and unmanageable, and finally an irresistible rush was made for the doors. They did not resist an instant, and gave way as though they had been made of paper. In the fierce tumult which followed the glass was all broken out of them, a boy being hurled bodily through one of the panes, with a most painful result to him, for he fell cut and bruised inside. There was not an inch of available space between the street and the main entrance that was not occupied by men, women, or children, indiscriminately huddled in together. The potted plants were overturned and annihilated under the feet of the throng; the glass in the large pictures which adorned the walls was broken, and the pictures themselves dragged to the floor. The box-office was besieged by a solidly-packed and howling mob, the regular line entirely overwhelmed, and a grand struggle ensued to get as near the box-office—which had not been opened—as possible. Then the crowd itself essayed to get into some sort of order.

"The more powerful forced themselves to the front and started a new line without any regard for those who had been first in position before the barriers were overthrown. It twisted itself about the lobby, forming curves and angles that would have made the typical snake retire into obscurity for very envy. This line was pressed upon from all sides by unfortunates who had been left out of the original formation of it. The air was thick and sultry, the crowd perspired and blasphemed, and the storming of the box-office became imminent. Just at this juncture Captain Short arrived with a large squad of police, and under the influence of a copious display of suggestive-looking locusts [the truncheons of the American police are made of locust wood] the crowd sullenly fell back and formed a somewhat orderly line. A line of season-ticket holders was also formed to purchase tickets for the next Patti night, and these were admitted through the inner door and served from the manager's office. In addition the crowd was notified that no Patti tickets would be sold from the box-office, but that all must go inside. This produced a yell of anger and turned bedlam loose again, as it broke up the line. But the police made a grand charge and forced hundreds outside, against the indignant protests of many who claimed that they had been in the regular line all the forenoon, only to be deprived of their rights by the police. The sale which followed seems to have given more satisfaction than that for the first Patti night."

Prior to the opening of the sale I discovered that some thirty speculators had somehow got to the inside barrier close to the office before the bonâ fide public, who had been waiting outside so long. I found that they had broken a window on the stage; afterwards clambering up and passing through the lobby of the theatre to the inner barrier, before the outer doors had been opened. I then saw that they intended to secure the whole of the tickets offered for sale. I therefore, in passing a second time, quietly nudged one of them, winked suggestively, and pointed to the upper circle ticket office; leading the willing dupes who followed me through a door in the main wall to an inner office. No sooner had the last one gone through than I had the door locked. I thus "corralled" between 25 and 30 of these speculative gentry, and kept them for over two hours, during which time the tickets were disposed of. This cleared my character with the general body of the public, who at once saw that I was in no league whatever with the speculators, or they would have turned King's evidence after my treatment of them.

While I was performing this manœuvre, the rush and jamb in the main vestibule became so great that the police officers were obliged to draw their clubs to maintain order.

On that evening we performed the opera Puritani, in which Mdme. Gerster again sang, to the delight of the numerous audience. About this time I discovered that the head usher had been in the habit of secreting a lot of stools and hiring them out to those who were standing at an extra charge of 12s. apiece. I at once sent for Captain Short, the esteemed Chief of Police, who said to the usher—

"Have the kindness to ask that lady to get up and take that stool away."

"All right," said the usher. "Please hand me that stool, madam."

The lady responded—

"But you made me pay 12s. for it; at all events, return me my money."

The Captain said—

"Give the lady back her 12s."

140

The answer was—

"We never return fees."

The Captain then gave instructions for one of his officers to take the usher off to the Southern Station and lock him up on a charge of misdemeanour.

The following morning I was again notified to attend the Police Court. My counsel, General Barnes, pleaded for a postponement for one week, on the ground that he was busily engaged in the Sharon case. To this the prosecuting attorney objected, saying that the outraged public demanded the speedy settlement of Mapleson, and the case was therefore set for the following morning.

When the case was called I was not present, being unavoidably detained at the bedside of one of my bass singers, who had suddenly died of pulmonary apoplexy. The deceased, Signor Lombardelli, was a great favourite in the Company.

General Barnes, however, appeared, demanding a postponement of the case, and intimating that a trial by jury would be demanded.

"If this should be conceded the case will go over until next May or June," replied the Clerk of the Court, "by which time the accused will be in Europe."

He therefore protested against the postponement. The Judge said sternly that it would not be granted, and the case was therefore set for the morrow.

On the following morning I came up to the Police Court, which was crowded. Police Captain Short was first called for the prosecution, and testified that the Opera-house was a place of amusement, but that it had been turned into a place of danger every evening since I had been there. Stools and standing spectators were in the main passages, and in case of a panic the consequences would have been most disastrous. Officer O'Connell testified that on the particular night in question there were 57 people standing in one little passage-way having about a dozen small folding stools amongst them. I was then placed on the witness stand, when I stated that I was the manager of the Opera Company, but not of the theatre. I had simply control of the stage, whilst the manager was responsible for the auditorium, and had provided me with the delinquent ushers. The box book-keeper was afterwards placed on the stand, who swore that I had ordered him to sell one-fifth less tickets than the manager had stated the house would hold. The defence only desired to make out the point that I was not the responsible manager. The Judge, however, decided otherwise, and found me guilty.

I was to appear the following morning to hear sentence. A heavy fine was imposed. But it was ultimately reduced to 75 dollars, which the Judge, evidently a lover of music, consented to take out in opera tickets.

That evening Patti appeared as "Leonora" in Il Trovatore. Standing room on the church steps opposite the main entrance to the theatre was again at a great premium, and a force of policemen under Captain Short was early on duty keeping the vestibule clear of loiterers, and allowing none but those who intended to witness the opera to be present.

I will not go into details of the performances either of Signor Nicolini as "Manrico," or of Patti as "Leonora." The representation was one unbroken triumph, and, as usual, the stage was piled up with set pieces and flowers.

About this time a report was brought to me as to the examination I had caused to be made of the bogus tickets, which could only be recognized after being soaked in water, when it appeared that the real ones consisted of three plies of cardboard and the bogus ones only of two.

But even after all this explanation, so disappointed and indignant were those who held the bogus tickets that they insisted, not only upon their money being returned, of which I had never received a penny, but also on their travelling and hotel expenses being repaid them. Many had come hundreds of miles in order to visit the opera.

Having arranged to give a concert on the following Thursday at the Pavilion, a large building capable of holding some 8,000 or 9,000 people, and in order to prevent a recurrence of the scenes I had just encountered and the daily trouble experienced throughout this engagement, I resolved to put up the choice of seats to auction.

The auction took place in the Grand Opera-house, and was attended by over 500 people, who had first to procure tickets of admission to attend the sale. A huge diagram was placed on the drop curtain, showing the seats that were to be sold divided into blocks. The auctioneer, who occupied the conductor's desk, explained that the whole of the seats would be placed on sale to the public and that none would be withheld, the bidders merely to name the premiums they wished to give for the privilege of purchasing the tickets. The first bidder gave 12s. premium per seat for the first choice of six seats for the concert, and other sums varied from 10s. down to 2s. 6d., the premiums alone reaching some £1,000, in addition to the sale of tickets.

This plan gave great satisfaction to the public, as whatever advance they then paid on the ticket went into the manager's pocket instead of the speculators'.

When the great concert took place the vast building was nearly full. Nine thousand persons had paid from one to five dollars each. The rain meanwhile was coming down in sheets, and several speculators who had obtained large numbers of tickets were now left out in the cold—and in the rain—with their purchases. Inside, at the back of the gallery, a brisk business was done in telescopes, for such was here the distance from Patti that, though her voice could be clearly heard, her features could not be seen.

A subscription was now started for the benefit of the widow of the late basso, Signor Lombardelli. Patti had contributed 150 dollars, when Gerster, to show that she was a greater artist, gave 1,000. I contributed 600; Galassi, Arditi, and the others 100 dollars each.

The following morning Lombardelli's funeral took place, which caused a great stir in the city. There was a full choral service; the orchestra and the whole Opera Company taking part in it, including the principal artists. Not only was San Francisco in full fête at this extraordinary funeral, but numbers of the Chinese came down from their city (called "Chinatown") in order to be present.

That evening a great reception was given by the San Francisco Verein in honour of Mdme. Gerster. The guests commenced to arrive early, and the entertainment was carried on till midnight. It is to be noted that the night for the compliment to Gerster was that of the Patti concert at the Pavilion.

On the following evening Gerster appeared as "Margherita" in Faust, the house being again crowded from floor to ceiling. That same night Patti's admirers gave a grand ball in her honour at the Margherita Club, for which 500 invitations were issued. An immense floral bower had been constructed for the occasion, the sides of the room being beds of choice flowers and roses in full bloom, while four enormous horse-shoes, all of flowers, adorned each corner of the room. Suspended from the roof was a great star with the word "Patti" in electric incandescent burners.

The Italian Consul, the Russian Consul, and several officers from the Russian flagship then in San Francisco Bay were present. The Queen of Song was escorted into the ballroom by Count Brichanteau, the band playing the "Patti Valse," composed expressly for the occasion by Arditi. A formal reception was afterwards held by the members of the Club; and later on a gorgeous supper was served in the Pavilion, which

142

had been specially erected, decorated with large Italian and Union flags. Dancing was kept up until an early hour the following morning.

While the rivalry between Patti and Gerster was at its height it was made known that General Crittenden, Governor of Missouri, had given Patti a kiss. Thereupon Mdme. Patti was interviewed, when she spoke as follows:—

"I had just finished singing 'Home, Sweet Home' last Thursday evening, when a nice-looking old gentleman, who introduced himself as Governor Crittenden, began congratulating me. All of a sudden he leaned down, put his arms around me, drew me up to him, and kissed me. He said, 'Madame Patti, I may never see you again, but I cannot help it;' and before I knew it he was kissing me. When a gentleman, and such a nice old gentleman, too, and a Governor of a great State, kisses one so quick that one has not time to see and no time to object, what can one do?"

The following dialogue on the subject between Mdme. Gerster and a reporter who had interviewed her was afterwards published:—

"THAT PATTI KISS."

MODEST REPORTER: "I suppose, Mdme. Gerster, you have heard about that kissing affair between Governor Crittenden and Patti?"

Mdme. GERSTER: "I have heard that Governor Crittenden kissed Patti before she had time to resist; but I don't see anything in that to create so much fuss."

REPORTER (interrogatively): "You don't?"

GERSTER: "Certainly not! There is nothing wrong in a man kissing a woman old enough to be his mother."

CHAPTER V.

LUNCHEON ON H.M.S. "TRIUMPH"—OPERA AUCTION—CONCERT AT MORMON TABERNACLE—RETURN TO NEW YORK—RETURN TO EUROPE—SHERIFFS IN THE ACADEMY—I DEPART IN PEACE.

I NOW received an invitation from the Admiral commanding Her Britannic Majesty's Pacific Squadron, whose flag-ship, the Triumph, had entered the bay. Several of my leading artists were also invited. The steam pinnace was sent on shore to take us on board. After visiting the ship and receiving all possible courtesies from the officers, we entered the grand saloon, in which an elegant déjeuner had been prepared, comprising all the delicacies of the season. We had scarcely begun our repast when an ominous whisper was passed by one of the officers to the captain of the ship to the effect that most of the band had deserted to go and play for Mapleson, who had offered them £12 a week each, and it was therefore impossible that any music could be given during the luncheon. Not even "God Save the Queen" could be played. The captain, in lieu of communicating this to the admiral, informed me of it privately. I thereupon expressed my surprise, as I had heard nothing about it, and I further gave my word that I would never permit one of the musicians who had deserted to take part in any performance at my theatre.

With this the captain was satisfied. It was rather hard lines to see the men on shore who had deserted the ship, and yet be unable to send a boat's crew to bring them back, after the many months of labour that had been spent in instructing them.

As the opera business kept on increasing, I determined to give an extra week in San Francisco, and to put up the privilege of purchasing seats to auction. Considerable doubt was felt, however, as to the probable result of this venture, and many declared that their purses and patience had been so thoroughly exhausted by the enormous drain of the past two weeks that I had but slender chance of continued patronage for so high-priced an entertainment.

I will, however, describe the sale. At twelve a.m. I opened the doors of the theatre, admission tickets being required to admit the purchasers, so as to keep out the rougher element, as well as the "scalpers." The auctioneer notified that the choice of every single seat in the house would be offered on sale. Upon the drop curtain were colossal diagrams of the different portions of the house, and as fast as each seat was sold it was erased by the auctioneer's assistant, who was in the orchestra with a fishing rod and black paint, with which he crossed off from the diagram each seat as it was sold.

The bids made were for choice of seat and were in addition to the regular price of the tickets.

The arrangements were most satisfactory. I had no representative present to guard my interests, but left all to the auctioneer and the public. The proscenium boxes reached 240 dollars premium for the five nights, on three of which I guaranteed that Gerster would sing, whilst Patti would sing on the other two.

Boxes were sold all round the house at an average of 120 dollars premium, each purchaser calling out from the auditorium the seat he would prefer, which was accordingly marked off, and a ticket handed to him by which he could obtain the seat selected on payment at the box office. Numbers of speculators somehow or another got mixed up with the public, and thus obtained sundry tickets. The premiums for the five nights reached £3,000.

Nothing but standing room and the gallery was left for the paying public. Notwithstanding this, the line I have already told the reader of still existed, and was as long as ever. This I could not account for, and on inquiry I found that numbers who had placed themselves in line never intended purchasing tickets, but waited there only for the purpose of selling their places. An order was thereupon issued by the police calling upon those nearest the office to produce their money to show that they were bonâ-fide purchasers. Those who could not do so were immediately removed. This difficulty, however, was met by some enterprising Jews, who lent out money for the day, simply that it might be shown to the police.

Friday was selected for the benefit and farewell of Gerster in L'Elisir d'Amore. Patti had chosen for her benefit La Traviata; which, however, was changed at the request of some 500 people, who signed a petition requesting me to substitute Crispino.

Whilst occupied one morning in my room on the fourth story at the Palace Hotel, counting with my treasurers several thousands of pounds, the atmosphere suddenly became dark. A sort of wind was blowing round the apartment, and my senses seemed to be leaving me. I could not make out what it was. The Hotel rocked three inches one way and then three inches another; the plates and knives and forks jumping off on to the floor, whilst my money was rolling in all parts of the room. I made a rush for the door, and then for the street, realizing now that there was an earthquake. Although it lasted but ten seconds the time appeared at least half an hour. On leaving the hotel I met the landlord.

"Don't be frightened," he said.

"Well, but I am."

"Nonsense! My hotel is earthquake-proof as well as fire-proof," he said, handing me a card, on which I found this inscribed: "The Palace Hotel. Fire-proof and earthquake-proof."

He afterwards explained to me that everything employed in the construction of the building was either wood or iron, no plaster or stone being used. Indeed, although this hotel is six stories high, with open corridors looking into the main courtyard the length of the entire building, it is wound round the exterior with no less than four miles of malleable iron bands. The proprietor, Mr. Sharon, said it might move into another street, but could not fall down.

To such an extent had Patti's superstitious feeling with regard to Gerster been developed that she at once ascribed the earthquake to Gerster's evil influence. It was not merely a malicious idea of hers, but a serious belief.

Meanwhile money was no consideration to those amateurs who had it. Tickets were gold. They were seized with avidity apart from any question about price. Hundreds were content to wait throughout the night, with money in their hands, to ensure the possession of even standing room, whilst thousands who, in their impecuniosity, could not hope to cross the threshold of the musical Valhalla, where Patti and Gerster were the divinities presiding, thronged the side walks, and gazed longingly at the dumb walls of the theatre, and the crowd of idolaters pouring in to worship.

At eight o'clock a.m. a second line of enthusiasts began to occupy the centre of the road leading to the Grand Opera, although the doors were not to be thrown open until six hours afterwards. A line was formed down Mission and Third Street, extending almost to Market Street. Ticket speculators passed up and down the line, and did a brisk business, tickets in some instances reaching £20 apiece.

Captain Short again arrived with 60 extra policemen, but he was pushed out with all his men, the crowd quite overpowering them. The 17 nights' performances produced £40,000. The receipts of the first Patti night did not fall far short of £5,000.

On the morning of our departure from San Francisco four young men were arrested, charged with the wholesale forgery of opera tickets. They had issued 60 bogus tickets for the opening night alone, and this caused all the confusion and wrangling. They were proved to have made a purchase of printer's ink, and to have bought one Patti ticket as a model, from which they had copied the remainder. They were duly convicted.

We left San Francisco late that evening, being accompanied by Mr. de Young, the proprietor of the leading newspaper, and his charming wife, and we arrived in due course at Salt Lake City on Tuesday evening, where Mdme. Patti dressed in her own railway car, which afterwards conveyed her to the concert. At the end of the concert she returned to the car, where a magnificent supper had been prepared for her, and the train then started for the East.

Meanwhile, the Mormons had been enthusiastic at the idea of their magnificent Tabernacle echoing with the tones of Adelina Patti. President Taylor, the Prophet of the Mormon Church, assisted in the preparations made to receive the great songstress. A special line of railway had been laid down from the regular main line of Salt Lake City to the Tabernacle, and on it the special train ran without a hitch up to the very door of the building. Upwards of 14,000 people were present, the event being considered one of extraordinary importance throughout the whole of Utah territory; and the proceeds amounted to nearly £5,000.

We left Salt Lake city after the concert about 1 a.m., and reached Omaha on the following Friday, when Mdme. Gerster appeared as "Lucia di Lammermoor." The train consisted as usual of four baggage cars, four coaches for the principals, four coaches for the chorus and orchestra, four sleeping cars, including the extra boudoir cars, La Traviata, La Sonnambula, and Semiramide, also the Lycoming, my own private car, followed by the car of Adelina Patti. The inhabitants were struck by the elegant style and finish of our equipment, and as the train rolled into the station curious crowds came to look at it, and also to catch a glimpse of the two leading stars, Adelina Patti and Etelka Gerster.

Several artists who had to perform that evening left for the town. Mdme. Patti went for a drive with Nicolini. During her absence a limited number of notabilities were allowed to inspect her car, which had cost £12,000. It was without doubt the most superb and tasteful coach on wheels anywhere in the world. The curtains were of heavy silk damask, the walls and ceilings covered with gilded tapestry, the lamps of rolled gold, the furniture throughout upholstered with silk damask of the most beautiful material. The drawing-room was of white and gold, and the ceiling displayed several figures painted by Parisian artists of eminence. The woodwork was sandal wood, of which likewise was the casing of a magnificent Steinway piano, which alone had cost 2,000 dollars. There were several panel oil paintings in the drawing-room, the work of Italian artists. The bath, which was fitted for hot and cold water, was made of solid silver. The key of the outer door was of 18-carat gold.

On Patti's being interviewed she spoke with unbounded enthusiasm of her trip to California, and expressed at the same time a wish to sing in Omaha the following year. One of the most constant companions of the Diva is the famous, world-renowned parrot, which has mastered several words and sentences in French and English. On Patti whistling a particular tune, the bird imitates her exactly. The reporter wished for its biography, and asked whether it was true that whenever Mapleson entered the car the bird cried out: "Cash, cash!" The parrot had really acquired this disagreeable habit.

That evening Mdme. Patti attended the opera, and received a perfect ovation. At the close of the performance the whole Company started for Chicago, which we reached the following Sunday, when I received telegraphic news of the sad state Cincinnati was in. The riots had assumed terrible proportions, the streets were full of barricades, the gaol had been burned down by petroleum, and the prisoners released from it; whilst absolute fighting was taking place in the streets, and numbers had been killed or wounded.

According to the pictures sent me in an illustrated paper, the militia were firing upon the populace; the Court House had been destroyed by fire, as well as the gaol; and the struggle had already been on for over three days. I therefore telegraphed at once to Fennessy, at Cincinnati, the impossibility of my coming there, the singers one and all objecting to move.

To my great regret I was obliged to cancel my Cincinnati engagement, and we started our train in the direction of New York. On the succeeding Monday we opened the season, during which we produced Romeo and Juliet, with Patti and Nicolini, and gave performances of Elisir d'Amore, followed by Semiramide, in which I was glad to be able to reinstate Scalchi as "Arsace." She having been thrown out of her engagement by the collapse of Mr. Abbey, I readily re-engaged her, not only for that year, but also for the year following.

Mdme. Patti afterwards sailed for Europe, leaving by the Oregon, which was to start early on the Saturday morning. She decided to go on board the day previously, but as it was Friday she drove about the city until the clock struck twelve before she would embark. The following day I shipped off the remainder of my Company.

I myself was compelled to remain behind in consequence of a deal of trouble which was then gathering, and which began by the attachment of the whole of the Patti benefit receipts at the suit of the Bank of the Metropolis. This bank had discounted a joint note of guarantee which the stockholders of the Academy of Music had given me early in the season to enable me to defeat the rival house, which I succeeded in doing.

My losses during the New York season having exceeded £1,200 a week, I was compelled to draw the maximum amount authorized. Nothing at the time was said about my repaying any portion of the money, although I felt morally bound, in case of success, to do so. The stockholders had really acted for the preservation of their own property, my own means having been already swamped in the undertaking. I worked as economically as

I possibly could to achieve the purpose for which their assistance had been given; and, in fact, drew some £800 less than I was entitled to. Judge, therefore, of my surprise when I learned of their harsh course of proceedings, beginning with what appeared to be the repudiation of their own signatures.

The Secretary having requested my attendance before the Directors, it had been hinted to me by friends that I was to be invited to a banquet at Delmonico's in recognition of the energy and skill with which, through unheard-of difficulties, I had at last conducted my season to a successful issue. All, however, that the Secretary had to say to me was that unless I immediately took up my guarantors' joint note seizure would be made on the whole of my worldly belongings.

Just at this time most advantageous offers were made to me from the rival Opera-house, then without a manager. But as I still had an agreement with the Academy, I did not enter into the negotiation, explaining my inability to do so, and at the same time relying fully on the justice and liberality of my own Directors and stockholders.

I felt sadly injured at their sending the Sheriff in on the very night of Patti's benefit to lay hands on all my receipts in order to squeeze the guarantee money out of me.

The next day Sheriff Aaron and his satellites took entire charge of the Academy. They commenced by unhanging all my scenery, and it was only with difficulty that I got permission to remove a small writing desk containing a few sheets of paper and half-a-dozen postage stamps. In vain did I remonstrate with the Directors, urging that if they were dissatisfied with my management they could easily set me at liberty from my next year's lease, which would be a great saving to them, inasmuch as by its terms they had to find the theatre for me free, and pay all the gas, service, and other expenses. All my approaches were met with silence, and I was again obliged to decline the tempting offer from the rival theatre, at which I should have had the use of the magnificent house and a very heavy subsidy to boot.

As the Metropolitan Opera Directors could wait no longer, they now opened negotiations with Mr. Gye.

In the meantime the myrmidons of the law, assisted by my regular scene-shifters and carpenters, set to work removing everything into the Nilsson Hall adjoining the Academy, of which I held the lease, whilst other assistants made out an inventory. As there were hundreds of scenes and thousands of dresses, the work continued for many days.

I met shortly afterwards one of the most prominent men of the Academy Board of Directors, who informed me that the Bank had not made application to him, nor, in fact, to any of his friends who had guaranteed the payment of the advance made on their joint bond; and he urged me to insist upon the Bank's making direct application to the signatories of the documents before proceeding to such extremities.

At length I induced the Bank to make the application suggested, and I must say that all the gentlemen punctually paid up. I afterwards ascertained that the trouble had been caused by two individuals who were unwilling to honour their own signatures. All this turmoil and fuss, however, had given new encouragement to the rival directors, who on learning of all the bother, and finding that I could not obtain my release from the Academy, prosecuted their negotiations with Mr. Gye to manage their Opera-house.

It was not until the third week in May that I was able to take my departure from New York. Some three or four hundred people met me at the wharf on my leaving. On the table in the saloons of the steamer were the most gorgeous flower devices sent by my friends of New York, Philadelphia, and Boston. One piece was five feet in height; another consisted of a large crown of roses supported on four rounded arms of metal, covered with vines and blossoms holding an inscription in the centre: "J. H. M., the Invincible," worked in forget-me-nots on a background of red and white carnations. In fact, such magnificent tributes had scarcely ever been offered even to my prime donne.

A tug followed the steamer up the bay with a band of music on board; and, to tell the truth, I was very glad to get out of the place in order that I might have a little relaxation.

CHAPTER VI.

ROYAL ITALIAN OPERA LIQUIDATES—GETTING PATTI OFF THE SHIP—HENRY WARD BEECHER'S CIDER—PATTI'S SILVER WEDDING—A PATTI PROGRAMME OF 1855—A BLACK CONCERT.

AFTER my departure the Directors of the Metropolitan Opera-house, convinced that they could make no arrangement with me in consequence of my engagement with the Directors of the Academy, which had still a year to run, took further steps towards securing Mr. Gye as manager; and it was proposed that he should open his season at the new theatre on November 10th, to continue for thirteen weeks. The negotiations were conducted on his behalf by his agent, Mr. Lavine. The stockholders of the Metropolitan Opera reserving seventy of the best boxes for themselves, Mr. Gye was to have the house rent free, together with a guarantee against loss, and £200 for each performance. This sum was ultimately raised to £300 for each performance.

Seeing another opera looming in the distance, I at once set to work by re-engaging Mdme. Adelina Patti on her own terms of £1,000 a night; likewise Mdme. Scalchi, Galassi, and Arditi, thus forming a very strong nucleus to start with. I afterwards learned that Gye had been making overtures to Mdme. Patti, Galassi, and others; but fortunately they had already signed contracts with me.

The Metropolitan Directors next dispatched their able attorney, George L. Rives, to Europe for the purpose of completing the arrangements with Gye.

Shortly after my return to London I learned that the Royal Italian Opera, Limited, had gone into liquidation. This, of course, snuffed out at once Gye's contract with the Metropolitan Opera Directors, who being now left without an impresario contemplated diverting the grand building to other purposes. They ultimately, however, resolved to try a German Opera rather than have no Opera at all, and they dispatched their energetic secretary, Mr. Stanton, to Europe for the purpose of engaging artists, Dr. Damrosch being appointed orchestral conductor.

During the summer months I visited various parts of the Continent for the purpose of obtaining the best talent I could find for the coming contest. Various meetings were held by my Academy stockholders in New York when they at length began to realize the justice of my demands for assistance, as it could not be expected that 200 of the best seats, for which no payment whatever was to be made, should be occupied for listening to Mdme. Patti, who was receiving £1,000 a night. After various meetings, a resolution was passed by which they agreed to give me a nightly assessment of four dollars a seat for the proscenium boxes, three for the other boxes, and two for the seats elsewhere, which during my season it was estimated by them would produce some £6,000; and a cable was sent me to that effect in order to obviate the trouble we had all fallen into in the previous year. At the same time the Directors passed a resolution to keep the theatre closed in case I did not accept their promised support.

About this time a young singer named Emma Nevada was attracting considerable attention in Europe, and after some difficulty I succeeded in adding her name to my already powerful list, which, however, did not include that of Madame Christine Nilsson, as I had contemplated; that lady having cried off at the last moment without any valid reason, after I had accepted all her conditions.

In due course the New York prospectus was issued, and a very fine subscription was the result, the demand for boxes being particularly brisk.

We sailed from Liverpool, and arrived in New York on the 1st November. I had a few hours only to give preliminary instruction regarding the commencement of my season when a telegram arrived to the effect that the Oregon, with Mdme. Patti on board, had been sighted off Fire Island.

I at once ordered the military band to go down to the Blackbird; but as no further telegram reached me from Sandy Hook they went on shore for beer. It was late in the evening when the expected telegram arrived, and the vessel had to start immediately. The only musicians I had now on board wherewith to serenade Patti were a clarinet, a trombone, and a big drum.

Stretched from mast to mast was a huge tarpaulin with the word "Welcome!" on both sides, in letters three feet long. In the lower bay of quarantine I met the Oregon, and as my steamer came alongside a small group appeared, and I at once recognized Patti. Handkerchiefs were waved, and three cheers given by my friends on board the Blackbird. We had a ladder with us which just reached from the top of our paddle-box to about two feet below the sides of the vessel. I was on the point of clambering up when the captain shrieked out—

"Patti cannot be taken out to-night without a permission from the health-officer."

I at once tendered a permit I had obtained from the barge office, allowing Patti to go on shore. I passed it to the captain, who, on reading it, said—

"That is all right, but the health-officer must give me a permit before I will let her out of the ship."

I, therefore, had to steam my vessel to quarantine, and it was nearly two hours before I could find health-officer Smith, through whose kind assistance I obtained a permit to take Patti off the ship. On my returning the whole of the passengers gave three hearty cheers as Patti was let over the side into my boat, followed by Nicolini, the maid, the parrot, and the diamonds.

Mdme. Patti, Nicolini, the maid, the parrot, and the diamonds duly arrived at the Windsor Hotel that evening, and the chief of the party was, of course, interviewed forthwith as to how she had passed the previous summer.

"Delightfully," was the Diva's reply. "We had lots of Americans stopping with us at my Castle, and the place grows dearer and dearer to me every year."

She was very much grieved to hear of poor Brignoli's death, which had occurred the previous day, and she sent a magnificent wreath to be placed on his coffin. I attended the funeral on behalf of my Company.

When the arrival of Patti became known in New York great excitement prevailed. The day afterwards the steamship Lessing arrived from Hamburg with an entire German Company for the Metropolitan Opera-house. I now felt quite at my ease, having no anxiety whatever as to the result of their season.

I opened brilliantly on the Monday following the arrival of Patti, with her inimitable performance of "Rosina" in Il Barbiere.

On Sunday I was invited by Henry Ward Beecher to visit Plymouth Church, at Brooklyn. On this occasion a number of railway guards and pointsmen had been asked; and never shall I forget the sermon he preached to them. It was magnificent, and in every way impressive. At the conclusion of the service I was invited to Mr. Beecher's house to luncheon, where there were some twenty of his relations and intimate friends present.

As the water came round he may possibly have observed a distressed look on my countenance. But certain it is that within a few minutes afterwards he said he thought he had a bottle of cider which I might prefer to the beverage then before us; and, although it was labelled cider, I discovered that the bottle contained something resembling excellent old "Pommery sec."

Two nights afterwards I invited him to my box at the opera, scarcely hoping that he would come; but shortly after the overture had commenced I was surprised to find him sitting at my side. He remained there all that evening, the eye of every one in the audience being fixed upon him.

Shortly afterwards my new prima donna, Mdlle. Emma Nevada, arrived, and in due course made her first appearance, in La Sonnambula, when a remarkable scene occurred. At the close of the performance the audience, instead of rushing to the doors as usual, remained, rose to their feet, and called the prima donna three times before the curtain.

This was followed by a production of Gounod's Mirella, in which Emma Nevada again appeared with brilliant success; and afterwards by La Gazza Ladra, with Patti and Scalchi in the leading rôles.

On the 24th November, it being the 25th anniversary of Patti's first appearance at the New York Academy of Music, great preparations were made for the purpose of celebrating her silver wedding with the New York operatic stage.

The opera selected for the occasion was Lucia di Lammermoor, being the same work in which she had appeared exactly 25 years previously on the Academy boards. Patti's first "Edgardo," Signor Brignoli, was to have appeared with her. But his sudden death necessitated an alteration of the original programme, and it was decided to give an opera which the Diva had never sung in America, namely, Martha.

The following account of Patti's début, which appeared in the New York Herald, of November 25th, 1859, will be read with interest:—

"DÉBUT OF MISS PATTI.

"A young lady, not yet seventeen, almost an American by birth, having arrived here when an infant, belonging to an Italian family which has been fruitful of good artists, sang last night the favourite rôle of débutantes, 'Lucia di Lammermoor.'

"Whether it is from the natural sympathy with the forlorn fiancée of the Master of Ravenswood which is infused into the female breast with Donizetti's tender music, or from a clever inspiration that to be unhappy and pretty is a sure passport to the affections of an audience, we cannot say. Certain it is, however, that the aspirants for the ovations, the triumphs, the glories, that await a successful prima donna almost always select this opera for their preliminary dash at the laurels. The music affords a fine opportunity to show the quality and cultivation of the soprano voice, and it is so familiar as to provoke comparison with first-rate artists, and provoke the severest criticisms by the most rigid recognized tests.

"All these were duly and thoroughly applied to Miss Adelina Patti a day or two since by a very critical audience at what was called a show rehearsal. It was then ascertained that Miss Patti had a fine voice, and that she knew how to sing. The artists and amateurs were in raptures. This was a certificate to the public, who do not nowadays put their faith in managers' announcements, unless they are endorsed. With an off-night and an opera worn to bits, the public interest in Miss Patti's début was so great as to bring together a very large audience, rather more popular than usual, but still numbering the best-known habitués and most critical amateurs. The débutante was received politely but cordially—an indication that there was not a strong claque, which was a relief. Her appearance was that

150

of a very young lady, petite and interesting, with just a tinge of schoolroom in her manner. She was apparently self-possessed, but not self-assured.

"After the first few bars of recitative, she launched boldly into the cavatina—one of the most difficult pieces of the opera. This she sang perfectly, displaying a thorough Italian method and a high soprano voice, fresh and full and even throughout. In the succeeding cabaletta, which was brilliantly executed, Miss Patti took the high note E flat, above the line, with the greatest ease. In this cabaletta we noticed a tendency to show off vocal gifts which may be just a little out of place. The introduction of variations not written by the composer is only pardonable in an artist who has already assured her position. In the duet with the tenor (Brignoli) and with the baritone (Ferri), and the mad scene, Miss Patti sang with sympathetic tenderness—a rare gift in one so young—and increased the enthusiasm of the audience to a positive furore, which was demonstrated in the usual way—recalls, bouquets, wreaths, etc., etc. The horticultural business was more extensive than usual.

"Of course we speak to-day only of Miss Patti's qualifications as a singer. Acting she has yet to learn; but artists, like poets, are born, not made. The mere convenances of the stage will come of themselves. She is already pretty well acquainted with them. So far as her voice, skill, method, and execution are concerned, we are simply recording the unanimous opinion of the public when we pronounce the début of Miss Patti a grand success.

"Everyone predicts a career for this young artist, and who knows but the managers may find in her their long-looked-for sensation?"

On repeating the character two days afterwards, said the same paper, "the prima donna was twice called before the curtain, and the stage was literally covered with the flowers thrown before her. The success of this artist, educated and reared amongst us, with all the vocal gifts of an Italian, and all the cleverness of a Yankee girl, is made. Everybody talked of her, wondering who and what she is, where she has been, and so on.

"She was brought out at the Academy to save the season. The manager had a good Company, plenty of fine artists, everything required for fine performances, but the great outside public, always thirsting for something new, wanted a sensation.

"They have it in 'Little Patti,' who not only pleases the connoisseurs and is the special favourite of the fair, but who has all the material for a great popular pet."

The jubilee performance was a brilliant success. At the close of the opera, after the usual number of recalls, accompanied by bouquets, etc., the curtain rose, and at the rear of the stage was an immense American eagle about to soar, beneath which was the word "Patti," and over it "1859-1884." The band of the 7th Regiment approached the footlights, and the musicians played a march that Cappa, the bandmaster, had composed in honour of Mdme. Patti twenty-five years before. Patti walked up to him, and said, with a choking voice: "I thank you for your kindness from the bottom of my heart."

She was afterwards recalled innumerable times, and on reappearing she brought on with her Mdme. Scalchi. At the close of the opera a carriage with four milk-white steeds which I had arranged for was standing to convey its precious burthen to her hotel. Following this we had 100 torch-bearers, for the most part admirers and supporters of the opera. Mounted police were on each side of Patti's carriage. At the end of the procession was a waggon full of people letting off Roman candles and large basins of powder, which, when ignited, made the streets and sky look most brilliant. The route was up Broadway to Twenty-third Street, and thence up Madison Avenue to Patti's hotel.

I on this occasion was to have taken the command of the troops as brigadier. My horse, however, never reached me. It was found impossible to get it through the crowd.

151

This did not prevent the illustrated papers from representing me on horseback, and in a highly military attitude.

Later on two other bands arrived, and took their stations under Patti's windows. This terminated the festivities in honour of the twenty-fifth anniversary of her first appearance on the American operatic stage.

I may here mention that, as a matter of fact, Adelina Patti did not make her first appearance on the American stage in 1859. I find, too, that she sang at Niblo's Saloon in 1855, and subjoin the programme of one of her concerts given in that year:—

GRAND VOCAL AND INSTRUMENTAL CONCERT,

IN AID OF THE

Hebrew Benevolent Societies,

AT NIBLO'S SALOON,

On Tuesday Evening, Feb. 27th, 1855.

The management announces that MRS. STUART, in consequence of the severe indisposition of her mother, will not be able to fulfil her engagement this evening; also, that MME. COMETANT cannot appear in consequence of her severe indisposition. The management have much pleasure in announcing that the services

of

SIGNORINA ADELINA PATTI

Have been secured, in connection with whom the following

artistes have volunteered:—

SIGNOR BERNARDI,

SIGNOR RAPETTI,

HERR CHARLES WELS,

T. FRANKLIN BASSFORD,

MR. SANDERSON.

PROGRAMME:

PART FIRST.

1   Grand Duet, on "William Tell," Piano and Violin—;Mr. Rapetti and Mr. Wels Osborne and De Beriot

2   Grand Cavatina, of Norma, Casta Diva—;Signa. Adelina Patti   Bellini

3   "La Chasse du jeune Henri," Overture for Piano—;Mr. Bassford Gottschalk

4   Aria, from "Don Sebastian"—;Sig. Bernardi   Donizetti

5   Ballad, "Home, Sweet Home"—;Signa. Adelina Patti   Bishop

6   Grand Duo concertando on airs of "Norma," for Two Pianos—;Messrs. Wels and Bassford   Wels

---

PART SECOND.

1   "Coronation March," from the Prophet, arranged and performed by Mr. Sanderson, his First Appearance in public   Meyerbeer

2   Aria, from the Opera Le Châlet—;Sig. Bernardi   Adam

3   {a. The Eolian Harp}

{b. Triumphal March} Composed and performed by   C. Wels

4   Jenny Lind's Echo Song—;Signa. Adelina Patti   Eckert

5   Violin Solo, from La Sonnambula   Sig. Rapetti

6   Grand Fantasia, for Two Pianos, performed by Messrs. Bassford and Wels, composed by   T. Franklin Bassford

_____

Conductor   Mr. Charles Wels.

_____

The Two Grand Prize Pianos, used on this occasion, are from the Music Stores of Messrs. Bassford and Brower, and are for sale at 603, Broadway.

Doors open at 7 o'clock. To commence at 8 o'clock.

TICKETS ONE DOLLAR

To be had at the Music Store of Messrs. Hall and Son, Bassford and Brower, 603, Broadway, and Scharfenberg and Louis, and at the door.

Going still further back, I may add that Adelina Patti made her very first appearance on the operatic stage in 1850, at Tripler's Hall, New York; where she sang and acted both. She was seven years old at the time.

The season continued until the latter part of December.

On my applying to the Academy Directors for an instalment of the £6,000 which had been promised me in accordance with the assessment made, I was informed by the Secretary that the assessment would only be allowed to me on Patti nights. This reduced my £6,000 by three-fourths, I having based my calculations on the amount that had been cabled to me. I in no way blame the stockholders, who had been most heavily assessed, and had paid up without a murmur. Some three-fourths of their contributions had been used for other purposes, including the decoration of the theatre.

Finding the President of the Academy Directors obdurate, I at once announced the farewell performances of Mdme. Adelina Patti, and shortly afterwards made arrangements for her appearance, together with that of the whole Company, at Boston, where I opened towards the close of December, glad, indeed, to get away from the Academy.

Our success in Boston was very great. Amongst the productions was Gounod's Mirella, in which Nevada, Scalchi, De Anna, and other artists appeared. Afterwards, of course, came Semiramide, with Patti and Scalchi; one of our surest cards.

We remained at Boston two weeks, concluding, what was then supposed to be Patti's positive farewell to the Bostonians, with a magnificent performance of Linda di Chamouni.

At the conclusion of a representation of Mirella given the following morning we started for Philadelphia, where we had a very remunerative season, the house being crowded nightly to the ceiling.

The American theatres are much better kept than ours. They are dusted and cleaned every day, so that a lady in America can go to the play or to the opera without the least danger of getting her dress spoiled; which in England, if the dress be of delicate material, she scarcely can do. The American theatres, moreover, are beautifully warmed during the winter months; so that the risk of bronchitis and inflammation of the lungs to which the enterprising theatre-goers of our own country are exposed has in the United States no existence.

Apart from the risk of getting her dress injured by dirt or dust, a lady has no inducement to wear a handsome toilette at a London Opera-house, where the high-fronted boxes with their ridiculous curtains prevent the dresses from being seen. At the American Opera-houses the boxes are not constructed in the Italian, but in the French style. They are open in front, that is to say, so that those who occupy them can not only see, but be seen. As for the curtains, they are neither a French nor an Italian, but exclusively an English peculiarity. What possible use can they serve? They have absolutely no effect but to deaden the sound.

An interesting feature in every American Opera-house is the young ladies' box—a sort of omnibus box to which young ladies alone subscribe. The gentlemen who are privileged to visit them in the course of the evening are also allowed full liberty to supply them with bouquets, which are always of the most delicate and most expensive kind—costing in winter from £4 to £5 a-piece. The front of the young ladies' box is kept constantly furnished with the most beautiful flowers that love can suggest or money buy; and if, as it frequently does, it occurs to one or more of the young ladies to throw a few of the bouquets to the singers on the stage, their friends and admirers are expected at once to fill up the gaps.

Whilst at Philadelphia the head-waiter of the hotel informed me that a very grand concert was to take place, for which it was difficult to obtain tickets, but that a prima donna would sing there whom he considered worthy of my attention. In due course he got me a ticket, and I attended the concert, which was held in one of the extreme quarters of the city. On entering I was quite surprised to find an audience of some 1,500 or 2,000, who were all black, I being the only white man present. I must say I was amply repaid for the trouble I had taken, as the music was all of the first order.

In the course of the concert the prima donna appeared, gorgeously attired in a white satin dress, with feathers in her hair, and a magnificent diamond necklace and earrings. She moreover wore white kid gloves, which nearly went to the full extent of her arm, leaving but a small space of some four inches between her sleeve and the top of her glove. Her skin being black, formed, of course, an extraordinary contrast with the white kid.

She sang the Shadow Song from Dinorah delightfully, and in reply to a general encore gave the valse from the Romeo and Juliet of Gounod. In fact no better singing have I heard. The prima donna rejoiced in the name of Mdlle. Selika. Shortly afterwards a young baritone appeared and sang the "Bellringer," so as to remind me forcibly of Santley in his best days. I immediately resolved upon offering him an engagement to appear at the Opera-house in London as "Renato" in Un Ballo in Maschera, whom Verdi, in one version of the opera, intended to be a coloured man; afterwards to perform "Nelusko" in L'Africaine, and "Amonasro" in Aida. Feeling certain of his success, I intended painting him white for the other operas.

After some negotiation I was unable to complete the arrangement. He preferred to remain a star where he was.

After the final performance of our Philadelphia engagement we started at about 3 a.m. with the whole Company for New Orleans, our special train being timed to reach that city by the following Sunday. On arriving at Louisville the gauge was broken, and the track became narrow gauge, which necessitated the slinging of every one of my grand carriages to have new trollies put under them to fit the smaller gauge. This was so skilfully managed whilst the artists were asleep that they were unaware of the operation.

CHAPTER VII.

PANIC AT NEW ORLEANS—THERMOMETER FALLS 105 DEGREES—BANQUET AT CHICAGO—THE COUNT DI LUNA AT MARKET—COFFEE JOHN—AN AMERICAN GEORGE ROBINS—MY UNDERTAKER.

ON getting down to New Orleans we found a great change in the temperature, and although it was the month of January the thermometer stood at about 75°. It had been raining exactly six weeks prior to our arrival, and only ceased as our train went in, fine weather immediately afterwards making its appearance.

154

Our opening opera was La Sonnambula with Nevada, which was followed by La Traviata with Mdme. Patti. Prior to the last act a panic was caused in the theatre by the falling of some plaster from the front of the dress circle. Someone near the exit to the stalls shouted "Fire," a cry which was repeated by numbers of men in the lobby. Consternation was seen in the faces of the audience, and a general rush was made for the doors. The situation was serious in the extreme; but the presence of mind of some gentlemen present, aided by the equal coolness of several ladies, had the effect of allaying the general fright.

Many ladies, on the other hand, fainted from excitement, whilst numbers of persons left the theatre, so that the last act was given with a very bare house.

"A great deal of excitement," wrote a local journal, "was manifested in the street, and rumour magnified the incident. It took the shape of a fearful accident in the minds of some people, and it was some time before the public was assured that no damage had resulted to life or limb. One young lady fainted as she was about to enter her carriage in front of the theatre. She fell to the side walk, slightly cutting her mouth, and was unconscious for a few minutes. With the assistance of Dr. Joseph Scott, her friends succeeded in reviving her, and she was placed in a carriage and driven home. Mr. David Bidwell was this morning waited upon by the Item reporter, who informed him of the many rumours regarding the safety of the St. Charles Theatre. Mr. Bidwell said: 'The whole trouble comes from the fall of a small piece of plastering, three feet long by one foot and a half wide, in the left part of the theatre, back to the parquette seats. The plastering at that place had been disturbed during the Kiralfy engagement by the moving out of some scenery. I had the spot repaired during the wet weather, and, from the dampness, the plastering did not hold. As regards the solidity of the theatre, you can state that it is the strongest building of its kind; the walls are in places four feet thick. Everything inside is sound and substantial, having been recently repaired and renovated. Mr. William Freret, the architect, has just been in here, and made a thorough inspection. He finds everything in first-class condition, and sound as can be. The public should not give credence to silly rumours, but listen to the voice of common sense and reason, and accept this satisfactory explanation.'"

The City Surveyor, with various architects, visited the theatre the following day to report; but all certified that the building was solid, and that probably the stamping of so many feet in applauding Patti had caused the fall of the plaster. However it may have been, my receipts being so considerably injured, I was compelled, after paying damages to the manager for not completing the engagement, to remove the Company and rent the Grand French Opera-house for the ensuing week. When my announcement was made several ladies called upon me, and a meeting was convened at one of their houses at which the élite of the city were present. A number of gentlemen had been invited to tea, and before being allowed to leave the room each of them was required to subscribe for at least one box. In this manner the whole of my boxes for the remainder of the season were disposed of.

I had a deal of trouble in getting the theatre into working order, it having been closed for a considerable period. The corridors had to be whitened and the dressing-rooms to be papered, and all the business had to be conducted in French, as my stage carpenters and employés were all of that nationality. The manager of the other theatre had refused to allow any of his staff to assist.

During this time the great New Orleans Exhibition had been opened, to which thousands of people were attracted. My attention, however, was drawn to the Woman's Work Department, in great need just then. I therefore organized a grand benefit matinée on their behalf, which was promptly responded to by many of the ladies of New Orleans. Many of my principal artists took part in the concert, and I was assisted by a splendid Mexican cavalry band. A large sum of money was realized, which was afterwards handed over to the treasurer of the Woman's Department.

After a performance of Les Huguenots we all left that night for St. Louis. The temperature was now intolerable, the thermometer marking 75 degrees. But on reaching St. Louis the following Monday afternoon we were overtaken by a blizzard. It was literally raining ice. The streets were impassable, it being difficult to stand upright or to move a step; whilst the thermometer stood 30 degrees below zero (62° below freezing point)— being a fall of 105 degrees. I need scarcely say everyone caught sore throat, even to the chorus. One or two of the ballet girls were blown down and hurt on leaving the train, and it was with considerable difficulty that I made a commencement that evening, two hours after our arrival, with a performance of La Sonnambula. This was followed by Semiramide with Patti and Scalchi, and by Lucrezia with Fursch-Madi. All the artists not taking part in these works were ill in bed during the week.

Prior to our leaving St. Louis a magnificent banquet was tendered to me by the Directors of the newly-organized Opera Festival Association of Chicago. The day originally fixed was the Wednesday during that week; but it had afterwards to be transferred to Thursday, all the trains to Chicago being snowed up, whilst several thousands of freight cars blocked the line for miles. I ventured after the performance on the only train allowed out of the station for Chicago, where I arrived the following day, and visited the huge glass building, formerly the exhibition, where I marked out what I considered would be the dimensions necessary for the construction of the New Grand Opera-house. In doing so I must have rather miscalculated my measurements, as I was shortly afterwards informed that if carried out the theatre would be a mammoth one.

In the evening I attended the banquet given in my honour, which was laid for fifty covers in the large room of the magnificent Calumet Club. The banqueting hall was picturesquely decorated with flowers. The tables were curved in the form of a huge lyre, bearing the coat of arms of the Association.

At the head of the table, which formed the base of the lyre, sat the President, Ferd. W. Peck, and at his right hand I was placed as the guest of the evening. Next to me was the Mayor, and next him the Hon. Emery A. Stores, the Vice-President of the Association. At President Peck's left hand sat the Hon. Eugene Carey and George Schneider, the treasurer of the newly-formed Association. All the city notabilities, more or less, were present on this occasion. At the conclusion of the banquet the President rose, introducing me as "The Napoleon: the Emperor of Opera," giving at the same time a brief outline of the work proposed to be accomplished. My speech was a very short one. I said: "After twenty-four years' experience in the rendition of opera I feel that my greatest success is about to be achieved here in Chicago. Never before have such opportunities been afforded me. I have this morning been over the Exposition building with an architect, and have fixed upon a large, comfortable auditorium. I also visited the hall where the extra chorus was practising, and I must say I was surprised at its excellence in every way. Never have I heard a better chorus, even in the Old World."

The Mayor afterwards rose and paid me the highest compliments.

In the small hours of the following morning, when we separated, I went to the station and thence returned to St. Louis.

At the close of the week we left St. Louis with the whole of the troupe, some 180 strong, reaching Kansas City late that evening. Most of the members of the Company went to the Coates House, Mdme. Patti, however, remaining in her private car, where the following day I paid her a visit. No sooner had I entered than we were shunted and sent some four miles down the line, much to the surprise of Nicolini, who had been speaking to me on the platform but a moment previously. We were detained a considerable time, and Mdme. Patti experienced a great shock as suddenly a goods truck, which had got uncoupled, came running down. This caused a great concussion, which broke most of the glass, and sent Nicolini's cigars, jams, the parrot, the piano, the table, and the flowers all pell-mell on to the floor. Mdme. Patti, however, took it in good part, and, assisted by her maids, commenced gathering up the broken ornaments and smashed bottles. The floor ran with Château Lafite.

Mdme. Patti visited the opera that evening, the Mayor of the town conducting her down the passage way to her proscenium box amidst such a storm of applause as is rarely heard in an Opera-house. Ladies burst their gloves in their enthusiasm, and men stood on their seats to get a view of the Diva. On reaching the box the audience rose and cried: "Brava!"

After the performance that night the train moved on in the direction of Topeka, where, through the politeness of the railway officials, I got Patti's car attached to the San Francisco express, which conveyed her to her destination in about three and a half days.

The rest of the Company remained in Topeka to give a performance of Il Trovatore, Mdme. Dotti being the "Leonora," Mdme. Scalchi "Azucena," De Anna the "Count di Luna," and Giannini "Manrico." The success was immense, the house being full, and the receipts reaching £700.

In connection with Topeka, I must mention rather a curious incident. We had exhausted our stock of wine in the train, and those artists taking part in the performance, on entering the hotel near the theatre where it was proposed to dine, were surprised and annoyed at having water placed before them; the baritone vowing, with a knife in his hand, that unless he could have a more stimulating beverage he would refuse to play the "Count di Luna" that evening.

Inquiry was made high and low, but there was not a drop of wine or spirits of any kind officially known to be in the town. Going along the street on my return to the hotel, I met a gentleman with whom I was acquainted, and through his kindness I was enabled to obtain from a medical practitioner a prescription. The prescription was in the Latin language, and the chemist evidently understood its meaning. There was no question of making it up. He simply handed me three bottles of very good hock.

At the conclusion of the opera, it being a most delightful evening, the various choristers and others made purchases of all kinds of comestibles, and it was a most ridiculous thing to observe some going down with chickens carried by the neck, others with cauliflowers and asparagus. The "Count di Luna" with a huge ham under his arm, and "Manrico" with a chain of sausages, took their provisions down to the cars to be cooked for supper, during which the train started for St. Joseph.

We reached St. Joseph the following day, where Mdlle. Nevada appeared in La Sonnambula, greatly pleasing the audience, which packed the theatre full.

We arrived the next afternoon at half-past four at Omaha, where we remained one day, my advance agent having failed to conclude any arrangements for our appearance there.

Shortly afterwards we started for Cheyenne, arriving in the Magic City, as it is called, in about a couple of days; when, to my great astonishment, no announcement whatever had been made of our visit, my advance agent again, for some unaccountable reason, having gone on the road towards San Francisco without notifying even a word.

Our coming there was quite an unexpected event. Arrangements were immediately made to give a performance. This entailed a delay of a couple of days, which delighted me, although it caused some loss, as it enabled me to drive over the beautiful country and visit once more the charming Club, where I had a right royal welcome from my numerous friends of the previous year.

At four o'clock the 3rd Cavalry band, in full uniform, came to serenade me at my hotel.

The opera selected was Lucia di Lammermoor, and the receipts came to some £700.

At the close of the performance we started for Salt Lake City, where we arrived on the following Thursday. Here, to my great regret, I was compelled to change the bill in consequence of Mdlle. Nevada's indisposition, at which the inhabitants and the Press grumbled as if it were my fault. Reports of course were circulated that she had not received her salary.

Whilst at Salt Lake City many of the artists and orchestral players wandered about, visiting various places of interest; and some were attracted to a restaurant kept by one "Coffee John," in whose window was exposed a huge turtle, bearing this tragic inscription on its head: "This afternoon I am to have my throat cut;" whilst on its back was a ticket for a private box, with the statement that Coffee John had paid 40 dollars for it, and was going to visit the opera that evening.

In order to patronize this enthusiastic amateur several of our principal artists went in and ordered luncheon. Coffee John was very polite, promising to applaud them on hearing them sing, and allowing many of them to go into the kitchen to prepare their own macaroni. The price of the luncheon was very moderate, so everyone decided to go and dine at Coffee John's later on.

When dinner was over they asked the waiter how much they had to pay.

"Six dollars a head," said the waiter.

"Corpo di Bacco!" exclaimed one of the artists; "dat is too dear. Where is Coffee John, our friend, our friend?"

"He has gone to dress for the opera," replied the head waiter, "and I dare not disturb him."

As there were twelve diners the bill came to 72 dollars, so that Coffee John, who had paid 40 dollars for his box, occupied it for nothing that evening, and profited, moreover, largely by the transaction. The waiter told the astonished artists that his governor had paid 40 dollars to hear them sing without kicking, and that he expected liberal treatment in return; finally, he thought the best plan for them would be to pay their six dollars each and clear out; which they eventually had to do.

Mdlle. Nevada had taken cold at Cheyenne, and contracted what turned out to be a severe illness; and I lost her services for no less than four weeks afterwards.

The night before we reached Salt Lake City Mdme. Scalchi's parrot died, which caused the excellent contralto to go into hysterics and take to a bed of sickness. I had announced Il Trovatore, in which the now despondent vocalist was to have taken the part of the vindictive gipsy. This I considered would amply compensate for the absence of Nevada. Only half an hour before starting for the theatre I was notified by Mdme. Scalchi's husband that she would be unable to appear that evening. I insisted, however, upon her going at all events to the theatre, as I considered the death of a parrot not sufficient reason for disappointing a numerous public. I threatened at the same time to fine her very heavily if she refused.

About an hour afterwards the call-boy came down, up to his waist in snow, to the door of my car—some little distance from the station—stating that Mdme. Scalchi had again gone into hysterics, and was lamenting loudly the loss of her beloved bird.

On my arriving at the theatre with another "Azucena," taken suddenly from the cars (this one was lamenting only that she had not dined), I found that it wanted but five minutes to the commencement of the overture. There was Mdme. Scalchi dressed as "Azucena," and it was impossible even to obtain possession of her clothing, for she was almost in a fainting condition. At last, however, she divested herself of her gipsy garments; and she was replaced by my new "Azucena," Mdlle. Steinbach.

After the opera was over we started for San Francisco.

On reaching Ogden early in the morning I received a telegram from San Francisco notifying Mdme. Patti's arrival there, but adding that she would not come out in Semiramide in conjunction with Mdme. Scalchi, though that was the opera announced for my opening night. La Diva wanted a night entirely to herself.

As every seat had been sold for the first performance, and places were at a high premium, I did not see how it was possible to make any alteration in the bill. I therefore declined. Towards the latter part of the following day, at Winnemucca, I got another telegram saying that Mdme. Patti would appear in Il Barbiere. This I declined, knowing that opera to be, in America at least, most unattractive. Nearly at every station did I receive telegrams, some of which I answered. At last I effected a kind of compromise by substituting Linda. This change caused me a loss of some £600 or £800.

On the road I had received a telegram from my auctioneer, the famous Joe Eldridge, desiring to know if he should reserve any seats or offer the whole to the public. I replied that not a single seat was to be reserved; he was to sell all. He took me at my word, and the following day I received a telegram that not only had he sold the whole of the pit and dress circle and boxes, but also the whole of the gallery for every night of the season, and that the premiums on the tickets alone amounted to something like £15,000 for the two weeks' season; and, although over 3,000 tickets of admission for every night of the whole season had been sold, the demand, instead of abating, kept on increasing. In many cases as much as 150 dollars per seat premium had been paid. The sale altogether surpassed that of the previous year.

I was afterwards informed by an eye-witness of the indefatigable exertions Joe Eldridge had gone through on the day of the auction. On entering the orchestra he first of all gave a graphic description of each of the different prime donne who were to take part in the season's performances, explaining also the enormous value the tickets would reach as soon as the whole of the Company arrived. He then, feeling warm, took off his hat. After a few lots had been sold he removed his cravat, afterwards his coat, followed later by his waistcoat and his shirt-collar, which he threw off into the stalls. Then, as the business became more exciting, off went his braces. Afterwards he loosened his shirt, tucking up both sleeves; and he was in a state of semi-nudity before he got rid of the last lot.

On leaving the theatre after the sale this highly esteemed gentleman, I regret to say, was attacked by pneumonia, which carried him off in a few hours. His death was a sad shock to all, for he was a general favourite.

The San Francisco Daily Report wrote on the subject:—

"Joe Eldridge arrived in San Francisco in 1849, and after visiting various parts of the State returned to San Francisco, in the house of Newhall and Co. About this time he lost his right leg in a very remarkable manner. He was in the habit of signalling each sale by a hearty slap of his hand on his right thigh at the word 'gone.' The constant concussion

159

brought on a cancer, and the leg had to be amputated. This misfortune, which would have depressed most men, more or less, for the rest of their lives, had no effect on his energy or his high spirits. He was a most charitable man, and beloved by all who knew him, being one of the founders of Mill's Seminary, whilst he was a pillar of strength at Dr. Stone's first Congregational Church."

One word as to Joe Eldridge's method of doing business. No one could get such prices as he obtained; and these he often secured by pretending to have heard bids which had never been made.

"Nine dollars," an intending purchaser would say.

"Ten dollars," Joe would cry.

"I said nine," the bidder would explain.

"Eleven!" shouted Joe. "I know your income, and you ought to be ashamed of yourself. Twelve!" he would then exclaim, supported and encouraged by the laughter and applause of the public. "And if you say another word I'll make it thirteen."

A very different sort of man was the auctioneer by whom poor Eldridge was succeeded. He called me the spirited "impresio," and sang the praises of Mdme. Bauermeister, whose name he pronounced "Boormister," and Mdme. Lablache, whom he described as the famous "Labiche." Rinaldini was another of my singers whose name, sadly as he mutilated it, had evidently taken his fancy. Mdme. Bauermeister, Mdme. Lablache, and Signor Rinaldini are excellent artists. But it was a mistake to insist so much on their merits while passing over altogether those of Mdme. Patti, Mdlle. Nevada, and Mdme Scalchi.

In due course we arrived at San Francisco, where the usual crowd was awaiting us. During the latter part of the journey one of my corps de ballet became seriously indisposed, and died the following Tuesday in St. Mary's Hospital. She was but sixteen years of age, and had been with me eight years, being one of my Katti Lanner school children. She had taken cold in the dressing-room at Cheyenne. During the journey, the train being twenty-three hours late, she received the attention of Dr. Wixom, Mdme. Nevada's father, also of Dr. Palmer, Mdme. Nevada's present husband.

On the day of the funeral some magnificent offerings were placed on the coffin, consisting of pillows of violets with the initials of the deceased, anchors of pansies, lilies, violets, roses, etc., likewise a beautiful cross of violets and camellias. I attended the funeral personally, accompanied by my stage manager, Mr. Parry, and seven of the ballet girls, including a sister of the dead girl, who all carried flowers. The affair was strictly private, the experience of the previous year suggesting this on account of the crowd on the former occasion. The whole of the flowers were afterwards placed upon the grave; and a celebrated photographer, I. W. Tabor, produced some beautiful pictures which I sent to London to the family of the deceased, who received them before the news of her death.

At the conclusion of the funeral, which had been conducted by Mr. Theodore Dierck, of 957, Mission Street, the spirited undertaker begged to be appointed funeral furnisher to the Company, he having had charge of the Lombardelli interment in the previous year, which, he said, "gave such satisfaction;" and I was not astonished, though a little startled, on my last visit to find over his shop this inscription:

"Funeral furnisher by appointment to Colonel Mapleson."

CHAPTER VIII.

PATTI AND SCALCHI—NEVADA'S DÉBUT—A CHINESE SWING—A VISIT FROM ABOVE—RESCUED TREASURE—GREAT CHICAGO FESTIVAL—AMERICAN HOSPITALITY.

FOR our opening night at San Francisco, as already explained, the opera substituted at Mdme. Patti's request for Semiramide was Linda di Chamouni. Of course the house was crowded, and the brilliancy of the occupants of the auditorium baffled all description. An assembly was there of which the city might well feel proud. The costumes worn by the ladies were mostly white. The leaders of fashion were, of course, all present; Mrs. Mark Hopkins, of Nobs' Hill, conspicuously so, as she was attired in a costume of black velvet, with diamond ornaments, the value of which was estimated at 200,000 dollars. The best order prevailed. The majority entering the theatre on the opening of the doors were accommodated in their various seats without any crushing. Patti was greeted with even more demonstrativeness than she had hitherto received. Mdme. Scalchi on entering must have felt proud that she was none the less welcome for appearing as "Pierotto" in lieu of "Arsace."

Notwithstanding all this there was a coolness about the house in consequence of Mdme. Patti's having insisted upon this change in the opera. Consequently numbers of tickets for the first night instead of being at a premium were sold at a discount. Mdme. Nevada was announced for the second evening, but, unfortunately, she had not yet recovered from her Cheyenne cold, which developed gradually almost to pneumonia. She kept her bed in San Francisco for over three weeks, causing me the greatest annoyance as well as loss, since I was obliged to engage Mdme. Patti to sing a great many extra nights beyond her contract, all of which, of course, I had to pay for. Il Trovatore was consequently performed the second evening in lieu of La Sonnambula. The following night I brought out La Favorita with Scalchi, De Anna, Giannini, and Cherubini, which was a great success; followed by Lucrezia Borgia, in which Fursch-Madi pleased the audience.

These changes and disappointments tended to mar the whole engagement. The following night, however, the opera boom really commenced, the work being Semiramide, which fully justified the anticipations that had been formed of it. The largest and most brilliant audience ever gathered in a theatre were there to hear Patti and Scalchi sing in two of the most difficult rôles in the whole range of opera.

Scalchi fairly divided the honours of the evening with Mdme. Patti; and in the duets they electrified the audience, who, not content with encoring each, insisted upon some half-dozen recalls. The stage was literally strewn with flowers; and the ladies of the audience vied with one another in the elegance of their toilettes. Not only were all the seats occupied, but even all the standing room, and the Press unanimously accorded me the next morning the credit of having presented the best operatic entertainment in that distant city the world of art could afford.

A similar audience greeted Patti and Scalchi at the performance of Faust the following week, whilst on the next Saturday Mdme. Patti appeared as "Annetta" in Crispino e la Comare, which is, without doubt, her best part.

About this time the auction took place for the second season of two weeks, which I determined to commence the following Monday. The particulars of this I have already given.

The proceeds were very handsome, but nothing like those of the previous sale. I decided, therefore, that all unsold tickets should be disposed of at the box-office of the theatre in order that the general public might have an opportunity of attending the opera prior to our departure.

During the following week, being the first of this extra season, Mdme. Patti appeared in Semiramide, La Traviata, and Martha. At each performance there were nearly 3,000 persons assembled in the theatre. On the following Monday, it being our last week,

I induced Mdlle. Nevada to make her first appearance, on which occasion the receipts reached the same amount as Mdme. Patti's. Mdlle. Nevada, perhaps because she is a Californian, drew probably the largest audience we had had.

On her entering the stage some 3,000 or 4,000 persons shouted and applauded a welcome as if they were all going mad. She was hardly prepared for her reception. She had looked forward for many years to appearing in her native city and singing a great rôle before the people amongst whom she had spent her early life; and this was a momentous occasion for her. The enthusiasm of any other public would have spurred her on. But she was here so much affected that, although she sustained herself splendidly, yet after the curtain fell she was unable to speak.

At the conclusion of the opera she was recalled several times, and large set pieces of flowers, some six feet in height, were handed up, numbers of the leading florists having been busy putting them in shape all the fore part of the day. New dresses were ordered for that occasion, and an invitation to get a seat in a box was looked upon as a prize.

Long before half-past seven the vestibule of the theatre held a mass of fashionably-dressed ladies and gentlemen, all waiting to be shown to their places in order to be present on the rising of the curtain.

During all the first act the singer was critically and attentively listened to, scarcely with any interruptions; but when the curtain fell after the duet with "Elvino" the pent-up enthusiasm of the audience broke loose. Nevada was called out, and with shouts, cries, and every manner of wild demonstration. Flowers were carried down the aisles, thrown from the boxes and dress-circle, until the stage looked like the much-quoted Vallambrosa. Again and again the prima donna was called out, until she was fairly exhausted. Amongst the set pieces handed up to the stage was a large floral chair built of roses, violets, and carnations on a wicker frame, and Nevada, as the most natural thing to do, sat plumply down in it, whereat the house fairly howled with delight. On the back of the chair were the words, "Welcome home!"

The following night Aida was performed with the great cast of Patti, Scalchi, De Anna, and Nicolini, when the largest receipt during the whole engagement was taken. To describe that evening would be impossible; it would exhaust all the vocabulary. The gratings along the alley-way were wrenched off by the crowd, who slid down on their stomachs into the cellars of the theatre to get a hearing of Patti and Scalchi.

On this day we discovered the "Chinese swing," of which so much was said in the papers, and which had, doubtless, been in operation throughout the season. In the alley-way leading to the theatre is a lodging-house facing a sort of opening into the building used for ventilation. An ingenious fellow had rigged up a swing, and so adjusted it that he could toss people from his house on to the roof of the theatre to the ventilation hole. Once there, the intruder passed downstairs through the building, got a pass-out check on leaving it, which he immediately sold for two dollars, and then repeated the swing act again. We arrested one man who had performed the trick four times. The police had to cut the ropes and take the swing away.

So many devices were resorted to for entering the theatre without payment that I had to put it during this performance in a state of siege, as it were, and to close the iron shutters, as people came in from ladders through the windows of the dress-circle unobserved in many instances.

The following evening Mdlle. Nevada made her second appearance, performing the character of "Lucia" in Donizetti's opera, when the receipts were almost equal to those of the first night. Mdme. Patti performed the next night Il Trovatore to similar receipts. The next day I produced Gounod's Mirella, when the Grand Opera-house was again crowded brimful, people considering themselves lucky when they could get standing room without a view of the stage or a glimpse of the singers. The following morning was devoted to a performance of Faust, in which Patti took her farewell as "Margherita."

Just at this time a strange complaint was made against me by a body of "scalpers," who accused me of having put forward Adelina Patti to sing on a night for which Nevada had been originally announced. This I had, of course, done simply from a feeling of liberality towards my supporters. No one could reasonably accuse me of paying £1,000 a night to Mdme. Patti with the view of injuring the scalpers. They had, however, got more tickets into their hands than they were able to dispose of at the increased rates demanded by them. They, therefore, banded together, employed a lawyer to proceed against me for damages, and as a preliminary procured an order laying an embargo on my receipts.

The Sheriff's officers dropped into the gallery pay-box through a skylight on to the very head of the money-taker, who was naturally much surprised by this visitation from above; and they at once seized two thousand dollars.

It was very important for me not to let this money be taken, as it would have been impounded; and being on the point of taking my departure for Europe I should have been obliged to go away without it.

The only thing to do was to find securities—"bondsmen," as the Americans say. It was already nearly four o'clock (I was giving a so-called matinée that afternoon), and at four the Sheriff's office closed. I insisted on the money being counted, and one of the Sheriff's officers who was employed in counting it proposed in the most obliging manner to do the work very slowly if I would give him 50 dollars. This generous offer I declined, though it would have had the effect of giving me more time to find bondsmen. I soon, however, discovered seated in the theatre two friends who I knew would stand security for me. But it was necessary to find a Judge who would in a formal manner accept the signatures.

The performance was at an end, and fortunately there was at this moment a Judge on the stage in the act of making a presentation to Mdme. Patti, doing so, of course, in a set speech.

I did not interrupt the oration; but as soon as it was over, and whilst Mdme. Patti was weeping out "Home, Sweet Home" as if her heart would break, I presented to the Judge my two bondsmen. I at the same time took from my waistcoat pocket and handed to him my ink pencil, and he at once signed a paper accepting the bondsmen, together with another ordering the release of the sequestrated funds.

Armed with these documents, I drove post haste to the Sheriff's office, and got there at two minutes to four, just as the last bag of silver was going in. All the bags were now got out and heaped together in my carriage. The story was already known all over San Francisco. An immense crowd had assembled in front of the Sheriff's office, and as I drove off bearing away my rescued treasure I was saluted with enthusiastic cheers.

When a year later I returned to San Francisco I thought the case would possibly be brought to trial; but the lawyer representing the "scalpers" told me that he had been unable to get any money out of them, and that if I would give him a season ticket he would let the thing drop. The thing accordingly dropped.

On reaching Burlington on the Thursday morning following I was desirous of having a general rehearsal of L'Africaine, which was to be performed on the second night of the Chicago Opera Festival, and which had not been given by my Company during the previous twelve months. I could not rehearse it at Chicago, lest the public should think the work was not ready for representation. I resolved, therefore, to stop the train at Burlington in order to rehearse it at a big hall which I knew was there available. But lest news should get to the Chicago papers that the Company had stayed at Burlington merely for the purpose of rehearsing L'Africaine, I determined, if possible, to give a public performance, and on seeing the manager of the theatre, arranged with him for one performance of Faust. For five hours I rehearsed L'Africaine in the hall, and in the evening we had a most successful representation of Faust at the theatre. Dotti was the "Margherita," Scalchi "Siebel," Lablache "Martha," Del Puente "Valentine," Cherubini "Mefistopheles," and Giannini "Faust." There was no time for putting forward announcements by means of bills, and the fact that a performance of Faust was to be given that evening was made known by chalk inscriptions on the walls. The receipts amounted to £600. Patti honoured the performance with her presence in a private box, and a somewhat indiscreet gentleman, Dr. Nassau, paid her a visit to remind her that it was over twenty-nine years since she had sung under his direction at the old Mozart Hall, "Coming through the Rye," "The Last Rose of Summer," Eckert's "Echo Song," and "Home, Sweet Home." He substantiated his statements by one of the original programmes which he had brought purposely to show her. She received him coldly.

We left Burlington immediately after the night's performance, reaching Chicago the following Sunday morning, when I immediately paid a visit to the large Opera-house that had been constructed, and was astonished at its surpassing grandeur.

A vast deal had, indeed, been done, and still had to be done in the few remaining hours to complete it for the reception of the public, the building being one of the most stupendous, and the event one of the most brilliant Chicago had ever known. It was impossible to realize the magnitude of the task which had been undertaken, or the splendid manner in which it had been performed, the auditorium being probably one of the finest ever constructed for such a purpose. An increased chorus had been organized of 500 voices, whilst the orchestra had been augmented by a hundred extra musicians. A new drop curtain had been painted. The scaffolding was being removed from the ceiling, revealing decorations both brilliant and tasteful. The opening of the proscenium measured no less than 70 feet, with an elevation of 65 feet at the highest point of the arch, and a projection of 20 feet in front of the curtain. There were two tiers of proscenium boxes, and between the main balconies, which rose to a height of 30 feet, extending over and above the dress circle, there was a further space of 50 feet for standing accommodation in case of overcrowding. To ensure proper warmth the great auditorium was closed in, and all parts of the building supplied with steam pipes for heating, upwards of four miles in length. Amongst the features of the hall were two beautifully-arranged promenades or grand saloons, one decorated in the Japanese and the other in the Chinese style. Dressing-rooms for ladies and gentlemen had been constructed all over the building. The acoustic properties were simply perfect; sounding-boards, stage drop deflectors, and other scientific inventions being brought to bear.

The advance sale of seats on the first day of the opening reached over $50,000. In consequence of the vast size of the building new scenery had to be painted, which I entrusted to Mr. Charles Fox, with a numerous staff of assistants; this alone costing £6,000. Each scene was nearly 100 feet wide.

The house after the opening of the doors presented a surprisingly brilliant and attractive appearance, looking, in fact, like a permanent Opera-house. The orchestra was in excellent form, and numbered 155 musicians, under the direction of Arditi. The opera performed was Semiramide. The stage band and chorus numbered some 450, and there were 300 supernumeraries; so that when the curtain rose the effect was most magnificent. The audience was worthy of the occasion. There must have been over 5,000 people seated and some 4,000 or 5,000 standing. There were 80 ushers to attend to the occupants of the stalls; and at the commencement of the overture there was not one vacant seat. At the close of each act many of the vast audience repaired to the promenade and refreshment-rooms, to be recalled to their places by six cavalry trumpeters who came on the stage to sound a fanfare prior to the commencement of each act.

A leading daily paper wrote, the following morning:—

"The promises made by the Festival Association have been fulfilled to the letter, and the great temple of Art stood ready for the thousands for whom it was built. Not a single pledge made in reference to this building but what has been discharged, and the Manager is entitled to the thanks, and, indeed, the gratitude of the refined and music-loving classes of this community for the very thorough and self-sacrificing way in which all essentials and minor details of comfort and convenience have been achieved."

On the second night L'Africaine was performed, when a similar gathering attended. The audience was just as brilliant as on the previous evening, everyone being in full evening dress. Mdme. Fursch-Madi gave an effective interpretation of the title rôle, De Anna as "Nelusko" created quite a sensation, and Cardinali was an admirable Vasco di Gama.

On the third evening Gounod's Mirella, an opera never before heard in Chicago, was chosen for the first appearance of Mdlle. Nevada, and given with immense success, the part of the gipsy being taken by Mdme. Scalchi. This was followed on Thursday night by Linda di Chamouni, in which Mdme. Patti and Mdme. Scalchi appeared together. The Semiramide night had been thought a great one, but the audience on this occasion consisted of probably 2,000 more. Where they went to or where they stood it was impossible to say. Certain it is that 9,000 people paid for seats, irrespective of those who remained standing.

On the following evening Mdlle. Nevada appeared as "Lucia," and scored another triumph; whilst Patti and Scalchi drew 11,000 persons more for the morning performance. This was really a day for memory. The attendance consisted mostly of ladies, all tastefully, and often elaborately, dressed in the very latest fashion. Weber's Der Freischütz was performed in the evening, which terminated the first week of the Festival.

The second week we opened with La Sonnambula to an audience of some 8,000 persons, the next night being devoted to the presentation of Verdi's Aida, with the following great cast:—

"Aida"	...	...	...	Patti.
"Amneris"	...	...	...	Scalchi.
"Amonasro"	...	...	...	De Anna.
"Rhadames"	...	...		Nicolini.

Some 12,000 people attended this performance. The disagreeable weather did not seem to keep anyone away, and the streets were blocked with carriages for many squares, as far as the eye could reach. I was assured afterwards by an inspector that but for the aid of the rain, which came down in sheets, it would have been impossible to cope with the vast crowds who still poured in, attempting to enter the building.

About this time a complaint came to me from behind the scenes that Mdme. Patti and Mdme. Scalchi were unable to force their way from their dressing-rooms on to the stage, the wings and flies being crowded with some 2,000 persons, who during the first act had been joining in the applause of the singers with the audience in front. Together with these were some 500 supernumeraries with blackened faces, in oriental garb, chasing round to try to find their places, others with banners arranging their dresses. At length, with the aid of the police, Mdme. Patti was enabled to leave her dressing-room, but was surrounded immediately by crowds of ladies with pens and ink and paper, requesting autographs just as she was going on to sing her scena.

The boxes of the house were filled to overflowing, some containing as many as twelve persons. The flowers on the arm-rests in front were of the most expensive kind.

The march in the third act was really most impressive. There were 600 State Militia on the stage, each Company marching past in twelves, the rear rank beautifully dressed, the wheels perfect. The finale of the act, with the military band and the 350 extra chorus, together with the gorgeous scenery and dresses, was something long to be remembered. Well might the audience cheer as it did on the fall of the curtain.

The following night Rigoletto was given, then Il Trovatore, and the night after that Lohengrin.

At the close of the second act of Lohengrin there came a call from all sides of the house, and I was compelled to appear before the curtain, when I addressed the audience in the following words:—

"Ladies and gentlemen,—I am rather unprepared for the flattering compliment which you pay me in thus calling for me. I assure you that I join with you in my appreciation of the successful termination of this opera season, and I can bestow nothing but the most cordial thanks for the liberal support which the people of Chicago have given their Opera Festival. It is an evidence of their taste, and I hope will prove the forerunner of many more similar meetings. (Applause.) There are several persons who deserve special mention and thanks, but I shall have to be content simply with testifying to the earnestness of purpose with which all have laboured who were in any wise connected with the Festival. I therefore thank them all. It is no small thing to present thirteen different operas in two weeks' time, yet the attendance and manifestations of appreciation on the part of the audience will justify me in claiming that success has crowned my efforts; and the knowledge that we have given you all we promised and have satisfied you repays us for all our work."

President Peck likewise came forward and thanked the people of the city for their generous attendance at the first Opera Festival. It had been a success in every respect, and the management had done its best to accommodate and please the public.

A leading journal, in giving a review of the Opera Festival, said:—

"The Great Operatic Festival is now over, and only the memories of its magnificence and importance are left. The last note has been sung at the Chicago Operatic Festival, without doubt the greatest musical undertaking that has ever been accomplished anywhere. In no great city of Europe or America could 190,000 people have been able to attend the opera in two weeks. In the first place, the accommodations of even the largest Opera-houses are not such that 10,000 people could be present at any one performance. The Operatic Festival Association have been untiring in their earnest endeavours to present all the operas in the best possible manner. Each performance has been given as announced, and the casts have been uniformly good. Thirteen operas have been produced, all of which were mounted in a manner never before equalled. Many of the stage pictures, as in Semiramide, Mirella, L'Africaine, Aida, and Faust, have been simply superb, and will be long remembered for their beauty. The pictorial charm of the scene on the banks of the Nile in Aida was also most poetic. The processions, and the way in which they were controlled, indicated that the stage manager was a man of taste and ability."

Prior to my departure, 18th April, 1885, my attendance was requested by the Mayor, Mr. Carter H. Harrison, at the City Hall, when I was amply repaid for all the labour I had bestowed upon the Festival by the magnificent presentation which was then made me, and which I value more than anything of the kind I have ever received. It was nothing less than the freedom of the City of Chicago—a compliment I can say with safety that has never been paid to any other Englishman, and what is more, is never likely to be. Chicago, as everyone at all connected with America must know, will within a very few years be the first city in the United States, and probably in the world.

The success of the Chicago Festival was due in a great measure to the personal efforts of Ferdinand W. Peck, the President, from whom I immediately afterwards received a notification to attend the final committee meeting, when the following testimonial was presented to me, magnificently engrossed on parchment:—

At a Meeting of the
CHICAGO OPERA FESTIVAL ASSOCIATION
held April 18th, 1885,
The following Resolution was unanimously adopted:
Resolved
That the Chicago Opera Festival Association
Recognizes the satisfactory manner in which
COLONEL JAMES HENRY MAPLESON
has fulfilled his obligations under his contract with
this Association,
And they desire to express their high appreciation
of his liberality in the presentation of all the operas
produced, without which the grand success of the
FESTIVAL
could not have been achieved. In attestation of
the above the Officers and Board of Directors have
hereunto subscribed their names:
FERD. W. PECK, President,
WILLIAM PENN NIXON, Vice-President,
LOUIS WAHL, Second Vice-President,
    A. A. SPRAGUE   brace pointing to the right
    GEORGE M. BOGUE
    EUGENE CAREY
    HENRY FIELD   directors.
    R. T. CRANE
    JOHN R. WALSH
    GEORGE F. HARDING
GEORGE G. SCHNEIDER, Treasurer.
S. G. PRATT, Secretary.
"ADDRESS
"Tendered to Col. J. H. Mapleson by the Musicians and Citizens of the City of Chicago.

"SIR,—Now since the last note has died away, and lingers only in the ear of memory to warm and cheer the heart, and the great musical triumph of our city, the Chicago Opera Festival, is over, we extend to you in these words what we had expected to say to you amid music and song, had not the manifold duties that engrossed your time rendered us unable to do so.

"It is, indeed, as musicians, lovers of music, and citizens that we can cordially thank you in the name of the mighty people of that great and haughty city, the Queen of the North and the West. For this city, whose history has been the wonder of the world, whose greatness and energy in all things in which it engages are acknowledged by all, now yields this tribute to you, sir, as the one by whose direction, management, enterprise, and energy the greatest musical success ever given within its walls was accomplished.

"We might say more, but in our city's characteristic mode we express by deeds far better than by words. For two weeks our citizens night after night were turned away from the vast temple of music under your control, for the halls were crowded by others. They brought with them a hope that blossomed into unexpected realization, and the keen business men and tired toilers of the city lived a new life and shook the very ground with their applause.

"Never had music received such homage here. Again, we thank you for what you have done, and while we say farewell we also bid you welcome, for we hope to see you year after year in some vast Opera-hall in which ten thousand people can be seated, as proposed to be erected by some of our citizens, where you may win new laurels to your fame in your heaven-inspired mission of procuring and giving music for the people.

"With congratulations we remain—

FREDK. AUSTIN, 1st Regt.
   Military Band Leader,   Committee on
—Address and
   Resolutions.
A. ROSENBECKER, Drct. 1st Regt.
   Grand Orchestra,
ALBERT KLEIST, Pres. of C.
   Musical Sy.,
E. B. KNOX, Col. 1st Rgt. Inf.
   I.R.G.,
GEO. W. LYON, P.,
CHAS. N. POST,

"Done at Chicago, April 21st, 1885."

This may be the place to mention, what I am reminded of whenever I have to speak of America, the cordial, lavish hospitality with which English visitors are received in that country. Apart from the favour shown to me by railway and steamboat companies, who, so far as I was personally concerned, carried me everywhere free, the committees of the leading clubs offered me in all the principal cities the honours and advantages of membership. Not only was I a member of all the best clubs, but I was, moreover, treated in every club-house as a guest. This sometimes placed me in an awkward position. More than once I have felt tempted, at some magnificent club-house, to order such expensive luxuries as terrapin and canvas-back duck; but unwilling to abuse the privileges conferred upon me, I condemned myself to a much simpler fare. It seemed more becoming to reserve the ordering of such costly dishes for some future occasion, when I might happen to be dining at a restaurant.

It must be admitted that in many of the conveniences of life the Americans are far ahead of us, and ahead are likely to remain; so averse are we in England to all departures from settled habits, inconvenient, and even injurious as these may be. Every opera-goer knows the delay, the trouble, the irritation caused by the difficulty, when the performance is at an end, of getting up carriages or cabs. This difficulty has, in the United States, no existence.

When the opera-goer reaches the theatre an official, known as the "carriage superintendent," presents a large ticket in two divisions, bearing duplicate numbers. One numbered half is handed by the "carriage superintendent" to the driver. The other is retained by the opera-goer, who on coming out at the end of the representation exhibits his number, which is thereupon signalled or telegraphed to a man on the top of the house, who at once displays it in a transparency lighted by electricity or otherwise. The carriages are all drawn up with their hind wheels to the kerbstone, so that the approach to the theatre is quite clear. The illuminated number is at once seen, and the carriage indicated by it is at the door by the time the intending occupant is downstairs in the vestibule.

It is astonishing how easily this system works.

CHAPTER IX.

"COUNT DI LUNA" INTRODUCED TO "LEONORA"—A PATTI CONTRACT—THE STING OF THE ENGAGEMENT—A TENOR'S SUITE—A PRESENTATION OF JEWELLERY—"MY DON GIOVANNI"—A PROFITABLE TOUR.

THE public are under the impression that the closest intimacies are contracted between vocalists in consequence of their appearing constantly together in the same works. Under the new system, by which the prima donna stipulates that she shall not be called upon to appear at any rehearsal, this possible source of excessive friendship ceases to exist. It now frequently happens that the prima donna is not even personally acquainted with the singers who are to take part with her in the same opera; and on one occasion, when Il Trovatore was being performed, I remember the baritone soliciting the honour of an introduction to Mdme. Patti at the very moment when he was singing in the trio of the first act. The "Manrico" of the evening was exceedingly polite, and managed without scandalizing the audience to effect the introduction by singing it as if it were a portion of his rôle.

To show that the stipulation I have just spoken of is made in the most formal manner, and to give a general idea of the conditions a manager is expected to accept from a leading prima donna, I here subjoin a copy of the contract between Mdme. Patti and myself for my season at Covent Garden in 1885:—

"THE ENGAGEMENT contracted in London Sixth day of June 1885 BETWEEN JAMES HENRY MAPLESON Operatic Manager, henceforward described as Mr. Mapleson and ADELINA PATTI, Artiste Lyrique, henceforward described as Madame Patti.

"Article 1.—Mr. Mapleson engages Madame Patti to sing and Madame Patti engages to sing at a series of Eight Operatic Representations in Italian or high class Concerts to be given under his direction from Sixteenth June and ending the Sixteenth July One thousand eight hundred and eighty five in London in such manner that two of such Representations or Concerts (as the case may be) may be given in each week of such period and so that an interval of at least two clear days may elapse between each Representation or Concert unless the contracting parties otherwise agree.

"Article 2.—Mr. Mapleson engages to pay to Madame Patti or her representative for such series the sum of Four thousand pounds and for all additional Representations or Concerts the sum of Five hundred pounds each; such payment to be made in advance in sums of Five hundred pounds each before 2 o'Clock in the afternoon of the day on which a Representation or Concert is to be given.

169

"Article 3.—The repertoire to comprise the Operas of Martha, Traviata, Trovatore, Lucia di Lammermoor, Il Barbiere di Seviglia, Crispino, Rigoletto, Linda, Carmen and Don Giovanni; and thereof 'Il Barbiere,' 'La Traviata,' 'Martha' and 'Zerlina' in Don Giovanni shall be assigned exclusively to Madame Patti during the entire Operatic Season. The Airs to be sung at the Concerts (if any) are to be selected by Madame Patti.

"Article 4.—The selection from such Repertoire of the Opera to be given at her re-entrée shall be selected and be fixed exclusively by Madame Patti; but with that exception the choice therefrom of the Operas to be given at the several representations shall be Tuesdays and Saturdays, and the days of the week on which Concerts (if any) shall be given shall be fixed by the mutual agreement of the contracting parties; and Mr. Mapleson engages to adhere thereto except in case of sudden, necessary change through the illness of other principal Artistes in the cast of the chosen Opera.

"Article 5.—Madame Patti shall be free to attend Rehearsals, but shall not be required or bound to attend at any.

"Article 6.—Madame Patti will at her own expense provide all requisite costumes for the Operas selected.

"Article 7.—Mr. Mapleson engages that Madame Patti shall be announced daily during the series of Representations or Concerts in a special leaded advertisement among the Theatrical Advertisements over the Clock as well as in the Operatic Casts or Concert Programmes in all Journals in which he may advertise his Operas or Concerts and likewise that her name shall appear in a separate line of large letters in all Announce Bills of Operas or Concerts in or at which she is to appear and that such letters shall be at least one third larger than those employed for the announcement of any other Artiste in the same Cast or Programme.

"Article 8.—Madame Patti is not to be at liberty to sing elsewhere during this engagement except at State Concerts.

"Article 9.—In the event of Madame Patti not appearing in Opera or at Concert on the day for which she may have been announced to sing owing to her indisposition such intended appearance shall be treated as postponed if such indisposition be of a temporary character, and for every such non-appearance a substituted Representation or Concert shall be given before the Sixteenth July One thousand eight hundred and eighty five, but if such indisposition continues during a period longer than two succeeding Operatic or Concert nights provided by the first Article the number of non-attendance nights shall be counted off the Eight agreed for Representations or Concerts as if Madame Patti had actually appeared thereat. In the case of such postponement the payment of the Five hundred pounds shall be postponed until the morning of the day on which the substituted Representation or Concert shall be given; but in the case of counting off the day as wholly gone no salary shall be payable by Mr. Mapleson therefor; but beyond such postponement or deduction from payment, as the case may be, he shall have no ground of complaint nor claim for non-attendance or otherwise. And he engages to announce her indisposition or withdraw her name from all advertisements and other announcements of performance at the earliest time and with all due diligence and publicity.

"Article 10.—In the event of an Epidemic of Cholera, Small pox, Fever or other contagious or deadly disease breaking out within the range of the London Bills of Mortality Madame Patti shall be at liberty to cancel this Engagement by notice in writing as provided in the Twelfth Article, and thereupon she shall be no longer required nor bound to continue the Representations or Concerts, and thereupon the Two thousand pounds deposit in the Eleventh Article mentioned, and no more, shall be repayable to him if he shall have duly performed his several engagements herein.

170

"Article 11.—Mr. Mapleson, as a preliminary obligation performable by him (and on performance of which Madame Patti's obligations under her engagements herein depend) hereby engages to deposit the sum of Two thousand pounds Cash with Messrs. Rothschild, at their Counting-house in New Court, St. Swithin's Lane, London, on or before the Tenth June One thousand eight hundred and eighty five to the credit of Madame Patti, as part guarantee for Mr. Mapleson's fulfilment of this engagement. Such Two thousand pounds are to be applied by Madame Patti as payment for the last four actual Representations or Concerts, or (as the case may be) retained by her as her own property for and on account of damages sustained by her through the nonperformance of this engagement by Mr. Mapleson.

"Article 12.—Should Mr. Mapleson fail to make such deposit in full by the day named Madame Patti shall be at liberty at any time afterwards, and notwithstanding any negotiation, withdrawal of notice, waiver, extension of time for depositing, or acceptance of part payment of such Two thousand pounds to put an end to this Engagement by lodging with Mr. Mapleson's Solicitors, Messrs. J. and R. Gole in London, a letter signed by her, announcing her determination of this Engagement; and thenceforth this Engagement shall be at an end except so far as regards the Agreement next following, that is to say, That on such failure and determination Mr. Mapleson shall, and he hereby agrees to pay to Madame Patti on demand the sum of Four thousand pounds as and for compensation to her for expenses incident to this Engagement and for loss of time in procuring other engagements of an equal character.

"ADELINA PATTI."

About the sum payable per night to Mdme. Patti by the terms of the above agreement I say nothing. Five hundred pounds a night was only half what I had paid her in the United States; and soon afterwards at Her Majesty's Theatre I myself offered to give the famous vocalist six hundred and fifty per night. The sting of the contract lies for the manager, pecuniarily speaking, in the clause which empowers the singer to declare herself ill at the last moment, while guaranteeing her against all the consequences sure to arise from her too tardy apology. The manager has suddenly to change the performance, and, worse by far, to incur the charge of having broken faith with the public; for however precisely the certificate of indisposition may be made out, there are sure to be some knowing ones among the disappointed crowd who will whisper, as a great secret known to them alone, that the prima donna has not been paid, and that the certificate is all a sham.

What an unfair clause, too, is that by which, if the manager does not pay in advance to the prima donna at the exact time prescribed the whole of the sum payable to her for all the performances she binds herself to give, he will by such failure render himself liable for the entire sum without the prima donna on her side being called upon to sing at all.

The clause liberating the prima donna from attending rehearsals will be condemned by all lovers of music. During the three or four years that Mdme. Patti was with me in America she never once appeared at a rehearsal. When I was producing La Gazza Ladra, an opera which contains an unusually large number of parts, there were several members of the cast who did not even know Mdme. Patti by sight. Under such circumstances all idea of a perfect ensemble was, of course, out of the question. It was only on the night of performance, and in presence of the public, that the concerted pieces were tried for the first time with the soprano voice. The unfortunate contralto, Mdlle. Vianelli, had never in her life seen Mdme. Patti, with whom, on this occasion, she had to sing duets full of concerted passages. At such rehearsal as she could obtain Arditi did his best to replace the

171

absent prima donna, whistling the soprano part so as at least to give the much-tried contralto some idea of the effect.

In addition to the clauses in the prima donna's written engagement, there is always an understanding by which she is to receive so many stalls, so many boxes, so many places in the pit, and so many in the gallery. How, it will be asked, can such an illustrious lady have friends whom she would like to send to the gallery? The answer is that the distinguished vocalist wishes to be supported from all parts of the house, and that she is far too practical—high as may be the opinion she entertains of her own talents—to leave the applause even in the smallest degree to chance.

There are plenty of great singers—though Mdme. Patti is not one of them—who carry with them on their foreign tours a chef de claque as a member of their ordinary suite. Tenors are, at least, as particular on this score as prime donne; and if one popular tenor travels with a staff of eight, his rival, following him to the same country, will make a point, merely that the fact may be recorded in the papers, of taking with him a staff of nine.

Signor Masini, the modest vocalist who wished Sir Michael Costa to come round to his hotel and learn from him how the tempi should be taken in the Faust music, went not long since to South America with a staff consisting of the following paid officials: A secretary, an under-secretary, a cook, a valet, a barber, a doctor, a lawyer, a journalist, an agent, and a treasurer. The ten attendants, apart from their special duties, form a useful claque, and are kept judiciously distributed about the house according to their various social positions. The valet and the journalist, the barber and the doctor are said to have squabbles at times on the subject of precedence.

The functions of the lawyer will not perhaps be apparent to everyone. His appointed duties, however, are to draw up contracts and to recover damages in case a clause in any existing contract should seem to have been broken. The hire of all these attendants causes no perceptible hole in the immense salary payable to the artist who employs them; and the travelling expenses of a good number of them have to be defrayed by the unfortunate manager.

Only an oriental prince or a musical parvenu would dream of maintaining such a suite; and soon, I believe, the following of a vocalist with a world-wide reputation will not be considered complete unless it includes, in addition to the other gentlemen who wait upon the Masini's and the Tamagno's, an architect and surveyor.

It will perhaps have been observed that by one of the clauses of Mdme. Patti's engagement the letters of her name are in all printed announcements to be one-third larger than the letters of anyone else's name; and during the progress of the Chicago Festival, I saw Signor Nicolini armed with what appeared to be a theodolite, and accompanied by a gentleman who I fancy was a great geometrician, looking intently and with a scientific air at some wall-posters on which the letters composing Mdme. Patti's name seemed to him not quite one-third larger than the letters composing the name of Mdlle. Nevada. At last, abandoning all idea of scientific measurement, he procured a ladder, and, boldly mounting the steps, ascertained by means of a foot-rule that the letters which he had previously been observing from afar were indeed a trifle less tall than by contract they should have been.

I can truly say, "with my hand on my conscience," as the French put it, that I had not ordered the letters to be made a shade smaller than they should have been with the slightest intention of wounding the feelings or damaging the interests either of Mdme. Adelina Patti or of Signor Nicolini. The printers had not followed my directions so precisely as they ought to have done.

In order to conciliate the offended prima donna and her irritated spouse, I caused the printed name of that most charming vocalist, Mdlle. Nevada, to be operated upon in this way: a thin slice was taken out of it transversely, so that the middle stroke of the letter E disappeared altogether. When I pointed out my revised version of the name to Signer Nicolini in order to demonstrate to him that he was geometrically wrong, he replied to me with a puzzled look as he pointed to the letters composing the name of Nevada: "Yes; but there is something very strange about that E."

To return to my narrative. At the conclusion of the great Chicago Festival, we left, in the middle of the night, for New York, and reached it on Monday morning, where we opened with Semiramide to as large an audience as the Academy had ever known. On the Friday following, on the occasion of my benefit, the receipts reached nearly £3,000, the house being crowded from floor to ceiling.

At the close of the opera I was called before the curtain, and on quitting the stage, with Adelina Patti on my right and Scalchi on my left, I was met by Chief Justice Shea, who approached me and said—

"Colonel Mapleson, a number of our citizens who represent significant phases of social life and important business interests in this metropolis desire to testify in a public and notable manner that they understand and laud the superb success which has followed your efforts to establish Italian Opera in this city. It is seldom that public men are understood. It is very seldom that they are offered an acknowledgment beyond the few earnest friends that cluster around them. Those citizens to whom I refer recognize that your career amongst us has not been a mere chance success, but the result of patience, energy, and the intelligent courage which comes of ripe experience. They think this an apt occasion on which publicly to express the sincerity of that opinion. Sir, allow me on their behalf to offer you this memorial."

I was then handed a magnificent ebony case, fitted with a crystal glass, containing the following:—A valuable repeater watch set in diamonds, a gold chain with diamond and ruby slides, diamond and ruby charm in the shape of a harp, a pair of large solitaire diamond sleeve buttons, a diamond collar stud, a horse-shoe scarf pin (nine large diamonds), three diamond shirt studs, a gold pencil-case with a diamond top and a plain gold pin with a single diamond; the whole being valued at £1,300.

The ebony case and crystal glass I still possess. The contents, together with everything else, went to keep the Company together during the disastrous retreat from Frisco of the following year, as to which I will later on give details.

I thanked the Chief Justice briefly for the gift and the public for their patronage, and with difficulty left the stage amidst ringing cheers and waving of pocket-handkerchiefs: I say with difficulty, because at that critical moment, as I was picking up a bouquet, the buckle of my pantaloons gave way; and as my tailor had persuaded me, out of compliment to him, to discard the use of braces, it was only with great difficulty that I could manage to shuffle off the stage, entrusting meanwhile some of the jewellery to Patti and some to Scalchi.

At New York, as previously at Philadelphia, Chicago, and San Francisco, lively complaints were made of the vanity and levity of my tenor, Cardinali, who was an empty-headed, fatuous creature unable to write his own name or even to read the love-letters which, in spite, or perhaps in consequence of his empty-headedness, were frequently addressed to him by affectionate and doubtless weak-minded young ladies. Cardinali possessed a certain beauty of countenance; he had also a sloping forehead, and a high opinion of his powers of fascination.

At San Francisco he got engaged to a young lady of good family, who was one of the recognized beauties of the city. A date had been fixed for the marriage, and the coming event was announced and commented upon in all the papers. The marriage, however, was not to take place forthwith; and when my handsome tenor got to Chicago he was much taken by one of the local blondes, to whom he swore undying love.

At Philadelphia he got engaged to another girl, who became furiously jealous when she found that he was receiving letters from his Frisco fiancée. Not being able to decipher the caligraphy of the former beloved one, he entrusted her letters for reading purposes to the chambermaids or waiters of the hotel where he put up.

At New York Cardinali formed an attachment to yet another girl, who fully responded to his ardour. He used to get tickets from me in order that he might entertain his young women in an economical manner at operatic representations; and one day, when he had taken the girl whom he had met at New York to a morning performance, he asked permission to leave her for a moment as he had to speak to a friend. This friend turned out to be a lady with whom he had arranged to elope, and the happy pair left for Europe by a steamer then on the point of starting. He did not, as far as I know, change his partner during the voyage, and I afterwards lost sight of him.

We remained at New York a week, giving six extra performances, and left the following Sunday for Boston. There, too, we stayed a week, terminating the season on the 2nd May, on which day Mdme. Patti sailed for Europe, followed by the Company. These frequent voyages across the Atlantic were my only rests. They greatly invigorated me, bracing me up, as it were, to meet the fresh troubles and trials which were sure to welcome me on my arrival.

It was a most fortunate thing that the Directors of the Royal Italian Opera Company, Covent Garden, Limited, had thought proper to dispense with my services the previous year by reason of my having, in conjunction with their own general manager, engaged Mdme. Patti. Otherwise I should have been obliged to hand them £15,000, being half the net profit of this last American tour, to which, by the terms of our agreement, they would have been entitled.

I ascertained on my return that for want of £2,000 the Company had collapsed.
CHAPTER X.

MY COVENT GARDEN SEASON—PATTI'S LONDON SILVER WEDDING—RETURN TO NEW YORK—DIFFICULTIES BEGIN—RIVAL REHEARSALS—GRAND OPERA AND OPERETTA.

ON my return to London I opened Covent Garden for a series of Italian Opera performances, in which Mdme. Patti was the principal prima donna, and but for Mdme. Patti's twice falling ill should certainly have made some money.

On the opening night I was notified as late as seven o'clock that Mdme. Patti would be unable to appear in "La Traviata," having taken a severe cold. This was a dreadful blow to me. On inquiry I found that madame's indisposition arose from a morning drive she had taken on the previous day over some Welsh mountains during the journey from her castle to the station. Signor Nicolini, either from fear of the bill at the Midland Hotel, where they were to put up, or from some uncontrollable desire to catch an extra salmon, had exposed la Diva to the early morning air; an act of imprudence which cost me something like a thousand pounds.

The season nevertheless promised to be unusually successful. But within a few days I met with another misfortune, la Diva having taken a second cold, of which I was not notified until seven p.m. There was scarcely time to make the news public before the carriages were already setting down their distinguished burdens before the Opera vestibule.

I had no alternative but to introduce a young singer who, at a moment's notice, undertook the difficult part of "Lucia di Lammermoor." I allude to the Swedish vocalist, Mdlle. Fohström, who afterwards made a very successful career under my management. Of course, on this occasion she was heavily handicapped, as people had gone to the theatre only for the purpose of hearing Mdme. Patti; whose two disappointments caused me considerable loss.

I ended my season about the third week of July, when Mdme. Patti appeared as "Leonora" in Il Trovatore, renewing the success which always attends her in that familiar impersonation.

On this night, the final one of the season, Mdme. Patti concluded her 25th consecutive annual engagement at Covent Garden. Numbers of her admirers formed themselves into a committee for the purpose of celebrating the event by presenting her with a suitable memorial, which consisted of a very valuable diamond bracelet. At the termination of the opera I presented myself to the public, saying—

"Ladies and Gentlemen,—Whilst the necessary preparations are being made behind the curtain for the performance of 'God Save the Queen,' I crave your attention for a very few moments. My first reason for doing so is, that I desire to tender my sincere thanks for the liberal support you have accorded my humble efforts to preserve the existence of Italian Opera in this country. When I state to you that I had barely ten days to form my present Company, including the orchestra and chorus, I feel sure you will readily overlook any shortcomings which may have occurred during the past season. My second reason is to solicit your kind consent to present to Mdme. Patti in the name of the Committee a testimonial to commemorate her twenty-fifth consecutive season on the boards of this theatre."

The curtain then rose, and disclosed Mdme. Adelina Patti ready to sing the National Anthem, supported by the band of the Grenadier Guards, in addition to the band and orchestra of the Royal Italian Opera. This was the moment chosen for the presentation of a superb diamond bracelet, subscribed for by admirers of the heroine of the occasion. Its presentation was preceded by my delivery of the following address from the Committee of the Patti Testimonial Fund:—

"Madame Adelina Patti,—You complete this evening your 25th annual engagement at the theatre which had the honour of introducing you, when you were still a child, to the public of England, and indirectly, therefore, to that of Europe and the whole civilized world. There has been no example in the history of the lyric drama of such long-continued, never interrupted, always triumphant success on the boards of the same theatre; and a number of your most earnest admirers have decided not to let the occasion pass without offering you their heartfelt congratulations. Many of them have watched with the deepest interest an artistic career which, beginning in the spring of 1861, became year after year more brilliant, until during the season which terminates to-night the last possible point of perfection seems to have been reached. You have been connected with the Royal Italian Opera uninterruptedly throughout your long and brilliant career. During the winter months you have visited, and have been received with enthusiasm at Paris, St. Petersburg, Berlin, Vienna, Madrid, and all the principal cities of Italy and the United States. But you have allowed nothing to prevent you from returning every summer to the scene of your earliest triumphs; and now that you have completed your twenty-fifth season in London, your friends feel that the interesting occasion must not be suffered to pass without due commemoration. We beg you, therefore, to accept from us, in the spirit in which it is offered, the token of esteem and admiration which we have now the honour of presenting to you."

The National Anthem, which followed, was received with loyal cheers, and the season terminated brilliantly.

After the performance an extraordinary scene took place outside the theatre. A band and a number of torch-bearers had assembled at the northern entrance in Hart Street, awaiting Mdme. Patti's departure. When she stepped into her carriage it was headed by the bearers of the lighted torches; and as the carriage left the band struck up. An enormous crowd very soon gathered; and it gradually increased in numbers as the procession moved on. The carriage was surrounded by police, and the procession, headed by the band, consisted of about a dozen carriages and cabs, the rear being brought up by a vehicle on which several men were standing and holding limelights, which threw their coloured glare upon the growing crowd, and made the whole as visible as in the daytime. The noise of the band and of the shouting and occasional singing of the very motley gathering, which was reinforced by all sorts and conditions of persons as it went along, awakened the inhabitants throughout the whole of the long route, which was as follows: Endell Street, Bloomsbury Street, across New Oxford Street and Great Russell Street, down Charlotte Street, through Bedford Square by Gower Street, along Keppel Street, Russell Square, Woburn Place, Tavistock Place, Marchmont Street, Burton Crescent, Malleton Place to Euston road, halting at the Midland Railway Hotel, where Mdme. Patti was staying. Along the whole of this distance the scene was extraordinary. The noise, and the glare of the coloured lights, and the cracking of fireworks which were let off every now and then, aroused men, women, and children from their beds, and scarcely a house but had a window or door open, whence peered forth, to witness the spectacle, persons, many of whom, as was apparent from their night-dresses, had been awakened from their sleep. Not only were these disturbed, but a number of horses were greatly startled at the unusual sound and noise. The procession, which left Hare Street just before midnight, reached the Midland Hotel in about half an hour, almost the whole distance having been traversed at a walking pace. When Mdme. Patti reached the Hotel she was serenaded by the band for a time, and more fireworks were let off. The great crowd which had assembled remained in Euston Road outside the gates, which were closed immediately after the carriages had passed through.

My season having thus terminated, I at once started for the Continent in order to secure new talent for the forthcoming American campaign.

For my New York season of 1885-6, after some considerable trouble, I succeeded in forming what I considered a far more efficient Company than I had had for the previous five years; except that the name of Adelina Patti was not included, she having decided to remain at her castle to take repose after her four years' hard work in America. I subjoin a copy of the prospectus:—

"ACADEMY OF MUSIC, NEW YORK.

Season 1885-86.

PRIME-DONNE—SOPRANI E CONTRALTI.

Madame Minnie Hauk, Madame Felia Litvinoff, Mdlle. Dotti, Mdlle. Marie Engle, Madame Lilian Nordica, Mdlle. de Vigne, Mdlle. Bauermeister, Madame Lablache, and Mdlle. Alma Fohström.

TENORI.

Signor Ravelli, Signor de Falco, Signor Bieletto, Signor Rinaldini, and Signor Giannini.

BARITONI.

176

Signor de Anna and Signor Del Puente.

BASSI.

Signor Cherubini, Signor de Vaschetti, Signor Vetta, and Signor Caracciolo.

DIRECTOR OF THE MUSIC AND CONDUCTOR.

Signor Arditi.

PREMIÈRE DANSEUSE.

Madame Malvina Cavalazzi.

The following were the promised productions:—

For the first time in New York Massenet's famous opera MANON: words by MM. H. Meilhac and Ph. Gille. Mr. Mapleson has secured the sole right of representation, for which M. Massenet has made several important alterations and additions. "The Chevalier des Grieux," Signor Giannini; "Lescaut," Signor Del Puente; "Guillot Morfontaine," Signor Rinaldini; "The Count Des Grieux," Signor Cherubini; "De Bretigny," Signor Caracciolo; "An Innkeeper," Signor de Vaschetti; "Attendant at the Seminary of St. Sulpice," Signor Bieletto; "Poussette," Mdlle. Bauermeister; "Javotte," Mdme. Lablache; "Rosette," Mdlle. de Vigne; and "Manon," Mdme. Minnie Hauk. Gamblers, croupiers, guards, travellers, townsfolk, lords, ladies, gentlemen, &c., &c. The action passes in 1721. The first act in Amiens; the second, third, and fourth in Paris. The last scene, the road to Havre.

Also Vincent Wallace's opera, MARITANA. For the first time on the Italian stage, by special arrangement with the proprietors. The recitatives by Signor Tito Mattei. "Don Cæsar de Bazan," Signor Ravelli; "The King," Signor Del Puente; "Don Josè," Signor De Anna; "Il Marchese," Signor Caracciolo; "La Marchesa," Mdme. Lablache; "Lazarillo," Mdlle. De Vigne; and "Maritana," Mdlle. Alma Fohström. Mdme. Malvina Cavalazzi will dance the Saraband.

Likewise Auber's FRA DIAVOLO. "Fra Diavolo," Signor Ravelli; "Beppo," Signor Del Puente; "Giacomo," Signor Cherubini; "Lord Allcash," Signor Caracciolo; "Lorenzo," Signor De Falco; "Lady Allcash," Mdme. Lablache; and "Zerlina," Mdme. Alma Fohström.

Ambroise Thomas' opera, MIGNON, will be also presented. "Mignon," Mdme. Minnie Hauk; "Wilhelm," Signor Del Falco; "Lothario," Signor Del Puente; "Laertes," Signor Rinaldini; "Frederick," Mdlle. De Vigne; "Giarno," Signor Cherubini; "Antonio," Signor De Vaschetti; and "Filina," Mdlle. Alma Fohström."

The list of singers, which I give above in extenso, would have done honour to any theatre in Europe. But, alas! the magic name of Patti not being included had at once the effect of damaging seriously the subscription. In addition to this, a strong leaning showed itself on the part of my New York supporters towards the German Opera at the Metropolitan House; while a newly-formed craze had been developed for Anglo-German Opera, or "American Opera," as it was denominated. The prospectus of the latter setting it forth as a "national" affair, everyone rushed in for it, and considerable sums of money were subscribed. Its projectors rented the Academy of Music where I was located. The upshot of it was that a considerable number of intrigues were forthwith commenced for the purpose, if possible, of wiping me entirely out. I will mention a few of them in order that the reader may understand the position in which I was placed. Just prior to leaving England, and after I had completed my Company, I was informed by the Directors that I should be called upon to pay a heavy rental for the use of the Academy, my tenancy, moreover, being limited to three evenings a week and one matinée.

Having made all my engagements, I was, of course, at their mercy, and it was with the greatest possible difficulty that I could even open my season, as they began carpentering and hammering every time I attempted a rehearsal. However, I succeeded in making a commencement on the 2nd of November with a fine performance of CARMEN, cast as follows:—

"Don José," Signor Ravelli; "Escamillo (Toreador)," Signor Del Puente; "Zuniga," Signor De Vaschetti; "Il Dancairo," Signor Caracciolo; "Il Remendado," Signor Rinaldini; "Morales," Signor Bieletto; "Michaela," Mdlle. Dotti; "Paquita," Mdlle. Bauermeister; "Mercedes," Mdme. Lablache; "Carmen" (a Gipsy), Mdme. Minnie Hauk.

The incidental divertissement supported by Mdme. Malvina Cavalazzi and the Corps de Ballet.

This was followed by an excellent performance of Trovatore, in which Mdlle. Litvinoff, a charming Russian soprano from the Paris Opera, made a successful appearance, supported by Lablache, De Anna, the admirable baritone, and Giannini, one of the favourite tenors of America, who after the Pira was encored and recalled four times in front of the curtain. I afterwards introduced Mdlle. Alma Fohström, who had made such a great success during my London season at the Royal Italian Opera, Covent Garden.

On the occasion of my attempting a rehearsal two days afterwards of L'Africaine, I found the stage built up with platforms to the height of some 30 feet, which were occupied by full chorus and orchestra.

Remonstrance was useless, the Secretary of the Academy being "out of the way," whilst the conductor, Mr. Theodore Thomas, was closed in and wielding the bâton with such vigour that no one could approach him. I said nothing, therefore. In spite of formidable obstacles, the march and the procession in the fourth act of the opera had to be rehearsed under the platform, and, as good luck would have it, the opera went magnificently.

Rehearsals of Manon had now to be attempted; but whenever a call was put up, so surely would I find another call affixed by the rival Company for the same hour; and as they employed some 120 choristers, who had about an equal number of hangers-on in attendance on them, the reader can guess in what a state of confusion the stage was.

The public has but little idea of the difficulties by which the career of an opera manager is surrounded. An ordinary theatrical manager brings out some trivial operetta which, thanks in a great measure to scenery, upholstery, costumes, and a liberal display of the female form divine, catches the taste of the public. The piece runs for hundreds of nights without a change in the bill, the singers appearing night after night in the same parts. The maladie de larynx, the extinction de voix of which leading opera-singers are sure now and then, with or without reason, to complain, are unknown to these honest vocalists; and if by chance one of them does fall ill there is always a substitute, known as the "understudy," who is ready at any moment to supply the place of the indisposed one.

The public, when it has once found its way to a theatre where a successful operetta or opéra bouffe is being played, goes there night after night for months, and sometimes years, at a time. The manager probably complains of being terribly over-worked; but all he has really to do is to see that some hundreds of pounds every week are duly paid in to his account at the bank. To manage a theatre under such conditions is as simple as selling Pears' Soap or Holloway's Pills.

The opera manager does not depend upon the ordinary public, but in a great measure upon the public called fashionable. His prices are of necessity exceptionally high; and his receipts are affected in a way unknown to the ordinary theatrical manager. Court mourning, for instance, will keep people away from the opera; whereas the theatre-going public is scarcely affected by it. The bill, moreover, has to be changed so frequently, so

178

constantly, that it is impossible to know from one day to another what the receipts are likely to be.

What would one give for a prima donna who, like Miss Ellen Terry or Mrs. Kendal, would be ready to play every night? Or for a public who, like the audiences at the St. James's Theatre and the Lyceum, would go night after night for an indefinite time to see the same piece!

Finally, at a London Musical Theatre the prima donna of an Operetta Company, if she receives £30 or £40 a week, boasts of it to her friends. In an Italian Operatic Company a seconda donna paid at such rates would conceal it from her enemies.

CHAPTER XI.

HOUSE DIVIDED AGAINST ITSELF—REV. H. HAWEIS ON WAGNER— H.R.H. AND WOTAN—ELLE A DÉCHIRÉ MON GILET—ARDITI'S REMAINS— RETURN TO SAN FRANCISCO.

TO return to my difficulties at the New York Academy of Music, I was at length compelled to rehearse where I could; one day at the Star Theatre, another at Steinway Hall; a third at Tony Pastor's—a Variety Theatre next door to the Academy.

In the midst of these difficulties I caught a severe cold and found myself one morning speechless. I was surprised that afternoon to find a bottle of unpleasant sticky-looking mixture left with the hall-keeper, accompanied by a letter strongly recommending it from an admirer, who had heard, with sorrow, that I had taken cold. Not liking the smell of it, I sent it to an apothecary's for analysis, when it was found to contain poison. Fortunately I had not tasted it.

Finding myself so heavily handicapped, I decided, pending the preparation of Manon, to get ready Auber's Fra Diavolo, which had to be rehearsed under the same difficulties. I, however, succeeded in producing it on the 20th November, and an excellent performance we gave. Fohström was charming as "Zerlina," and in the rôles of the two brigands, Del Puente and Cherubini were simply excellent. I have seen many performances of Fra Diavolo in London with Tagliafice and Capponi, whom I considered admirable; but on this occasion they were fairly surpassed in the brigands' parts by Del Puente and Cherubini. The part of "Fra Diavolo" was undertaken by Ravelli, and the scenery and dresses were entirely new; the former having been painted on the roof of the theatre, either late at night or early in the morning, with the finishing touches put in on the Sundays.

The majority of my stockholders were careful to remain away, thus leaving a very bare appearance in the proscenium boxes. They, too, were siding with the enemy, or had not quite recovered from the three-dollar assessment which they had been called upon to pay for Patti the previous year. All these intrigues, however, marked in my mind the future downfall of the Academy and its stockholders, the house being now "divided against itself."

I will quote from the Evening Post, a paper hostile to my enterprise, a criticism on the Fra Diavolo performance:—

"Fra Diavolo, as presented at the Academy last evening, was by far the most enjoyable performance given by Mr. Mapleson's Company for a long time. There was an element of brightness and buoyancy in the acting and singing of all the principals that admirably reflected the spirit of Auber's brilliant and tuneful score. Next Monday, when the season of German Opera opens at the Metropolitan with Lohengrin, there will be doubtless hundreds who will be unable to secure seats. All such we earnestly advise to proceed straight to the Academy next Monday, where Fra Diavolo will be repeated; not only because they cannot fail to enjoy this performance, since it is an entertaining opera entertainingly interpreted, but because Mr. Mapleson ought to be encouraged, when he undertakes to vary his old repertory.... Ravelli sang admirably last evening, and so did Fohström, who acted her part with much grace and dainty naïveté. Lablache, Del Puente, and Cherubini were unusually good and amusing. The Academy, we repeat, ought to be crowded on Monday next."

The production of Fra Diavolo gave great satisfaction. Meanwhile, I made another attempt to continue my rehearsals of Manon. Not only was I excluded from the stage by the hammering and knocking of this new Anglo-German Opera Company, but they turned one of the corners of the foyer into a kind of business office, where their chatterings greatly interrupted my rehearsals with pianoforte. These, at least, I thought, might be managed within the theatre.

On ordering an orchestral rehearsal at Steinway Hall the following morning I was surprised to find that Mr. Thomas and his orchestra had actually gone there before me; and I had to dismiss my principal singers, chorus, and orchestra for a couple of hours, when with difficulty I was enabled to make a short rehearsal.

This went on day after day much to my annoyance. The Directors now began troubling me to pay the rent; to which I replied that I would willingly do so as soon as they performed their portion of the contract by allowing me to rehearse.

About this time I was challenged to meet the Rev. H. Haweis, author of Music and Morals, in a discussion on Wagner to be held at the Nineteenth Century Club, at which a great number of the fashionables of New York were present. After a brief introductory address, Mr. Courtlaudt Palmer, President of the Club, introduced the Rev. Mr. Haweis. His paper was a running series of anecdotes about Wagner, many of them keeping the audience in a continual laugh. He then made an onslaught on Italian Opera, assuring the audience that its days were numbered, that Wagner for the future was the one composer of dramatic music, and that every support should be given to his works now being represented at the Metropolitan Opera-house.

When he had concluded I rose and said, "You have told us much about Wagner, but nothing about his music. I trust I am not unparliamentary when I say that if he is to be judged by the effect of his works on the public—works that have now been for years before the world—Wagner is an operatic failure, and that what the Rev. Mr. Haweis has told us about his operas is sheer nonsense. One question he puts to me is: 'Did I ever lose money by Wagner?' I say emphatically, 'yes.' I once brought over all the material for his trilogy, the Ring des Nibelungen, from Munich to London, where it was to have been produced (according to one of the conditions of the agreement) under the supervision of Wagner himself. The master did not come; but his work was produced under a conductor of his own choice, and when the series had been twice given about six thousand pounds had been lost.

"My time will come yet. I labour under many difficulties now; but when New Yorkers are tired of backing German and American Opera, and will only subsidize me with one per cent. of the millions they are going to lose, I will return and give them Italian Opera."

I remember an interesting and, I must admit, not altogether inexact account of my production of the Ring des Nibelungen being given in the Musical Journal of New York.

"The series," wrote the American journalist, "was given under the special patronage of the Prince of Wales, who loyally remained in his box from the rising to the going down of the curtain, although he confessed afterwards that it was the toughest work he had ever done in his life. When Wotan came on the darkened stage and commenced his little recitative to an accompaniment of discords the Prince took a doze, but was awakened half-an-hour later by a double forte crash of the orchestra, and, having fallen asleep again, was startled by another climax fifteen minutes afterwards, when he found Wotan still at it, singing against time. At the end of five weeks Mapleson's share of the losses was 30,000 dollars; and the Prince told him confidentially that if Wotan appeared in any more operas he should withdraw his patronage."

By dint of perseverance, together with the aid of various managers, I succeeded in producing Wallace's Maritana. I first performed it over in Brooklyn, where it met with the most unqualified success, nearly every piece of music being encored, while Ravelli roused the audience to frantic enthusiasm by a finely-delivered high C from the chest at the conclusion of "Let me like a soldier fall." On a third encore he sang it in English. I then returned to the New York Academy with this opera, thus fulfilling the second of my promises in the prospectus.

It wanted now but nine days to the conclusion of my season, and as I had given to the public, despite the grumbling and cavilling, all the singers announced in my prospectus, I strained every nerve to produce the last of my promised operas, which caused more difficulty than all the others put together. This was Manon, which I succeeded in placing on the stage with entirely new scenery and dresses, and with a magnificent cast.

Glad indeed was I to shake the dust off my feet on leaving the Academy, where during a course of some eight or nine years I had given the New York public every available singer of eminence, including Adelina Patti, Etelka Gerster, Albani, Fursch-Madi, Scalchi, Campanini, Aramburo, Mierzwinski, Galassi, De Anna, Del Puente, Foli, and other celebrities. I confess I was not chagrined when I gradually saw after a couple of seasons had passed the downfall of the Anglo-German-American Opera Company, which from the very beginning had failed to benefit musical art in any way. Not a single work by an American composer was given, the repertory being entirely made up of translations of German operas. I also read without any deep regret of the total break-up of the Academy with all its belongings. It is now the home of a "variety show."

This New York season of 1885 was a most disastrous one financially, as it necessitated my closing for nearly a fortnight in order that the promised productions should all be given. It was with great difficulty that I could start the tour, as every combination seemed to be against me.

However, I opened at Boston with Carmen early in January, 1886, to a crowded house; the other performances of that week being Fra Diavolo, Manon, Maritana, Traviata, and Carmen for a matinée, the receipts of which exceeded even those of its performance on the previous Monday.

During the second week Faust, Don Giovanni, Rigoletto, Martha, etc., were performed. We left the next day for Philadelphia, where we remained until the middle of the following week. From there we went on to Baltimore, Washington, Pittsburg, Chicago, opening in the last-named city very successfully with a performance of Carmen; when a violent scene occurred during the third act from which may be said to date the disastrous consequences which followed throughout the whole of the route; one paper copying from another, with occasional exaggerations, so that in every town we visited the public expected a similar disturbance. Hence a general falling off in the receipts.

It was in the middle of the third act, when "Don José," the tenor (Ravelli), was about to introduce an effective high note which generally brought down the house, that "Carmen" rushed forward and embraced him—why I could never understand. Being interrupted at the moment of his effect, he was greatly enraged, and by his movements showed that he had resolved to throw Madame Hauk into the orchestra. But she held firmly on to his red waistcoat, he shouting all the time, "Laissez moi, Laissez moi!" until all the buttons came off one by one, when she retired hastily to another part of the stage. Ravelli rushed forward and exclaimed, "Regardez, elle a déchiré mon gilet!" and with such rage that he brought down thunders of applause, the people believing this genuine expression of anger to be part of the play.

Shortly afterwards, on the descent of the curtain, a terrible scene occurred, which led to my receiving this letter the following morning:—

"Palmer House, Chicago,

"February 9th, 1886.

"DEAR COLONEL MAPLESON,

"The vile language, the insults, and threats against the life of my wife in presence of the entire Company, quite incapacitate her from singing further, she being in constant fear of being stabbed or maltreated by that artist, the unpleasant incident having quite upset her nervous system. She is completely prostrate, and will be unable to appear again in public before her health is entirely restored, which under present aspects will take several weeks. I have requested two prominent physicians of this city to examine her and send you their certificates. Please, therefore, to withdraw her name from the announcements made for the future.

"As a matter of duty, I trust you will feel the necessity to give ample satisfaction to Miss Hauk for the shameful and outrageous insults to which she was exposed last night, and Mr. Ravelli can congratulate himself on my absence from the stage, when further scenes would have occurred.

"I fully recognize the unpleasant effect this incident may have on your receipts, more especially so should I inflict upon him personally the punishment he deserves.

"I am, dear Colonel Mapleson,

"Very truly yours,

"(Signed) E. DE HESSE WARTEGG."

The following day I received this, other epistle:—

"February 10th.

"DEAR SIR,

"My client, Baron Hesse Wartegg, has applied to me for advice concerning the indignities which Signor Ravelli, of your troupe, has offered to Mdme. Minnie Hauk on the stage. Signor Ravelli has uttered serious threats against the lady, and has on several occasions in presence of the public assaulted her and inflicted bodily injuries, notably on Monday evening last, during the performance of Carmen. My client wishes me to invoke the protection of the law against similar occurrences, as Mdme. Hauk fears that her life is in imminent danger. Under these circumstances I am compelled to apply to the magistrates for a warrant against Signor Ravelli, in order that he may be bound over to keep the peace. The law of this State affecting offences of this character is very severe, and should the matter be brought to the cognizance of our courts, Miss Hauk will not only have ample protection, but Mr. Ravelli will be punished. It is her desire, however, to avoid unpleasant notoriety, which would doubtless reflect on your entire troupe, and on your undertaking to execute a bond for 2,000 dollars to guarantee the future good conduct of Ravelli I shall proceed no further. I respectfully invite your immediate attention to this, and beg you will favour me with an early reply. Should I fail to hear from you before to-morrow evening I shall construe your silence as a refusal to secure proper protection for Miss Hauk and proceed accordingly.

"Miss Hauk and her husband are actuated by no other motives but those which are prompted by the lady's own safety. Please favour me with an early answer.

"Very respectfully yours,

"(Signed) WILLIAM VOCKE,

"Attorney for Miss Minnie Hauk."

I had no option but to give the bond.

That evening Signor Arditi, on leaving the theatre, caught a severe cold, which confined him to his bed, developing afterwards into an attack of pneumonia. The assistant conductor, Signor Sapio, was attacked by a similar malady; also Mdlle. Bauermeister, who was soon indeed in a very dangerous condition.

The following evening Mdlle. Fohström appeared as "Lucia di Lammermoor," and met with very great success.

With much persuasion I induced Miss Hauk to reappear as "Carmen", replacing Ravelli by the other tenor, De Falco.

During the ensuing week Arditi's condition became worse and worse. As we were engaged to appear the following evening at Minneapolis we were compelled to leave him behind as well as various other members of the Company, who were also indisposed. Prior to my departure I saw the doctor, who informed me that he considered Arditi's case hopeless; on which I prepared a cable for his wife asking what was to be done with his remains. This I left confidentially with the waiter.

I managed to get with the remnants of my Company to Minneapolis, where a severe attack of gout developed itself, which confined me to my bed; I in turn being left behind whilst the Company went on to St. Paul.

On the Company leaving St. Paul I managed to join the train on its road to St. Louis, where we remained a week. On the last day of our stay there I was pleased to see Arditi again able to join the Company, though in a very delicate state. Mdme. Hauk arrived at St. Louis the last day we were there. The following week we performed in Kansas City, where for the opening we gave Carmen with Minnie Hauk, followed by Faust with Mdme. Nordica as "Margherita." The following night at Topeka we played Lucia di Lammermoor with Fohström.

During these lengthened journeys across the Continent to the Pacific Coast the whole of the salaries ran on as if the artists were performing regularly.

As a rule we all travelled together; but occasionally, when the distance between one engagement and the next was too great, and the time too short, we separated. Sometimes one town in which we performed was four or five hundred miles away from the next. In that case the train was either divided into two or into three pieces, as the case might be. For instance, when we left for Chicago the engineer saw that he was unable to get to that city in time for our engagement the same evening. He therefore telegraphed back to Pittsburg, and the railroad officials there telegraphed on to Fort Wayne to have two extra locomotives ready for us. Our train was then cut into three parts, and sent whizzing along to Chicago at a lively rate, getting there in plenty of time for the evening's performance. It was wonderful, and nothing but a great corporation like the Pennsylvania Railroad Company could accomplish such a feat. By leaving at two o'clock in the morning we arrived at four the same afternoon at our next destination, in ample time to perform that evening; my hundred and sixty people having travelled a distance of four or five hundred miles with scenery, dresses, and properties.

We afterwards visited St. Joseph and Denver, opening at the latter with Carmen on a Saturday at the Academy of Music. Early the next morning we decided to give a grand Sunday concert at the Tabor Opera-house; but as no printing could be done, and no newspapers were published, the announcements had to be chalked upon the walls. With some difficulty we got a programme printed towards the latter part of the day, but notwithstanding this short announcement, so popular was the Company that the house was literally packed full. We played at Cheyenne the following evening, afterwards visiting Salt Lake City, where we presented Carmen. The irascible Mr. Ravelli again showed temper, and by doing so caused great inconvenience. I replaced him by one of the other tenors of the Company.

Of course I was blamed for this. Ravelli, however, had declared himself to be indisposed, and I at once published the certificate signed by Dr. Fowler.

The opera went exceedingly well.

Immediately after the performance we started for San Francisco, where we arrived the following Sunday afternoon, opening with Carmen on the Monday night before a most distinguished audience. Signor Ravelli performed "Don José," but in a very careless manner, omitting the best part of the music. He made little or no effect, whilst Minnie Hauk, who had not recovered from her previous fatigues, obtained but a succès d'estime.

Meantime a sale of seats by auction, which had been held, was an entire fiasco.

The second evening Mdlle. Fohström made a most brilliant success. The third night was devoted to Massenet's Manon, in which Miss Hauk did far better than on the opening night. The following evening we performed La Traviata, in which Mdme. Nordica made her appearance, Signor Giannini undertaking the rôle of "Alfredo." During this time great preparations were being made for a production of L'Africaine. The whole of the scenery and dresses, even to the ship, had been brought to the Pacific coast, at a considerable outlay; no less than £900 being paid for overweight of baggage through transporting this costly vessel across the plains.

The performance was a fine one, and the work was rendered admirably throughout, the great ballets and the processions gaining immense applause.

In the meantime a great deal of unpleasantness was going on in the Company, which greatly crippled my movements, besides diminishing my nightly receipts.

Although Ravelli, who was really the cause of all the trouble, had been ill for nearly three weeks, he refused to sing any more unless his full salary were paid him for the whole of the time. This, of course, I refused, and law proceedings were the consequence.

De Anna, the baritone, had an engagement for the whole six months of our American tour; and there was a clause in his contract which provided that during the interval of eight days, about the latter part of December, whilst the Company was idle, the salary should be suspended. But on our resuming the tour Mr. De Anna immediately notified me that unless I paid him for those eight days he would stop singing. This was the commencement of my trouble with him. Prior to our arrival his salary was handed to him, half in cash, and half in a cheque payable at San Francisco. He presented his cheque at the bank before the money had been placed there, and notified me that in consequence of non-payment he refused to sing that evening. Thereupon the treasurer went down to his hotel with the money, which was only a small amount of some £50 or £60. But he refused to accept it and surrender the cheque. The money was again tendered to him, and again refused.

De Anna, following suit with Ravelli, immediately inserted an advertisement in the daily papers setting forth that the part of "Nelusko" in L'Africaine was one of the most arduous rôles in the répertoire of a baritone, and that he alone was capable of performing it; while he at the same time respectfully informed the public that he did not intend to do so.

In the production of L'Africaine, however, Del Puente undertook the rôle of "Nelusko," and met with signal success, so that the recalcitrant baritone was left out in the cold and not missed. This tended still further to rouse his ire, and he resorted to a series of daily statements of some kind or other with the view of discrediting the Opera.

It was, indeed, a trying matter to me. The baritone, De Anna, refused to sing, and Ravelli was in bed with a bad cold; so, too, was Mdlle. Fohström. News, moreover, arrived from Minneapolis that Mdme. Nordica's mother, who had been left there, was at the point of death. Nordica insisted on rushing off at a moment's notice to make the journey of five days in the hope of reaching her while she was yet alive; and the rest of the Company were in open rebellion.

The season, however, despite these almost insurmountable difficulties, was a complete artistic success; and the Company I presented to my supporters in San Francisco was one that would have done honour to any European Opera-house. But, again, the name of la Diva being missing, the patronage accorded me was of a most scanty kind. The wealthy and luxurious inhabitants of the suggestively named "Nobs' Hill" remained carefully away.

I managed, however, to give the twenty-four consecutive performances promised, together with three Sunday concerts, the penultimate performance being devoted to my benefit.

CHAPTER XII.

THE RETREAT FROM FRISCO—HOTEL DANGERS—A SCENE FROM "CARMEN"—OPERATIC INVALIDS—MURDEROUS LOVERS—RAVELLI'S CLAIM—GENERAL BARNES'S REPLY—CLAMOUR FOR HIGHER PRICES—MY ONWARD MARCH.

SAN Francisco, or Frisco, as the inhabitants pleasantly call it, is at the end of the American world; it is the toe of the stocking beyond which there is no further advance. For this reason many persons who go to Frisco with the intention of coming back do, as a matter of fact, remain. It is comparatively easy to get there, but the return may be difficult. It is obviously a simpler matter to scrape together enough money for a single journey than to collect sufficient funds for a journey to and fro; and the capital of California is full of newly-settled residents, many of whom, having got so far, have found themselves without the means of retracing their steps.

At the period of the operatic campaign conducted by me—which, beginning most auspiciously, ended in trouble, disaster, and a retreat that was again and again on the point of being cut off—contending railway companies had so arranged matters that access to San Francisco was easier than ever. The war of rates had been carried on with such severity that the competing railway companies had at last, in their determination of outstripping one another, reduced the charge for carriage from Omaha to Frisco to a nominal sum per head. £20 (100 dollars) was the amount levied for conveying a passenger to Frisco direct; but on his arrival at the Frisco terminus £19 was returned to him as "rebate" when he gave up his ticket.

The rates from Frisco to New York had also been considerably reduced; and it was not until, after a series of pecuniary failures, we were on the point of starting that, to our confusion and my despair, they were suddenly raised. I had a force of 160 under my command, with an unusual proportion of baggage; and this hostile move on the part of the railway companies had the immediate effect of arresting my egress from the city.

Ravelli, possibly at the suggestion of his oracular dog (who always gave him the most perfidious counsel), had laid an embargo on all the music, thus delaying our departure, which would otherwise have been effected while the railway companies were still at war. They seemed to have come to an understanding for the very purpose of impeding my retreat. Ravelli suffered more than I did by his inconsiderate behaviour, for he was entirely unable, with or without the aid of his canine adviser, to look after his own interests.

It must be understood that in America a creditor or any claimant for money, bonâ-fide or not, can in the case of a foreigner commence process by attaching the property of the alleged debtor. This may be done on a simple affidavit, and the matter is not brought before the Courts until afterwards.

All the foreigner can do in return is to find "bondsmen" who will guarantee his appearance at a future period, or, in default, payment of the sum demanded; and it has happened to me when I have been on the point of taking ship to be confronted by a number of claimants, each of whom had procured an order empowering him either to arrest me or to seize my effects. I used, therefore, on my way to the steamer, or it might be the railway station, to march, attended by a couple of "bondsmen" and a Judge. The "bondsmen" gave the necessary security, the Judge signed his acceptance of the proffered guarantee, and I was then at liberty to depart.

Once, as I have already shown, I had to suffer attachment of my receipts at the hands of a body of "scalpers," who, when I had liberated the money through the aid of two friendly "bondsmen" and a courteous Judge, abandoned their claim; though when next year I returned to Frisco they could, of course, had it not been absolutely groundless, have pressed it before the proper tribunal.

Among other extraordinary claims made upon me immediately after the affair of the "scalpers" was one for 400 gallons of eau de Cologne. Some such quantity had, it was alleged, been ordered for fountains that were to play in front of the Opera-house; but the dealers, in lieu of eau de Cologne, had furnished me chiefly with water of the country. They swore, however, that I really owed them the money they demanded, and an attachment was duly granted.

It was through the treachery, then, of the dog-fearing Ravelli that our misfortunes in Frisco were brought to something like a crisis. In seizing the music in which the whole Company had an interest the thoughtless tenor was, of course, injuring himself and preparing his own discomfiture. The effect of his action was in any case to stop for a time my departure. We had evacuated the city, and now found ourselves blocked and isolated at the railway station. The railways would not have us at any price but their own. The hotel keepers were by no means anxious for our return, and some of the members of my Company had a healthy horror of running up hotel bills they were unable to pay. This may in part at least have been inspired by the following notice which, or something to the same effect, may be found exhibited in most of the Western hotels:—

An Act to Protect Hotel and Boarding-house Keepers.

"Be it enacted by the General Assembly of the

State of Missouri as follows:—

"Section I.—Every person who shall obtain board or lodging in any hotel or boarding-house by means of any statement or pretence, or shall fail or refuse to pay therefor, shall be held to have obtained the same with the intent to cheat and defraud such hotel or boarding-house keeper, and shall be deemed guilty of a misdemeanour, and upon conviction thereof shall be punished by a fine not exceeding five hundred dollars, or by imprisonment in the county gaol or city workhouse not exceeding six months, or by both (such) fine and imprisonment.

"Section II.—It shall be the duty of every hotel and boarding-house keeper in this State to post a printed copy of this Act in a conspicuous place in each room of his or her hotel or boarding-house, and no conviction shall be had under the foregoing section until it shall be made to appear to the satisfaction of the Court that the provisions of this section have been substantially complied with by the hotel or boarding-house keeper making the complaint.

"Approved March 25th, 1885."

I had, counting principals, chorus, ballet, and orchestra, 160 persons under my care, and by the terms of the hotel notice just reproduced the penalties incurred by my Company, had they quartered themselves upon innkeepers without possessing the means of paying their bills, would have amounted in the gross to £16,000 in fines and eighty years in periods of imprisonment. It was evidently better to bivouac in the open than to run the chance of so crushing a punishment.

A deputation of the chorus waited upon me, saying that as their artistic career seemed to be at an end, it would be as well for them to take to the sale of bananas and ice creams in the streets; whilst others proposed to start restaurants, or to blacken their faces and form themselves into companies of Italian niggers.

Some of the female choristers wished to take engagements as cooks, and one ancient dame who in her early youth had sold flowers on the banks of the Arno thought it would be pretty and profitable to resume in Frisco the occupation which she had pursued some thirty or forty years previously at Florence.

All these chorus singers seemed to have a trade of some kind to depend upon. In Italy they had been choristers only by night, and in the day time had followed the various callings to which now in their difficult position they desired to return. All I was asked for by my choristers was permission to consider themselves free, and in a few cases a little money with which to buy wheelbarrows. I adjured them, however, to remain faithful to me, and soon persuaded them that if they stuck to the colours all would yet be right. For forty-eight hours they remained encamped outside the theatre. Fortunately they were in a climate as beautiful as that of their native land; and with a little macaroni, which they cooked in the open air, a little Californian wine, which costs next to nothing, and a little tobacco they managed to get on.

From the "Morning Call."

"The scene outside the Grand Opera-house looked very much like Act 3 from Carmen—about 100 antique and picturesque members of Mapleson's chorus and ballet, male and female, were sitting or lying on their baggage where they had passed the night. As these light-hearted and light-pursed children of sunny Italy lay basking in the sun they helped the hours to pass by card playing, cigarette smoking, and the exercise of other international vices. One could notice that there was a sort of expectant fear amongst them seldom seen in people of their class."

What above all annoyed them was that they were not allowed to go to their trunks, an embargo having been laid not only on my music, but on the whole of the Company's baggage. One of them, Mdme. Isia, wished to get something out of her box, but she was warned off by the Sheriff, who at once drew his revolver.

The Oakland steamer was ready to carry us across the bay to the railway station as soon as we should be free to depart. But there were formalities still to go through and positive obstacles to overcome. At last my anxious choristers, looking everywhere for some sign, saw me driving towards them in a buggy with the Sheriff's officer. I bore in my hand a significant bit of blue paper which I waved like a flag as I approached them. They responded with a ringing cheer. They understood me and knew that they were saved.

187

How, it will be asked, did the Company lose its popularity with the American public to such an extent as to be unable to perform with any profitable result? In the first place several of the singers had fallen ill, and though the various maladies by which they were affected could not by any foresight on my part have been prevented, the public, while recognizing that fact, ended at last by losing faith in a Company whose leading members were invalids.

One of the St. Louis papers had given at the time a detailed account of the illnesses from which so many members of my Company were suffering.

"An astonishing amount of sickness," said the writer, "has seriously interfered with the success of the Italian Opera. Fohström and Dotti sang during the engagement, but both complained of colds and sore-throats, and claimed that their singing was not near as good as it usually is. Minnie Hauk had a cold and stayed all the week in St. Paul. Mdlle. Bauermeister could not sing on account of bronchitis. Signor Belasco was compelled to have several teeth pulled out, and complained of swollen gums. Mdme. Nordica was sick, without going into particulars. Signor Rigo was sick after the same fashion. Signor Sapio was attacked by quinsy at Chicago, and returned to New York. Signor Arditi, the musical conductor, was confined to his bed with pneumonia. Mdme. Lablache had a bad cold and appeared with difficulty. Many of the costumes failed to appear because Signor Belasco, the armourer, was taken sick en route, and held the keys of the trunks."

The illness from which so many of the members of my Company were suffering might, in part at least, be accounted for by their reckless gaiety at St. Paul. The winter festival was in full swing, and the ice-palace and tobogganing had charms for my vocalists, which they were unable to resist. They went sliding down the hill several times every day. The ladies would come home with their clinging garments thoroughly wet. They caught cold as a matter of course, and the sport they had had sliding down hill took several thousand dollars out of my pocket.

Minnie Hauk was nearly crazy on tobogganing; so was Nordica. Signori Sapio and Rigo tried heroically to keep up with the ladies in this sport, and were afterwards threatened with consumption as a reward for their gallant efforts.

But it was above all the conflict between Ravelli and Minnie Hauk in Carmen that did us harm, for the details of the affair soon got known and were at once reproduced in all the papers. It has been seen that Mr. von Wartegg found it necessary to bring Ravelli before the police magistrate and get him bound over on a very heavy penalty to keep the peace towards Mdme. von Wartegg, otherwise Mdme. Minnie Hauk; and the case, as a matter of course, was fully reported.

What could the public think of an Opera Company in which the tenor was always threatening to murder the prima donna, while the prima donna's husband found himself forced to take up a position at one of the wings bearing a revolver with which he proposed to shoot the tenor the moment he showed the slightest intention of approaching the personage for whom he is supposed to entertain an ungovernable passion? "Don José" was, according to the opera, madly in love with "Carmen." But it was an understood thing between the singers impersonating these two characters that they were to keep at a respectful distance one from the other. Ravelli was afraid of Minnie Hauk's throttling him while engaged in the emission of a high B flat; and Minnie Hauk, on her side, dreaded the murderous knife with which Ravelli again and again had threatened her. Love-making looks, under such conditions, a little unreal. "I adore you; but I will not allow you under pretence of embracing me to pinch my throat!"

"If you don't keep at a respectful distance I will stab you!"

Such contradictions between words and gestures, between the music of the singers and their general demeanour towards one another, could not satisfy even the least discriminating of audiences; and the American public, if appreciative, is also critical.

With some of my singers ill in bed, others quarrelling and fighting among themselves on the public stage, my Company got the credit of being entirely disorganized, and at every fresh city we visited our receipts became smaller and smaller. The expenditure meanwhile in salaries, travelling expenses, law costs, and hotel bills was something enormous. The end of it all was that at San Francisco we found ourselves defeated and compelled to seek safety in flight.

We did our best at one final performance to get in a little money with which to begin the retreat; and I must frankly admit that the hotel-keepers on whom the various members of my Company were at this time quartered did their very best to push the sale of tickets, for in that alone lay their hope of getting their bills paid.

It has been seen that at one time I was threatened with a complete break-up: my forces seemed on the point of dispersing.

I succeeded, however, in keeping the Company together with the exception only of Ravelli, Cherubini, and Mdlle. Devigne, who afterwards started to give representations on their own account, and soon found themselves in a worse plight than even their former associates who had the loyalty and the sense to remain with me. After much aimless rambling they turned their heads towards New York, which, in the course of two months, they contrived by almost superhuman efforts to reach.

Before leaving, Ravelli, as I have shown, dealt me a treacherous blow by getting an embargo laid on my music as if to secure him payment of money due, but which was proved not to be owing as soon as the matter was brought before the Court. That there may be no mistake on this point I will here give exact reproductions of Ravelli's claim as set forth in due legal form, and of my reply thereto. Apart from the substance of the case, it will interest the reader to see that an American brief bears but little resemblance to the ponderous document known by that name in England. An American lawyer sets forth in plain direct language what in England would be concealed beneath a mass of puzzling and almost unintelligible verbiage. I may add that law papers in America are not pen-written but type-written, being thus made clear not only to the mind, but also to the eye. In America a lawyer arrives in Court with a few type-written papers in the breast-pocket of his coat. In England he would be attended by an unhappy boy groaning beneath the weight of a whole mass of scribbled paper divided into numerous parcels, each one tied up with red tape.

I will now give the documents in the case of Ravelli against Mapleson, which, after being heard, was dismissed, but which, in spite of the admirable rapidity of American law proceedings, caused me several days' delay, and, as a result, incalculable losses; for apart from the sudden rise in the railway rates I missed engagements at several important cities along my line of march.

"Superior Court City and County of San Francisco,
State of California.
"LUIGI RAVELLI, Plaintiff, v. J. H. MAPLESON,
Defendant.
"Complaint.
"Plaintiff above named complains of defendant above named, and for cause of action alleges:

189

"That between the 4th day of February 1886, and the 4th day of April 1886 the Plaintiff rendered services to the defendant at said defendant's special instance and request, in the capacity of an Opera singer.

"That for said services the said defendant promised to pay plaintiff a salary at the rate of twenty-four hundred dollars per month.

"That said defendant has not paid the said salary or any part thereof, and no part of the same has been paid, and plaintiff has often demanded payment thereof.

"Wherefore plaintiff demands judgment against the defendant for the sum of forty-eight hundred dollars and costs of suit and interest.

"FRANK & EISNER & REGENSBURGER,

"Attorneys for Plaintiff."

"State of California, City and County of San Francisco.

"LUIGI RAVELLI being duly sworn says that he is the Plaintiff in the above entitled action. That he has heard read the foregoing complaint and knows the contents thereof. That the same is true of his own knowledge except as to the matters therein stated on his information and belief and as to those matters he believes the same to be true.

"LUIGI RAVELLI

"Sworn to before me this 10th day of April 1886.

"SAMUEL HERINGHIE,

"Dep. Co. Clerk."

In reply to the above my attorney and friend, the invincible General W. H. L. Barnes, put in the following "answer and cross complaint":—

"In the Superior Court of the State of California in and for the City and County of San Francisco.

"LUIGI RAVELLI, Plaintiff, v. J. H. MAPLESON, Defendant.

"Now comes J. H. Mapleson defendant in the above entitled action by W. H. L. Barnes his attorney and for answer to the complaint of Luigi Ravelli the plaintiff in the above entitled action respectfully shows to the Court and alleges as follows:

"The defendant denies that between the 4th day of February A.D. 1886 and the 4th day of April 1886 or between any other dates plaintiff rendered services to the defendant at defendant's special instance or request or otherwise in the capacity of an opera singer or otherwise except as hereinafter stated.

"Defendant denies that for said alleged services or otherwise or at all this defendant promised to pay plaintiff the salary of twenty-four hundred dollars per month or any sum except as is hereinafter stated.

"Defendant admits that he has not paid the said plaintiff for his alleged services since the 4th day of February A.D. 1886; but he denies that the same or any part thereof is due to plaintiff from the defendant.

"And further answering the defendant alleges and shows to the Court as follows:

"That heretofore to wit on or about the 22nd day of July A.D. 1885 at the City of London, England, the plaintiff Luigi Ravelli and this defendant made and entered into a contract in writing in and by which it was agreed substantially as follows:—

"1st: That said Ravelli engaged as primo tenore assoluto for performances in Great Britain, Ireland, and the United States with the defendant, said engagement to begin at the commencement of the season about the 1st of November A.D. 1885 and to close at the end of the American season, the salary of said plaintiff to be twenty-four hundred dollars per month payable monthly. The said Ravelli agreed to sing in Concerts as well as in

190

Operas, but not to sing either in public nor in private houses in the Kingdom of Great Britain, Ireland, or the United States during 1885-6 without the written permission of the defendant. The said plaintiff also agreed in and by said contract to conform himself to the ordinary rules of the Theatre, and to appear for rehearsals, representations, and concerts at the place and at the precise time indicated by the official call, and in case the said plaintiff should violate said undertaking, the defendant had the right to deduct a week's salary from the compensation of the plaintiff, or at his option to entirely cancel the said agreement as by said contract now in the possession of the defendant, and ready to be produced as the Court may direct, reference being thereunto had may fully and at large appear.

"And the defendant further says that after the making of said contract, said plaintiff commenced to render services as an Opera singer under said contract, and so continued down to about the 8th day of February 1886 at which time this defendant was in the City of Chicago, State of Illinois, and was then and there with his Opera Company engaged in giving representations of Operas, and the like at the Columbia Theatre in said City. That on the night of said day, and while the Opera Company of this defendant was engaged in giving a representation of the Opera known as Carmen in which Madame Minnie Hauk assumed the rôle of 'Carmen,' and the said Ravelli the rôle of 'Don José,' the said Ravelli while on the stage, and in the presence of the audience violently assaulted said Madame Minnie Hauk and threatened then and there to take her life, and shouted at her the most violently insulting epithets and language; that his conduct caused said Madame Minnie Hauk to become violently ill, and she so continued, and from time to time was unable to perform, thereby compelling this defendant to change the operas he had proposed and advertised to give, causing great public disappointment, and great pecuniary loss to this defendant.

"And the defendant further says that from about the 8th day of February 1885 to and until the 20th of February 1885 plaintiff refused to perform any of the parts set down for him to sing, or to attend rehearsals, or to obey calls as they were sent to him, and generally conducted himself in a brutal and insubordinate manner. That on the 20th of February at said City of Chicago this defendant with great difficulty persuaded him to act and sing in the part of 'Arturo' in the Opera of I Puritani, but before said last named day, he had been regularly and formally notified and called to the rehearsals of the Opera of Mignon, and to rehearse, and sing the part of 'Guglielmo,' and he refused so to do, and tore up the calls, or notices sent to him therefor, and threw them in the face of defendant's messenger. The said Ravelli was announced to the public to sing the rôle of said 'Guglielmo' in said opera of Mignon in all advertisements and notices for the 19th day of February A.D. 1885, but wholly refused and neglected so to do, and also neglected and refused to appear and sing in the rôle of 'Don José' in Carmen, announced in bills and advertised for February 20th, 1885.

"That after this defendant had as aforesaid persuaded said Luigi Ravelli to sing in the part of I Puritani, he continued to sing until the 13th March, at which time this defendant was with his Company at the City of Denver, in the Territory of Colorado, at which time and place he again without reason or excuse neglected and refused to sing in a public concert advertised and given in said City by this defendant.

"That thereafter and until the 6th of April 1885 said Ravelli was insubordinate, disrespectful, and self-willed in all his relations with this defendant, and falsely pretended to be unable to sing with the exception of two occasions, and on each of such occasions, without permission of this defendant, and without notice, he wilfully omitted the various principal airs and songs in the presence of the public who had paid to hear him sing the same, thereby causing this defendant great annoyance and loss by reason of the disappointment of the public, and the ill-will of the public towards this defendant caused thereby. That during the past four weeks during which this defendant has been with his said Company in the City and County of San Francisco the said Ravelli has repeatedly wilfully broken his contract, disappointed the public and greatly injured this defendant in his enterprise in business. He has sung only twice during all said period, and on his first appearance wilfully and maliciously omitted to sing a principal part of the music set down for him to sing, thereby disappointing the public, interrupting and injuring the representation and inflicting great injury and loss on this defendant.

"That on the 10th of April last the said Luigi Ravelli was duly called to rehearsal, and to sing certain music selected by himself, and which he had requested this defendant to insert in the Concert programme for April 11th, but refused to rehearse or sing at said concert although this defendant had caused to be prepared said music and the band parts thereof to be written out, and arranged to suit the pleasure and caprice of said plaintiff.

"That said Ravelli not only refused to sing, but then and there declared he would sing no longer for this defendant, and falsely and maliciously inserted advertisements and notices in certain of the public newspapers of San Francisco, which notices and publications were greatly to the injury of this defendant.

"That all of which doings of said plaintiff were in breach of his contract with this defendant, and greatly to this defendant's damage, and to his damage in the sum of five thousand dollars.

"And this defendant further says that he has repeatedly condoned the violations by said plaintiff of said contract with this defendant and his violence and brutality towards persons of the Company other than this defendant in the hope that he will ultimately come to his senses, and behave himself as he should; but that all this defendant's forbearance towards him has been of no effect, and has led only to repeated and further violations of his contract.

"Wherefore this defendant alleges that all and singular the said acts and doings of said Ravelli have constituted, and are so many breaches of his said contract with this defendant and that the same have been to the damage of this defendant over and above the amount of salary to which the said Ravelli would have been entitled had he properly conducted himself in the respects aforesaid, the full sum of five thousand dollars.

"Wherefore the defendant demands that the said complaint be dismissed, and that he may have and recover of the plaintiff as damages for the breach of his said contract with this defendant the sum of five thousand dollars, together with the costs of the action and disbursements incurred in defending this action.

"W. H. L. BARNES,

"Attorney for Defendant."

"State of California, City and County of San Francisco.

"J. H. MAPLESON being duly sworn deposes and says that he is the defendant in the above entitled action, that he has read the foregoing answer and cross-complaint and knows the contents thereof; that the same is true of his own knowledge except as to those matters which are therein stated on his own information and belief and that as to those matters that he believes it to be true.

"J. H. MAPLESON.

"Subscribed and sworn to before me this 16th day of April A.D. 1886.

SEAL.   "GEO. F. KNOX,

    "Notary Public."

The suit having been promptly terminated in my favour (General Barnes wins all his cases, even when they are not quite as good as mine was) I had to pay a few dollars for law expenses, and the embargo on the music and baggage was raised. But we could not start on our long journey with something like ten dollars among the whole one hundred and sixty of us, and I had still many difficulties to contend with before I could make a start. In London or Paris I should have begun by parting with my valuable jewellery, but this I could not do in an American city without everyone getting at once to know of it. That jewellery cannot pass from hand to hand without some reasonable proof of ownership being given is undoubtedly an excellent thing, though it did not suit my particular case. In England we are such lovers of liberty that a low-class pawnbroker or a receiver of stolen goods is free to purchase or to accept as a pledge whatever may be offered to him without asking inconvenient questions, or troubling himself in any way as to how the property came into the hands of the person anxious to dispose of it. In America the vendor or pledger of any article of value must give his real name and address, and at the same time brings as reference some respectable person, whose name and address must also be given. This reminds me (if for a few moments I may be allowed to depart from the thread of my story) that in America spirits cannot legally be sold to anyone under the age of fifteen, nor under any circumstances to women. In England we are so wonderfully free that women and children may buy penn'orths of gin at any public-house; and one enterprising publican is said to have made a large fortune by establishing in his drink-den a metal counter low enough to suit the convenience of small children.

I was obliged to leave a fifty-pound ring at one hotel as security for the payment of a singer's bill, and, oddly enough, when this ring was afterwards forwarded me in a registered letter to New York it was seized at the moment of my opening the packet by a creditor, or rather a claimant, who, for a pretended debt, had procured an attachment against my effects; so that it was not until after I had gone through several formalities that I could get it finally into my possession.

I remember a case in which an American manager, whose receipts had been attached, made a point of putting the money, as it was paid at the doors, into his pockets, which in a very short time were laden with coin. To attach the money that a man carries in his pockets a special order known as a "garnishee" is necessary; and the attachment of money carried on the person cannot be obtained unless the bearer admits that he has it about him, or can be proved on sworn evidence to have made such an admission within the hearing of another person.

When an attachment has once been obtained the order of attachment can be sent on by telegraph to be enforced, wherever the person against whom it has been granted possesses property. On the other hand, as a counterbalancing advantage, a manager may pledge his receipts by telegraph, and one man may at any time send money to another by the same means at quite a nominal charge. Deposit the money at a telegraph office, and the clerk telegraphs to the office of the place where your correspondent is staying that a sum equal in amount to the one deposited is to be forthwith paid. Our post-office orders are issued at usurious rates, and within limited hours. One cannot, however, but foresee the day when we shall be reasonable enough in this, as in so many other matters of practical life, to imitate the Americans.

It was absolutely necessary for me at the last moment to part with a certain amount of jewellery, and this I contrived to do without, I hope, attracting too much attention. I was spared the annoyance of seeing the details of each separate sale recorded in the newspapers.

I calculated that the losses caused to me by Ravelli's preposterous conduct amounted to at least 10,000 dollars. At some of the cities along the great line of railway, where I had engaged to give performances, I was unable, having lost the dates that had been fixed, to get others; and at one city, where the manager gave me another date, he stopped the whole of the receipts; which he said were due to him as damages for the injury done to him by not performing on the evening originally appointed.

On the morning of our departure—our escape, I may say—from the city where, a year before, we had been so prosperous, and whence I had borne away not a small, but a very considerable fortune, I was awakened about one o'clock in the morning by a Chinaman, a negro, and several Italian choristers, all crying out for money. But I satisfied every claim before I left; and I was more astonished than delighted to find myself complimented on having done so by one of the San Francisco papers, in which it was pointed out that I could easily have saved myself the trouble and pain in which I had been involved by taking a ticket and travelling eastward on my own account, leaving the Company to take care of themselves in the Californian capital.

I was not in a position to give gratuities to all who, in my opinion, deserved them. But John O'Molloy, the gasman of the Opera-house, had stood by me manfully in all my troubles; and I could not leave without making him a small present. In doing so I rendered the poor fellow a truly tragic service; inasmuch as, for the sake of the twenty-five dollar note which I gave him, he was the same evening robbed and murdered.

On the whole, though in the midst of my difficulties I had been worried a little by interviewers, the San Francisco papers gave me good words at parting. One of them explained my pecuniary failure not by the scandal which Ravelli's conduct had caused, but by my having played to popular prices, instead of the exceptionally high ones which I had charged when the year before Patti was singing for me, and receiving at the time payment at the rate of £1,000 a night.

"Opera," said the journal in question, "is regarded as a luxury, to enjoy which its votaries are willing to pay liberally. High prices are its illusion, and when put down to current rates the romance of the thing is destroyed. Mapleson did not appear to understand this, and his deficiency of the knowledge has caused him to leave us almost a bankrupt by his San Francisco venture. It is admitted on all hands that he had a splendid troupe, but the fact of his performing to what are known as popular prices, and complications arising with certain members of his troupe, seem to deprive him of his usual success."

"By the way," said a writer in the paper called Truth, "I notice that Mapleson is said to be indebted to Ravelli for 6,000 dollars, though an artist notoriously never permits an impresario to owe him more than a few performances. [It was proved in Court that I owed him nothing.] At home, as everybody knows, in their own country they receive in about a year as much as they are paid in a month in America, the streets of which the average Italian singer imagines to be paved with gold coins. As to the success or failure of the venture of the impresario they are supremely indifferent, but pertinaciously continue to demand the utmost farthing, no matter how badly things may be going. Lyric artists are, as a rule, the most grossly ignorant people on all subjects, except their own special art, and money. They are intensely conceited and abominably selfish, and regard an impresario as their natural prey. The sums that Ravelli has received from Mapleson in the last few years are beyond question sufficient to maintain the tenor in comfort and luxury for the rest of his life. Yet the moment he fails to receive his quid pro quo he refuses to render his services, denouncing his manager as a swindler, and abandons him at a moment when by loyalty and a little patience he could have aided in relieving the ill-fortune which must inevitably be anticipated in operatic affairs. Of course on general commercial principles the labourer is worthy of his hire; but in operatic matters the hire is, as a rule, so entirely out of proportion to the services rendered, and the conditions of the enterprise so unlike any other venture, that a little latitude certainly ought to be allowed."

I found on my arrival at Chicago that one of the Chicago papers had, at the beginning of my troubles, published the following telegram from its correspondent at San Francisco:—

"Mapleson is fighting his last week of opera at San Francisco in the teeth of dissensions, his first tenor having published a card to the purport that Mapleson had not fulfilled his obligations with him, and that he would not sing unless he published an announcement over his own name. The San Francisco Chronicle, the leading paper, therefore calls on all music lovers to rally in force for Mapleson's benefit on the 16th. The absurd prices Mapleson pays his operatic cut-throats makes the opera business a ruinous one. Covered with trophies and a due proportion of scars from his many campaigns, Mapleson will march his forces into Chicago to-morrow, Sunday, bivouacing for the night at the Chicago Opera-house, where his principal members will be heard in a sacred concert.

"The different performances given, notwithstanding all these operatic troubles, have been of that high standard which Mapleson alone has ever presented to us. Mapleson remains with us another week. Such performances as he has given are in but few places to be found. No Opera Company existing to-day has a better troupe of singers. There appears to exist a general impression among certain of the newspapers that Colonel Mapleson is operatically dead, and entirely out of the hunt. By his advent here, he proves to the public that he is still on deck."

My plan of retreat was well devised, and with a little good luck might have been thoroughly successful. As it was, it at least enabled us, without too much delay, to reach New York, and from New York to take ship for Liverpool.

Unable to command the railroad in a direct way from Frisco to New York, I determined to undertake a series of engagements at certain selected points all along the line. If the first of these proved successful I should be in a better position for my second encounter. It was certain in any case that at each fresh city I should be able to levy contributions; and with the money thus raised I could lay in a new stock of provisions and continue my advance by rail in the direction of New York, ready to stop at the first city whose population and resources might make it worth my while to do so.

Going back a little I must here explain that before leaving San Francisco, in order that Mdme. Minnie Hauk might be fresh for the proposed performance at Omaha, I had sent her on two days in advance—a distance of not more than 1,867 miles; whilst Mdme. Nordica was placed at another strategical point 2,500 miles away, at Minneapolis. She had to attend her sick mother, but was prepared to rejoin us when called upon to do so. Mdlle. Alma Fohström, not having sufficiently recovered from her late indisposition, was left behind at San Francisco, 2,400 miles from the scene of my next operations.

From Louisville, Kentucky, I telegraphed Mdme. Minnie Hauk to come on at once to play Carmen for the second night of our season; and she arrived in good time. She sang the same evening.

Mdme. Nordica received orders to join us at Indianapolis, where she was to appear in La Traviata, which she duly did the following Friday; whilst Mdlle. Alma Fohström, now recovered, was brought on from San Francisco to Cincinnati, a distance of some 2,500 miles, to perform in Lucia di Lammermoor. She also arrived punctually, and sang the same night.

I mention this small fact to show what can be accomplished with a little discipline. The reason why Mdme. Minnie Hauk was sent on to Omaha beforehand was in order that, by announcing her arrival in that city, I might give confidence to the public, it having been reported that my Company was broken up. Hence there was no booking; though had we arrived punctually for the opera on the promised date, my receipts, which I had already pledged to the Railway Company to get out of San Francisco, would certainly have been not less than £500 or £600. Mdme. Minnie Hauk, moreover, would have been saved a détour of some 2,400 miles.

Altogether I lost about £2,000, as I missed Omaha on the Friday, Burlington on the Saturday, Chicago on the Sunday, and my first performance in Louisville on the Monday.

Notwithstanding my all but insurmountable difficulties the performances never stopped, an announced opera was never altered, and the whole of the promised representations actually took place in each city; the press notices, which I still preserve, being unanimous as to the excellence of the representations.

I may mention that the travelling on these lines averages some 25 miles an hour only, there being several very steep gradients on the road. In some instances the train goes up over 3,000 feet in 57 miles, and down again; whilst the height of several mountains traversed by the train reaches from 7,000 to 8,000 feet.

CHAPTER XIII.

DEL PUENTE IN THE KITCHEN—SCALDING COFFEE—CALIFORNIAN WINE—THE SERGEANT TAKES A HEADER—THE RUSSIAN MOTHER—I BECOME A SHERIFF—A DUMB CHORUS—DYNAMITE BOMBS.

WHEN the Company started for the steamer which was to ferry us across to the railway station, further trouble arose in consequence of the increased sums demanded (now that the rates had been got up) for the Pullman cars which I had ordered for the principal artists; amounting to a considerable sum. But this difficulty was ultimately surmounted, and we left early on Wednesday evening for Omaha, where we were due on the Friday following.

My private car, moreover, had been let, and I was forced to engage an ordinary Pullman, with no facilities whatever for cooking or even heating water. Hasty purchases had now to be made of wine, coffee, etc., and a few tins of preserved meats; and a start was made for Omaha.

I was obliged to make arrangements not only for provisioning my principal artists, but also for cooking their food. I bought, when we were on the point of starting, a couple of hams and some cans of tinned meat, wine, and several gallons of whisky; the latter being intended not for internal consumption, but simply for cooking purposes. I found that there was no kitchen in the train, and I was obliged to improvise one as best I could. Del Puente, besides being an excellent singer, is a very tolerable second-rate cook; and I appointed him to the duty of preparing the macaroni (which I must admit he did in first-rate style), and of acting generally as kitchenmaid and scullion. I myself officiated as chef, and saw at the close of each day that the eminent baritone washed up the plates and dishes and kept the kitchen utensils generally in good order.

Early every morning I prepared the coffee for breakfast; and I believe no better, and certainly no hotter coffee was ever made than that which one day just before the breakfast hour I upset, through a jolt of the train, over my unhappy legs.

The fresh invigorating air of the mountains and of the spacious plains may have had something to do with it; but to judge from results, I may fairly say that my cooking was appreciated. My eight principal artists were, moreover, in charming temper. All professional jealousy and rivalry had been forgotten, except perhaps on the part of Del Puente, who did not quite like the secondary position which I had assigned to an artist who had previously refused all but leading parts.

At most of the principal stations we were able to purchase eggs, chickens, tomatoes, and salad. There was generally, moreover, a cow in the neighbourhood; and wherever we had an opportunity of doing so we laid in a supply of fresh milk.

While on the subject of cows, I must say a word as to the cruel fate which these unhappy beasts meet with at the hands of the railway people. In front of every train there is a "cow-catcher," which, when a cow gets on the line, shunts the wretched animal off and at the same time breaks its legs. I begged the driver more than once to stop the train and put the mutilated animal out of its misery with a revolver shot, but it was not thought worth while.

When a cow is destroyed by the "cow-catcher" the owner can claim from the railway company half its value; and it is said that in bad times when cattle are low in the market, or worse still, unsaleable, they are driven on to the line with a view to destruction. I have often in a day's journey perceived hundreds of the bleached skeletons of the animals killed outright by the "cow-catcher," or maimed and left to die. An inspector, appointed by the railway company, passes from time to time along the line and, after settling up, marks in the left ear and at the tip of the tail the dead beasts for which the company has paid. The former owner disposes of the carcasses and hides; the latter alone possessing appreciable value. The former are left on the ground to become food for the crows; though the Indians will sometimes cut away portions of the meat when they come upon a beast which is still fresh.

During our eight days' journey I acted not only as cook, but also as butler; and our various wines, all of Californian growth, were excellent. They cost from 8d to 10d a bottle, and I was not alone in regarding them as of excellent quality. Singers are not great wine drinkers, but they are accustomed to wines of the first quality; and I may say in favour of the wines of California that they were appreciated and bought for conveyance to Europe by artists of such indubitable taste as Patti, Nilsson, and Gerster. The cost of carriage renders it impossible to send the wines of California to Europe for sale. But someday, when, for instance, the Panama Canal has been cut, there will be a market for them both in England and on the Continent. They are, of course, of different qualities. But the finest Californian vintages may be pronounced incomparable. I remember once being entertained in company with some of my leading artists by Surgeon-General Hammond, at his house in Fifty-eighth Street, New York, when some Californian champagne was served which we all thought admirable. Our facetious host disguised it under labels bearing the familiar names of "Heidsieck" and "Pommery-Greno;" and we all thought we were drinking the finest vintages of Epernay and of Rheims. Then under the guise of Californian champagne he gave us genuine Pommery and genuine Heidsieck; the result being that we were all deceived. The wine labelled as French, but which was in fact Californian, was pronounced excellent, while the genuine French wines described as of Californian origin seemed of inferior quality.

On arriving at Cheyenne I found it would be impossible to reach Omaha in time to perform Carmen, which was announced for the following evening; or Burlington, where Lucia was billed for the Saturday; or Chicago for our Sunday concert, for which every place had been taken. All had to be abandoned. Our special train was consequently diverted off to the right in the direction of Denver, where I telegraphed to know if they could take us in for a concert the following Sunday. On receiving a negative reply, I telegraphed to Kansas City, where my proposition was accepted. I consequently wired the

Kansas manager the names of the artists and the programme containing the pieces each would sing. Through the manipulation of the telegraph clerks scarcely one of the artists' names was spelt right, whilst the pieces they proposed to sing, as I afterwards found, were all muddled up together.

In due course our party reached Denver, where we took half an hour's stop for watering the train and obtaining ice for the water tanks in the different cars, after which we started on our road to Kansas City.

Shortly after leaving Denver one of my sergeants belonging to the corps of commissionaires—several of whom I had brought from London—was taken ill and reported to be suffering from sunstroke received many years previously in India.

During our brief stoppage at Denver one of the other sergeants had purchased him some medicine which he was in the habit of taking. About two o'clock in the morning he became very violent, and it was found necessary to cut the bell-cord running through the carriage in order to tie him down. I then gave orders to the sergeant-major to place him in a bed and have him watched by alternate reliefs of the other sergeants, changing every two hours.

About four in the morning, in the midst of a terrific thunderstorm, accompanied by torrents of rain, I was alarmed by the sudden entry of the sergeant-major, stating that the invalid under his charge had opened the window and taken a header straight out.

There was great difficulty in stopping the train in consequence of the absence of the bell-cord; but we ultimately succeeded in doing so. Numbers of us went out to look for the poor man's remains, the vivid flashes of lightning assisting us in our search. As the water on each side of the railway was several feet deep, and as the sergeant was nowhere to be found on the line, we concluded after three hours' search that he must be drowned, and again started the train, leaving word at the first station of the misfortune that had happened.

In consequence of this delay we did not reach Kansas City until half-past ten at night, when a portion of the public met us to express in rather a marked manner their extreme disapprobation. It was afterwards explained to me that nearly every seat in the house had been sold, and that had we arrived in time we should have taken at least £800, which, in my straitened circumstances, would have been of considerable assistance.

We prosecuted our journey straight through to Louisville, Kentucky. But here, too, we failed to arrive at the proper time. The train being so many hours late, we did not reach our destination till eleven o'clock at night, when the audience, who had been waiting some considerable time, had gone home very irate. Minnie Hauk having rejoined us the following evening we played Carmen to but a moderate house, in consequence of the public having lost all confidence in the undertaking. In settling up with the manager he deducted the whole of my share of the receipts, stating that they would partly compensate him for the losses incident to our non-arrival the first night, as well as on the previous night, and for the general falling off in the receipts caused by these mishaps. We afterwards went to the station to take the train for Indianapolis; but on arriving there I found that the Sheriffs had seized and attached, not only all the scenery, properties, dresses, and everybody's boxes, but the whole of my railway carriages; and it was only with the greatest possible difficulty, by giving an order on the next city, that I got the train released. I had, of course, to pay the Sheriff's costs, which were exceedingly heavy.

On arriving at Indianapolis very meagre receipts awaited us, these being absorbed entirely by the railway people on the order which I had given from Louisville. There were likewise sundry claims from San Francisco. During the whole of my stay in Indianapolis I was unable to obtain even a single dollar from the management. I, however, arranged by anticipating the coming week's receipts to clear up all my liabilities and get under way for Cincinnati, where the results of our engagement were something atrocious. The theatre was almost empty nightly, the public, by reason of the threatened riots, being afraid to go out in the streets.

I was now forced, in order to meet the large demands for railway fares, to drop at successive stations scenery, costumes, and properties. At one place an immense box, containing nothing but niggers' wigs, mustachios, and beards, made by Clarkson, of London, passed from my hands into those of the Sheriffs, who held an attachment against it. When I found it necessary to part at one station with L'Africaine, at another to separate myself from William Tell, and at a third to cast away the whole of Il Trovatore and a bit of Semiramide, I felt like the Russian mother who, to secure her own safety, threw her children one after the other to the wolves.

I cannot, however, say that the wolves of the law are worse in America than in other countries. They bear the same honoured names that one is accustomed to among the members of the profession in happy England. I was interested, moreover, to learn that the Levys, the Isaacs, the Aarons, and the Solomons of the United States are all related to the Levys, Isaacs, Aarons, and Solomons of our own favoured land. I had so much to do with them, from the beginning of the retreat from Frisco until my arrival at New York, and the eve of my departure for Europe, that they ended by treating me as their friend, and made me free of their guild. They entertained me also at dinner, and gave me a badge; and when my health was drunk I was assured that in future I should be treated like a brother: for, said the speaker, referring to the fact that I myself was now a Sheriff, "Dog doesn't eat dog."

To return to my story, contracts having been given out for repairing the roads and repaving the city, in consequence of some league amongst the various contractors all the streets had been left unpaved at the same time; and as soon as every paving stone was up a general strike took place. It was impossible for a carriage to pass along anywhere without getting upset by the hillocks of stones. Suddenly we heard that the anarchists were rising, and now the city was filled with State militia accompanied by numerous Gatling guns for the purpose of clearing the streets. These things in combination so injured the business of the Opera that the theatre was empty every night. In many instances choristers were afraid to go through the streets to fulfil their duties.

We were now rejoined by Mdlle. Fohström, also by Mdme. Nordica; but all looked very unpromising. Our previous mishaps had been so much written about, telegraphed, and in every way exaggerated by the various papers, that all confidence seemed to have been withdrawn from us, and it was with the greatest possible difficulty we could carry through our performances.

As if in imitation of the paviours of Cincinnati, portions of my Company now began to strike. First the band struck, then the chorus, then the ballet.

One night, when Lucia di Lammermoor was being played, a delegation of choristers notified me that unless all arrears were paid up they would decline to go on the stage. Argument was useless. The notification was in the form of an ultimatum. The choristers would not even wait until the close of the performance for their money, but insisted upon having it there and then.

I therefore had to begin the opera with the entrance of "Enrico," leaving out the small introductory chorus, which was not missed by the public. We thus got through the first act; also the first scene of the second act. The curtain was now lowered just before the marriage scene; and negotiations were again attempted, but still without success. I felt it necessary to improvise a chorus for the grand wedding scene, and it consisted of the stage-manager, the scene-painter, several of the programme-sellers, the male costumier, the armourer and his assistants, together with several workmen, ballet girls, etc., who, elegantly attired in some of my best dresses, had a very imposing effect. I gave strict instructions that they were to remain perfectly silent, and to act as little as possible; at the same time telling the principal singers to do their very best in the grand sextet.

The result was an encore and general enthusiasm. Everyone, too, was called before the curtain at the close of the act, and one of the leading critics declared that the finale was "nobly rendered."

Finding how well I could do without them the chorus now came to terms.

A concert was given on the following Sunday night which closed the engagement. The whole of the receipts had been absorbed by lawyers, sheriffs, railway companies, and the keepers of the hotels at which the principal members of the troupe put up. The hotel-keepers, moreover, had seized all the boxes. The train was drawn up at the station; but after waiting two hours the engine was detached and taken away into the sheds.

In the meantime dark groups of choristers were congregated in different parts of the city, and things did, indeed, look gloomy. During the night I succeeded in paying the different hotel bills; and ultimately in the small hours of the morning the train was got together and started for Detroit, I remaining behind to make arrangements for paying off the remaining attachments.

On the Company's arriving at Detroit it was discovered that Minnie Hauk's boxes containing her Carmen dresses had been left behind. As they could not possibly reach her in time I had to arrange by telegraph to have new dresses made for her during the afternoon. It took the whole of my time to release the fifty or sixty attachments that had been issued against the belongings of the various members of the Company, and I arrived in Detroit early the following morning with the things which I had at last triumphantly released. The whole of a Pullman car was filled with the various articles I had set free, including the Carmen dresses, sundry stacks of washing, various dressing bags, and piles of ballet girls' petticoats, beautifully starched.

Our artistic success in Detroit was great, and, after performing three nights, we left after the last performance for Milwaukee.

We passed from Detroit to Milwaukee, where but a few days beforehand the mob had been fired upon, with some eighteen killed and several wounded. The whole town was in a state of alarm; neither Fohström's "Lucia" and "Sonnambula," nor Minnie Hauk's "Carmen," nor Nordica's "Margherita" in Faust could attract more than enough cash to pay the board bills and fares to Chicago, for which city we left early the following morning.

The scenes that had taken place there must be fresh in the mind of everyone.

Bombshells had been thrown by the Anarchists; numbers of people had been killed, and the public of Chicago was in the same frame of mind with regard to the opera as so many of the previous cities. It preferred to remain indoors.

Our musical operations were seriously interfered with by the strike, which was promptly responded to by a lock-out. The clothing manufacturers closed their shops, throwing but of employment nearly 2,000 superintendents—"bosses," as the Americans call them—and 25,000 hands. The hands had demanded ten hours' pay for eight hours' work, with 20 per cent. advance on trousers, and 25 per cent. on vests and coats. The "bosses" demanded an advance of from 35 to 50 per cent. on all kinds of work; and it was resolved by the employers not to reopen until all the firms had made a successful resistance to these claims on the part of the workmen. The metal manufacturers and furniture makers had been threatened in like manner by their men; and they also refused to yield to the strikers. At the same time from 30,000 to 40,000 men were on strike at Cincinnati, where the suburbs were occupied by a whole army of troops. It now appeared that the disturbances at Chicago were closely connected with those at Cincinnati. Some of the Socialists on strike were armed, to the number of 600 or 700, with effective rifles, and they controlled the manufacture of dynamite shells. The shells which the rioters had been using at Chicago had been made at Cincinnati, and it was said that the Chicago Socialists had on hand for immediate use a supply of these infernal machines. At Milwaukee, some seventy or eighty miles from Chicago, nineteen Anarchists and Socialists had just been arraigned on a charge of riot and conspiracy "to kill and murder." In the streets of Chicago placards were posted on the walls announcing that groups of more than three persons would be dispersed by force; so that a husband and wife proceeding in company with two of their children to hear Il Trovatore or Lucia di Lammermoor ran the risk of being fired into by Gatling guns.

CHAPTER XIV.

SUBTERRANEAN MUSIC—THE STRIKER STRUCK—TUSCAN TAFFY—A HEALTHY "LUCIA"—I RECOVER FROM THE UNITED STATES—A BEKNIGHTED MAYOR.

WE opened our Chicago season with a grand concert prior to the commencement of the regular performances in order to let the public know that all the Company was present in the city after the conflicting reports that had been circulated.

Notwithstanding all our recent reverses, my Company was intact, except that the refractory tenor Ravelli had been replaced by Signor Baldanza, and the basso Cherubini by Signor Bologna. Here, again, in Chicago, my usual stronghold for Italian Opera, the reports of our troubles had been exaggerated and enlarged upon, so that the general public had lost all confidence, notwithstanding the fact that, through Mrs. Marshall Field's influence, a party of the most distinguished citizens had secured the whole of the boxes for the entire season.

The Chicago engagement was expected to recoup us for our losses in the West. But, unfortunately, this hope was not realized; and in consequence of the wild reports that got into general circulation, and, of course, into the newspapers, the Company began to clamour for their pay. I referred them to Mr. Henderson, the Manager of the Chicago Opera-house; and his office was crowded daily with prime donne, chorus people, dancers, musicians, property men, bill-board men, and supernumeraries, all demanding money. "Lucia" was begging for dollars and cents; "Manrico" insisted on having at least three meals a day; while the "Count di Luna," who shared his rival's apartments, protested that unless he had a pint of good wine before he went on he could not get out his F's with due effect in Il Balen.

Mr. Henderson proclaimed his managerial life a burden, but made no other response.

Of the orchestral players the drum was the noisiest; though the hautboy and the piccolo were every whit as emphatic. It was a united and determined strike, the keynote of which was, "No pay no play."

Only two weeks' pay was owing to them, and it was agreed that Mr. Henderson, the Manager, should give them one week's salary on account. But when the musicians assembled to receive it they suddenly, through the persuasiveness of one of their body, insisted upon having all arrears paid up; otherwise they would not enter the orchestra.

Finding they were obdurate and would not take the money that was offered them, I was forced to seek musicians from among the various musical societies of the city, and called a rehearsal as soon as I was ready. After the new orchestra had been brought together, a hasty rehearsal was ordered for 7.30 that evening; and not long after the opening of the doors the public was regaled with the sounds of my new orchestra, who were practising underneath the pit, from which they were separated only by a very thin flooring.

On Arditi's notifying Signor Bimboni, the accompanist and under-conductor, that he would require him to assist on the piano in the orchestra, Bimboni replied: "Bless you! I have struck too."

Nothing discouraged, though somewhat wrath, Arditi succeeded in unearthing an accompanist, who struggled bravely with the pianoforte score.

During the performance, Parry, our stage manager, met Bimboni near the stage door, and reproached him sharply for deserting his post. This altercation led to blows. Bimboni struck out wildly, and soon went down with a black eye and a bruised face as a souvenir of the encounter.

The chorus, finding that I had provided another orchestra, and had threatened to find other choristers, gave in; and I must say we succeeded in giving a very excellent performance, despite all difficulties.

The next day all was again serene, and I was enabled to continue my representations until the close, finishing up the season with success. The Chicago engagement concluded with a benefit tendered to me by most of the prominent citizens. They thus showed their appreciation of my efforts as a pioneer; for I was the first manager who had introduced into their city grand opera worthy of the name.

Amongst the signatures to the document embodying this fact were the following well-known names:—The Hon. Carter H. Harrison, Judge Eugene Carey, Marshall Field, Ferd. W. Peck, J. Harding, Professor Swing, George Boyne, Irving Pearce, A. A. Sprague, George Schneider, John R. Walsh, J. McGregor Adams, George F. Harding, S. S. Shortball, J. Russell Jones, Edson Keith, C. M. Henderson, Hon. J. Medill, Potter Palmer, John B. Drake, N. K. Fairbank, T. B. Blackstone, A. S. Gage, &c.

On being called before the curtain I thanked the public for the liberal support they had given to my undertaking; also the press for the encouraging notices which it had published daily, notwithstanding all my troubles. These had been fully made known to everyone by means of the daily papers, which really took more interest in my affairs than I did myself.

In regard to the strike of my orchestra, an account of which was published in the Inter-Ocean, Mr. David Henderson, manager of the Chicago Opera-house, said to an interviewer:—"The new orchestra played this evening in a satisfactory manner. The Musical Union held a meeting during the day, and decided, I am told, that the members of the Colonel's orchestra did wrong in taking the stand in the matter of wages that they did; that is, in demanding from me back salaries. After the meeting several of them expressed a desire to come back; but I only took those needed—five or six in all. The rest are out of employment. The orchestra is now better than before, and everything is going along smoothly. At the conclusion of the engagement of the Company, Sunday night, a number of the principals and of the chorus and executive staff will return with Colonel Mapleson direct to London. I ought to add that since the beginning of the engagement he has not touched one cent of the box-office receipts. I have distributed the money as equitably as I could, giving to each artist, on present and past salaries, as much as the receipts would permit. I have learned that the Colonel is not as much in arrears to his Company as newspaper reports led the public to believe. Some of the leading people have been, as near as I can ascertain, only behindhand some three or four performances, before coming to Chicago. The orchestra that left, I understand, have two weeks' salaries due to them, that were incurred during the past eight weeks since the Colonel's bad business in California, and through the lengthened voyage. The best proof of the belief on the part of his company that the Colonel intends doing what is right by its members is the willingness with which every one of them has consented to appear at his benefit, Saturday evening, without compensation."

"The Mapleson Opera Company," wrote the Tribune, "with the Colonel's trials and tribulations, have pretty well filled the public eye the past week. Outside of the Columbia Theatre, with the McCaull people there has been nothing to talk about but the Colonel. There are times when Mapleson, unconsciously, perhaps, appeals to sympathy. He is the only living man to-day with nerve enough to go into the business at all, who can govern and control the average opera singer. The latter is the most trying beast on earth. Male or female, Italian or Greek, German or 'American,' they are all alike. A more obstreperous, cantankerous, and altogether unreasonable being than an opera singer it is hard to find in any other walk of life. The Italian contingent of the guild is the worst to get along with. The Italian singer is rapacious, improvident, ungrateful, and wholly inconsiderate of his manager. At the same time he is a vain fool whom a word of flattery will move. Mapleson speaks Italian fluently, and hence when trouble arises he seeks the complainer, gives him a lot of Tuscan taffy, and the idiot goes off and sings as if nothing had happened. The Mapleson season at the Chicago Opera-house has had its difficulties, yet it has scored successes. The leading people have stood by the Colonel. He has had trouble with the orchestra, but that was quickly remedied. Yesterday Giannini, whom Mapleson picked up, as it were, out of the gutter in New York, where the Milan Company dropped him, and to whom he has since paid thousands of dollars, whether he earned it or not, made a strike just before the matinée. Giannini wanted 600 dollars. Mapleson offered 400 dollars. Giannini refused it, and would not sing. Then the Colonel began to talk Italian in his charming way, and the result was that the tenor went back, dressed, and sang, and that, too, without a 'cent,' and did it with meekness. La Sonnambula, which gave Mdlle. Fohström her last chance to appear, drew a good house at the matinée, and the Colonel's benefit in the evening was a gratifying tribute. There were no more breaks, and the audience showed a warm appreciation throughout. The programme was just what Colonel Mapleson's admirers wanted. Last night's performance ended the season. From here the company scatters. The principals seek their homes in Europe, and the Colonel travels post-haste to London, where he is to superintend the Patti appearance in June. Mapleson is disgusted with his present season's experience, but he is by no means disheartened. He threatens to come back at an early period."

At the end of some three weeks we learned that Sergeant Smith, the commissionaire who jumped out of the window in his shirt, had been discovered comfortably asleep and unhurt. Some difficulty was experienced in marching him along in the costume in which he then was to the hospital, whither it was thought prudent first to take him until some clothing could be provided. Whilst he was detained there a lady who had come to visit a sick gardener recognized the sergeant as having crossed on the same boat with her some six months previously. He readily accepted her offer of the vacant place, and forthwith began work; and it was only after many inquiries as to how the missing body had been disposed of that we discovered the man was still alive. On this being made known several articles came out in various journals, some giving the life of Sergeant Smith, and saying where and how he had won his numerous medals, whilst others expatiated generally on the valour and endurance of the British army.

In due course the gallant sergeant joined the main body and donned his uniform.

While we were at Chicago another Opera Company, calling itself the Milan Grand Italian Opera Company, was giving performances, and an amusing incident happened during a representation of Lucia. The audience was waiting for the appearance of the heroine in the third act. But they waited and watched in vain. The chorus stood in mute amazement, while the musicians in the orchestra looked somewhat amused. The audience stamped their feet and clapped their hands, while the gallery hissed repeatedly. The curtain was rung down, and there was a wait of a few minutes, when finally Signor Alberto Sarata, the manager of the Company, appeared on the stage, and said that Miss Eva Cummings, who had been singing the part of "Lucia," had suddenly become ill, and was quite unable to continue her performance. The opera would, therefore, go on without her. He had scarcely finished speaking when "Lucia" herself came on to the stage, and declared that she was in perfect health, and that she wanted her salary. This announcement was received with mingled cheers and hisses.

The prima donna bowed gracefully first to one side of the house, then to the other, and was about to follow the manager, who had already left the stage, when she found that the curtain was held fast by invisible forces. From one exit she went to the other, but still was unable to escape from the presence of the public.

"I will get off this time, anyhow!" she exclaimed, and with a rush pushed the curtain back. The invisible forces still resisted; but after a time "Lucia" succeeded in making her way to the wings.

Then the curtain went up, and "Edgardo" began to bewail the death of a "Lucia" who had not died.

Towards the close of our Chicago engagement attachments, writs, summonses, etc., began to fall thick and fast, which had to be dealt with speedily in order to ensure our departure.

I therefore made arrangements for a farewell Sunday concert in order to raise the wind for the purpose.

I cannot allow this opportunity to pass without tendering my sincere thanks to my esteemed and valued friend, President Peck, who very kindly came to the rescue by affording me the monetary assistance I required to enable us to get out of the city.

As fast as one attachment was released another came on. The last one I got rid of about 2 a.m., and left the theatre satisfied that all was serene. On seating myself at the Pacific Hotel, with a view to supper, I was called to the door, and notified that the waggons I had seen properly started had all been arrested and were at the corner of Dearborn Street. Placing down my knife and fork I hastened off; and by the aid of my friend Henderson, who gave bonds, the attachment was released. Meanwhile the whole of the Company was on the qui vive for the entraining order, the steam having been up some ten hours and the train not yet started.

At the station I came across the remnants of the Milan Opera Company which had been stranded some fortnight previously, and whose members were supplicating aid towards getting to New York. I thereupon had the great pleasure of affording them all a free passage in my train; and after sundry salutations from my numerous friends who came to see me off we took our departure. The Company reached Jersey City very early the following Tuesday morning, and went straight on board the boat which was to sail late that afternoon. I meanwhile crossed over into New York, where I attended at the Inman Steamship Office, and arranged for them to give a passage to my Company and to take an embargo on my belongings for their protection, as well as mine.

I must here set forth that every year on entering the port of New York the Customs authorities had charged me duty at the rate of some 50 per cent. on all my theatrical costumes, scenery, and properties, although the majority of them had originally been manufactured in the United States. Explanation was useless. The tax was invariably levied, though I always paid it under protest. I maintained that the things which accompanied me were tools of my profession, and were entitled under the State law to enter free; but inasmuch as I did not wear the clothing myself, it was contended that the property could not be so entered. To be free of duty the costumes, it was argued, must be the personal property of each performer. Mdme. Sarah Bernhardt on entering the United States brought some thousands of pounds worth of beautiful dresses, which were seized, she refusing to pay the amount of import duty claimed. Her case was heard, and it was decided from Washington that her dresses, since she wore them herself, were the tools of her profession or trade, and must be allowed to enter free. My case was different. But I instituted law proceedings against the United States, which, in consequence of various delays, lasted some four or five years. A decision was at last given in my favour. An order was, in fact, issued to refund me the duty I had previously paid, together with 6 per cent. interest.

On leaving the Inman Company's office I met my attorney, who informed me that the money that I was entitled to in the action I had won against the United States was payable to me on demand. This was, indeed, good news, and through my attorney's indefatigable exertions I was enabled to obtain the final signature of the Customs House authorities to the cheque which had been drawn to my order, and through his kindness to get it cashed.

I had, before leaving Chicago, received a letter from the ticket speculator Rullmann, to whom I was indebted upon a libretto contract, suggesting I should embark at Jersey City to avoid difficulties at New York. Angelo also recommended this course, saying that at New York there would be a plant put upon me, in order to delay my departure. As I was a resident of New York, and stood well there, I decided to start from that city; and it was a good thing I did so, as I afterwards learned that preparations had been made at Jersey City to prevent my starting, the "plant" having been prepared there. As I had a deal of business in New York the day of my departure, I decided to sail from Castle Garden in the health-officer's steamer, which was kindly placed at my disposal, the Captain of the Inman steamer having agreed, on my hoisting the health flag, to heave-to when outside in order to allow me to get on board.

Prior to leaving New York I arranged with the Mayor of Liverpool, through the medium of the cable, to give a grand concert at the Liverpool Exhibition building with the whole of my principal artists, for which I was to receive two-thirds of the gross receipts; and as the papers stated that the Exhibition was a very great success, I anticipated sufficient results to enable me, after landing, to take the Company on to London and send the choruses over to Italy.

We arrived in Liverpool three days before the time fixed for the proposed concert.

On landing I at once looked at the morning papers, when to my astonishment no announcement whatever of the concert had been made. On presenting myself at the Mayor's office I was informed that his Worship, who had just been knighted, had gone to the north to rest himself, leaving no instructions whatever with regard to the concert. A few bills had been ordered at the printers', but the proofs had not been corrected.

Feeling myself placed in a very trying position, I set personally about the arrangements, every obstacle meanwhile being thrown in my way by the executive, who contended that the Mayor had no right to enter into any arrangement without their sanction. I at last got placed up in the Exhibition two bills; which had vanished, however, by the next morning.

The concert-room was in a most chaotic state, stray pieces of wood, broken chairs, etc., lying about the floor. I had to arrange the room myself, and even number the seats.

The evening of the concert arrived; but the public as well as my own artists were debarred from entering the doors unless they first paid for admission to the Exhibition, the whole of the gate money having been pledged to some banker in Liverpool.

The concert gave great satisfaction, but the receipts only reached some £70 or £80; of which to the present moment I have been unable to obtain my share.

As I had to pay Mdlle. Fohström £50, Del Puente £40, and all the others in proportion, I found myself, counting the hotel bills, some £180 out of pocket.

The day after the concert we all reached London. As it was now the 18th of June it was too late to think of giving a London season; and my doings were limited to my benefit, which took place at Drury Lane under the immediate patronage of Her Majesty the Queen and H.R.H. the Prince of Wales. Mdme. Patti volunteered her services on this occasion, the Theatre, kindly placed at my disposal by Mr. Augustus Harris, being crowded.

CHAPTER XV.

BACK IN THE OLD COUNTRY—THE LONDON SEASON—SLUGGISH AUDIENCES—MY OUTSIDE PUBLIC—THE PATTI DISAPPOINTMENTS—THE "SANDWICH'S" STORY.

SHORTLY afterwards I organized a very strong opera party, determining, during the coming September, to revisit the English provinces, which I had rather neglected during the previous seven or eight years. I, therefore, arranged to visit Dublin, Cork, Liverpool, Manchester, Glasgow, Edinburgh, Birmingham, etc., etc., resolved on giving a series of excellent performances. Engagements were concluded with Mdlle. Alma Fohström, Mdme. Nordica, Mdlle. Dotti, Mdlle. Marie Engle, Mdme. Hastreiter, Mdlle. Bianca Donadio, Mdlle. Jenny Broch, together with Signor Frapolli, Signor Runcio, Signor Del Puente, Signor Padilla, Signor Ciampi, Signor Vetta, a promising young basso, and Signer Foli; my conductors being Signor Arditi and Signor Vianesi.

My performances were admirably given; which was readily acknowledged by the whole of the provincial Press. But during the seven or eight years I had been away a younger generation had grown up and the elder ones had gone elsewhere. Inferior English Opera seemed now to be preferred to my grand Italian Opera; and it was only after I had been playing three or four nights in a town that the public began to understand the superiority of the latter.

In Dublin we had to feel our way with the performances, which culminated on the last night with a crowded house. I was anxiously expecting the arrival of Mdlle. Fohström, who had been delayed in Russia through the illness of a relative. She made her appearance at Dublin in the latter part of September to one of the most crowded houses I have ever seen.

We afterwards visited Cork, where I fear, as in Mdme. Gerster's case some years previously, Mdlle. Fohström took the germs of typhoid fever, which developed some ten days afterwards. Whilst singing at the grand concert of the Liverpool Philharmonic the lady found herself scarcely able to move, much to the astonishment of myself as well as the Committee. She, however, got through her work, and came on to Manchester, where she lay in bed for nearly three months, which was, of course, a great drawback to our success.

At Manchester, which is a great musical centre, our receipts the first week were miserable. But with the commencement of our second and last week they gradually increased, until there was not standing room. I endeavoured in vain to buy off another Company in order to continue our success.

Again, in Glasgow, where our old triumphs had been evidently forgotten, we played to most miserable receipts until the second week, when gradually the business grew until we had to refuse money. In fact, I had to re-take the theatre, and return there a fortnight afterwards, when on my last performance of Il Flauto Magico people were paying 10s. for standing room, while private boxes fetched London prices.

We next moved on to Birmingham, where my sole consolation was the admirable articles, making over a column in each of the daily papers, which appeared the morning after each representation, according the most unstinted praise to my really excellent performances. We afterwards left for Brighton, where we closed up just before Christmas.

Very early in the following month I started my Spring concert tour, visiting some forty cities in as many days, and meeting with great artistic success in every place we stopped at. My party consisted of Mdme. Nordica, Mdme. Marie Engle, Mdme. Hélène Hastreiter, and Mdlle. Louise Dotti; likewise Signori Runcio, Del Puente, and Vetta, with M. Jaquinot as solo violinist. No more excellent artistic party could have been put together; but here, again, the provincial public, not knowing my singers, attended with great caution; preferring old names to the young voices I had with me.

In Liverpool, as well as in Bradford, both said to be great musical centres (?), the receipts were nil.

We finished up in Dublin, where, as usual, the houses were crowded with large and appreciative audiences. The Irish, thoroughly understanding music, and judging for themselves, crammed the hall, and encored every piece.

In England, as a rule, singers take some years to acquire a reputation; but having once got it, they can never get rid of it.

I recollect hearing Mr. Braham sing when he was 82; and he was applauded. We are a conservative nation, and value old friends as we do old port wine.

Both on the Continent and in America I have been frequently interrogated as to why the London opera season is held at a time when it is next to impossible for so many patrons and supporters of music to attend on account of the numberless fêtes, flower shows, balls, garden parties, races, &c., that are taking place; to say nothing of the Crystal Palace, the Alexandra Palace, and (as regards the present season of 1888) the Irish, Danish, and Italian Exhibitions.

I, of course, could make no reply, being fully aware that alike in France, Spain, Austria, Germany, Italy, Russia, America, etc., the opera season begins generally about the third week in October; at a time when all outdoor attractions have ended. In the countries above mentioned dances and balls are, it is true, given during the winter months, whereas in London these social gatherings generally take place when the weather is extremely hot; and, as a rule, the smaller the house the greater the number of the guests invited.

In former times the London season was set by the opera; and its beginning usually coincided with the arrival of the singers from abroad, who in those days had to cross in sailing vessels, and would only come in fine weather.

Returning to London in the latter part of February, I decided on opening the Royal Italian Opera early in March; for which purpose I formed an admirable Company, consisting in the prima donna department of Mdlle. Alma Fohström, Mdlle. Emma Nevada, Mdlle. Jenny Broch, Mdlle. Marie Engle, Mdlle. Lilian Nordica, Mdlle. Louise Dotti, Mdlle. Hélène Hastreiter, Mdlle. Borghi, Mdlle. Bauermeister, Mdme. Lablache, Mdlle. Rosina Isidor, and Mdme. Minnie Hauk; my tenors being Signor Ravelli, M. Caylus, and Signor Garulli; my baritones Signor Padilla, Signor Del Puente, and M. Lhérie;

with Signor Miranda, Signor Vetta, Signor de Vaschetti, and Signor Foli as basses, Signor Ciampi as buffo, and Signor Logheder as musical conductor—in which capacity he proved most efficient. I moreover introduced two danseuses of remarkable excellence, Mdlle. Dell'Era and Mdlle. Hayten; both of whom must have left a favourable impression.

The novelties I produced were Leila (Bizet's Pêcheurs de Perles); and Gounod's Mirella, for the first time since twenty-five years. Thus Mirella was practically a new opera. Both works were newly mounted, and both made their mark artistically.

But the season being a short one, and having no spare capital, I could not resort to my old Faust and Carmen plan and hammer the music of Leila into people's heads. Consequently my production of the work did not meet with the financial success it should have done. The day will, however, come when it will form an attractive gem in the operatic crown. Leila is readily accepted all over the Continent; and even in Italy has been the mainstay of some twelve or fourteen opera-houses. Here, unfortunately, at its first production, many of the Pressmen were absent; and at its repetition no further notice was taken of it—though numbers of the public rely entirely upon what the newspapers say for their opinions and views.

The same fate awaited Gounod's Mirella—another most charming opera, in which Mdlle. Nevada sang to perfection.

The season continued for upwards of eight weeks, and was a pronounced success, both artistically and financially. It terminated about the middle of May. As I knew that London would be full of strangers on account of Her Majesty's Jubilee, I rented Her Majesty's Theatre, and on taking possession of it discovered it to be in a most desolate state. There was not a scene or a rope in working order, and the interior of the theatre was in a most deplorable condition, entailing upon me considerable expense for cleaning and restoring, painting, papering, carpeting, etc. There was nearly a mile of corridors and staircases to whiten, paper, paint, and carpet.

I opened a fortnight afterwards, when I again brought forward a powerful Company, including such valuable new-comers as Mdlle. Lilli Lehmann, Mdme. Trebelli (after an absence of eight years), and Mdlle. Oselio.

The season commenced most auspiciously on Saturday, June 4. But soon there was a difficulty with the orchestra, for there were now two other Italian Operas going on. It was impossible to induce the players I had engaged to attend rehearsals. There were Philharmonic, Richter, and other concerts in full swing; and although I paid them weekly salaries I could never command the services of my musicians for rehearsal, even though I closed my theatre at night for the purpose. I therefore had to suspend the representations for a week and form another orchestra, in order that I might sufficiently rehearse Boito's Mefistofele, which I had then in preparation. Ultimately I succeeded in bringing out that work, when, as on its first performance, it met with considerable success. This was followed by the rentrée of Mdlle. Lilli Lehmann in Beethoven's Fidelio, which was probably the grandest and most perfect performance given in London for many years. In the meantime I placed Bizet's masterpiece, Leila, in rehearsal.

About this time the Royal Jubilee excitement began, followed by extremely hot weather; and notwithstanding the brilliant performances given the house was empty nightly, the public preferring the free show they got out of doors, in the shape of processions, illuminations, etc., to performances at the theatre, where the temperature was now averaging 90°, notwithstanding all I did to keep it cool.

In fact, the only receipts I got for the purpose of paying my way were from the letting of the exterior of my theatre instead of the interior; seats on the roof fetching £1 apiece, whilst windows were let for £40. These receipts helped to provide the sinews of war for carrying on my arduous enterprise.

I now bestirred myself in order to obtain some attraction that would replenish the depleted operatic chest. My efforts seemed rewarded when I secured the services of Mdme. Adelina Patti, at the small salary of £650 per night. Mdme. Patti in due course made her first appearance at Her Majesty's Theatre in her favourite rôle of "Violetta" in La Traviata, when there was £1,000 in the house. My hopes, however, of recouping my heavy losses were dashed almost instantly to the ground. Mdme. Patti having accepted an invitation from a wealthy banker for a trip up the river, to be followed by a dinner, she took a violent cold, from having been placed in a draught with a light muslin dress on. The next evening Mdlle. Lilli Lehmann again made the old theatre ring with her magnificent impersonation of "Fidelio." The house, however, was nearly empty, all attention being directed to the next night, which was to be Patti's second appearance—in Il Barbiere di Siviglia.

At five o'clock, however, on the evening of the performance, Signor Nicolini came in to inform me that Patti was too ill to sing, but that I might rely upon her services the following Saturday, when she would appear as "Margherita" in Faust, transferring the Barbiere performance to the following Tuesday. He himself added to the programme an announcement to the effect that she would introduce in the lesson scene the valse from Romeo and Juliet.

It being too late to substitute another opera, I had no alternative but to close the theatre that evening, leaving hundreds of carriage folks who had sent their coachmen home to get away as best they could, disappointed, and declaring (in many cases) that there was no reliance to be placed on Mapleson!

On the following Friday, finding that the booking for the second Patti night was very light, the public having lost all confidence, as is generally the case after a disappointment, I suggested to Mdme. Patti and to Nicolini that a small allowance ought to be made towards the vast expenses I had incurred (rent, salaries to artists, band, chorus, &c.) while keeping the theatre closed, which her incautiousness of the previous Sunday up the Thames had alone prevented me from opening.

The following day Signor Nicolini offered to contribute a sum of £50. I replied that that would be scarcely enough for the orchestra, and that the entire representation would be jeopardized. He thereupon went home, stating that Mdme. Patti would not sing that evening unless the orchestra was duly secured.

I immediately made arrangements with my orchestra, and notified the fact to Mdme. Patti by half-past three o'clock through her agent at her hotel, who, after seeing her, informed me that it was all right. She was then lying down in view of the evening performance, for which her dresses had already been looked out by herself and her maid.

Just as I was leaving the hotel Mr. Abbey came downstairs, and accompanied me to the ticket-office, adjoining the theatre, the proprietors of which were large speculators for the occasion. On ascertaining that some four or five hundred of the best seats had not been disposed of—the public naturally holding back until Mdme. Patti should have made her reappearance after the disappointment they had experienced—Mr. Abbey informed me that Mdme. Patti should not sing that evening. I may here mention that the full £650, being the amount of her honorarium, was already deposited to her credit at the bank, so that it was not on the score of money matters that her services were refused.

I waited until eight o'clock for the arrival of Mdme. Patti, her room being prepared for her; but no message was sent, nor any notification whatever, that she was not coming down. After the previous disappointments the public had met with I could not find heart to close the theatre. I, therefore, informed the numbers who were then getting out of their carriages and gradually filling the grand vestibule that I would perform the opera of Carmen, and that I invited all present to attend as my guests; adding that their money would be returned to them on presentation of their tickets. This, of course, it was.

As to the gratuitous representation of Carmen (with Trebelli in the principal part), it went off admirably. The audience was numerous and enthusiastic; and among the distinguished persons who honoured me with their presence, was, I remember, H.R.H. the Duchess of Edinburgh.

I wrote to Mdme. Patti the following day, entreating her not further to disappoint the public, and to stand by the announcement Signor Nicolini had given me of her appearance the following Tuesday in Il Barbiere. To this I had no reply; and I afterwards learned that Mdme. Patti had gone off by a special morning train to Wales, to avoid meeting the chorus and employés who, hearing of her probable flight, had assembled in large bodies at Paddington to give her a manifestation of their disapprobation.

I was now placed in a most difficult position, and left to struggle on as best I could, having some three weeks' rent still to pay for the use of the theatre until the end of the month; together with the salaries of singers, choristers, bill-posters, supernumeraries, orchestra, etc., etc. These unfortunate people were actually following me in the street, clamouring for money. There were, moreover, some sixty Italian choristers, whose travelling expenses had to be provided for to send them home to Italy. In fact the Opera Colonnade had become a regular Babel, and it was only by dint of hard work amongst my numerous friends that I was enabled to collect funds and see the last of my chorus singers depart.

This affair threw me into contact with several supernumeraries as well as bill-board men, and I was very much interested to hear their different histories. One man, who had been a "Sandwich," gave me the following account of his life:—

THE "SANDWICH'S" STORY.

"I was formerly," he said, "a captain in the—— Regiment, and many a time have I paid my six guineas for a box at your Opera, both in Edinburgh and in London. Subsequently I began to take a great interest in the turf, and soon met with heavy losses, which compelled me to give various promissory notes. This at last came to the knowledge of my colonel, who recommended me to leave the regiment without delay. Having nothing to live upon, and being a fair performer on the cornet à piston, I joined a travelling circus, and ultimately came across your Opera Company in Philadelphia, where I was one of your stage band. Later on I joined a party who were bound for the diamond fields in South Africa, where I was most unsuccessful; and I had to work my passage home in a sailing ship, till I got to London, where I became a supernumerary under your management at Drury Lane.

"During your third season an aunt of mine died, and I found myself the possessor of £10,000. My cousin, who was largely interested in building operations, which he assured me paid him at least 60 per cent., induced me to place half my fortune in his speculations. His houses were in the west part of London, which had been considerably overbuilt; and being mortgaged they would have been lost but for my paying away the remainder of my fortune with the view of saving them. In spite of this the mortgagee foreclosed, and I again became a supernumerary, when, in the mimic fight in the second act of Trovatore, one of my companions by mere accident with a point of a spear put my eye out.

210

"I was now no longer qualified for engagement even as a supernumerary, and I became a 'sandwich' man. My duties during the last four and a half years have been to parade Bond Street and Regent Street, receiving as payment ninepence a day."

On my handing the poor man his salary and settling up he at first declined to take the money, saying that I had done him so many kindnesses at different periods of his life that now, when I was in trouble myself, he could not think of taking his week's pay. I, however, not only insisted upon his accepting it, but gave him a sovereign for himself. The unfortunate gentleman, as he showed himself to the last, went away blessing me.

CHAPTER XVI.

MASTER AND MAN—"DON GIOVANNI" CENTENARY—MOZART AND PARNELL—BURSTING OF "GILDA"—COLONEL STRACEY AND THE DEMONS—THE HAWK'S MOUNTAIN FLIGHT—AMBITIOUS STUDENTS AND INDIGENT PROFESSORS—A SCHOOL FOR OPERA—ANGLICIZED FOREIGNERS—ITALIANIZED ENGLISHMEN.

ALTHOUGH an operatic impresario cannot reasonably count on making his own fortune, it is often a source of satisfaction to him to reflect that he in his lavish expenditure makes the fortune of singers, officials, and various people in his service. At the time when I was in my greatest trouble through the disappointments I had to put up with from some of my leading singers, I heard that an enterprising Italian who had been employed by me for many years had taken the New York Academy of Music for a brief season, and that he was actually performing the duties of manager.

Angelo was, or rather is, a very remarkable man. I engaged him many years ago as my servant at 10s. a week, and he is now said to be in possession of some thousands or even tens of thousands of pounds, which he gained while in my service by turning his opportunities and his talents to ingenious account. Angelo is well known in the United States, chiefly by the unwashed condition of his linen. Reversing the custom by which, in England and America, gentlemen who cannot trust their memory to keep appointments write with a black pencil the time and place on one of their wrist-bands, Angelo used to write on his wrist-band, as nearly as possible black, with a piece of white chalk which, primarily with a view to billiards, he used to carry in his pocket. I mention this as an example of his proneness to imitation, and also of his economical habits.

How, it will be asked, did he amass a fortune in my service when I was paying him only at the rate of 10s. a week?

He began by starting a claque of which he constituted himself chief, and which was at the service of any of my singers who chose to pay for it. He was always ready, moreover, to act as interpreter. There was no language which he did not speak in courier fashion more or less well; and as in a modern operatic Company artists from such outlandish countries as Spain and Russia as well as from Italy, France, and Germany are to be found, Angelo's talents were often called into requisition by singers who did not understand one another and who were altogether ignorant of English.

Angelo knew where to buy cheap cigars, and he used to make the members of my Company buy them as dear ones. He speculated, moreover, largely and advantageously in vermuth, which he sold in the United States for at least a dollar a bottle more than he had paid for it in Italy. Campanini acted as his friend and accomplice in these vermuth sales. Entering a bar, in no matter what American city, the great tenor would call for a glass of vermuth. "Pah!" he would exclaim when he had tasted what the bar-keeper had offered him. Then, after making many wry faces, he spat out the liquor which had so grievously offended him.

"Where did you get this horrible stuff?" he would then inquire. "Vermuth? It is not vermuth at all. What did the rascal who sold it to you charge for it?"

"Three dollars a bottle."

"And here is a gentleman," pointing to Angelo, "who has genuine vermuth of the finest quality and will sell you as much as you like for two dollars a bottle."

The bar-keeper thought, with reason, that an eminent Italian tenor like Campanini must know good vermuth from bad, and at once bought from Angelo a case or two of the true vermuth di Torino.

Angelo, in addition to his other talents, is a first-rate cook, and in the preparation of certain Italian dishes, dear to those born in the "land of song," has scarcely an equal. He was too important a personage to act as cook to any one singer; but on the Atlantic passage he would take a pound a-head from some thirty different vocalists in order to see that each of them was provided with Italian cookery during the voyage.

Angelo made most of his money, however, by speculating in opera tickets during my Patti seasons. He had, of course, peculiar facilities for getting (unknown to me) almost as many tickets as he wanted at box-office prices; and he could count as a matter of certainty on selling them at enormous premiums—often as much as two or three pounds a-piece.

During the retreat from Frisco, seeing that there would be a scarcity of food along the line, he laid in a stock of provisions, which he retailed at enormous profits.

Angelo had made himself a prominent figure in connection with my Company, and was frequently spoken of in the newspapers. On our arrival at New York he waited upon the Secretary of the Academy, as I found out some time afterwards, and actually took the building from him for a season of opera, which was to begin in the following October. He accompanied us, however, to London as though nothing had happened. He returned at the appointed time to America, taking with him a company which included Mdme. Valda, Giannini, and others. When his prospectus came out I noticed two announcements which struck me as strange in connection with his costumes and music. The former, said the prospectus, had been "lent" by Zamperoni, the latter by Ricordi and Mdme. Lucca. They would not, then, be liable to seizure. He had taken the precaution to secure what he considered a proper reception at New York. Thus he had hired a steam tug with a brass band on board. This excited the mirth of all the New York journals.

When the season began Angelo on the opening night occupied my box, wearing for the first time in his life a white shirt; and it was noticed that when he made memoranda on his cuffs he now did so with a black lead pencil.

After the first week, the salaries having become due, the theatre closed, and the would-be impresario found himself surrounded in his hotel by infuriated choristers, who, with drawn stilettos presented, formed a veritable chevaux de frise in front of him. Angelo appeared himself at the second floor window in order to hold parley with his aggressors at a safe distance, and for some days he remained confined to his hotel.

A public subscription was got up for the choristers to enable them to return to Europe, and Angelo himself now accepted an appointment as interpreter in Castle Garden, where he had to receive the emigrants, make known their wants, and give them instructions in whatever happened to be their native tongue; but he would do nothing for them unless they began by buying a certain number of his detestable but high-priced cigars. Even Dr. Gardini, the husband of the distinguished prima donna, Mdme. Gerster, was actually afraid in Angelo's presence to smoke any cigars but his. I remember on one occasion giving Dr. Gardini an Havanna of the finest brand. He knew that Angelo, who was acting at the time as chef de claque to Mdme. Gerster, would, if he came in, recognize at once its superior flavour; and when the door-keeper suddenly entered to tell me that

Angelo wished to speak to me for a moment, the doctor thought it politic to throw aside the cigar I had given him and replace it by one of Angelo's vile weeds.

As to Angelo's exact pecuniary position at this moment it is difficult to speak with certainty. Some say that he is without a shilling, and my baritone, Signor de Anna, declares that he accommodated him with that sum a few weeks ago when he was passing through New York. According to other accounts he is a millionaire, with his millions safely invested in Italian securities.

To return to my own managerial business. I now fitted out an expedition for the following October, when I proposed to make an operatic tour throughout Great Britain and Ireland. Some few days before my departure I was much astonished at an embargo being laid on all my costumes and music under a bill of sale, voluntarily given by me to two friends, in order to secure a sum which they had advanced as subscribers for the previous season; which, but for Mdme. Patti's refusal to sing, would have been completed. I thought that, under the circumstances, my friends might have waited until after the tour had started. This incident prevented me from getting away at the appointed time, and I was delayed in London for nearly a week with the whole of my artists and chorus on my hands. I, however, got over this difficulty, and left for Ireland with a most attractive Company.

We opened in Dublin about the middle of October with an excellent performance of Carmen; Minnie Hauk not having appeared there since ten years previously on our way to America for our first visit, when Bizet's opera was totally unknown. On this occasion we were rewarded with a very crowded audience. Mdme. Rolla made her début as "Michaela," in which she met with great success; Del Puente, of course, being the "Toreador."

On the following night Mdlle. Dotti appeared as "Leonora" in Trovatore, when the house was again crowded. The third night was devoted to the Barbiere, for which I expected Mdlle. Arnoldson, who did not turn up. The part was, therefore, undertaken by Mdme. Rolla, who met with great success. Some eight months previously it had been agreed with Ravelli, prior to his departure for South America, that he should return to me in Ireland for this engagement, and I must give him credit this time for having kept his word. He had been travelling continuously for over seven weeks, and, landing at Bordeaux, had to work his way on to Dublin, where he joined the Company. There was now no murderous feeling between him and Minnie Hauk; they seemed to be the best of friends. I felt sure, however, that this reconciliation would be only temporary. I remained in Dublin a fortnight, during which time I produced Le Nozze di Figaro, and Ernani, with Mdme. Rolla's excellent impersonation of "Elvira" and Signor De Anna's superb rendering of "Carlo V." This was followed by Don Giovanni, Faust, Rigoletto, Il Flauto Magico, in which the whole Company took part, the exceptionally difficult rôle of the "Queen of Night" being undertaken with great effect by Mdlle. Marie Decca. I afterwards left for Cork, where the Company met with great artistic success, the Press notices being more favourable than they had ever been on previous visits.

On the 29th October, being the centenary of Mozart's Don Giovanni, I was determined to celebrate the event with due circumstance; and the great opera was given with the following very efficient cast:—"Donna Anna," Mdlle. Louise Dotti; "Donna Elvira," Mdme. Rolla; "Zerlina," Mdme. Minnie Hauk; "Don Ottavio," Signor Ravelli; "Leporello," Signor Caracciolo; "Il Commendatore," M. Abramoff; "Masetto," Signor Rinaldini; and "Don Giovanni," Signor Padilla; conductor, Signor Arditi.

I had arranged at the close of the first act to place a bust of Mozart on the stage, executing at the same time the grand chorus of the Magic Flute while the High Sheriff of the County crowned the immortal composer. Alas! there was no bust of Mozart to be obtained. But the property-man reported that he had one of Parnell, which, by the removal of the beard and some other manipulation, could be made to resemble Mozart. The High Sheriff having declined to perform the ceremony in connection with the bust of Parnell, the Mayor of Cork immediately volunteered to replace him. The public soon got wind of what was going on; and, fearing a popular commotion—as this very day the city had been proclaimed in consequence of the Land League meetings—I had to content myself with performing the opera as Mozart originally intended.

The part of the dissolute "Don" was superbly rendered by Signor Padilla, the eminent Spanish baritone, whose appearance reminded me forcibly of Mario. He had just returned from Prague, where Mozart's centenary had been duly celebrated, the whole of the arrangements having been left in his hands. He told me many interesting stories concerning his researches in the museums and libraries that had been placed by the Government at his disposal during his stay there, which extended over some five or six weeks. He succeeded in ascertaining the correct date of the original production of Don Giovanni at Prague. The authorities in Paris insisted that it had been first performed on the 27th October, 1787, and they even went so far as to regulate their centenary performance by that day. Signor Padilla, however, obtained the original play-bill from the National Library, in which it was clearly set forth that Il Don Giovanni, Ossia, Il Dissoluto Punito was first produced on the 29th day of October, 1787.

In my representation the absurd scene of "Don Giovanni" surrounded by a lot of stage demons flashing their torches of resin all over him was, of course, omitted. He simply went below in the hands of the Uomo di Pietra.

This reminds me of an amateur operatic performance we once had at Woolwich, in which I took part for the benefit of some regimental charities.

I was dining at my Club with some friends when the performance was first suggested. It was decided to give Rigoletto, in which I was asked to undertake the part of the Duke; this to be followed by the last act of Don Giovanni.

I, of course, said "Yes," as I usually do to everything; and before the dinner was over so many bets had been made on the question whether or not I would appear as the "Duke of Mantua" that, on making up my book, I found I must either play the arduous part or pay some £300 or £400. I determined on the former course.

I, of course, kept the matter a profound secret from all connected with my theatre. On the night of the performance, on the rising of the curtain, I was horrified in the midst of my first aria at seeing Mdme. Titiens, Mdme. Trebelli, Sir Michael Costa, and Adelina Patti amongst the audience; and it required some nerve to pull myself together and continue the part. I succeeded, however, in obtaining the customary encore for the "La donna è mobile" and for the quartett; and on the whole I believe I acquitted myself well. So, at least, said the notices which, to my astonishment, appeared next morning in the daily papers.

A catastrophe occurred at the close of the last scene, where the late Colonel Goodenough, in the character of "Rigoletto," had to mourn over the corpse of the murdered "Gilda." At the rehearsal a man had been placed in the sack, but he was too heavy to be dragged out; and, as Colonel Goodenough was very nervous, the property-man made the sack lighter by placing inside some straw and two large bladders full of air. Just as the curtain was descending Goodenough, who was a very heavy man, threw himself for the final lament on to the corpse of his daughter, when a loud explosion took place, one of the bladders having burst.

The performance concluded with the last act of Don Giovanni, in which Colonel Stracey undertook the part of the dissolute "Don." The demons were gunners from the Royal Artillery. It was most ludicrous, every time the Colonel gave the slightest stage direction as to where these men were to go and when they were to take hold of him and carry him down, to see the eight demons all give the military salute at the same time. Stracey told them not to salute him, on which they said "No, Colonel!" and gave another salute.

On leaving Cork we had to return to Dublin, where, in consequence of enormous success, we were called upon to give an extra week. We finished up on the following Saturday evening with a performance of Wallace's Maritana, in the Italian language, to a house literally packed to the very roof. Ravelli sang the part of "Don Cæsar;" and being encored in "Let me like a soldier fall," gave it the second time in English.

We afterwards went to Liverpool, when suddenly Mdme. Minnie Hauk, without a moment's warning, left the Company. Two days afterwards I received a medical certificate from Dr. Weber, to the effect that the lady was in a precarious state of health, and utterly voiceless, so that it was necessary for her to go to a certain mountain in Switzerland to recover her health. It was the month of December.

I afterwards ascertained that en route she had sung at three concerts for her own benefit.

We next visited Nottingham, Manchester, Birmingham, Bristol, Brighton, etc., concluding at the last-named town just before Christmas with a memorable performance of Maritana, when the curtain had to be raised no less than five times.

On the termination of the season we returned to London, where the Company disbanded for the holidays, my Italian chorus being now sent back to Italy.

It costs £8 to get an Italian chorus singer from his native land to England; and this seems money wasted when one reflects that just as good voices are to be found in this country as in Italy. If such a thing as a permanent Opera could be established in London arrangements might be made by which it would look for its chorus to one or more of our numerous musical academies, which at present seem to exist and to be multiplied solely to deluge the country with music teachers, whose keen competition lessens daily the value of their services. When the Royal Academy of Music was established the Earl of Westmorland, who presided at the first meeting of the promoters, said, in reference to the expected advantages of such an institution, that he hoped to see the day when music lessons would be given in England at the rate of 6d. an hour.

A nice time music teachers will have when ten hours' work a day will give them an income of 30s. a week! But what, if not music teachers, are the pupils of our four leading musical academies to become? The Royal Academy of Music, the Royal College of Music, the Guildhall School of Music, and Dr. Wylde's London Academy of Music must send out annually some thousand or two well-taught musicians who have nothing to turn to but teaching.

Except among the richer classes almost everyone who studies music ends by teaching music to someone else. Such is his fate whatever may have been his ambition. What, except a music teacher, or an orchestral player, or, by rare good luck, a concert singer, is he or she to become? In other countries there is an established musical theatre with which the recognized Academy of Music is in connection, and which in some measure depends upon it as upon a feeder. The students of the Paris Conservatoire sing in the chorus of the Grand Opera; and those students who gain prizes, or otherwise distinguish themselves, obtain an appearance, as a matter of course, at the great Lyrical Theatre, for which they may be said to have been specially trained. In England, however, we occupy ourselves exclusively with the teaching of music, never in any manner dealing with the question what the students are to do when their period of study is at an end. In other countries there is together with one musical academy one Opera-house. Here we have four musical academies and not one permanent operatic establishment.

Such is the national mania for establishing schools of music that a few years ago some £200,000 was collected for establishing a new musical academy with, for the most part, the same professors as those already employed at existing academies; and an attempt, moreover, was made to shelve Sir Arthur Sullivan (who may yet, it is to be hoped, compose an opera), by placing him at the head of this quite superfluous establishment. More recently Sir Arthur refused to allow himself to be shackled in the manner contemplated; and not many years afterwards another composer, Mr. A. C. Mackenzie, who has already proved himself capable of writing fine dramatic music, was put on the retired list in similar fashion. Mozart, Rossini, Auber, Bellini, Verdi studied at no academy; and my friend Verdi was rejected from the Conservatorio of Milan as incapable of passing the entrance examination. We, however, hope everything from music schools though we have nothing to offer our composers or our singers when, in a theoretical sort of way, they have once been formed. The money wasted in establishing the Royal College of Music might have been usefully spent in founding a permanent lyrical theatre for which our young composers might have worked, on whose boards our young vocalists might have sung. Thus only, by practice in presence of the public, can composers and singers perfect themselves in their difficult art. It should be remembered too that for operatic music the best school is an operatic establishment where fine performances can be heard.

The unhappy students, meanwhile, receive but small benefit from their tuition, seeing that they are simply turned out to swell the ranks of indigent teachers. No capital in Europe has anything like so many music schools as London, and no capital in Europe is so entirely without the means of offering suitable work to students who have once qualified themselves for performing it. We have some twenty or thirty theatres in London without one school of acting; which is possibly a mistake. But it is not such a bad mistake as to have four large music schools without one lyrical theatre. Nothing can be more preposterous. Yet there is at this moment more chance of a fifth music school being established than of an Opera-house being founded at which the shoals of composers and vocalists shot out every year would have an opportunity of pursuing their profession.

Sixty years ago, since which time we are supposed to have made progress in musical as in other matters, the Royal Academy of Music, which has produced so many excellent singers, instrumentalists, and composers, was intimately connected with the King's Theatre. Its students sang in the Opera chorus, and every fortnight gave performances of their own, at which leading vocalists, choristers, and orchestra were exclusively from the Academy. These performances took place in the King's Concert Room, a sort of annexe to the theatre in which the performances of Italian Opera were given.

Nor in those days were singers who happened to be English ashamed to call themselves by their own names. The present custom of Italianizing English names as the only process by which they can be made fit for presentation to the public is much more modern than is generally known. Even in our own time two admirable vocalists, Mr. Sims Reeves and Mr. Santley, have had the manliness to reject all suggestions for Italianizing their names. The foreign musicians, often of the highest eminence, who have settled amongst us, seem, on the other hand, to have taken a pride in passing themselves off as Englishmen. Handel is always called in the bills of the period Mr. Handel; Costa (until he was knighted) was always Mr. Costa; Hallé (until he also was knighted) Mr. Hallé; Benedict (until the moment when he was empowered to adopt the "Sir"), Mr. Benedict;

Herren Karl Rosa, August Manns, Alberto Randegger, Wilhelm Ganz, and Wilhelm Kuhe (whose knighthood has not yet reached them), are Mr. Carl Rosa, Mr. Manns, Mr. Randegger, Mr. Ganz, and Mr. Kuhe. It cannot be a disgrace even for a musician to be an Englishman, or so many foreign musicians of eminence would not so readily have called themselves "Mr."

An English vocalist, on the other hand, will not hesitate to pass himself off, so far as a name can assist him in his enterprise, as some sort of foreigner. My old pal, Jack Foley, becomes Signor Foli, and the Signor sticks to him through life. We have a Signor Sinclair, a name which seems to me as droll as that of Count Smith at the San Francisco Hotel. Provincial managers have often entreated me to use my influence with Mr. Santley in order to make him change his name to Signor Santalini, which they assured me would look better in the programme, and bring more money into the house. A Mr. Walker being engaged to appear at Her Majesty's Theatre, called himself on doing so Signor Valchieri (Signor Perambulatore would certainly have been better); and a well-known American singer, Mr. John Clarke, of Brooklyn, transformed himself on joining my Company into Signor Giovanni Chiari di Broccolini. The English and American young ladies who now sing in such numbers on the Italian stage take the prefix not of Signora or Signorina, but of Madame or Mademoiselle. This, also, is confusing.

CHAPTER XVII.

FIGHT WITH MR. AND MRS. RAVELLI—AN IMPROVISED PUBLIC— RAVELLI'S DANGEROUS ILLNESS—MR. RUSSELL GOLE—REAPPEARANCE OF MR. REGISTRAR HAZLITT—OFFENBACH IN ITALIAN—WHO IS THAT YOUNG MAN?—FANCELLI'S AUTOGRAPH—RISTORI'S ARISTOCRATIC HOUSEHOLD.

IN the early part of January, 1888, I gave forty-two grand concerts in forty-two different cities, commencing in Dublin, where I was placed in a position of the greatest difficulty by the non-arrival of Padilla, the baritone, Ravelli, the tenor, and my principal soloist, Van Biene, who was laid up with rheumatism; so that it was only with the greatest difficulty that I could even make a beginning. In due course Ravelli arrived, but with such a cold that he was unable to speak. I, therefore, had to proceed to the south of Ireland minus a tenor and a baritone. I succeeded, however, in replacing the instrumentalist by M. Rudersdorf, the eminent violoncellist, who resides in Dublin.

Prior to going to Belfast, towards the latter part of the week, Signor Padilla joined us, and for the next evening in Dublin all was arranged for the appearance of Ravelli, who had been living the whole week with his wife in the hotel at my expense. On notifying him to go to the concert, he replied that he must be paid a week's salary for the time during which he had been sick or he would not open his mouth. He conducted himself in so disrespectful a manner that he deserved, I told him, to be taken to the concert-room by force. I had scarcely made a movement of my hand as in explanation when he thought I was going to strike him, and made a rush at me in a most violent way, kicking up in the French style in all directions, while his wife assisted him by coming behind me with a chair.

I knew that if I injured him in the slightest degree there would be no concert that night. Meanwhile he was going full tilt at me to strike me in any way he possibly could, and it taxed my ingenuity to stop all action on his part without injuring him. It was fortunate I did so, as, after he had calmed down, seeing me in earnest, he dressed himself and went on to the concert. All this occurred only half an hour before its commencement. Afterwards Ravelli sang with comparative regularity.

Business, however, was not what it ought to have been, in consequence of the absence of favourite names from the programme. The musical excellence of my Company was beyond question, but the public must have old names of some kind or other, whether with voices or not, to ensure an audience.

We reached Leicester some four days afterwards. On the Company arriving in a body at the hotel, the hostess looked at us with amazement, and asked me if I had not come to the wrong town, since no announcement whatever had appeared as to any concert taking place. I thereupon made inquiries and found the landlady's statement to be perfectly true. All the printed matter—bills and programmes—previously sent on was discovered hidden away; and the person who had undertaken the arrangement of the concert, being in difficulties, had been unable even to announce our coming in the newspapers.

I, of course, insisted upon giving the concert, and as evening approached some half-dozen people who were accidentally passing purchased tickets. The performance proceeded in due form, and Ravelli, much to his disgust, obtained an encore from his audience of six.

In a hall adjoining I heard excellent singing, as if from a large chorus. I at once saw a way of giving encouragement to my artists, who were going on with the concert. On entering I found that the local Philharmonic Society was practising. It included many of the leading ladies and gentlemen of Leicester, and numbered altogether some two or three hundred singers.

I told the conductor that a capital concert was going on in the adjoining hall, to which I invited all present. If he would suspend the rehearsal they could go and help themselves to the best seats. Great astonishment was evinced amongst the six members of our public when they suddenly found the room filling with a well-dressed and distinguished audience, who were so delighted with the excellence of the performance that they encored every piece. Prior to the close of the concert I thought it was better to address a few words to my visitors, in which I stated that the concert, having been given secretly, without the knowledge of the town, I should look upon it as a private rehearsal only; and that it was my intention to return to Leicester some two or three weeks afterwards, when the public performance would take place. On leaving the hall my new audience booked some £20 or £30 worth of seats to make sure of obtaining places at my next visit.

When I returned shortly afterwards the Concert Hall was packed from floor to ceiling, and I was even requested to come back and give a third entertainment. The Press declared that no better concert had ever been given in Leicester.

We afterwards visited Cheltenham, Bristol, Exeter, and some twenty other cities, in each of which we were considerably handicapped by amateurs giving concerts for the entertainment of other amateurs; neither performers nor listeners seeming to have any high idea of art.

On reaching Cardiff Ravelli, without any reason, in the middle of the concert, said that he was indisposed, and walked home. As there was no other tenor present, and as it was impossible to continue the performance without one, I volunteered my services. I had previously notified the public; and after I had sung in the Trovatore duet I was recalled twice, and on taking an encore was again twice recalled. This helped us for the moment. But I have no intention of again appearing as a vocalist.

Ravelli, after going home to bed, had requested me to send for a doctor, as he was in a desperate state. The next morning, prior to leaving the town, I gave instructions to the landlady that proper care should be taken of him, adding that I would return in three or four days to see how he was progressing. I requested her, moreover, to paste up the windows to prevent any draught blowing into the room.

I then started with the Company to Exeter. On reaching that city I received a telegram from the landlady, stating that after my departure Mr. Ravelli had gone to Paris by the next train with his wife.

From Exeter we passed on to Plymouth and Torquay, where we gave a morning concert, remaining in that delightful watering-place till the following Monday morning, when we left for Salisbury; after which we visited Southampton, Southsea, Cambridge, Leicester, and Nottingham. The concert tour being now at an end, I returned to London.

Although both Mdme. Minnie Hauk and Signor Ravelli had left me on the plea of sickness without being seriously indisposed, I took no steps against either of them. For a time, I must admit, I thought of having recourse to the good services of my friend and solicitor—strange conjunction!—Mr. Russell Gole; who during my career as impresario has brought and defended for me actions innumerable, and invariably, I believe, with the best results that under the circumstances could have been obtained. The reader has already heard of Mr. Gole's ingenious suggestion at a time when for six minutes I was in the position of a bankrupt. During those memorable six minutes Mr. Registrar Hazlitt had occupied the position of an impresario, and it would be difficult to say whether at that momentous crisis he or I was most out of place. When Mr. Gole reminded him that he was now ex-officio the manager of Her Majesty's Theatre, and that advice was expected from him as to the cutting of Lohengrin, the making up of the ballet girls' petticoats, and the pacification of an insubordinate tenor, he sent for the Book of Practice, and after consulting it rescinded the order, observing that he did so "in the interest of the public."

Once more, only a few weeks ago, I stood in the presence of Mr. Registrar Hazlitt, and, as in the days of Sir Michael Costa's disputed cheque, had Mr. Russell Gole by my side. Once more, too, when an order of bankruptcy was impending over me it was withdrawn partly through the instrumentality of my solicitor, but mainly, of course, through the goodwill of my creditors, who subscribed among themselves sufficient money to pay into Court a sum which was at once accepted in liquidation of all claims.

I am generally regarded and have got into the habit of looking upon myself as a manager of Italian Opera. But, accepting that character, I do not think I can be fairly accused of exclusiveness as towards the works of German or even of English composers. Nor can I well be charged with having neglected the masterpieces of the lyric drama by whomsoever composed. For a great many years past no manager but myself has given performances of Cherubini's Medea. Fidelio is a work which, from the early days of Mdlle. Titiens until my last year at Her Majesty's Theatre, with Mdlle. Lilli Lehmann in the principal part, I have always been ready to present. I was the first manager to translate Wagner's Tannhäuser and Lohengrin into Italian, and the only one out of Germany who has been enterprising enough to produce the entire series of the Ring des Nibelungen.

As regards English Opera, Macfarren's Robin Hood and Wallace's Amber Witch owe their very existence to me. It was I who, at Her Majesty's Theatre in 1860-61, brought out both those works, which had been specially composed for the theatre. I myself adapted Balfe's Bohemian Girl to the Italian stage, and in the course of my last provincial tour I gave for the first time in Italian, and with remarkable success, the Maritana of Wallace.

Casting back my recollection over a long series of years I find that the only composer of undisputed influence and popularity whose propositions I could at no time accept were those of Jacques Offenbach; whom, however, in his own particular line I am far from undervaluing. The composer of La grande Duchesse de Gérolstein, La Belle

Hélène, and a whole series of masterpieces in the burlesque style, tried to persuade me that his works were not so comic as people insisted on believing. They had, according to him, their serious side; and he sought to convince me that La Belle Hélène, produced at Her Majesty's Theatre with an increased orchestra, and with a hundred or more additional voices in the chorus, would prove a genuine artistic success. I must admit that I gave a moment's thought to the matter; but the project of the amiable maestro was not one that I could seriously entertain. I may here remind the reader that Offenbach began life as a composer of serious music. He was known in his youth as an admirable violoncellist, playing with wonderful expression all the best music written for the instrument he had adopted. He was musical conductor, moreover, at the Théâtre Français in the days when the "House of Molière" maintained an orchestra, and, indeed, a very good one. When Offenbach composed the choruses and incidental music for the Ulysse of M. Ponsard he did so in the spirit of Meyerbeer, who had undertaken to supply the music of the piece; and he then showed his aptitude for imitating the composer of Les Huguenots in a direct manner, as he afterwards did in burlesquing him.

Offenbach was destined not to be appreciated as a serious composer, though in one of his works, the little-known Contes d'Hoffmann, there is much music which, if not learned or profound, is at least artistic.

Had I agreed to Offenbach's offer, I was also to accept his services as conductor; which would have been more, I think, than Sir Michael Costa, who would have had to direct on alternate nights, would have been able to stand. Sir Michael was not only peculiarly sensitive, but also remarkably vindictive; and the engagement of Offenbach at a theatre where he was officiating would certainly have caused him no little resentment. He forgave no slight, nor even the appearance of one in cases where no real slight could possibly have been intended. When he left the Royal Italian Opera he was of opinion that the late Mr. Augustus Harris, who was Mr. Gye's stage manager at the time, should also have quitted the establishment; and carrying his hostile feelings in true vendetta fashion from father to son, he afterwards objected to the presence of the Augustus Harris of our own time, at any theatre where he, Sir Michael, might be engaged.

"Who is that young man?" he said to me one day when the future "Druriolanus" was acting as my stage manager. "He seems to know his business, but I think I heard you call him 'Harris.' Can he be the son of my enemy?"

I tried to explain to Sir Michael that the gentleman against whom he seemed to nourish some feeling of animosity could not be in any way his foe. But the great conductor would not see this. The father, he said, had shown himself his enemy, and he was himself the enemy of the son.

The hatred sometimes conceived by one singer for another of the same class of voice and playing the same parts, is, if not more reasonable, at least more intelligible. I shall never forget the rage which the tenor Fancelli once displayed on seeing the name of the tenor Campanini inscribed on a large box at a railway station with these proud words appended to it: "Primo Tenore Assoluto, Her Majesty's Opera Company." It was the epithet "assoluto" which, above all, raised Fancelli's ire. He rushed at the box, attacked the offending words with his walking-stick, and with the end of it tried to rub off the white letters composing the too ambitious adjective, "assoluto."

"Assoluto" was an epithet which Fancelli reserved for his own private use, and to which he alone among tenors considered himself justly entitled. Unfortunately, he could not write the word, reading and writing being accomplishments which had been denied to him from his youth upwards. He could just manage to scribble his own name in large schoolboy characters. But his letter-writing and his "autographs" for admiring ladies were done for him by a chorister, who was remunerated for his secretarial work at the rate of something like a penny Pickwick per month. The chorister, however, in agreeing to work on these moderate terms, knew that he had the illustrious tenor in his hands; and in moments of difficulty he would exact his own price and, refusing cheap cigars, accept nothing less than ready money.

Occasionally when the chorister was not at hand, or when he was called upon, to give his autograph in presence of other persons, Fancelli found himself in a sad plight; and I have a painful recollection of his efforts to sign his name in the album of the Liverpool Philharmonic Society, which contains the signatures of a large number of celebrated singers and musicians. In this musical Book of Gold Fancelli made an earnest endeavour to inscribe his name, which with the exception only of the "c" and one of the "l's" he succeeded in writing without the omission of any of the necessary letters. He had learned, moreover, to write the glorious words "Primo tenore," and in a moment of aspiration tried to add to them his favourite epithet of "assoluto." He had written a capital "A," followed by three "s's," when either from awkwardness or in order to get himself out of the scrape in which he already felt himself lost, he upset the inkstand over the page. Then he took up the spilt ink on his forefinger and transferred it to his hair; until at last, when he had obliterated the third "s," his signature stood in the book and stands now—

"FANELI PRIMO TENORE ASS—"

Some rude critics having declared of Signor Fancelli's singing that it would have been better if he had made a regular study of the vocal art, he spoke to me seriously about taking lessons. But he declared that he had no time, and that as he was making money by singing in the style to which he was accustomed it would be better to defer studying until he had finished his career, when he would have plenty of leisure.

About this time the strange idea occurred to him of endeavouring to master the meaning of the parts entrusted to him in the various operas.

"In Medea," he innocently remarked, "during the last two years I have played the part of a man named 'Jason'; but what he has to do with 'Medea,' I have never been able to make out. Am I her father, her brother, her lover, or what?"

Fancelli had begun life as a facchino or baggage porter at Leghorn, so that his ignorance, if lamentable, was at least excusable. On retiring from the stage he really applied himself to study; with what success I am unable to say. At his death he left a large sum of money.

It has often astonished me that singers without any education, musical or other, should be able to remember the words and music of their parts. Some of them resort to strange devices in order to supply the want of natural gifts; and one vocalist previously mentioned, Signor Broccolini, would write his "words" on whatever staff or stick he might happen to be carrying, or in default of any such "property," on the fingers and palm of his hand. In representing the statue of the Commander, in Don Giovanni, he inscribed beforehand the words he had to sing on the bâton carried by the Man of Stone; but to be able to read them it was necessary to know on which side in the scene of the cemetery the rays of the moon would fall. On one occasion he had majestically taken up his position on horseback, with the bâton grasped in his right hand, and reposing on his right hip, and was expecting a rush of moonlight from the left, when the position of the orb of night was suddenly changed, and he was unable to read one syllable of the words on which he depended. Having to choose between two difficulties, he at once selected the least, and, to the astonishment of the audience, transferred the Commander's bâton from the right hand to the left.

The vanity of an opera singer is generally in proportion to the lowness of his origin. This rule, however, does not seem to apply to dramatic artists, for I remember that when I once called upon Mdme. Ristori at Naples I found her principal actors and actresses, who had apparently begun life as domestic servants, continuing the occupations of their youth while at the same time impersonating on the stage the most exalted characters. "Sir Francis Drake" waited at table, the "Earl of Essex" opened the street door, "Leicester" acted as butler; and I have reason to believe that "Dirce" dressed "Medea's" hair.

Two more anecdotes as to the caprices and the exactions of vocalists. My basso, Cherubini, on one occasion refused to go on with his part in Lucia because he had not been applauded on entering.

An incident of quite an opposite character occurred at Naples during the Titiens engagement. Armandi, a tenor of doubtful repute, who resided at Milan, always awaited the result of the various fiascos of St. Stephen's night (26th December) which marks the beginning of the Carnival season, when some hundreds of musical theatres throw open their doors. He had a large répertoire; and, after ascertaining by telegraph where his services were most in need, and where they would be best remunerated, he would accept an engagement as a kind of stop-gap until another tenor could be found. Generally, at the close of the first evening he was paid for his six performances and sent back to Milan.

But on the occasion I am speaking of Armandi had stipulated in his contract that he should be paid the six nights and sing the six nights as well; for he was tired, he said, of being systematically shelved after a single performance.

The part in which he had to appear at Naples, where the leading tenor of the establishment had hopelessly broken down, was that of "Pollio" in Norma; but every time he attempted to sing the public accompanied him with hisses, so that he soon became inaudible. At the close of the first act he came before the curtain, and after obtaining a hearing begged the audience to allow him to finish the opera in peace, when he would leave the city. If they continued hissing he warned them that he would sing the remaining five nights of his engagement.

The public took the candour of the man in such good part that they not only applauded him throughout the evening, but allowed him to remain the entire season.

FINAL CHAPTER.

FIGURES are dull and statistics fatiguing; or I might be tempted to give the reader particulars as to the number of miles that I have travelled, the sums of money I have received and spent during my career as manager; with other details of a like character. I may mention, however, that for many years during our operatic tours in the United Kingdom and in the United States, our average annual travelling with a large company of principal singers, choristers, dancers, and orchestral players amounted to some 23,000 miles, or nearly the length of the earth's circumference. This naturally necessitated a great deal of preparation and forethought. The average annual takings were during this period over £200,000. All this involved so much organization and such careful administration, that a mere impresario might, without disgrace, have proved unequal to the work. The financial department, in particular, of such an enterprise ought, to be thoroughly well managed, to enjoy the supervision of a Goschen.

Difficulties, however, are only obstacles set in one's way in order to be overcome, and mine have never caused me any serious trouble. I am disposed by nature to take a cheerful view of things, and I can scarcely think of any dilemma in which I have been placed, however serious, which has not presented its bright, or at least when I came to think of it, its amusing side. When, moreover, one has had, throughout a long career, difficulties, often of a very formidable character, to contend with, the little inconveniences of life are scarcely felt.

I remember one day dining with a millionaire of my acquaintance who got red in the face, stamped, swore, and almost went into convulsions because the salmon had been rather too much boiled. He had led too easy a life; or so trifling a mishap would have had no effect upon him.

Often when affairs looked almost tragic, I have been able to bear them by perceiving that they had also their comic aspect. The reader, indeed, will have seen for himself that some of my liveliest anecdotes are closely connected with very grave matters indeed. Of such anecdotes I could tell many more. But I feel that I have already taken up too much of the reader's time, and, having several important projects on hand which will take up the whole of mine, I must now conclude.

APPENDIX.

SINGERS AND OPERAS PRODUCED BY ME.

The following is a list of the principal artists whom I first had the honour of engaging for this country, and, with two exceptions (marked by asterisks), of introducing for the first time to the British public:—

European Prime Donne.

*Adelina Patti,
Christine Nilsson,
Etelka Gerster,
Marguerite Chapuy,
Ilma di Murska,
Marie Roze,
Marie Marimon,
Emelie Ambré,
Caroline Salla,
Lilli Lehmann,
Eugénie Pappenheim,
Harriers Wippern,
Victoire Balfe,
Jenny Broch,
Elena Varese,
Marianina Lodi,
Alma Fohström,
Caroline Reboux,
Clarice Sinico,
Louise Sarolta,
Mathilde Sessi,
Bianca Donadio,
Matilda Bauermeister,
Zelie Trebelli,
Sofia Scalchi,
Anna de Belocca,
Borghi-Mamo,
Carolina Guarducci,
Caroline Bettelheim.

American Prime Donne.

*Emma Albani,
Clara Louise Kellogg,
Alwina Valleria,
Marie Vanzandt,
Emma Nevada,
Emma Abbott,
Marie Litta,
Lilian Nordica,
Louise Dotti,
Hélène Hastreiter,
Emma Juch,
Annie Louise Cary,
Kate Rolla,
Laura Harris-Zagury,
Lilian Lauri,
Marie Engle,
Genevieve Ward,
Minnie Hauk,
Nikita,
Etc., etc., etc.

Tenors.
Pietro Mongini,
Roberto Stagno,
Italo Campanini,
Luigi Ravelli,
Dr. Gunz,
Carlo Bulterini,
Ernesto Nicolini,
De Capellio-Tasca,
Victor Capoul,
Giovanni Vizzani,
Tom Hohler,
Allesandro Bettini,
Antonio Aramburo,
Giuseppe Fancelli.
Baritones.

Enrico Delle-Sedie,
Mariano de Padilla,
Charles Santley,
Enrico Fagotti,
Jean de Reszke,
Antonio Galassi,
Giuseppe Del Puente,
Innocente de Anna,
Pandolfini,

224

Agnesi,
Senatore Sparapani,
Colonnese,
Varese,
Badiali,
Paul Lhérie,
Giovanni Rota.
Basses.

Rokitansky,
Bagagiolo,
Medini,
Castelmary,
Belval,
Junca,
Behrens,
Novara,
Cherubini,
Foli.
Buffos.

Scalese,
Ciampi.
Bevignani,
Vianesi,
Logheder,
Fred Cowen,
Bisaccia,
Pasdeloup,
Etc., etc., etc.

Tragedian.
Tommaso Salvini.

The following celebrities ended their operatic career with me, having remained for many years previously under my management.:—

Thérèse Titiens,
Giulia Grisi,
Marietta Alboni,
Fanny Persiani,
Pauline Viardot,
Mario,
Antonio Giuglini,
Italo Gardoni,
Ignazio Marini,
Karl Formes,
Sir Michael Costa.

The following works were, in England, first produced under my management:—

Faust	Gounod.
Damnation de Faust	Berlioz.
Messe Solennelle	Rossini.
Ballo in Maschera	Verdi.
Forza del Destino	Verdi.
I Vespri Siciliani	Verdi.
Carmen	Bizet.
Leila (Pêcheurs de Perles)	Bizet.
Mirella	Gounod.
Falstaff (Merry Wives of Windsor)	Nicolai.
Don Bucefalo	Cagnoni.
Hamlet	Thomas.
Rinnegato	Orczy.
Nicolo de Lapi	Schira.
Esmeralda	Campana.
Mefistofele	Boito.
Talismano	Balfe.
Ruy Blas	Marchetti.
Medea	Cherubini.
Iphigénie	Gluck.
Deux Journées	Cherubini.
Seraglio	Mozart.
Ring des Nibelungen	Wagner.

The following revivals, among others, were given by me with entirely new scenery, dresses, and decorations:—

Fidelio	Beethoven.
Freischütz	Weber.
Oberon	Weber.
Aida	Verdi.
Flauto Magico	Mozart.
Anna Bolena	Donizetti.
Lohengrin	Wagner.
Dinorah	Meyerbeer.
Semiramide	Rossini.

CPSIA information can be obtained
at www.ICGtesting.com
Printed in the USA
LVHW051413010321
680268LV00047B/3300